Time and Money
The Economy and the Planets

Second Edition

Books by Robert Gover

One Hundred Dollar Misunderstanding
Here Goes Kitten
J.C. Saves
The Maniac Responsible
Poorboy at the Party
Tomorrow Now Occurs Again
On the Run with Dick and Jane
Two Brothers

Novella

Getting Pretty on the Table

Nonfiction

Voodoo Contra:
Contradictory Meanings of the Word

Time & Money:
The Economy and the Planets

Time and Money

The Economy and the Planets

Second Edition

Robert Gover

Hopewell Publications

TIME AND MONEY: The Economy and the Planets
Copyright © 2005, 2011 by Robert Gover.

All rights reserved. No part of this book may be reproduced or transmitted in any form or by any means, electronic or mechanical, including photocopying, recording, or by any information storage or retrieval system, without permission in writing from the publisher, with exception of reviews.

Published by Hopewell
Publications, LLC
PO Box 11
Titusville, NJ 08560-0011
(609) 818-1049

info@HopePubs.com
www.HopePubs.com

International Standard Book Number: 9781933435367

Library of Congress Control Number: 2010942041

First Edition

Printed in the United States of America

*for
Alvina Star,
my mentor*

*and for
Carolyn,
patient and beloved wife*

———

All charts created in Solar Fire™

Cover photos courtesy of NASA

Praise for Gover's other books:

One Hundred Dollar Misunderstanding

"What a find! I've been recommending it to everyone." - Henry Miller

"Robert Gover has written a special book, a freak of a novel; he has faced up to race, sex and money issues in American life by caricaturing two amorous antagonists in a series of burlesque monologues, extended exercises of style."
- Herbert Gold, *New York Times Book Review*

"There is always a division between what a society does and what it says it does, and what it feels about what it says and does. But nowhere is this conflict more vividly revealed than in the American middle class's attitude toward sex I hope this book will read by every adolescent in the county, which is most of the population."
- Gore Vidal, *Esquire Magazine*

The Maniac Responsible

"…a work of art. Brilliant." - *Newsweek*

"Real and powerful." - *Dallas Times Herald*

On the Run with Dick and Jane

"Gore Vidal has called this novel 'A literary Halley's comet' And like that comet, it is not likely to be forgotten by those who experience it."
- Thomas E. Kennedy, author of *In the Company of Angels*

Table of Contents

INTRODUCTION 1
    TIME FACTOR 2
    BELIEFS AND EVIDENCE 3
    MONEY 3
    MONEY AND MAYAN ASTROLOGERS 4
    WHAT'S THE ECONOMY FOR? 6
    TIMES AND FORTUNES 6
    USA'S BIRTH TIME 9

ECONOMIC PLANETARY CYCLES 11
    SATURN-URANUS CYCLES 11
    SATURN-NEPTUNE CYCLES 12
    SATURN-PLUTO CYCLES 14
    URANUS-NEPTUNE CYCLES 15
    URANUS-PLUTO CYCLES 15
    NEPTUNE-PLUTO CYCLES 16

THE CORPORATOCRACY & 911 18
    SATURN-PLUTO OPPOSITION 20
    MOST DEVASTATING 21
    WE'S AND THEIR THEY'S 23
    SIMILAR TO 911 24
    RETURNING TO THE 20TH CENTURY 25
    JIM CROW, DRUGS, VIETNAM 25
    WHY DID THEY DO IT? 27

MONEY 31
    MAMMON AND PUBLIC DEBT 32
    JEKYLL ISLAND CONSPIRACY 33
    A MOST UNHAPPY MAN 35
    EZRA POUND'S PASSION 36
    FED'S IMPACT ON SOCIETY 38
    "FOLLOW THE MONEY" 40
    BEN FRANKLIN'S PAPER MONEY 41
    CHINA'S BEN FRANKLIN BANK 43
    PRIVATE V. PUBLIC CONTROL 43
    PLUTO: CONCEPTION AND BIRTH 45
    WILL THE FED BE NATIONALIZED? 45
    RISKY BUSINESS 47

Table of Contents

 BRAIN-DAMAGING HUBRIS 48
GRAND CROSS AND GREAT DEPRESSIONS 51
 GREAT DEPRESSION DEFINED 51
 GRAND CROSS IN US HISTORY 52
 HOW TO VERIFY 53
 X IN A BOX 53
 ANOTHER WAY TO VISUALIZE 54
 GREAT DEPRESSION OF THE 1780S 55
 GREAT DEPRESSION OF THE 1840S 57
 GREAT DEPRESSION OF THE 1870S 59
 GREAT DEPRESSION OF THE 1930S 59
 NO GRAND CROSS, NO GREAT DEPRESSION 61
 URANUS-NEPTUNE CROSSROADS 65
 NEPTUNIAN SPECULATIVE BUBBLE 65
 ECONOMIC INDICATORS 66
 THE OMINOUS GAP 66
 MONETARISTS AND KEYNESIANS 67
 WHO GETS HOW MUCH 67
 GOOD NEWS AND BAD 68
 URANUS-PLUTO SQUARE DIRECT HITS 69
STOCK MARKET PANICS 71
 A COMMON SIGNATURE 72
 PANIC OF 1837 73
 PANIC OF 1857 74
 BLACK FRIDAY, 1869 74
 BLACK FRIDAY 1873 75
 PANIC OF 1893 75
 RICH MAN'S PANIC, 1903 76
 PANIC OF 1907 77
 CRASH OF 1920 77
 THE BIG CRASH OF '29 77
 WITCHDOCTORS AND ECONOMISTS 78
 THE POWER OF INCANTATION 79
 BLACK MONDAY 1987 80
 SCARE OF 1997 81
 RECORD HIGHS 82
 NASDAQ LOSES 78 PERCENT 82

Table of Contents

9/11/01 84
SUMMARY OF PAST PANICS 85
LOOKING AHEAD 86
SECOND EDITION UPDATE 86
THE MAYA CALENDAR 89

URANUS, PLUTO, AND REVOLUTION 90
BACON'S REBELLION 91
WITHOUT PRECEDENT 92
SEEDS OF CLASS WAR 93
INDIAN TRIBES UPSET 94
A CERTAIN DISDAIN 95
KILL ALL OR KILL SOME 95
SLAVES AND SERVANTS UNITED 96
23 REBEL LEADERS HANGED 96
RIGHTS AND FREEDOMS 97
SEEDING REVOLUTIONS 98
ENGLISH LANGUAGE AND CULTURE 100
THE STAMP ACT 102
"SONS OF LIBERTY" 103
HOSTILITIES ESCALATE 103
THE BOSTON MASSACRE 104
REVOLUTIONARY FERVOR 104
URANUS-PLUTO TRINE 106
PAINE'S IMMORTAL ESSAY 107
DIVINITY AND COMMON SENSE 107
COHESION 108
TOM PAINE'S URANUS 110

AMERICAN AND FRENCH REVOLUTIONS 111
ENEMY OF MY ENEMY 112
VICTORY AND GREAT DEPRESSION 114
STAR-CROSSED LOVERS 114
FRANCE IN 2015 117
PLUTO AND ADAM SMITH 118

DRUMBEATS OF CIVILIZATION 119
ZIONISM AND TERRORISM 124
PHASES 124

Table of Contents

    REVOLUTIONS: AMERICAN, FRENCH, INDUSTRIAL 125
    THE INQUISITION 125
    FALL OF ROME 126
    CHANGING RELIGIOUS BELIEFS 127
    ECONOMIC DEMOCRACY 127
    OLD GODS OBLITERATED 128
    ST. AUGUSTINE 128
    JESUS: GOD OR HUMAN? 129
    20TH CENTURY 130
    SPIRITUAL KNOWLEDGE LOST 131
    EVIL REDEFINED 131
    CULMINATION OF TRENDS 132
    INVASIONS THEN AND NOW 132
    ONSET OF DARK AGES 133
    PARALLELS 134
    BRIBERY INSTITUTIONALIZED 135
    LAWYERS AND INQUISITORS 136
    CHANGE OR BE CHANGED 138
    INTERESTING SIMILARITY 139
    UNINTENDED CONSEQUENCES 139
    ARABS AND INDIANS 140

COLUMBUS RUNS AGROUND 141
    CHRISTIANS AND CANNIBALS 142
    FREEDOM FROM STATE RULE 142
    PONCE DE LEON FINDS FLORIDA 143
    CULTURE CLASH 144
    AZTEC ASTROLOGERS 144
    ENGLISH CLOTHES 145
    IN THE LONG RUN 146
    WELCOMING THEN SLAUGHTERING 147
    "HE WHO IS RICH" 149
    SUCCESSFUL AD CAMPAIGN 150
    JAMESTOWN JOYS AND SORROWS 150
    INDIANS AND RUNAWAYS 151
    HURRICANES 152
    DUTY TO GOD AND KING 152
    WITCHES 155
    ALL THE GOLD 155

Table of Contents

PLEASURES AND PHILOSOPHIES 156
20 AFRICAN SLAVES 156
COST-EFFECTIVE LABOR 158

JOHN LAW'S LONG SHADOW 159

PROMOTIONS THEN AND NOW 159
MONEY AS VALUE ITSELF 160
REPEATEDLY FORGOTTEN 162
SPECULATIONS USEFUL AND FOOLISH 162
WILDERNESS SPECULATIONS 163
PRICES TO GREAT HEIGHTS 164
PRICE AND VALUE 164
MONEY FROM THIN AIR 165
PIRACY AND BUSINESS AS USUAL 166
"WE THE PEOPLE" 166
"GREATLY ABUSED" 167
ARMED FARMERS 168
REBELLIOUS LOWER CLASS 168
SAM ADAMS READS RIOT ACT 169
"YOUR LIFE OR MINE" 170
PLANETS AND REVOLUTION 171
SAVAGES AND DEMOCRACY 171
COMMON PROPERTY OF ALL 172
"IMPUDENCE OF DEMOCRACY" 173
BILL OF RIGHTS 173
INEFFICIENCY OF SLAVERY 174

GOLD AND THE DOLLAR 177

"TO REGULATE THE VALUE THEREOF" 178
RISE OF THE BANKERS 180
A MAJOR RESTRUCTURING 181
MERCURY-PLUTO OPPOSITION 182
GOLD ABANDONED 183
NOT EVERYONE CONVINCED 184
TWO VIEWS OF INFLATION 186
PRODUCTION AND PROFITS 187
HIT "ENTER" 187
AMERICAN TAXPAYER-OWNED 188
WHO'S TO BLAME? 189

Table of Contents

    A Zero-Sum Game 189

THE INSTITUTIONALIZED OXYMORON 193

    Forms of Democracy 194
    Veneer of Democracy 194
    Capitalist Delusions 195
    "Bribe-ocracy" 196
    Free Market Tyranny 196
    Christianity and Democracy 197
    Another Perspective 197
    Public Relations 198
    Help the Poor, Kill Welfare 198
    Reforms and Threats 199
    "Provide Jobs" 199
    Free Thought and Kiddy Porn 200
    Doing God's Work 200
    Hate Socialism, Love Social Security 201
    Ongoing Class War 201
    Every 110 to 130 Years 202
    Before USA Was Born 202
    Women's Right to Vote 203
    Changes and the Masses 206

PLUTO AND CLASS CONFLICT 207

    Muckrakers and Plutocrats 207
    A Thrill for Investors 208
    Trust Buster Teddy 209
    The Fed 209
    Auspicious Timing 210
    The Fed's Mission 211
    People and Wealth 212
    Money Defined 212
    Bankers Are Human 213
    Exporting the Oxymoron 213
    Self-Fulfilling Prophecy 214
    Divining the Future 214
    Over There 215
    "The Greater Good" 216
    Artificial Community 216

Table of Contents

    Conscription 217
    Russian Revolution 218
    "Enemy of My Enemy" 219
    Unexpected Effects 219
    State-Run Capitalism 220
    The Soviet Pluto 221

DOWN AND DOWN AND DOWN 222
    Concentrations of Wealth 222
    Insatiable Wants 223
    A More Awesome Panic 224
    Economic Catch 22 224
    Earthbound Time 225
    Forecasting Economic Conditions 226
    McWhirter's System 226
    The Missing Time Factor 227
    Reading the Stars 227
    Finger of Blame 228
    Great Depression Reviewed 229
    Stocks and Overall Economy 231
    Contrast: 1929 and 1987 233
    Grim Scenarios 234
    After the Crash 235
    Overcoming Common Sense 235
    Store Invaders 236
    The Bonus Army 236
    People Help Themselves 237
    Juries Refuse to Convict 238
    Inherited Script 240
    Flying Squadrons 240
    Leaders Lose Control 240
    War Means Jobs 241
    Capitalism Survives 242
    Human Labor Replaced 242
    Uranus and Keynesians 243
    Targeting Civilians 246
    Theories and New Realities 247

"BREAK ON THROUGH TO THE OTHER SIDE" 248

Table of Contents

    UNCANNY UNEXPECTEDNESS 249
    A MYSTIFYING TIME 250
    RIOTS AND LOVE-INS 250
    DRUGS, RADICALS, INFORMANTS 251
    THE DOMINO THEORY 252
    MEKONG AND MISSISSIPPI 253
    LUNCH COUNTER WARRIORS 253
    BEGINNING, MIDDLE, AND END 254
    CONSERVATIVES SHOCKED 258
    FLOW OF REVOLUTIONARY IDEAS 260
    KINGS, COMMONERS, AND GOLD 260
    GOLD AND PRICES 261
    URANUS AND ACTS OF GOD 262
    GRISHAM'S LAW 262
    ANOTHER KEYNESIAN STIMULUS 263
    DRUG WAR CASUALTIES 264
    PLUTOCRATS FIGHT BACK 265
    COMMUNIST MENACE BONANZA 265
    COMMUNIST CAPITALISTS 266
    WIDENING DISPARITY 267

WALL STREET DANCES, MAIN STREET WEEPS 268
    DREAMER AND SHOCKER 269
    THE BULL STUMBLES 270
    SPLIT TRENDS 272
    IRAQ'S SWITCH 272
    SPECULATIVE BUBBLE 273
    CHAOTIC HEALTH CARE SYSTEM 274
    FAITH IN FREE ENTERPRISE 274

YOU GET THE VOTE, WE GET YOUR OIL 276
    ARMIES AND ENVIRONMENTS 277
    RISE OF THE EURO 277
    PROTECTING THE DOLLAR 279
    POLL-VOTE DISCREPANCY 281
    HE WHO SELLS WHAT ISN'T HIS'N, MUST PAY THE PRICE OR GO TO PRISON 282
    OCCUPIED IRAQ VOTES 284
    WE'LL TAKE CARE OF YOUR OIL 284

Table of Contents

ISLAMIC TERRORISTS AND MOTHER NATURE 286
- "OUR FINEST PEOPLE" 287
- MONEY AND DEMOCRACY 287
- MAGICAL EUPHEMISMS 288
- TRANSLATION DIFFICULTIES 290
- UNDOING SOCIAL SECURITY 291
- HEADS I WIN, TAILS YOU LOSE 292
- "GREENSPAN'S WHOPPER" 294
- 2008 ELECTION 295
- GRISHAM'S LAW 297
- "CHANGE OR BE CHANGED" 298

EMPIRES AND REVOLUTIONS 299
- BOSTON TEA PARTY 299
- A WORLD-ALTERING MISTAKE 300
- REBIRTH OF CORPORATE TYRANNY 302
- "CORPORATIZED GOVERNMENT" 303
- THE MOST FREE SPEECH MONEY CAN BUY 304
- THE CORPORATE "FOOD CHAIN" 305
- SEA WHALES AND CEO WHALES 306
- A WORLD ACCORDING TO WAL-MART 307
- TREE OF POSSIBILITIES 308
- CORPORATOCRACY 309
- HUMPTY DUMPTY 310
- UPCOMING URANUS-PLUTO SQUARE 311
- MIND CONTROL 313

SECOND EDITION ADDENDUM 315
- BALLOONING DEBT 316
- PREDICTION 317
- CULTURAL SCRIPT 318
- HIS OWN PETARD 319
- SECRETS REVEALED 321
- PUBLIC UTILITY MONEY 323
- WINTER SOLSTICE LUNAR ECLIPSE 324

BIBLIOGRAPHY 326
ASTROLOGICAL CHARTS 329
INDEX 331

Note on Second Edition

Why a second edition? Since the first edition was published in 2005, I have become convinced that the USA's monetary system is the root cause of the economic malaise that has overcome us since the predicted crash of 2008. I have added information about the money system for this edition. I believe it will be imperative that we gain an understanding of how our privatized Federal Reserve's creation and distribution of money plunders our society. Without that understanding, the present economic malaise could be extended indefinitely. The Fed's natal Sun-Pluto opposition was hit hard by the 2010 Winter Solstice and simultaneous Lunar Eclipse, indicating a major transformation in our privatized, banker-run money system. It is unsustainable in any case and will either crash with dire consequences, or be changed and renew our national/international economy.

Introduction

One way of stating the basis of astrology is that the Earth, and thus we Earthlings, are part of a much larger environment. If you could look down on our Solar System from light-years above the North Pole, you'd see a community of planets moving counterclockwise around a Sun. You'd see that the paths of the planets are flat, and elliptical rather than circular. From that perspective, it would be obvious that Earth is part of this community we call the Solar System. We passengers on planet Earth are a minuscule part of this Solar System environment just as it is a minuscule part of the surrounding universe.

Astrology is also how we measure time. There is clock time, the cycles of days and nights, minutes and seconds, and the four seasons we experience as our planet orbits the Sun. And there is "Solar System time," measured by the cycles of primary angles made by the planets as seen from Earth. Clock time duplicates every 24 hours. In Solar System time, even though we measure it in earth-bound clock time, no two moments are ever exactly the same.

What we experience each year as winter is due to the Earth's rocking motion as it rolls around the Sun. Every winter brings cold but some winters are much colder than others. Planetary cycles are not so regular and they occur in an ever-changing celestial context. Every 28 days when the Sun and Moon come conjunct at the Lunation or New Moon, the other planets are in different angular relationships—by longitude, latitude, or degrees above or below the Ecliptic (the Sun's path)—to each other and each Lunation.

Robert Gover

Time Factor

In *Astrology and Stock Market Forecasting*, published in 1936, Louise McWhirter said: "The way conditions exist today, man is the victim of the business cycle. With detailed charts and graphs, he can tell you when business began to pick up, and when a recession started, but he cannot tell you these factors in advance, with all his statistical research, because he has no time factor."

Astrology provides that time factor. Saturn takes 28-30 Earth years to complete one orbit around the Sun, Uranus averages 84 years, Neptune 165 years, Pluto 248 years. Those four outermost are the "astro-economic indicators." By reviewing history to find what patterns they formed during past great depressions, we can gauge when another great depression is likely. Incidentally, Uranus is pronounced "*your*-an-us," nor "your *anis*."

The inner planets are those closest to the Earth: Moon, Mercury, Venus, the Sun, Mars and Jupiter. They are of secondary concern because they move too swiftly to mark years or decades of major economic cycles.

Every time the USA has gone through a great depression, the outermost, slowest moving planets have formed what astrologers call a grand cross with the USA's natal Sun and Saturn. Every time Uranus has returned to early Gemini where it was when the USA was "born" July 4, 1776, America has experienced its worst wars. Every time Uranus and Pluto have moved into conjunctions or 90-degree squares and simultaneously come conjunct, opposite or square sensitive points in the US birth chart, America has experienced social changes or upheavals. (Planetary angles are explained below.)

Other wars occur when the US natal Uranus is "afflicted" by transiting planets, as happened when the World Trade Center and Pentagon were attacked. Saturn and Pluto form 180-degree oppositions three times a century, the latest being in effect on September 11, 2001. The previous Saturn-Pluto opposition coincided with the tempestuous period we now call The Sixties; the one before that with what we now call The Great Depression (1930s).

Astrologers speak of the planets influencing but not controlling us. We have free will, intelligence, historic memory, and judgment. We don't freeze to death in winter because we're prepared. We can also prepare for economic winters and times of radical social change.

Beliefs and Evidence

A kind of dialogue occurs between an entity's cultural assumptions and the planetary influences. Our cultural assumptions contain our most basic and unquestioned beliefs. We tend to interpret evidence according to our beliefs, and too often find what we believe should be rather than what the evidence indicates. I synthesize this human proclivity in the phrase, *belief trumps evidence*. A capitalist and socialist viewing Third World poverty will prescribe different remedies based on their different beliefs.

Astrology has been called God's newsletter. The basic message it brings is that we humans are not in charge here. We must harmonize with God's will or suffer consequences. By adding astrology to economic forecasting, we can much more intelligently predict when the next economically difficult period will arrive. For example, the first edition of this book predicted a major downturn beginning early in 2008, and that's exactly what has happened.

Although humans have been stargazing for millennia, no one has discovered the why or how of these coincidences or synchronicities or correlations. All we know for sure is that certain planetary cycles and angles coincide with certain types of events here on planet Earth.

Money

Just as baffling as the effect of the planets on our lives, and paralleling the development of astrology, is the development of money. An interesting perspective on money in the 20th Century came from a former director of the Bank of England, Lord Josiah Stemp, who in 1937 said, "The modern banking system manufactures money out of nothing.

The process is perhaps the most astounding piece of slight of hand that was ever invented...If you want to be slaves of the bankers, and pay the cost of your own slavery, then let the banks create money."

As far back as 700 BC people found they could expand economic well-being by using things like cowry shells, seeds, rare stones and bits of metal to facilitate trading. In the past three centuries it was deemed more convenient to keep precious metals in vaults and use paper money that could be exchanged for those precious metals. "...the paper bill was originally the equivalent of a receipt showing that the bearer owned an amount of precious metal, but the paper receipt was more convenient and transportable."

But paper money has brought out humankind's proclivity for self-destructive greed, and this proclivity has mushroomed during the last quarter of the 20th Century and first years of the 21st Century. "Money has become almost pure abstraction delinked from anything of value." (*When Corporations Rule the World* by David C. Korten, 2001, Barrett-Koehler Publisher, page 179.) "There are two common ways to create money without creating value," continues Korten. "One is by creating debt. Another is by building up asset values. The global financial system is adept at using both of these devices to create money delinked from the creation of value." (Page 181.)

This we have done and it has led to a growing problem. One past US Treasury secretary, Nicholas F. Brady, put it this way: "If the assets were gold or oil, this phenomenon (unrestrained creation of more and more dollars) would be called inflation. In stocks, it's called wealth creation."

With the delinking of money from the gold standard and the invention of computers, coupled with our human urge to amass wealth, "The global financial system has become a parasitic predator that lives off the flesh of its host—the productive economy." Page 185.

Money and Mayan Astrologers

We must keep the distinction between finances and the economy clear. I define the economy as all our efforts to produce and distribute food, clothing and shelter, and the amenities, arts and sciences. Our modern, industrial economy, national and global, needs capital investments. Investors usually seek as much profit as quickly as possible. Their profits may or may not benefit the overall economy. When trillions of dollars are made or lost in instantaneous computerized trades having nothing to do with the production of goods and services, the prediction of Mayan astrologers centuries ago is validated.

The Maya, like other Native Americans, believed that Mother Nature is the kingpin capitalist. From the perspective of the ancient Mayan astrologers, the abstracting of money from our Earthly environment means our modern world's financial system is ripe for radical change around 2012, change more revolutionary than any known in recorded history. That Maya prediction correlates with Western astrology's history of Pluto's 248-year visits to Capricorn, to be combined with an angle to Uranus which will be impacting in 2012. Uranus "rules" electricity.

"Assume that, for whatever reason, all the information in all the computers of the banks of the world were suddenly eradicated. This would mean that all accounts and holdings of money, stock, options, etc., would disappear. Although many individuals would regard this as a catastrophe, we may ask if anything of value would be lost. Obviously not! All natural resources, buildings, machines, human knowledge, goods, etc., that existed before, would remain untouched by such a hypothetical synchronistic crash in all the world's bank computers. In terms of real values, nothing would be lost and the world could easily pick up the day after (leaving aside the emotional effects this occurrence would have on many)."

The author of the above is Carl Johan Calleman, a biomedical scientist with a Ph. D. from the University of Stockholm. He has dedicated himself to studying the Mayan Calendar and has found correlations between it and economic history. He has concluded this:

"The correlation between (economic and Mayan cycles) is so strong that most economists could only dream of attaining a similar concordance to support their theories."

What's the Economy For?

The question running through this book is this: What's the economy for? The money profit of a few, or the well-being of all? What is the long-range goal of our economic busyness?

As I write this, it's become obvious that the global economy is way out of whack: it produces too much wealth for the few, too little for the many.

Columbus sailed forth to find a shortcut to India and obtain gold and the slaves to dig it up for him. That mission is the essence of what motivates modern global corporations. The costumes, tools and architecture have changed since Columbus, but essentially the same beliefs drive the search for wealth.

We respond to economic crises both individually and collectively. When the great depression of the 1930s arrived, the American nation suffered as a whole, most individuals suffered personally, but a few founded new family fortunes.

Times and Fortunes

The observable fact is that each nation and each individual has a relationship with planetary patterns as surely as the tides of the seas are moved by the Moon. One person's combination of planetary influences, beliefs, and economic circumstances may result in that person prospering while most around him suffer. An heiress and an orphan, born at the same time and place, will respond differently to an economic downturn. One of my grandfathers suffered during the great depression of the 1930s; the other grandfather grew abundant crops for his own family and had an excess to sell or share with those less fortunate.

Planetary cycles repeat but each moment in celestial time is unique. History repeats but never duplicates. Economic cycles repeat but in an ever-changing context. The astrological clock is complex.

My aim is to keep this presentation as simple as possible in order to communicate to as many as possible. So I will keep the focus on "transit

Time and Money

to natal" studies, showing that repeating planetary cycles and the major angles formed to certain points in the USA's horoscope coincide with times of major economic changes.

What I've done, to oversimplify, is sit with a history book in one hand and a table of daily planetary positions in the other hand, and search for similar planetary patterns which repeat with similar economic events—except that I've used a computer instead of a huge library.

The historic events referred to are easily checked. To communicate astrological information to readers who are not versed in the language of astrology, I try to keep it as simple as possible—while enabling other astrologers to check my charts and interpretations.

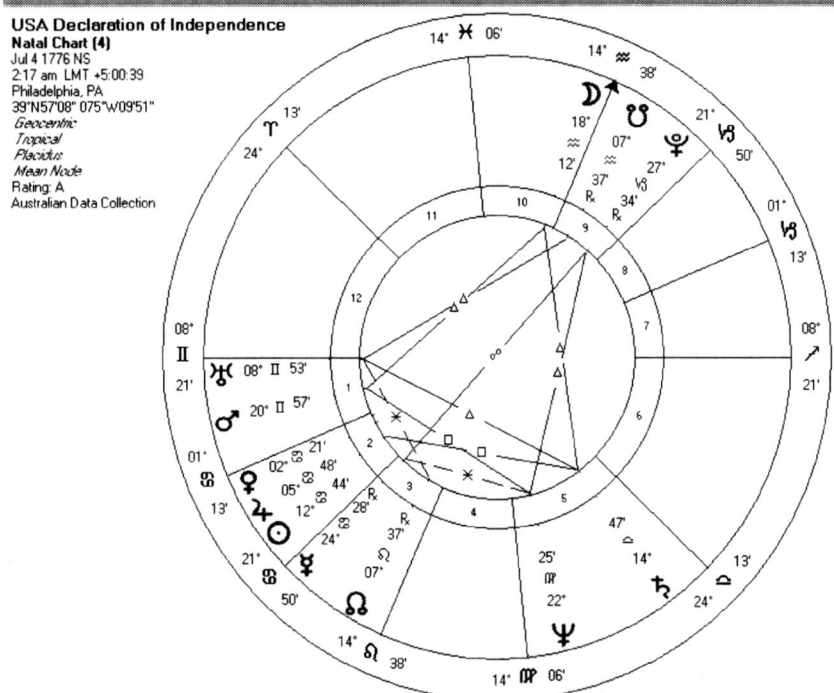

Let's begin with the USA's birth chart. The primary focus throughout this book will be the cluster of planets in the Signs of Gemini (at 9 o'clock) and Cancer (about 8 o'clock). The secondary focus will be on the opposition between Mercury shown at 24 Cancer opposite Pluto at 27 Capricorn.

Robert Gover

Notice:
1) Sun in Cancer *square* Saturn in Libra.
2) Mars in Gemini *square* Neptune in Virgo.
3) Mercury in Cancer *opposite* Pluto in Capricorn.

The Planets

☉	Sun	Soul/Ego
☽	Moon	Emotions/Mother/Moods
☿	Mercury	Thought/Communications/travel
♀	Venus	Love/Beauty/Art
♂	Mars	Strength/Force/Aggression
♃	Jupiter	Abundance/Good Fortune
♄	Saturn	Structures/Hardships
♅	Uranus	Surprise/Change/Genius
♆	Neptune	Mystery/Inspiration/Illusion
♇	Pluto	Birth/Death/Transformation

The Major Aspects

Name	Symbol	Exact degree
Conjunction	☌	0
Opposition	☍	180
Square	□	90
Trine	△	120
Sextile	✶	60

The term *within orb* is used to convey how close to exact an aspect is. An "allowable orb" may be 3, 7 or 10 degrees plus or minus exact, depending on the clusters of planets involved, and on who is interpreting. The planets rarely form exact aspects, and then but briefly. These are called "hits."

A *Grand Cross* aspect is created when four planets form simultaneous squares and oppositions to each other. This is a rare aspect which brings obstructions, tensions, frustrations, i.e. a grand cross to the US Sun-Saturn square has formed the last three times the USA has fallen into a great depression.

A *Grand Trine* aspect is also rare, and is formed by a triangle of three planets 120 degrees from each other, creating harmonious flows of energy, good fortune and opportunities.

A *T Square* is formed when planets are opposite each other and simultaneously both square another. T square afflictions to the US Mars-Neptune square by planets in either Sagittarius (opposite the US Mars) or Pisces (opposite the US Neptune) have coincided with stock market panics.

Biwheel charts are used for **transit studies**. Also called **comparison charts**, a biwheel is used to compare where the planets where at two different moments in time.

In this book, the USA's birth chart will be shown on the inner wheels, and the positions of the planets for a notable event on the outer wheels. Those notable events are great depressions, stock market panics, wars, social upheavals and other historic turning points.

USA's Birth Time

Among astrologers there is ongoing debate as to precisely what time on July 4, 1776, should be used to erect the USA's natal chart. Historic evidence suggests that the time was in the afternoon of July 4, with philosophical Sagittarius Rising. Another historic time used gives a Scorpio Rising chart. The Gemini Rising time I use is not based on historical evidence, yet it's been used by many astrologers over the past two centuries. This is because the most influential Founders were Masons, who understood the basics of astrology. As Masons, they would want to have Sun, Jupiter and Venus in the 2nd house of wealth. One could hardly ask for a more fortunate 2nd house trio than those, promising great prosperity. Indeed the USA soon became the world's wealthiest nation. This suggests the Founders, being Masons, would fix the time on July 4 between 2 am to roughly 2:30 am, placing these three most beneficent planets together in the "house of money."

History shows that Uncle Sam has behaved as an entity with Uranus conjunct Gemini Rising. The key words for Uranus here are "free and independent, original and unique, sharing exciting ideas." The USA has, since its formation, aggressively asserted its independence, promoted freedom and individuality, and come forth with some of mankind's most exciting ideas and inventions, prominent among these being political democracy and The Bill of Rights addendum to the Constitution.

The negative tendencies of Uranus in Gemini on the Ascendant are bullheadedness and aggressive proselytizing, and over its brief history the USA has shown these tendencies too. Uranus here often describes an eccentric genius who is by turns admired and ostracized, and in the community of nations, the USA has certainly been both.

Economic Planetary Cycles

Of primary importance in economic astrology are the four outermost planets—Saturn, Uranus, Neptune and Pluto—and the cyclical conjuncttions, squares and oppositions they form. These are sometimes called "synodic cycles," meaning they occur at roughly regular time intervals.

In this book I will be focusing mainly on two: Saturn-Pluto cycles and Uranus-Pluto cycles.

In other astrological specialties, Jupiter is considered among the distant planets, too, as compared to the inner planets, those closest to Earth: Moon, Mercury, Sun, Venus and Mars. Jupiter moves a little too swiftly to have the major economic impact of the outermost four.

Jupiter is expansive, the bringer of Great Good Fortune, although it can also amplify the negative influences of other planetary aspects. Conjunctions of Jupiter-Saturn occur every 20 years; Jupiter-Uranus every 14 years; Jupiter-Neptune every 13 years, and Jupiter-Pluto every 12.7 years.

Saturn-Uranus Cycles

The conjunction of Saturn and Uranus combine the systematized with sudden change or innovation. They occur every 45 years. The last time this conjunction occurred, the Berlin Wall came down and the Soviet Union "deconstructed," freeing former nations from the Soviet block and restructuring Russia as a single nation. In the USA this conjunction in 1989-1990 brought a rash of corporate mergers and restructurings. Both the Soviet and American economies restructured, and this theme was repeated around the world in various other nations.

Each conjunction is followed by 90-degree "waxing" squares, 180-degree oppositions, and 270-degree "waning" squares. The 270 degrees is arrived at by adding 90 degrees to the opposition's 180 degrees. Much like the phases of the Moon, the waxing phase is when the effects of a conjunction are most potent.

The Saturn-Uranus waxing square culminated in the late 1990s, and this period coincided with tremendous innovations in computers and Internet technologies. Rapid developments in computer technology upgraded autos and a long list of other things we use daily, from telephones to TV "clickers" to microwave ovens to factory assembly lines.

The Saturn-Uranus opposition will be in effect from 2008 through 2010 and will make five "direct hits." During those years we can expect a kind of restructuring of technologies as applied to Saturnian endeavors like big industries, government systems, personal electronics and, since Uranus brings the unprecedented, surprises we cannot anticipate.

Saturn-Neptune Cycles

This 36-year conjunction combines the practical and the intuitive, and/or the deceptive and the delusional. When favorably aspected by other planets, the matter-of-fact works harmoniously with the inspirational. When unfavorably aspected, self-delusion and delusions generally hold sway. The speculative mania of the late 1990s and the bursting of that stock market bubble is a good example of the Saturn-Neptune pair's effects. So was the Supreme Court decision called Bush v. Gore in December, 2000.

The latest Saturn-Neptune square culminated in 1998 and 1999, and the atmosphere it stimulated was epitomized by the 2000 Presidential Election, settled by the Supreme Court, in effect declaring George W. Bush the new President by stopping a Florida vote recount. Liberals felt defrauded and were outraged. Conservatives found the decision inspiring. Just about everyone who carefully analyzed it wound up confused. This Neptunian fog is neatly explored in "A Layman's Guide

Time and Money

to the Supreme Court Decision in Bush v. Gore by Mark H. Levine, Attorney at Law." Here's a sample of Levine's Q and A with a baffled non-lawyer:

Q: So Bush wins because hand-counts are illegal?
A: Oh no. Six of the justices (two-thirds majority) believed the hand-counts were legal and should be done.
Q: Is there an exception in this case?
A: Yes...This decision is limited to only this situation.
Q: C'mon. The Supremes didn't really say that. You're exaggerating.
A: Nope. They held "Our consideration is limited to the present circumstances...the problem of equal protection in election processes generally presents many complexities."
Q: What complexities?
A: They don't say.
Q: The votes can't be counted because the Florida Supreme Court "changed the rules of the election after it was held." Right?
A. Dead wrong. The US Supreme Court made clear that the Florida Supreme Court did not change the rules of the election. But the US Supreme Court found the failure of the Florida Court to change the rules was wrong.
Q: Huh?
A: The Legislature declared that the only legal standard for counting votes is "clear intent of the voter." The Florida Court was condemned for not adopting a clearer standard.
Q: I thought the Florida Court was not allowed to change the Legislature's law after the election.
A: Right.
Q: So what's the problem?
A: The US Supreme Court said the Florida Supreme Court should have "adopt[ed] adequate statewide standards for determining what is a legal vote"
Q: I thought only the Legislature could "adopt" new law.
A: Right.

13

Q: If the (Florida Supreme) Court had adopted new standards, it would have been overturned for changing the rules. And if it didn't, it's overturned for not changing the rules. That means that no matter what the Florida Supreme Court did, legal votes could never be counted.
A: Right. Next question.
(See http://www.iknowwhatyoudidlastelection.com/bush-supreme-court.htm.)

Saturn-Pluto Cycles

The conjunction, averaging 33.8 years, combines the desire to maintain the status quo with the pull for transformative change. When favorably aspected, Saturn's systemization works harmoniously with Pluto's transformations. When negatively aspected, the status quo may change for the worse. The last occurred in 1982 when President Ronald Regan dramatically expanded the military-industrial complex, launched the doomed "star wars" defense program, and curtailed the power of unions. Reagan's "supply-side" economics enriched conservatives, who view him as a hero.

The waxing Saturn-Pluto square culminated in January 1994 with Bill Clinton in the White House, feeling curtailed by Reaganomics and the push by conservative industrialists to join the World Trade Organization and expand "free" trade. The tendency during this pair's waxing square period is to become obsessive, demanding, controlling.

The Saturn-Pluto opposition, as we shall explore in more detail in the next chapter, coincided with the attack of September 11, 2001, the passage of the Patriot Act curtailing the inalienable rights of US citizens, the creation of the prison for "noncombatants" at Guantanomo Naval Base in Cuba and shipping prisoners to foreign lands to avoid US laws against torture. In brief, the Bush Administration took a big Saturnian step back to the mindset of Medieval feudalism.

Uranus-Neptune Cycles

This Uranus-Neptune conjunction occurs every 171 years. The last occurred in 1993 at 19 Capricorn, opposite a point between the US Sun and US Mercury. Each aspect formed by these two planets is within orb for extended periods and are usually seen as descriptive of generations. However, it's obvious from history that Uranus-Neptune cycles have an economic impact as well. The last was colored by a mildly beneficent 60 degree sextile from Pluto and 30 degree semi-sextile from Saturn. Uranian innovativeness worked with Neptunian inspiration to power the dot com stock bubble.

The next waxing square won't culminate to exact until 2039. The last waxing square made exact hits during 1868 to 1870, the tumultuous years following the Civil War. Actually, the Civil War occurred as this waxing square was applying. It followed the conjunction of 1821 and coincided with a Supreme Court decision that strengthened the powers of Congress and established the Bank of the United States, siding with Congress against states. This led in turn to the Second Bank of the US, destroyed by President Andrew Jackson, a states rights advocate.

Uranus-Neptune conjunctions, squares and oppositions are in effect for extended periods during which the forces of innovation grapple with the forces of a variety of Neptunian qualities: fear, inspiration, delusion, illumination. Neptune's diffusive effect is often the uncertainty associated with inspirations and delusions.

Uranus-Pluto Cycles

This conjunction occurs once every 127 years. The last conjunction defined The Sixties, combining Uranus' rebellious streak with Pluto's transformative effects. African Americans rebelled against their second-class citizen status; the youth of America rebelled against the government's right to force them to fight in foreign wars; women rebelled against traditional limitations imposed on them.

The waxing Uranus-Pluto square will make 7 direct hits between 2012 and 2015 but will be within orb from 2008 to 2019. Keeping in mind that waxing squares deliver the most energetic power of conjunctions, we can expect this upcoming decade to culminate what was seeded in The Sixties. What promises to make this period even more awesome than The Sixties is that the Uranus-Pluto square will form a lingering grand cross pattern with the US Sun-Saturn square. Rebellious movements seeded in The Sixties will sprout up stronger during the 2000-teens.

Neptune-Pluto Cycles

These occur twice per millennium, conjunction to conjunction, averaging 494 to 496 years. The last one occurred in 1892, although its effects were felt from the late 1870s to the early 1900s. It occurred conjunct the USA's Ascendant and Uranus in Gemini, indicating the USA would rise in prominence within the community of nations.

The Neptune-Pluto conjunction heralds major cultural changes. Although such changes are not always obvious immediately, upon looking back decades later it becomes obvious that humanity has taken a new path, that some old beliefs have been lost or forgotten, new beliefs arisen and been accepted.

Neptune and Pluto will form their square from 2061 to 2065, making nine direct hits during that time.

Neptune's effects are inspirational, delusional, vague and sometimes expansively good, sometimes contagiously fearful, depending on how the conjunction is aspected by the other planets, especially Saturn and Uranus.

Pluto is named for the god of the underworld and/or the great mystery from whence all things arise into manifestation and into which all things eventually disappear. Pluto rules births, transformations and deaths. He reminds us that nothing in our Earthly reality is permanent, for even mountains and seas had their origins and undergo transformations.

Time and Money

Columbus arrived in America during the waxing years after the Neptune-Pluto conjunction of 1398. We don't have photographs showing what the "new world" looked like then, but from journals written by early explorers we know the Western Hemisphere has gone through immense changes since then, and that the most dramatic occurred during the waxing period, from 1492 to 1572. How many natives perished from diseases brought from Old Europe to the New World is unknown; estimates range from several million to hundreds of millions.

The last Neptune-Pluto opposition made 11 direct hits between 1644 and 1648, when the first English settlers were struggling to stay alive and learn to survive in what is now the Eastern Coastal region of the USA.

Keep in mind, too, that when each of the four points of any of these cycles are reached by any of these outermost pairs of planets, the other bodies of our Solar System are arranged differently than the last conjunction, square or opposition.

The Corporatocracy & 911

I want to begin with the most recent event which has altered the USA's economic position in the community of nations. Astrologically it marks the first manifestation of Pluto's return to where it was when the 13 colonies, under British rule, were embroiled in the French and Indian War. The aftermath of that war became the years of turmoil and chaos leading to the American Revolution. Pluto takes an average of 248 years to orbit the Sun, so with the attack we now refer to simply as 911, we entered a second cycle in US history of Pluto in the wintry signs.

To recap: On the morning of September 11, 2001, hijacked airliners were used as bombs in suicide attacks on the World Trade Center in New York City and the Pentagon in Washington, DC when Pluto returned to where it had been for the outbreak of the French and Indian War, 12 Sagittarius, opposite the USA's natal Uranus and Mars in Gemini.

The most telling astrological pattern at the time was an opposition of Saturn in Gemini and Pluto in Sagittarius. Uncle Sam's natal Uranus and Mars in Gemini were impacted by this opposition. A reading of this combination: Sam's Uranus and Mars under affliction from Saturn and Pluto brings explosive (Mars), unprecedented surprises (Uranus), suffering and frustration (Saturn) leading to huge transformations (Pluto).

The Sun this day was conjunct the US Neptune in Virgo, square the US Mars, suggesting confusion, deception. Even three years later, many are not satisfied by official explanations, giving rise to suspicions that the Bush Administration has not revealed all it knows about this horrendous event. The Sun signifies the President. Conjunct Neptune suggests the leader's motives and actions aren't clear; they're shrouded in a Neptunian fog.

Many articles and books have been written, raising questions or explaining, for instance, why military fighter planes were not routinely scrambled as soon as it was known the first airliner had veered off its scheduled heading. Probably the most famous and widely distributed examination of this event and its aftermath is Michael Moore's documentary film "Fahrenheit 911," portraying President Bush as using this attack to link Saddam Hussein of Iraq to the Islamic militants who brought 911.

An immediate concern arising from 911 was why US intelligence operatives, seen by many as globally ubiquitous, had not alerted the Bush Administration that such an attack was being planned. During a Congressional hearing it came out that some in the intelligence community were aware, and had tried to alert the Bush Administration but were rebuffed. The suspicion grew that Bush and his inner circle used 911 as an excuse to invade Iraq as well as Afghanistan, where the attackers had been trained by Osama bin Laden and al Qaeda. Further confusing the situation and giving rise to more suspicions and speculations was the fact that, during the Soviet war in Afghanistan, the CIA had supplied and trained bin Laden and al Qaeda. Moreover, the CIA had sided with Saddam Hussein previously in the Iraq-Iran war.

The Bush Administration and corporatized media mounted a stunningly effective public relations campaign which convinced, by some polls, 70 to 80 percent of the American people that Hussein's Iraq was behind the attack of 911, had weapons of mass destruction and plans to use them against Americans. Those who disagreed with this fantasy were denigrated as "conspiracy theorists," further splitting an already divided public. One thing all could agree upon was that the USA and world would never be the same again, that 911 had "changed everything."

Robert Gover

Saturn-Pluto Opposition

The key planetary aspect on September 11, 2001 was the opposition of Saturn and Pluto, within orb of both the US Uranus and Mars-square-Neptune. This indicated the US establishment was up against the new and revolutionary—the unmovable battered by the unstoppable. Saturn-Pluto oppositions occur three times a century and indicate a major change is underway. Since those of established power resist change, Saturn-Pluto oppositions portend conflict.

The previous Saturn-Pluto opposition was in 1965 coinciding with the war in Vietnam and the social upheavals of The Sixties (Uranus-Pluto conjunct in Virgo and both conjunct the US Neptune, opposite Saturn), and before that, in 1931 during the Great Depression, when another Saturn-Pluto opposition hit the US Sun-square-Saturn. In both those periods, established assumptions were changed.

The worst wars in American history have occurred when Uranus has returned to its natal position in Gemini. Less severe wars have occurred when this point in the US chart was harshly aspected by transiting planets, as it was September 11. Uranus, when triggered by such a pattern, manifests the unexpected, and often shocking. It is said of Pluto that its effects have subtle beginnings but manifest dramatically. By 911, transiting Pluto's opposition to the US Uranus was separating while its opposition to the US Mars was applying. Hard aspects formed by the inner planets (Moon, Mercury, Venus, Mars and to some extent Jupiter) may bring transitory events, but the outermost planets (Saturn, Uranus, Neptune and Pluto) bring long-lasting changes.

One positive aspect on this day is that transiting Uranus and Neptune in Aquarius were forming a 120-degree trine to Uncle Sam's Mars and Uranus, focusing energy on the USA's war-making ability. But on the morning of 911 Mercury was on New York's eastern horizon and fiery Mars was involved, as well as the Sun conjunct the US Neptune. This mix taken together indicates immediate shock to be followed by Neptunian confusion and long-range Plutonian transformation.

Months before 911, I emailed some friends expressing the fear that our nation's capitol appeared likely to be hit by a suitcase nuke or other weapon of mass destruction. That we were attacked did not surprise me; how we were attacked did. My astrological reading suggested it could have been much worse.

The official explanation was that this event had been perpetrated by 19 Arab jihadis, 17 from Saudi Arabia. Clearly it had been engineered by people who were technologically savvy and willing to sacrifice their lives for their cause. Aimed at the World Trade Center and Pentagon, the objective was clearly to cripple the global empire and its military backup.

By mid-day, the World Trade Center's famous twin towers had disappeared from the Manhattan skyline, collapsed in on themselves, pancaked to piles of rubble, smothering the Wall Street area in poisonous smoke, dust and debris. Casualties were expected at first to be over 5,000, a figure later cut to under 3,000.

Evidence suggested this attack had been planned for years. Key members of this cadre had received pilot training inside the USA. Three of the hijacked airliners completed their missions; the fourth crashed and exploded in southwestern Pennsylvania. Presumably it had been on its way to deliver another attack on Washington. It was later surmised that passengers on this flight had heard of the previous hits and had jumped the hijackers, causing them to lose control of the airliner.

Most Devastating

It was the most devastating attack by a foreign entity on US soil in American history. From coast to coast, schools and businesses closed, all air traffic ceased, and vehicle traffic thinned on interstate highways as people went home to stare at televisions and find out from corporate-owned TV news what had happened.

The biwheel chart for 911 has the US natal chart on the inner wheel (the clock face) and the chart for the first strike on the WTC on the outer wheel (the celestial time when it occurred).

Robert Gover

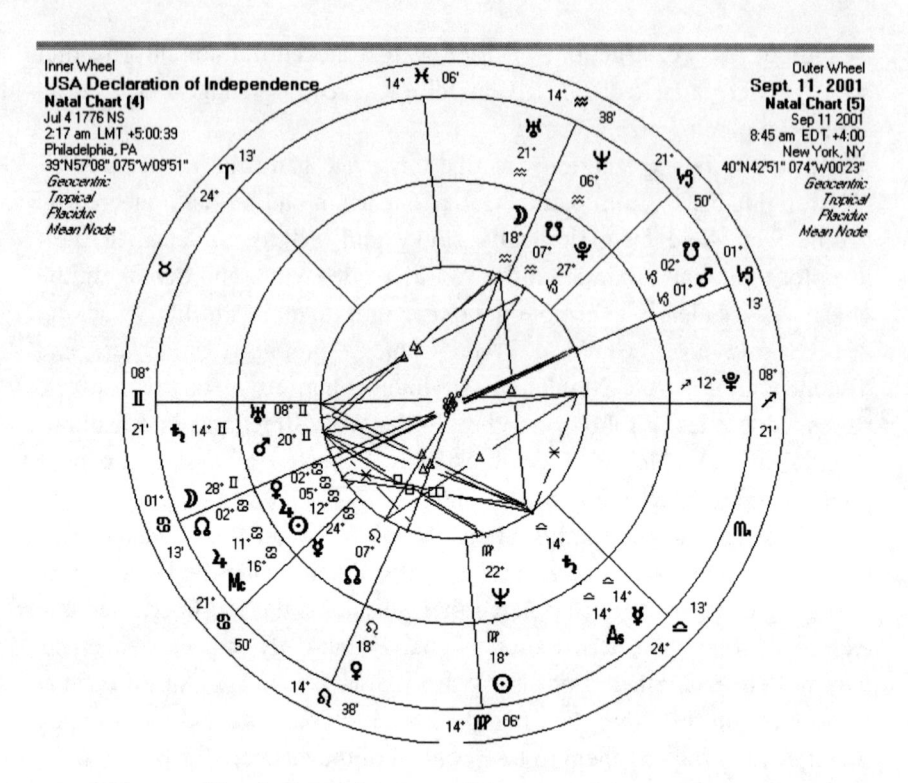

This combined chart shows a rich mix of harmonious trines and difficult oppositions and right-angle, 90-degree squares. Natal Uranus is involved in the grand trine with Mercury conjunct the US natal Saturn, in turn trine transiting Uranus and the US natal Moon, plus US Mars trine US Saturn, Moon and Uranus—all these harmonious angles had the American people united and primed to do whatever it would take to deal with this crisis. Americans had not been so united since World War II when we were shocked by the Japanese attack on Pearl Harbor. (Saturn and Uranus applying to a conjunction of the US Uranus, Pluto opposite its natal position.) In both instances, most of the world's peoples sympathized with Americans when they learned what had happened. There was one huge difference in the circumstances of the USA, however. In 1941, the USA was in danger of being dominated by foreign powers; in 2001 the USA was the single dominant power in the world.

Wherever in our Solar System the thrice-per-century Saturn-Pluto opposition forms speaks to what area of activity will be most impacted.

Time and Money

Pearl Harbor followed the Saturn-Pluto opposition of 1930 which afflicted the US Sun-square-Saturn, indicating this was predominantly an economic event. On 911, the Saturn-Pluto opposition impacted the USA's war-making Uranus and Mars-Neptune square, impacting primarily the financial section.

The USA quickly mobilized for war in the 1940s, cranking up its dormant productive capacity to supply the military. In 2001, the US military-industrial complex was the world's greatest. In the 1940s there was no doubt that the US was fighting for its independence and economic survival. In 2001, the USA faced a radical new threat to its monetary dominance.

We's and Their They's

Another way to describe the mood of a Saturn-Pluto opposition is this: *All the we's are good and all their they's are evil.* An especially adverse angle formed by this opposition to a nativity's chart can raise a lot of partisan passion. The 1960s Saturn-Pluto opposition involved Uranus, and created a T square with the US Mars, square the US Neptune. The passions of pro- and anti-war factions brought the Vietnam War home.

Shortly after 911, when the Bush administration and corporate-owned media were beating the war drums, Bush used the word "crusade" to characterize this war he envisioned. It's now clear that his intention was to morph al Qaeda attackers with Saddam Hussein. This propaganda spin succeeded. A majority of Americans were misinformed into believing that Saddam and Iraq were connected to 911 when in fact they were not.

The Crusades were launched by the Roman Catholic Pope about a thousand years previous to Bush, with Saturn at 13 Libra opposite Pluto at 11 Aries. Another coincidence: Crusaders used the severed heads of Arabs as cannon balls lobbed over the walls of Arab cities; now Iraqi insurgents sever the heads of Americans and other Westerners, and lob them over the worldwide Internet.

Many Americans were irked when the Iraq War was compared to the Vietnam War. During any Saturn-Pluto opposition, it's not always immediately clear what radical new is threatening what status quo. The Saturn-Pluto opposition of 1931 saw the German Third Reich's genocide of Jews and other "undesirables" while the Roosevelt Administration pushed socially beneficial legislation to uplift the American poor and middle class. Both radically changed previous status quos.

Similar to 911

In 1898, the Saturn-Pluto opposition came precise with Saturn at 14 Sagittarius and Pluto at 14 Gemini, almost a mirror image of the 2001 opposition. The American public was aroused by the media of this time when the US Navy Battleship *Maine* exploded in Havana Harbor. People chorused, "Remember the Maine!" President McKinley was pressured into asking Congress for a declaration of war. The major change during this period was that the USA departed from its "isolationism" and assumed the task of economically and militarily dominating the Western Hemisphere, called the Monroe Doctrine, launching America on the empire-building which climaxed on 911. How a nation deals with one Saturn-Pluto opposition creates the circumstances it finds itself in when the next arrives.

During the Saturn-Pluto opposition of 1866, in the swash of the Civil War, the Fourteenth Amendment was ratified to enfranchise former slaves but had unintended consequences—Jim Crow violence in the South segueing to the great depression of the 1870s, the longest (though not the most severe) in US history. Then the Fourteenth Amendment was twisted to bestow upon corporations all the rights of freed slaves but without the accompanying responsibilities of full citizenship. (Santa Clara County V. Southern Pacific Railroad)

Time and Money

Returning to the 20th Century

Construction of the World Trade Towers was begun about the same time the Vietnam War kicked into high gear, April of 1966. Many saw the towers as an assault on the New York skyline. At that time Saturn was in Pisces opposite Pluto in Virgo, and Pluto was conjunct Uranus, with both conjunct the US natal Neptune, which squares the warrior energy of the US natal Mars in Gemini. (See Chart 3)

On 911, Saturn was in Gemini, square where it had been in 1966, and Pluto was opposite in Sagittarius, square where it had been in 1966. (See Chart 4) My guess is that you'd have to search astronomical calculations back many millennia to find a previous time when Saturn in Pisces was opposite both Pluto and Uranus in Virgo. As a society, the USA is still trying to resolve the cultural conflicts of The Sixties.

Jim Crow, Drugs, Vietnam

The joke is that if you lived the Sixties you can't remember what happened because you were either zapped on drugs or clashing with police over Jim Crow or the Vietnam War, and in either case, things were happening so fast and furiously that no one had any idea how it would all shake out. The unprecedented became the norm, and you came to expect the unexpected. That was Uranus' influence at play.

From an astrological perspective it's the surprising geometry of the latest Saturn-Pluto opposition, combined with the 1960s pattern, which reprised memories of The Sixties. Then as now we were caught up in a foreign war which, unlike World War II, not all Americans believed was justified.

Americans had been split also over the Spanish-American War coinciding with the Saturn-Pluto opposition of 1898, and during the Reconstruction years coinciding with the opposition of 1863 following the Civil War when the first Civil Rights Bill was passed. As a nation, we have yet to finally resolve our peculiar racial separatism.

Robert Gover

What may we learn from the pattern formed by Saturn, Uranus, Neptune and Pluto during the mid-1960s (building of the Twin Towers and Vietnam War) concerning the Saturn-Pluto opposition of 911 and the morphing of the Iraq War and so-called "war on terror"?

Now (Iraq War) as then (Vietnam War), there was a disconnect between the American masses and their political leaders. Now as then the US Administration is being isolated by other nations and called arrogant, ignorant and hypocritical. There are important differences: the US military now is all volunteer, whereas then its foot soldiers were draftees; now the USA is energy-dependent on oil-producing nations; in the 1960s the USA was much less vulnerable to foreign oil-producers.

Back in The Sixties, the military-industrial complex was All-American. Now Congress has enabled big corporations to plunder countries all over the planet, including our own homeland by outsourcing American jobs to cheap labor countries and importing cheap labor from south of the border to "downsize" American workers.

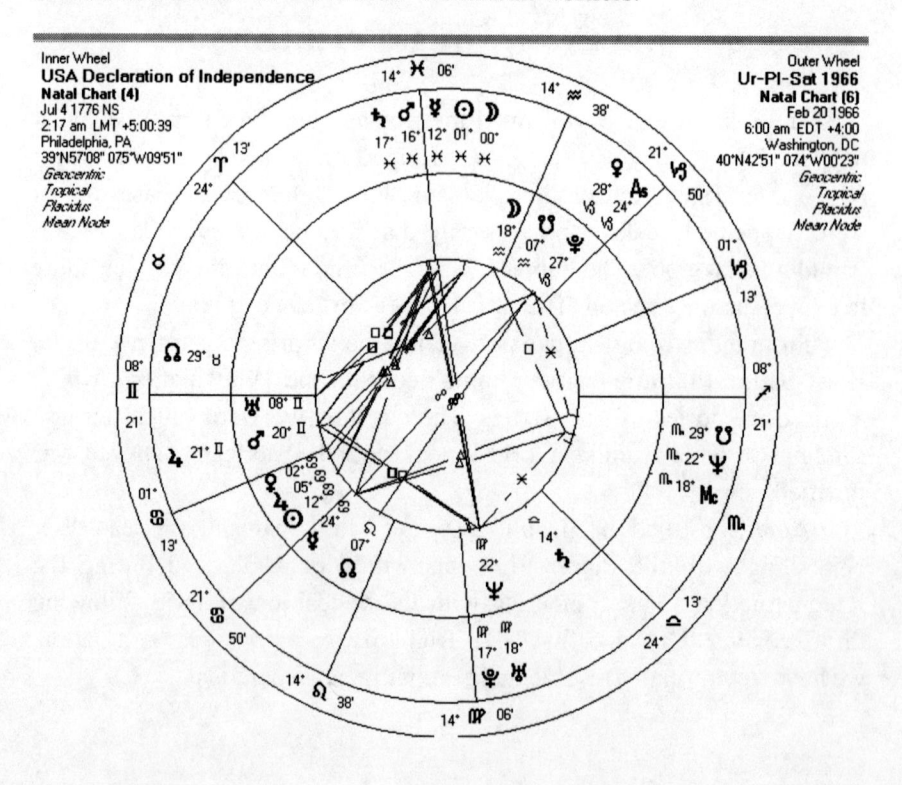

Time and Money

Because the global empire is headquartered in our nation's capitol, the inevitable blowback will manifest most dramatically in Washington, DC, as happened in the sixties. Both Saturn-Pluto oppositions—the 1960s and 2001—hit the same sensitive points in the USA's natal birth chart: the Mars-Neptune square.

Compare the previous chart showing where Saturn and Pluto were in 1966 with the previous chart showing where they were in 2001. Saturn, remember, takes about 30 years to orbit our Sun; Pluto takes about 248 years. From 1966 to 2001, Saturn made about one and a quarter orbits; Pluto made about one-quarter orbit. Both were thus 90 degrees square in 2001 where they had been in 1966.

We will get another reminder of the Sixties in late 2008 and early 2009 when Uranus is at 20 Pisces and Saturn is at 20 Virgo, again making right angles to the US Mars.

Why Did They Do It?

In the immediate aftermath of 911, Americans were shocked, sickened and Sun-conjunct-Neptune puzzled. Why did those Arabs attack us? What had we ever done to them?

John Perkins knows a lot about why they attacked. He is the author of *Confessions of an Economic Hit Man*, a book roundly rejected by the big media corporate publishers, which became an instant bestseller when it was finally published.

Perkins is a former member of the international banking community. There are others in banking and academia who know bits and pieces of the story which has been unfolding since 1970, unbeknownst to the American public. Perkins alone has had the rare combination of experience, eloquence and courage needed to write the book that clearly explains what the American public had no idea was happening.

Quoting from the preface:

"We (economic hit men or EHMs) are an elite group of men and women who utilize international financial organizations to foment

Robert Gover

conditions that make other nations subservient to the corporatocracy that runs our biggest corporations, our government, and our banks. Like our counterparts in the Mafia, we provide favors. These take the form of loans to develop infrastructure — electric generating plants, highways, ports, airports, or industrial parks. One condition of such loans is that engineering and construction companies from our own country must build all these projects. In essence, most of the money never leaves the United States; it is simply transferred from banking offices in Washington to engineering offices in New York, Houston, or San Francisco...

"Despite the fact that the money is returned almost immediately to corporations that are members of the corporatocracy...the recipient country is required to pay it all back, principal plus interest. If an EHM is completely successful, the loans are so large that the debtor is forced to default on its payments after a few years. When this happens, like the Mafia, we demand our pound of flesh, which often includes one or more of the following: control over United Nations votes, the installations of military bases, or access to precious resources, like oil or the Panama Canal. Of course, the debtor still owes us the money — and another country is added to our global empire."

The American empire is like no other in history. Previous empires sent soldiers to conquer other nations. The new global empire sends bankers. Previous empires conquered within single regions; the global empire now spans the world. It was metaphorically said that the sun never set on the British Empire; that is literally true of the new corporate global empire.

"The subtlety of this modern empire-building puts the Roman centurions, the Spanish conquistadors, and the eighteenth- and nineteenth-century European colonial powers to shame. We EHMs are crafty; we learned from history. Today we do not carry swords. We do not wear armor or clothes that set us apart. In countries like Ecuador, Nigeria, and Indonesia, we dress like local schoolteachers and shop owners. In Washington and Paris, we look like government bureaucrats and bankers. We appear humble, normal. We visit project sites and stroll through impoverished villages. We profess altruism, talk with local papers about the wonderful humanitarian things we are doing. We cover

Time and Money

the conference tables of government committees with our spreadsheets and financial projections, and we lecture at the Harvard Business School about the miracles of macroeconomics. We are on the record, in the open. Or so we portray ourselves, and so are we accepted. It is how the system works. We seldom resort to anything illegal because the system itself is built on subterfuge, and the system is by definition legitimate."

But, you might say, none of these less developed nations could have capitalized such projects themselves. Shouldn't they be happy that we invest so much money and energy into building up their infrastructures, even if it is American companies which do the building?

Perkins uses Ecuador as an example of what is happening everywhere else in the global empire. A trans-Andean pipeline built by the corporatocracy has leaked over half a million barrels of oil into fragile rain forests, more than twice the amount of oil spilled by the Exxon Valdez. Vast areas of rainforest, macaws and jaguars, and three tribes of Ecuadorian Indians have been devastated. Rivers have become flaming cesspools.

"Because of me and my fellow EHMs, Ecuador is in far worse shape today than before we introduced her to the miracles of modern economics, banking, and engineering. Since 1970 — during this period known euphemistically as the oil Boom — the official poverty level grew from 50 to 70 percent, under- or unemployment increased from 15 to 70 percent, and public debt increased from $240 million to $16 billion. Meanwhile, the share of national resources allocated to the poorest segments of the population declined from 20 to 6 percent...Unfortunately, Ecuador is not the exception. Nearly every country we EHMs have brought under the global empire's umbrella has suffered a similar fate."

All around the world, everywhere economic hit men have done their thing, a few elites have been magnificently enriched while the majority of people have greatly suffered. Osama bin Laden has become as popular in Latin America, Africa and East Asia as he is in the Middle East.

"For every $100 of crude taken out of the Ecuadorian rain forests, the oil companies receive $75. Of the remaining $25, three quarters must go to paying off the foreign debt. Most of the remainder covers military and other government expenses — which leaves about $2.50 for health, education, and programs aimed at helping the poor. Thus, out of every

Robert Gover

$100 worth of oil torn from the Amazon, less than $3 goes to the people who need the money most, whose lives have been so adversely impacted by the dams, the drilling, and the pipelines, and who are dying from lack of edible food and drinkable water."

Perkins points out that we Americans are educated to perceive our national foreign policy as altruistic. Over the years he was an EHM, highly educated people would offer such opinions as, "If they're going to burn the US flag and demonstrate against our embassy, why don't we just get out of their damn country and let them wallow in their own poverty?"

"Despite credentials," Perkins points out, *"such people are as uneducated as those eighteenth century colonialists who believed that the Indians fighting to preserve their lands were servants of the devil."*

It's no wonder we Americans are uninformed or misinformed. Our media uses the name of a country to tell us what a few elite beneficiaries of the global corporatized empire do. *"Today Ecuador announced its willingness to cooperate with the US in rooting out terrorists and drug dealers..."* Meaning the Ecuadorian elite will buy weapons from US manufacturers—with money borrowed from the World Bank to be repaid by the Ecuadorian people—to make war on those same people when they object to the situation the elites have gotten them into.

Is Perkins pessimistic about the future? Not at all. While this global corporatocracy has been taking over the US government and building a worldwide feudalistic corporate empire, more and more people are becoming aware of the difference between plutocracy masquerading as democracy, and true democracy. The corporatized media have spent billions to hoodwink the American people, but eventually the truth will come out. By 2005 it was becoming clear to millions of Americans that the USA had been added to the list of countries which were under the control of the corporatocracy, and there was nothing the people's duly elected politicians could or would do about it.

Money

Money is the lifeblood of society. Without a sane and sustainable monetary system, a modern society is dysfunctional.

A monetary system is not about your money or my money, it's about our money, the cash and credit we all use to buy and sell and keep track of who owes whom how much. Today, everybody needs money to live. If everybody has enough money to buy necessities, the whole society prospers.

Money became everybody's business with the industrial revolution (beginning around 1776) and massive population shifts from farms to cities. Before this migration, during medieval times most people, other than the aristocracy, grew their own food, made their own clothes, built their own homes, bartered, and had little need for money. Now money extends its tentacles into every facet of all our lives, from conception to casket.

When gold and silver and other precious metals were used as money, money was a form of wealth itself. Modern paper currencies are based on our faith in them as means of exchange, measure of value, and symbol of wealth. About 97% of what we now call money is credit. Modern money is not wealth itself. But just as the flag is often equated with the patriotism it symbolizes, money is often equated with the real wealth it symbolizes.

Since money is now as necessary to our lives as air and water, it's amazing that most of us know more about air and water than we know about money. In this and other ways, money is comparable to the great mystery from which we came into this life and into which we disappear when we die: Pluto's realm.

Robert Gover

Mammon and Public Debt

Control of money bestows God-like powers. "Give me control of a nation's money and I care not who makes the laws," said Mayer Amschel Rothschild a couple hundred years ago as he was pioneering what we now call "the New World Order."

Centuries ago, the God of anti-social greed was named Mammon. A good case can be made that today Mammon rules, for tremendous amounts of money are transferred from society at large to personal fortunes. This is done by both private loans at usurious interest rates and the creation of public debt for private gain.

Lending and borrowing money is as old as money itself. What's new in the past few centuries is public debt: Government borrowing from bankers to be repaid by an unwitting third party called "we the people." Public debt is not to be confused with private debt, all those corporate loans and personal mortgage, auto and credit card loans. Murray Rothbard[1] explained public debt this way:

"The public debt transaction...is very different from private debt...the government receives money from creditors, both parties realizing that the money will be paid back NOT out of the pockets or the hides of the politicians and bureaucrats (who borrowed it), but out of the looted wallets and purses of the hapless taxpayers, the subjects of the state. The government gets the money by tax-coercion; and the public creditors, far from being innocents, know full well that their proceeds will come out of that selfsame coercion. In short, public creditors are willing to hand over money to the government now in order to receive a share of tax loot in the future. This is the opposite of a free market, or a genuinely voluntary transaction. Both parties are immorally contracting to participate in the violation of the property rights of citizens in the future. Both parties, therefore, are making agreements about other people's property, and both deserve the back of our hand."

---

[1] "Repudiating the National Debt" by Murray Rothbard (1926–1995), posted on the von Mises web site January 16, 2004. Rothbard was professor of economics at the University of Nevada, Las Vegas, and vice-president for academic affairs at the Ludwig von Mises Institute. This article ran in the June 1992 issue of *Chronicles* (pp. 49–52).

Time and Money

This money borrowed by government is then sliced and diced and sold as Treasury Bonds and Bills. It cannot be completely repaid without leaving the American population money-less. All our money—currency and credit—has been borrowed from the banks of the Federal Reserve, the USA's privatized central bank. If everyone were to suddenly repay all debts in full, we'd be without the means-of-exchange money we need to function as a society. That's at once utterly illogical and literally true.

The vast majority of the American population believes government creates our money. Not so. More than 97% of what we call money is credit, loaned by the bankers of the Federal Reserve. In other words, the bankers of the Fed sell us the stuff we use as money. Money is created when loans are made. So most of what we call money is actually debts to borrowers and credits to lenders. Electronic transfers of credit become paper bills and coin money if or when people cash checks rather than deposit them.

Most people believe the *Federal* Reserve is an agency of the US Government. Why else would it be called "Federal"?

Many, if not most, politicians like this system. It means they don't have to notify taxpayers when they want to spend a lot of money, i.e., go to war. They borrow the money needed and spread the cost to taxpayers over coming generations. Executives of big banks and Wall Streeters love it too, for it means politicians will bail them out with taxpayer money when—as happened most recently in 2008—they screw up. Who suffers? The vast majority who don't understand the system. They lose jobs, homes, businesses, educations and opportunities.

Jekyll Island Conspiracy

A US senator and the world's most powerful bankers conceived what was to become the Federal Reserve System in secret during November 1910, at a retreat on Jekyll Island, Georgia. "Their expressed purpose was to standardize the nation's banking system. But they also intended to eliminate competition between banks and maximize profits by creating a central bank independent of government control. To do this, they would need to write the needed legislation and carefully navigate it though Congress in such a way as to not arouse fears by allowing the public to realize they were privatizing control of the nation's money. If they could manage this they might expand and achieve their long-range goal: A cartel of independent central banks that would dominate the world." [2]

Even today some historians deny that this conspiratorial meeting ever happened. But the cat got out of the bag in 1916 when B. C. Forbes, who would later found *Forbes* Magazine, was a reporter for *Leslie's Weekly*, and wrote:

"Picture a party of the nation's greatest bankers stealing out of New York on a private railroad car under cover of darkness, stealthily hieing hundreds of miles South, embarking on a mysterious launch, sneaking on to an island deserted by all but a few servants, living there a full week

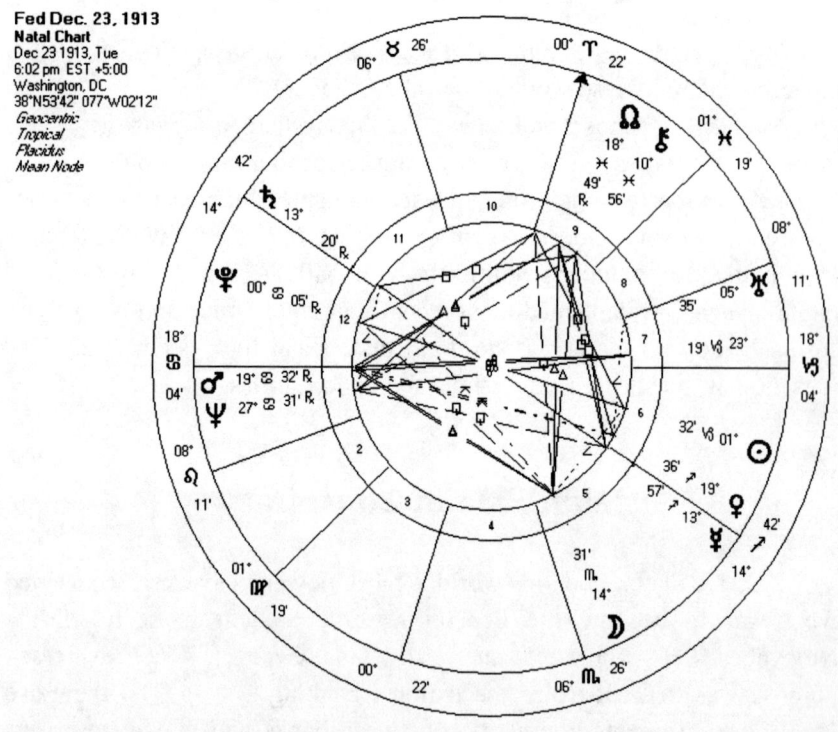

---

[2] G. Edward Griffin's *The Creature From Jekyll Island*, American Media, 2006.

under such rigid secrecy that the names of not one of them was once mentioned lest the servants learn the identity and disclose to the world the strangest, most secret expedition in the history of American finance... I am not romancing. I am giving to the world, for the first time, the real story of how the famous Aldrich currency report, the foundation of our new currency system, was written."

The most pertinent aspect in the Fed's birth chart is the Sun-Pluto opposition. It's pertinent now (2010) because Transiting Pluto is lingering in early Capricorn, conjunct the Fed's Sun, and thus also opposite the Fed's Pluto in the 12th house. T Pluto moved into Capricorn in January 2008 to coincide with the stock market plunge predicted five years ago in this book's first edition. T Pluto moving over the Fed's Sun opposite natal Pluto means the Fed is in for some kind of major transformation beginning in 2008. By that year there was a rising tide of concern, even outrage, as more individuals came to comprehend exactly what the Fed really is and how it impacts the overall US and world economy.

A Most Unhappy Man

In 1930 banker Paul Warburg wrote a book of 1,750 pages in which he described the meeting on Jekyll Island and its purpose without mentioning its location or the names of those who attended—except for Senator Aldrich. "I do not feel free to give a description of this most interesting conference concerning which Senator Aldrich pledged all participants to secrecy," wrote Warburg. "Even the fact that there had been a meeting was not permitted to become public."

The assumption that money is the private provenance of a few is a holdover from medieval times when a "divinely-appointed" aristocracy controlled money. Although we no longer believe that a few of us were God-ordained to control money, the assumption continues to be so deeply embedded in our culture that most are unaware of how it shapes our lives.

Ten years after signing off on the Federal Reserve Act, President Woodrow Wilson said: "I am a most unhappy man. I have unwittingly ruined my country. A great industrial Nation is controlled by a system of credit. Our system of credit is concentrated. The growth of the Nation, therefore, and all its activities are in the hands of a few men. We have come to be the worst ruled, one of the most completely controlled and dominated Governments in the world—no longer a Government of free opinion, no longer a Government by conviction and vote by the majority, but Government by the opinion and duress of a small group of dominant men."

In the 1920s, Congress asked one Fed member (Donald J. Winn, Assistant to the Board of Governors) if the Fed wasn't in fact a private corporation. Winn replied, "The Federal Reserve System was established by an act of Congress and is not a private corporation." He went on to explain: "The stock of the Federal Reserve Banks is held entirely by commercial banks that are members of the Federal Reserve System."

Say what? How can it NOT be privately held corporation when its stock is privately held by a few bankers? If some homeless guy said he didn't rob that convenience store, he merely gave it a credit advance, he'd be declared reigning clown of the criminal realm.

Ezra Pound's Passion

Poet Ezra Pound got himself in a world of trouble in the 1930s and 1940s by vociferously objecting to this heist we now affectionately call The Fed. He felt the need to flee the USA and go to Italy where he broadcast diatribes against those who had created it. Since most, if not all of the Fed's creators were of the Jewish faith, Pound railed against "the Jews." This got him vilified as an anti-Semite. If the conspirators had been Methodists, would Pound have railed against Methodists? Not likely. On the other hand, anyone who objected to the Fed was labeled a conspiracy nut by the media.

The US Government finally captured Pound and locked him up in an insane asylum. While there, he was visited by a young poet, Eustace Mullins. Mullins described this meeting in his book, *Secrets of the Federal Reserve:*

Time and Money

"In 1949, while I was visiting Ezra Pound...at St. Elizabeth's Hospital, Washington, D.C., Dr. Pound asked me if I had ever heard of the Federal Reserve System. I replied that I had not, as of the age of 25. He then showed me a ten dollar bill marked 'Federal Reserve Note' and asked me if I would do some research at the Library of Congress on the Federal Reserve System which had issued this bill. Pound was unable to go to the Library himself, as he was being held without trial as a political prisoner by the United States government. After he was denied broadcasting time in the U.S., Dr. Pound broadcast from Italy in an effort to persuade people of the United States not to enter World War II. Franklin D. Roosevelt had personally ordered Pound's indictment, spurred by the demands of his three personal assistants...I had no interest in money or banking as a subject, because I was working on a novel. Pound offered to supplement my income by ten dollars a week for a few weeks. My initial research revealed evidence of an international banking group which had secretly planned the writing of the Federal Reserve Act and Congress' enactment of the plan into law. These findings confirmed what Pound had long suspected. He said, 'You must work on it as a detective story.'"

When Ezra Pound ran out of money and could no longer pay young Mullins $10 a week for his research, Mullins appealed to various foundations for money to complete his task. All refused. He then wrote a book based on what he'd found so far, but 19 New York publishers rejected his manuscript. One editor, Devin Gerrity, president of Devin Adair Publishing Company, gave him some friendly advice: "I like your book but we can't print it. Neither can anybody else in New York. Why don't you bring in a prospectus for your novel, and I think we can give you an advance. You may as well forget about getting the Federal Reserve book published."

Mullins eventually did publish a small edition in 1952 via two of Ezra Pound's disciples, under the simple title *Federal Reserve*. A couple of years later an unauthorized edition was done by a New Jersey publisher under the title *The Federal Reserve Conspiracy*. In 1955, a German edition was put out by Guido Roeder but the entire edition of 10,000 copies were burned by "government agents," ordered to take this action by the US High Commissioner to Germany James B. Conant, who

Robert Gover

was President of Harvard University from 1933 to 1953. This was the only book burning in Germany since the days of the Nazi Party.

In 1968 another pirated edition appeared in California and Mullins tried to get the FBI and Postal Inspectors to act, but they refused. Then, in 1980, a second German edition came out and because the US Government no longer controlled the internal affairs of Germany, this edition survives. It's a duplicate of the one that was burned in 1955.

Fed's Impact on Society

The Fed was not designed to benefit society; it was designed to plunder society, making the Haves richer and the Have-nots poorer. By clever public relations and a lot of secrecy, it was navigated through Congress and passed while most congress persons had their minds on Christmas shopping and getting home for the holidays.

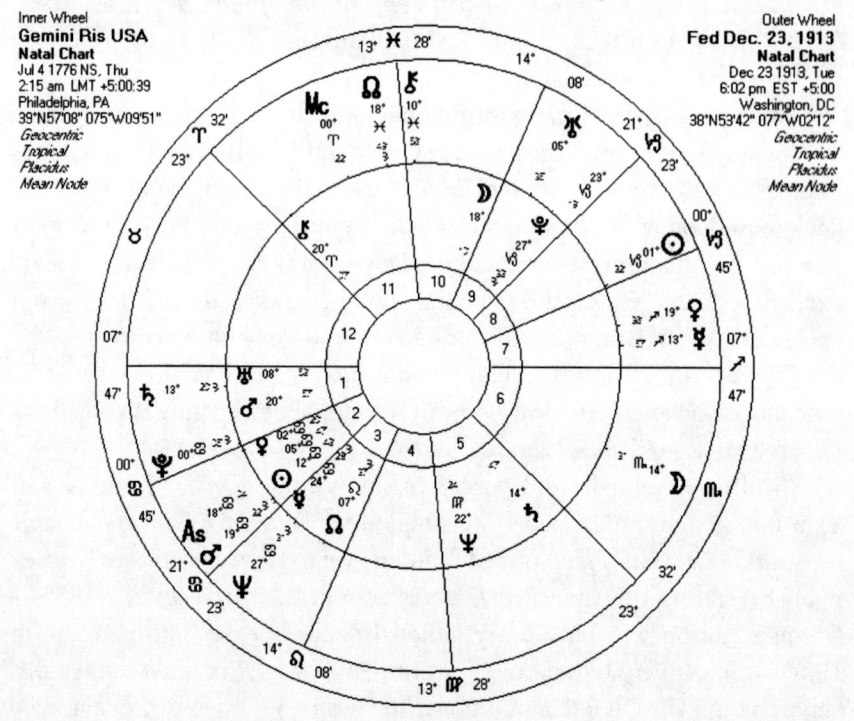

Time and Money

Let's inspect a biwheel chart for the Fed's impact on the USA's natal chart.

Notice on the outer wheel for the Fed's nativity that Saturn at 13 Gemini is conjunct the USA's Uranus and Mars, with those planets opposite the Fed's Venus and Mercury in Sagittarius. And all those planets are square the USA's Neptune in Virgo, indicating inspiration/illusion/delusion for the financial sector, and/or trouble for the nation from the financial sector. The Fed's Sun-Pluto opposition afflicts the USA's money planets Venus and Jupiter in Cancer, and the Fed's Mars hits the USA's economically-sensitive Sun-square-Saturn. The position of the Fed's Neptune conjunct the USA's Mercury and opposite the USA's Pluto indicates the deception that was perpetrated on the American public.

People who have studied the Fed and its impact describe it as the greatest heist in human history. The vast majority of the American population does not know that the Fed is not part of the Federal Government, and that the money it lends the government constitutes what is called "the national debt."

The national debt is also called government debt, public debt, federal, state, municipal or local government debt, or sovereign government debt. It's not to be confused with deficit—which is a budget shortfall (more annual spending than income). The national debt is now so much a part of the economy that it is taken for granted, as though it is as inevitable as sunrise and sunset.

Who owns the debt being repaid by American taxpayers for money borrowed from the Fed banks by the US Government? In 1952, Mullins says, he traced those people to a group called the London Connection. The conclusion was obvious. Although the USA gained its political independence during the Revolutionary War, we were resold into debt to British and European "divinely endowed" aristocrats by the creation of the Fed.

Robert Gover

"Follow the Money"

Today the general belief is that our money is printed by government, although simultaneously we are harangued by the mass media about the national debt and how each of us owes an astounding share of it, and what a crime it is to pass this horrendous debt onto our children and grandchildren. If money were really created by government, why would government borrow money from banks? This cognitive dissonance is evidence that secrecy persists. Even President John F. Kennedy got whacked shortly after he made a move to undermine the Fed's absolute money power. (Google Executive Order 11110. June 4, 1963 for details). Remember that famous line, "Follow the money," in Oliver Stone's movie "JFK"?

While it's true that Congress and/or the President appoint key members of the Fed, it's also true that the most powerful bankers recommend who should be appointed, and since the politicians depend on the most powerful bankers for campaign contributions, they do not bite the hand that feeds them.

When you watch the TV news and see that handsome face under the perfectly coifed hairdo blathering on about "the national debt," know that this purveyor of information is grossly misinformed, and that if he/she were not misinformed, you would not be seeing him/her on TV. The top brass of the cartel of corporations which now own and operate the American mass media are in cahoots with the bankers of the Fed and benefit from the system.

The Fed-run, debt-based monetary system is, after all, the opposite of a democratic institution. There are people in high places who understand that the Federal Reserve System is legalized thievery, but most would rather throw their mothers under a bus than chance ruinous loss of personal wealth and status by saying so publically.

"When society loses control over its money system, it loses whatever control it might have had over its destiny. It can no longer set priorities and the policies for achieving them. It can't solve problems which then develop into crises and continually mount up...Its leaders substitute public relations for actions and although the media is part of this pretense, an awareness slowly develops that there is 'nobody home' in Washington. Nobody is taking care of America. People stop voting and a deep sickness of the spirit develops." (*The Lost Science of Money* by Stephen Zarlenga, American Monetary Institute, 2002, page 656.)

Ben Franklin's Paper Money

Ben Franklin understood the difference between commodity money (gold and silver coins) and paper money (called "fiat money," declared legal tender by government). He understood what Aristotle pointed out a couple of millennia previous, that money's primary function is as a medium of exchange. In 1792, he published a pamphlet titled "A Modest Enquiry into the Nature and Necessity of a Paper Currency." His printing company rolled off paper money for Pennsylvania, New Jersey and Delaware. And he experienced first hand and with keen intelligence how well paper money worked for his own colony, Pennsylvania.

As the Revolutionary War was brewing, 1764, Franklin journeyed to London to petition Parliament to lift its restrictive bans and taxes so as to prevent what was building toward a bloody conflagration. The British aristocracy had banished their poor to the colonies and now wondered how in the world they had become so prosperous there. Franklin told them:

"That is simple. In the colonies we issue our own money. It is called Colonial Scrip. We issue it to pay the government's approved expenses and charities. We make sure it is issued in proper proportions to make the goods pass easily from the producers to the consumers...In this manner, creating for ourselves our own paper money, we control its purchasing power, and we have no interest to pay to no one."

The Bank of England, prototype of the USA's Federal Reserve, was created in 1694 when King George needed to borrow money to fight a war. He could not tax his subjects for wealth they did not yet have, so the Bank of England was established to lend the British Government whatever money it needed to fight wars, to be repaid from future tax collections. This worked so well for the British aristocracy that they outlawed the creation of money by colonies. That did not work for the American colonies. British Pounds went back and forth across the Atlantic but the colonists needed money to trade among themselves. So despite the ban, each colony created its own medium of exchange. Ben Franklin is sometimes called "the father of paper money" for his role in this illegal colonial enterprise.

After the USA became a separate and independent nation, a kind of psychological tug of war ensued between those who believed a privately owned central bank should issue the nation's money and those who believed government should issue money rather than borrow from banks. Two national banks were established (1782 and 1816). Each was abolished at the end of its 20-year charter. President Andrew Jackson abolished the second after a protracted the damaging battle with its president, Nicholas Biddle. The bankers retaliated by withdrawing credit, sending the nation into its second great depression in the 1840s.

President Abe Lincoln, to fight the Civil War without bankrupting the Union, had his government issue "greenback" dollars instead of borrowing the money from banks at 36 percent or higher. This being a radical departure from rule by a wealthy aristocracy (traditional lenders of money) the London Times expressed outrage:

"If that mischievous financial policy which had its origin in the North American Republic should become indurate down to a fixture, then that government will furnish its own money without cost. It will pay off its debts and be without a debt. It will become prosperous beyond precedent in the history of the civilized governments of the world. The brains and wealth of all countries will go to North America. That government must be destroyed or it will destroy every monarchy on the globe."

The Fed was created in 1913 after a chaotic period following the Civil War of private and state banks issuing a variety of reliable, unreliable and downright counterfeit currencies—to prevent the US Government from following in Franklin's and Lincoln's footsteps. The government could have, and in retrospect should have, brought order out of the chaos without handing creation of the nation's money over to those now often referred to as "banksters." But the group who met in 1910 on Jekyll Island was clever enough to pull the wool over the eyes of

Congress and the public. Few people understood how a monetary system works. Those who did understand it saw it as an opportunity to greatly enrich themselves and their heirs at the expense of taxpayers.

China's Ben Franklin Bank

Ironically, the Peoples Republic of China, established December 1, 1948, adopted the monetary system advocated by Ben Franklin and Abe Lincoln. Their People's Bank of China is an agency of their government.

American and European financiers have lambasted the Chinese system as "state control" in contrast to "free enterprise." Well, our system is free profits for a tiny minority—those who economist Thorstein Veblen called "a parasitic leisure class"—but an increasingly heavy burden for the vast majority. Novelist Gore Vidal called this system socialism for the rich, free enterprise for everyone else.

The current national debt numbers stagger the mind: $13 Trillion owned by the Federal Government to Treasury bond and bill holders at home and around the world. The bankers of the Fed lend money to government and then, via the Treasure Department, issue bonds and bills to monetize the debt, paying it down over decades with taxpayer money. By summer 2010, this debt amounted to 89% of GDP, and annual interest on this debt came to roughly $375 Billion.

Private v. Public Control

If the Fed were to be abolished, it would return the creation of money to the national government, presumably responsive to the public. I say "presumably" because as of 2010, the US Government was aptly described as "of, for and by the big banks and corporations." Politicians are dependent on campaign money to win reelection, and bankers and their best corporate customers control who gets most of that campaign money and who doesn't. If the Federal Government were to take back its Constitutional right and duty to create our money, it would be a small next step from today's big-money backed political campaigns to publicly funded political campaigns.

Government creation of our money would not change how banks make private loans to consumers and corporations, but it would remove much of the pressure on politicians to serve the wealthy instead of their electorate. Instead of a privatized central bank selling money to government, government would sell money to the banking system. Above all, this would relieve taxpayers of the unwitting obligation to repay a national debt. Today's national debt would be phased out as obligations to bond holders are repaid over time, ending that scam.

A publicly owned national bank would not mean the end of the difficult business of managing the nation's monetary system. Government created money would have to be balanced by need, keeping demand (money) in balance with supply (goods and services). But instead of all our busy economic activity being for the greater enrichment of the already rich, we'd be working for the material improvement of our whole society. Taxes would be greatly reduced, for eventually there would be no more national debt to pay. Private debts on mortgages, credit cards, corporate borrowing, etc., would continue as they are. But with government selling money to banks instead of banks selling money to government, the American taxpayer would be out from under an impossible burden.

Nationalizing the Fed would not end problems arising from the so-called "Fractional Reserve" system of lending—banks legally able to lend $10 for every $1 they hold as deposits. But it would put government in the catbird seat, freeing it from dependence on bankers and enabling it to regulate the banking industry as representatives of the electorate. And it would enable public access to banking information. Sweetheart deals and other scams would still be possible, but so would journalistic exposes. The public would no longer be kept in the dark about how the money system works. It would no longer be the private business of the super wealthy; it would become the concern of every voter. "He who controls the money, rules." Thus, public control of the money system would stimulate a purer democracy, as government monetary specialists would be working for the public. The system would become transparent.

Pluto: Conception and Birth

In his book *The Creature from Jekyll Island*, E. Edward Griffin compares trying to understand the banking game to isolated islanders suddenly transported to an American football game trying to comprehend why those strangely costumed players are colliding with each other and throwing an oddly shaped object around. The purpose of the banking game is to relieve customers of money while convincing them they are being served. This is done by employing some truly arcane and illogical rules and regulations developed over centuries. If government were to relieve the privatized Fed from its duty to create the nation's money, it would not disrupt most of the banking game, but it would relieve taxpayers of the obligation to repay what government borrows, since it would end the need for government to borrow.

Will the Fed be nationalized?

Transiting Pluto lingers conjunct the Fed's Sun opposite the Fed's Pluto till the summer of 2011 when it moves beyond a 7 degree orb of influence. Then Pluto moves retrograde, back and forth as seen from our perspective on Earth, and by September 2011 it returns to 4 Capricorn, again conjunct the Fed's Sun. The effects of Pluto are usually delayed. An exact Pluto aspect is often symbolized as the time of conception, leading to pregnancy and birth. We can expect the birth of whatever happens behind the scenes in Washington to manifest later, as the birth of whatever new comes out of the present T Pluto conjunction and economic angst that began with the crash of 2008.

By the winter Solstice 2012, Pluto will be at 8 Capricorn and square Uranus at 4 Aries. With both Uranus and Pluto still in the first third of these Cardinal Signs, we can expect something dramatic. And given that Uranus will be square the Fed's Sun-Pluto opposition at this time, we can expect that whatever manifests will involve the Fed's privatized monetary system.

Robert Gover

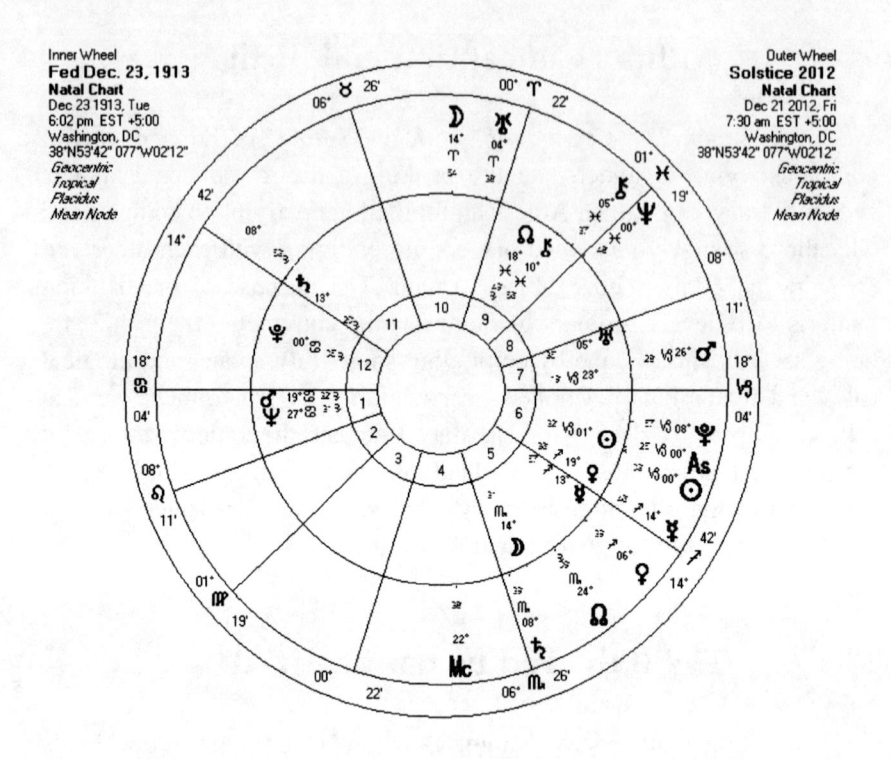

Uranus square Pluto indicates a clash of values. It's an aspect that has a long history of coinciding with revolutionary change. The Sun on this day conjunct the Fed's Sun and opposite its Pluto could trigger the kind of change needed for the monetary system to be wrested from the big banks and returned to control by a government agency responsive to public needs. The Solstice's Saturn conjunct the Fed's Moon in Scorpio indicates that whatever change occurs around this time will be long-lasting. The question is, will the conception indicated by Pluto's lingering over the Fed's Sun manifest at this time? With the Solstice's Mars conjunct the Fed's Jupiter there will be plenty of energy behind whatever manifests. And with the Solstice's Jupiter applying to a conjunction with the Fed's Saturn-Mercury opposition, it appears that the time may very well be ripe for the transformation needed to end the plundering of our society by "banksters."

Risky Business

One thing is certain: the present privatized, Fed-run money system is not sustainable, for it creates a slow but relentlessly growing gap between a decreasing number of Haves and a growing number of Have-nots. This gap has never been greater than it now is. No society can survive such a huge imbalance. Nor can any amount of generosity relieve the problems thus created. What's needed is a systemic change, a new script for the 21st Century. For in our modern, urbanized societies, money is no longer the privilege of a small aristocracy, it's now a necessity for everyone.

Changing the bankster-run monetary system is risky business, as the fates of Presidents Jackson, Lincoln and Kennedy hint. Lincoln and Kennedy were assassinated. Jackson would have been assassinated if his assassin's bullets had not been disabled by the wet atmosphere of the Washington of his day. Were these assassinations coincidences having nothing to do the control of the nation's money? Maybe, but maybe not. The three assassins involved were all declared crazies, with no connection to the bankers of their day.

As I write this, Congressman Dennis Kucinich, Democrat from Ohio, is trying to push through Congress a law written by Stephen Zarlenga's American Monetary Institute. But this new law would ask politicians to bite the hand that feeds their drive for wealth-based status, and we humans are instinctively status-driven creatures. Kucinich is also swimming against the tide of public ignorance, for about 99% of the population does not understand how the system works.

The ancient Greeks were concerned about a money system's ability to destroy *polis*, community, and had a very different perspective on the short-sighted greed of Mammon. Here is a quote from an article by classics scholar Richard Seaford, titled "Money Makes the (Greek) World Go Round: what the ancient Greek anxiety about money has to tell us about our own economic predicaments":

"Consider…the myth of Erysichthon, a full version of which can be put together from a few sources (notably Callimachus and Ovid). Erysichthon cuts down a sacred grove to make himself a banqueting hall

and is punished by being made insatiable. No food is enough—whether from land, sea, or air—to satisfy him. He is driven to sell his daughter in marriage, from which she returns to him, and the process is constantly repeated. In the end he eats himself. This myth contains a unique combination of unusual features: the transformation of nature into product, selling to obtain food, and eating the self. The constant return of the daughter from marriage excludes progeny (the future). The Greeks had a myth for many of our central concerns, and here is one for global warming: exploitation of nature produces pathological insatiability, the unlimited need for a source of income that sacrifices the future, and (eventual) self-destruction." [3]

Brain-Damaging Hubris

As though to echo this ancient Greek myth with chest-pounding bravado verging on brain-damaged hubris, Nelson Rockefeller, addressing the Bilderberg Group meeting in June 1991, said this:

"We are grateful to The Washington Post, The New York Times, Time Magazine and other great publications whose directors have attended our meetings and respected their promises of discretion for almost forty years. It would have been impossible for us to develop our plan for the world if we had been subject to the bright lights of publicity during those years. But, the world is now much more sophisticated and prepared to march towards a world government. The supranational sovereignty of an intellectual elite and world bankers is surely preferable to the national self-determination practiced in past centuries."

In other words, forget democracy, folks, you will henceforth be ruled by we who control money and thus governments. You want to vote? Fine. Line up and vote but know that whoever you elect will obey us, for we control what your elected representative will need. No one bites the hand that doles out the money and lives to tell about it.

Thus the privatized Fed's money game has grown dramatically since 1913, fulfilling the long-range intentions of the Jekyll Island conspirators, for the Fed is now the "lender of last resort" to the

---

[3] The Times Literary Supplement, London, June 17, 2009.

Time and Money

International Monetary Fund and World Bank, created at a meeting known as the Breton Woods Conference in July 1944. In effect, though not so stated, the IMF and World Bank are part of the USA's Federal Reserve System. Through a procedure known as SDR (Special Drawing Rights) these worldwide organizations lend credit money to mostly third-world countries. If the taxpayers of these countries cannot fully repay with interest, American taxpayers make up the difference.

This is how it works: the US issues a credit (money conjured from thin air) to the IMF of, say, $1 Billion dollars. The IMF lends these electronic digits in the form of SDRs to anther country, publicized as "aid," via elites chosen for their compatible ideology. These elites usually spend the billion on themselves. If the taxpayers of that country cannot repay the loan plus interest, the difference comes out of the hard-earned cash paid in taxes by Americans.

The stated intention of IMF and World Bank lending is to uplift the world's poor, but it has the opposite effect. Its unstated intention is to take over the world's monetary system and rule all humanity by controlling all humanity's money. As of 2010, it was slowly but steadily on track to achieve that goal.

IMF and World Bank SDRs go into the pockets of elites in Asia, Africa and Latin America. It is supposed that these elites will use the money to benefit their societies. But that's not what happens. Argentina went from prosperity to pauperism during the 1990s when its elites accepted "aid." In 1996 Tanzania fed its own people and exported food to other countries; after receiving $3 Billion in "aid," Tanzania nationalized its farms and factories, and sunk into poverty, received more "aid," and became one of the poorest nations on earth.

For the involved elites, "…money has probably never been easier to obtain than it is today; with no complicated projects to administer and no messy accounts to keep, the venal, the cruel and the ugly are laughing literally all the way to the bank…All they have to do—amazing but true—is screw the poor, and they've already had plenty of practice at that." [4]

---

[4] *Lords of Poverty: The Power, Prestige, and Corruption of the International Aid Business*, by Graham Hancock, Atlantic Monthly Press, 1994.

Robert Gover

The poverty created grows until it surrounds the wealthy elites whose "success" created it and who live isolated from their societies behind layers of security. Thus isolated, they eventually wind up "eating themselves" as in the Greek myth. In other words, the system eventually kills the goose that lays their golden eggs.

Sometime after 2012, under the lingering Uranus-Pluto square and grand cross to the USA's Sun-Saturn square, a series of crises leading to exceedingly harsh circumstances will force a drastic change in this privatized monetary system. The message of Pluto in primary angles with Uranus is, Change or be changed. A history of these primary angles is explored later in this book.

Chapter Endnotes:

- Also see *The Lost Science of Money—The Story of Power* by Stephen Zarlenga, American Monetary Institute, 2002; and *The Web of Debt: The Shocking Truth About Our Money System—The Slight of Hand That has Trapped Us in Debt And How We Can Break Free*, by Ellen Hodgson Brown, Third Millennium Press, 2007. Ellen Brown's web page has a blog with numerous articles and reader comments.

- For more information, including videos about this complicated subject, Google "debt based monetary system."

- Also see *Dishonest Money: Financing the Road to Ruin*, self-published in 2010 by Joseph Plummer, who skillfully makes the hide-and-seek complexities of banking comprehensible in common English.

- Astrologers are certainly aware that Pluto was "demoted" from "planet" to "dwarf" at a meeting of the International Astronomers Union convention in Prague, Czech Republic, August 24, 2006. Since it was first declared a planet back in 1929 and its orbit calculated historically by astronomers, astrologers have studied its apparent effects on earthly affairs and compiled a body of lore about it. Thus most astrologers, myself included, continue to call it a planet, even though its small size, remoteness from the Sun and extremely elliptical orbit make it an oddity. Like the Greek deity it is named for, it inhabits a separate Hades-like realm. When it forms primary angles to certain natal positions such as an entity's Sun, it consistently correlates with transformations that manifest as dramatic and long-lasting.

Grand Cross and Great Depressions

There have been four great depressions in US history: the 1780s, 1840s, 1870s and 1930s.

Great depressions are not to be confused with periods of less hardship or shorter periods of hardship, often inaccurately or vaguely called depressions or recessions.

Great Depression Defined

How can we distinguish recessions and depressions from great depressions? Dr. Ravi Batra provided this definition (*Great Depression of 1990*, Simon and Schuster, 1987):

"A recession usually lasts for one to three years, during which the rate of unemployment, while rising, is generally below 12 percent. When a recession lasts for more than three years, and/or the rate of unemployment lies between 12 percent and 20 percent, the economy may be said to be suffering from a depression. When unemployment remains high and business stagnates for six or more years, the nation's plight may be called a great depression. Thus, depending on its severity in depth and length, the downswing of the business cycle may be defined as a recession, depression, or great depression." (Page 106).

Since 1800, every time the USA suffered through a great depression, Saturn was found in mid-Capricorn forming a 90-degree square to one of the outermost planets in Aries. The great depression of the 1780s is somewhat anomalous. It unfolded with Mars in mid-Aries. But Mars soon moved out of this pattern. This great depression coincided with a T-square formed by Neptune in Libra conjunct the US Saturn and Uranus in Cancer conjunct the US Sun. (See chart page 41) Understand that in the Solar community, no planet by itself is good or bad. It's when these members of the Solar family move into certain angles to each other that their combined influence is experienced by us as good or bad. Malefic angles (0 degrees, 90 or 180 degrees) formed by the slower-moving Saturn, Uranus, Neptune and Pluto are notoriously the worst, with Mars a close runner-up and/or a trigger. Mars, Saturn, Uranus, Neptune and Pluto are often called "the malefics" because their adverse angles are experienced by us as troublesome or worse.

Grand Cross in US History

Never has a great depression occurred when Saturn was not in mid-Capricorn, or when it arrived in mid-Capricorn without forming a square to Pluto, Neptune, Uranus or Mars in mid-Aries. And this outer-planet grand cross pattern has never formed without coinciding with a great depression.

Of all the various aspects the planets form, the most difficult, demanding or "malefic" is the grand cross. And that aspect is what great depressions have coincided with as depicted by combining the time of each great depression with the time of Uncle Sam's birth. The result is called a synastry or biwheel chart: two astrological charts that show two moments in time depicted so they can be compared to one another.

The stressful period of 1893 to 1895 is often called "one of the worst depressions in history," and indeed it was extremely difficult. Crop failures were rife, and prices were the lowest they'd ever been to that point in US history. It was ushered in by what is now called "The Panic of 1893" when the primary economic measurement of that time, The Business Curve, dropped from 10 points above normal to 20 points below normal. But it was too brief to qualify as a great depression.

Another example of a difficult but brief period was the Oil Embargo of the 1970s, when the price of gasoline was driven skyward by the

OPEC cartel. We had what was dubbed "stagflation," a combination of stagnant activity and inflationary prices. But this didn't qualify as a great depression either.

How to Verify

There is nothing hidden or intuitive about this planetary pattern which has invariably repeated with great depressions. Anyone can verify it by checking an Ephemeris (a table of daily planetary positions) or by acquiring astrological software and erecting two charts: One chart for the USA's birth, July 4, 1776, Philadelphia, and the other for when a past great depression was at its depth. The two charts are then combined, creating a biwheel: a symbolic freeze-frame of two moments in time.

Until the 1990s, America experienced great depressions in roughly 30- and/or 60-year cycles. It takes Saturn 28 to 30 years to complete an orbit by transiting through each of the 12 constellations and/or Signs of the Zodiac. When Saturn returns to mid-Capricorn each 28-30 years without squaring Pluto, Neptune, Uranus or Mars in mid-Aries, (for instance, in the 20th Century during the 1900s, 1960s and 1990s) the country has experienced economic upheavals but not great depressions.

When Uncle Sam was born on July 4, 1776, in Philadelphia, the Sun was at 12 degrees and 44 minutes of Cancer, forming a 90-degree square aspect to Saturn at 14 degrees and 47 minutes of Libra. We round out to the nearest degree: Sun at 13 Cancer, Saturn at 15 Libra.

X in a Box

Uncle Sam was born when the Sun was in Cancer. The constellation Cancer is opposite Capricorn. And Libra (wherein resides Sam's Saturn) is opposite Aries. So by comparing Uncle Sam's birth chart with a second chart for a great depression, a grand cross pattern becomes evident, formed by transiting Saturn in Capricorn being 180 degrees opposite the US natal Sun in Cancer, while another malefic planet in

Aries is 180 degrees opposite the US natal Saturn in Libra. Since the planets involved are also thus 90-degrees square to each other, a box is also formed. It's this X-in-a-box pattern astrologers call a grand cross.

Another way to understand a biwheel chart is to imagine the US birth chart as a clock face. In a biwheel chart, the clock face is the inner wheel and remains stationary. The 12 planets depicted on the second chart, shown on the outer wheel, become the clock's hands. The combination tells us what celestial time it was for a certain event. This is called "reading the transits."

Because we humans are creatures of habit, we tend to apply solutions that have worked in the past, instead of finding new solutions to new problems. Belief trumps evidence. But each moment in cosmic time is unique, so beliefs formed in the past do not always provide solutions to new problems.

Another Way to Visualize

Another way to grasp the grand cross planetary pattern is to visualize mid-Capricorn as being at the 12 o'clock position, and mid-Cancer (the US Sun) being at 6 o'clock. Mid-Aries is thus at 9 o'clock and mid-Libra (Uncle Sam's Saturn) at 3 o'clock. In this schemata, all four great depressions in US history have occurred when Saturn was at 12 o'clock and another "malefic" planet was at 9 o'clock, putting them opposite and square Sam's natal Sun at 6 o'clock and Saturn at 3 o'clock.

These oppositions and squares are measured by longitude only, and need not be precisely exact. They are effective when they are "within orb"—that is, within 7 degrees of exact. When Saturn reaches 7 degrees of Capricorn, it has come within orb of an opposition to the US Sun at 14 Cancer. Planetary aspects have been found to be more powerful when "applying" than when "separating," much as ocean waves have more force when building up to a breaker. Keep in mind, also, that the larger, outermost planets orbit slowly as measured in Earth years: Saturn 28-30 years, Uranus 84 years, Neptune 165 years, Pluto 248 years.

Time and Money

Events corresponding to outer planetary patterns do not occur "like clockwork," so there is another term used by astrologers: "square by Sign." This means that although two outer planets are not quite within orb, they are in Signs of the Zodiac which are 90 degrees apart. By contrast, planets closer to Earth produce most noticeable effects when precisely conjunct, square or opposite. A good example of this is the Moon's phases. (For astrological purposes, the Sun and Moon are called planets.) A hurricane arriving with the Full Moon (opposition of Sun and Moon) is a lot more powerful than one arriving with the three-quarter Moon.

Great Depression of the 1780s

The first great depression in the new nation's history became an undeniable fact around December of 1783. Saturn, Uranus, Neptune, and "trigger" Mars were all involved in the 1780's grand cross, and this first great depression is viewed by economic historians as being especially severe.

Note on the biwheel chart for this one that Saturn was at 15 degrees Capricorn which puts it opposite the US natal Sun at 13 Cancer; meanwhile, Mars at 21 Aries is within orb or an opposition to Sam's natal Saturn at 15 degrees of Libra. Adding to this combination is Uranus conjunct US Sun and thus also opposite transiting Saturn, and Neptune conjunct US Saturn, thus also opposite transiting Mars. All our traditional "malefics" were involved except Pluto.

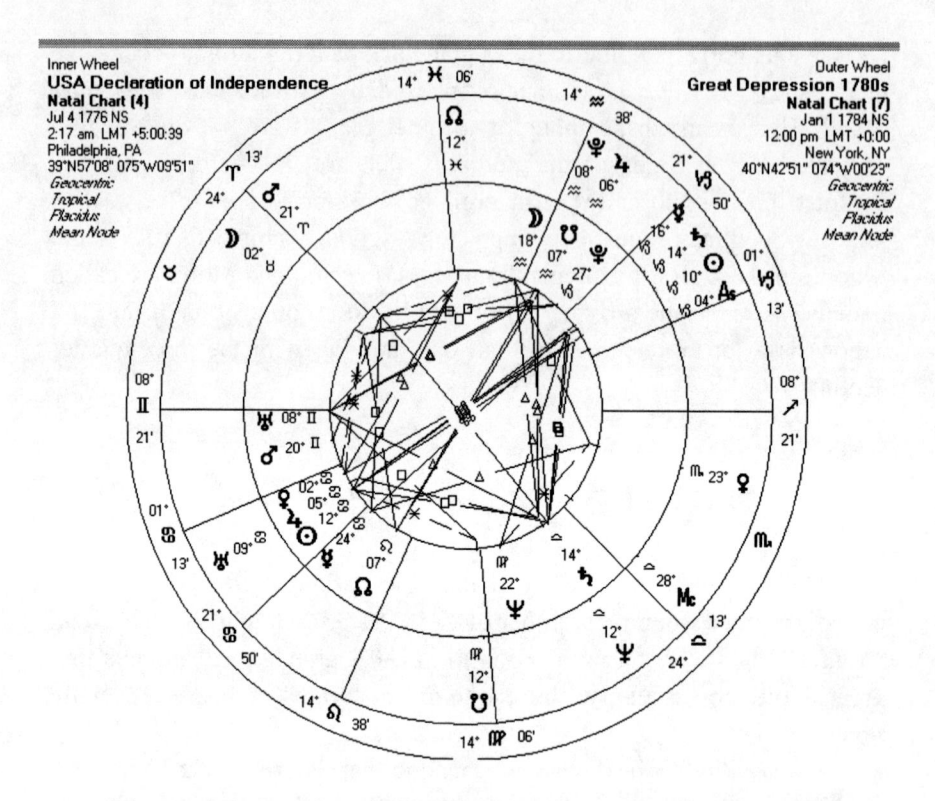

What was happening then? The planet Uranus was discovered on March 13, 1781, by Sir William Herschel of England. "Hershel's discovery did more than alter our concept of the Solar System. It heralded a period of revolution in politics and science that led to the birth of the United States and democracy in France." ("The Discovery of the Outer Planets" by astrologer Jeff Jawer, www.stariq.com.) "In the discovery of Uranus, we have a perfect example of the convergence of many ways, all leading to the same end: invention, revolution, and transcendence...the year 1781 was the year of Cornwallis' surrender to the American forces. ... Emmanuel Kant's Critique of Pure Reason...the beginning of the French Revolution..." Thomas Jefferson captured the mood of this time when, in 1787, he wrote, "I hold it, that a little rebellion, now and then, is a good thing, and as necessary in the political world as storms in the physical."

And the American rebellion was not ended by Cornwallis' surrender.

Time and Money

"Even more than their civilian neighbors, the (Revolutionary War) soldiers nursed grievances that they could attribute to incompetent, if not dishonest, government. They had left their farms and shops to fight the hated redcoats, but they could not even depend on the paltry sums their services had earned for them. Inflation had made their Continental currency almost worthless, and now the government set up by the Articles of Confederation was delaying payment of overdue wages and retracting its promises of lifetime pensions for officers." ("Shay's Rebellion" by Alden T. Vaughan, page 199, *Historical Viewpoints*.)

On each chart below, look first at around 2 o'clock on the outer wheels for Saturn in Capricorn; then look for another "heavy" at around 10 o'clock on the outer wheels in mid-Aries.

On each inner wheel, note that Uncle Sam's Sun (around 7 o'clock), being three 30-degree Signs away from the US Saturn, forms a 90-degree square with Saturn (about 5 o'clock).

The straight lines radiating like wheel spokes from the middle of each chart mark the 12 Signs of the Zodiac. The First House, the cusp of which at 9 o'clock, marks where dawn occurred at this time and place, and pertains to one's relations with one's world; the Second House, moving counterclockwise, found at about 8 o'clock, pertains to well-being, health, and money. Entities born with both Sun and Jupiter in the Second House are fortunate; they either inherit wealth or become rich, or go through life in an easy-come easy-go way. After the US declared itself a separate nation in 1776, it didn't take long for it to become the wealthiest on Earth. A number of the founders were Masons, and thus aware of astrological lore.

Great Depression of the 1840s

The second great depression in US history held the nation in its grip two cycles of Saturn or 60 years after the 1780s, during the 1840s when Saturn again arrived in mid-Capricorn, this time square to Pluto in mid-Aries. Again the grand cross pattern was formed with Sam's Sun and Saturn. Mars added to the stress by being at 14 degrees of Libra conjunct Sam's Saturn.

Robert Gover

While Saturn has "anchored" all four great depressions from mid-Capricorn, the planets occupying mid-Aries have been Mars (the 1780s), Pluto (the 1840s), Neptune (the 1870s) and Uranus (the 1930s). When Saturn has opposed Sam's Sun without forming a grand cross with Uranus, Neptune, Pluto or Mars, no great depression has happened.

If more than two planets are involved in a major aspect like the square, conjunction or opposition, the orb is extended to 10 or 11 degrees because such a cluster has been repeatedly observed to be effective within 10 or 11 degrees.

On the chart below for the great depression of the 1840s, again look for Saturn around 2 o'clock and this time Pluto around 10 o'clock forming the grand cross pattern by being at once opposite and square the US natal Sun and Saturn. Transiting Mars is again involved, this time down around 5 o'clock conjunct the US Saturn, adding oomph to this grand cross.

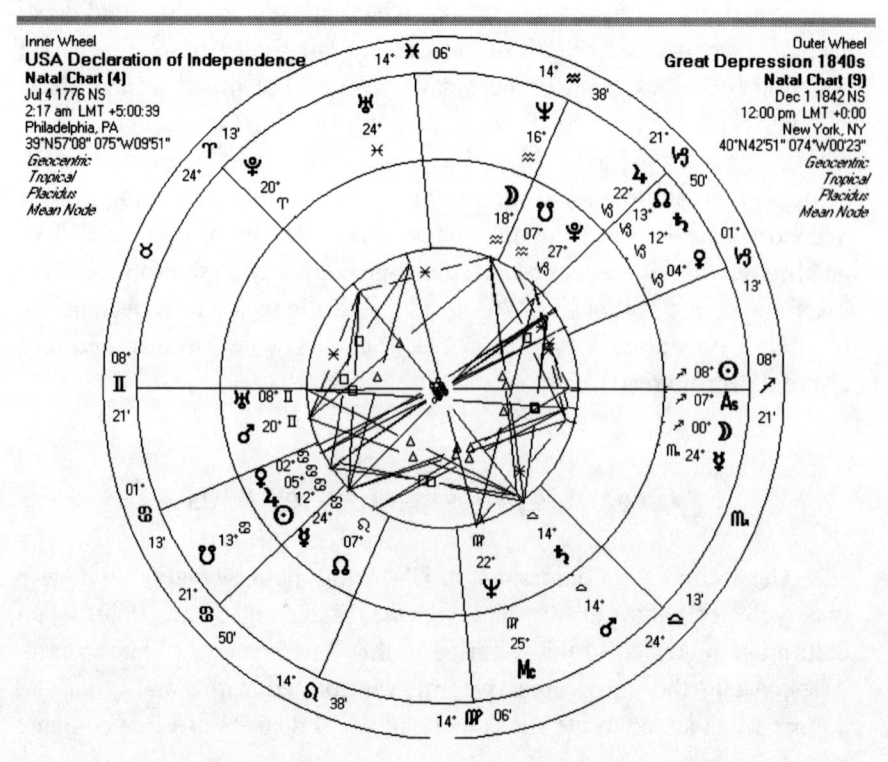

Great Depression of the 1870s

Thirty years (or one transit of Saturn) after the 1840s, the nation suffered its third great depression. This time Saturn in Capricorn formed a square with Neptune in Aries to create the grand cross with Sam's Sun and Saturn. For this date, we stretch the orb between Saturn and Neptune to 9 degrees but keep in mind that defining the economic bottom of any great depression is difficult and usually imprecise.

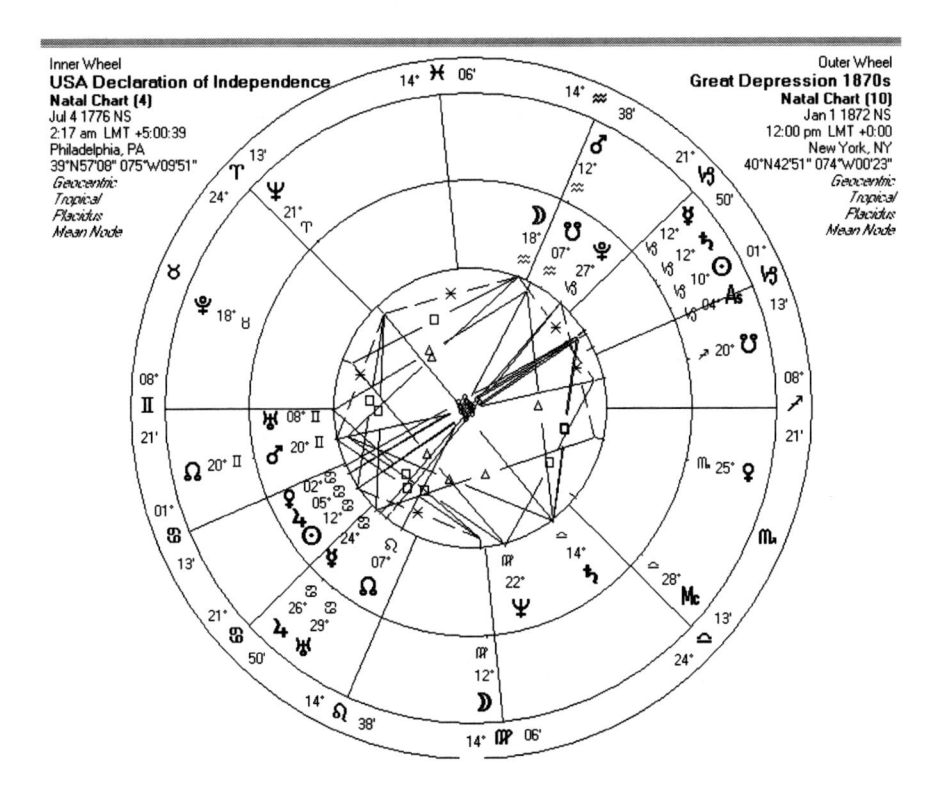

Great Depression of the 1930s

Sixty years later, the USA went through what is arguably the worst great depression of its history. I say arguably because historic data indicates the great depression of the 1780s was as bad or worse. We

Robert Gover

contemporaries are more aware of the 1930s because we have haunting photos of that time, and some still alive to tell us about it.

Although no two economists are likely to agree when the bottom of any great depression was reached, by January 1, 1931 it was clear that this crash was not going to rebound quickly. Fear that the whole economy would be impacted had become widespread, despite efforts by important people to propagate optimism.

Pluto was discovered by an Illinois farmboy turned astronomer, Clyde Tombaugh, whose early work so impressed the director of the Lowell Observatory in Flagstaff, AZ, that he was offered a job there. Tombaugh completed the task of finding Pluto, begun 25 years earlier, on February 18, 1930. It was calculated to be at 18 degrees Cancer then. Jeff Jawer in his essay "The Discovery of the Outer Planets," quotes a line written by poet T. S. Elliot in 1930 as "about as concise a definition of Pluto as one could make." Elliot's line: "Birth, and copulation, and death. That's all the facts when you come to brass tacks."

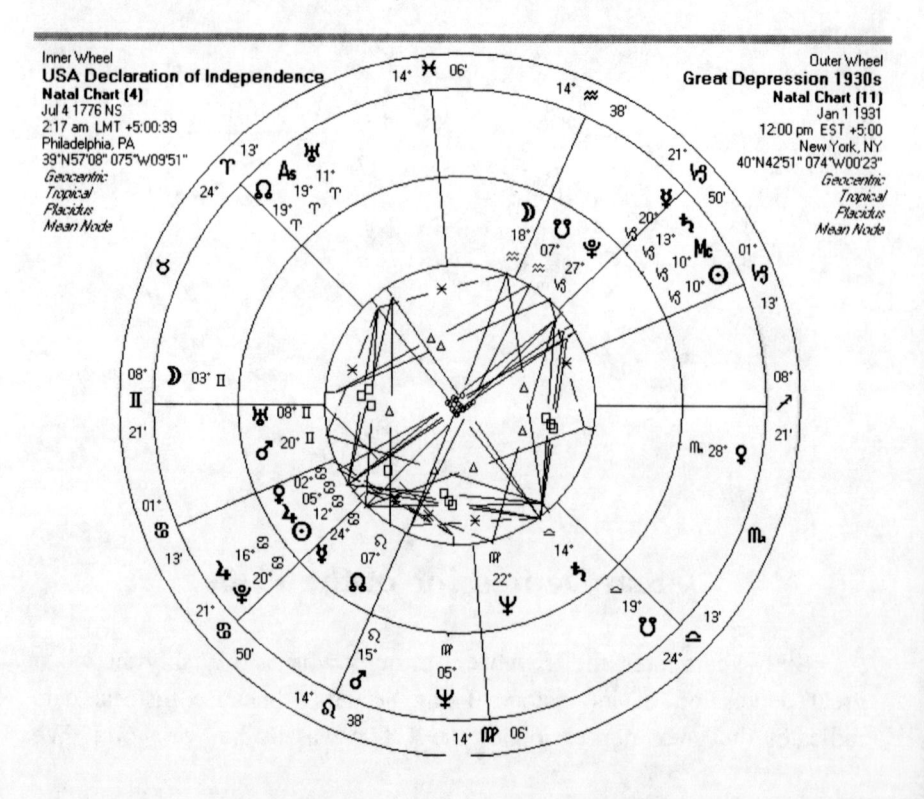

Time and Money

The biwheel chart for 1931 shows transiting Saturn at 13 Capricorn square Uranus at 11 Aries to form the grand cross with Sam's Sun and Saturn. Ominously, Jupiter and Pluto (which had moved a couple of degrees since being discovered the year before) were both in Cancer conjunct the US Sun and opposite transiting Saturn and thus also square transiting Uranus. So the grand cross to Uncle Sam's Sun-square-Saturn at this time, anchored by Saturn, included Uranus, Pluto and Jupiter. To make matters worse, Mars in Leo was opposite the US Moon in Aquarius. It's also notable that this great depression followed the Saturn-Pluto cyclical opposition that would reoccur to usher in The Sixties, and then to coincide with 9/11/01.

Understand that there is a lot happening up there in the infinite universe at any given moment. I am focusing attention on the larger bodies within our Solar System and ignoring the countless other celestial events in and beyond our Solar System. We could also include Lunations, progressions, eclipses, asteroids, planetary moons and rings, comets, perihelion positions and parallels and latitudes as well as longitudes of each single major event, greatly complicating the picture. We might venture beyond our Solar System into infinite space and chart many other constellations, or add Sirius (Polaris) to our calculations. My aim is to keep it simple so both lay readers and astrologers can appreciate the fact that great depressions correlate with grand cross patterns formed by the outermost planets to the US Sun-Saturn square.

No Grand Cross, No Great Depression

Following the great depression of the 1930s, Saturn next arrived in mid-Capricorn, opposite Sam's Sun, in the early 1960s. But there was no grand cross formed and no great depression occurred. What developed as The Sixties unfolded was a rare combination of the unprecedented (Uranus) and transforming (Pluto). More about Uranus-Pluto and the Sixties in a later chapter.

The first decade of the 20th Century was a rocky time for stocks. Two stock market panics rattled Wall Street (1903 and 1907), sending financiers down to Washington to seek help from government. After much

Robert Gover

wrangling in the halls of Congress, Wall Streeters got their way and in 1913 the Federal Reserve System was created as America's central bank.

Saturn's return to Capricorn in 1961 was another dicey time economically, but military spending provided an innovative mix of Keynesian stimulus delivered as corporate welfare. As in the early 1950s when the Korean "police action" stimulated the economy, working class American conscripts soon found themselves mired in a foreign land, this time Vietnam. Military hardware stocks were robust but millions lost their lives. The rationale for this war was "stopping communism." From the Vietnamese perspective, it was a war for independence, as the American Revolution had been.

The important thing to notice in the following three charts is that although Saturn is found again in mid-Capricorn, no other malefic squares Saturn from Aries. No grand cross, no great depression.

There are a lot of symbols included in these biwheel charts that are of interest only to other astrologers. For the non-astrologers, the ones to look for are Saturn, Uranus, Neptune, and Pluto, and upon certain occasions Mars and the Moon acting as "triggers."

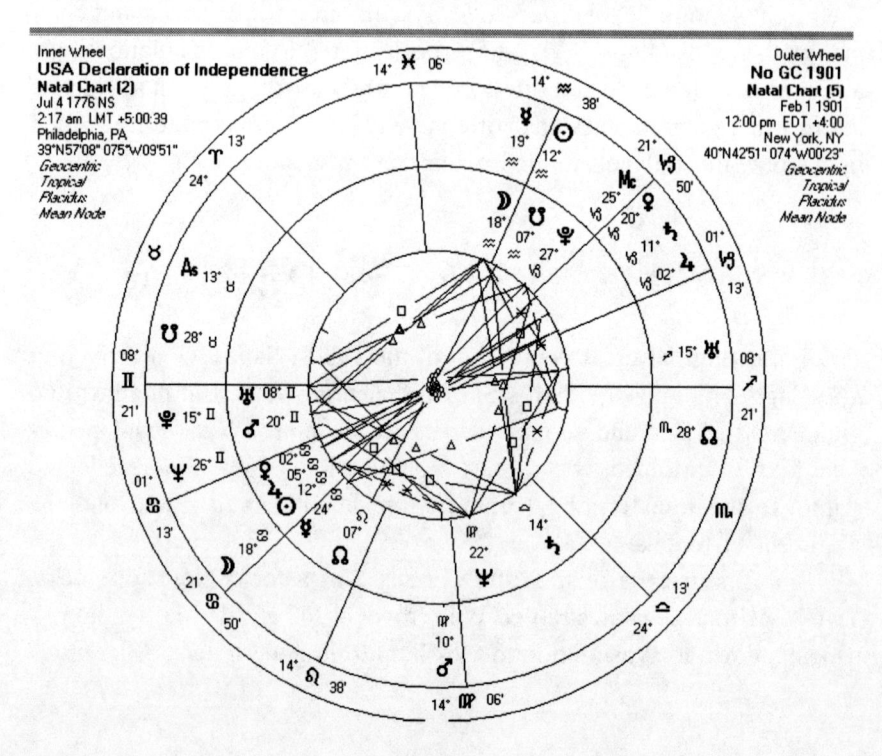

Time and Money

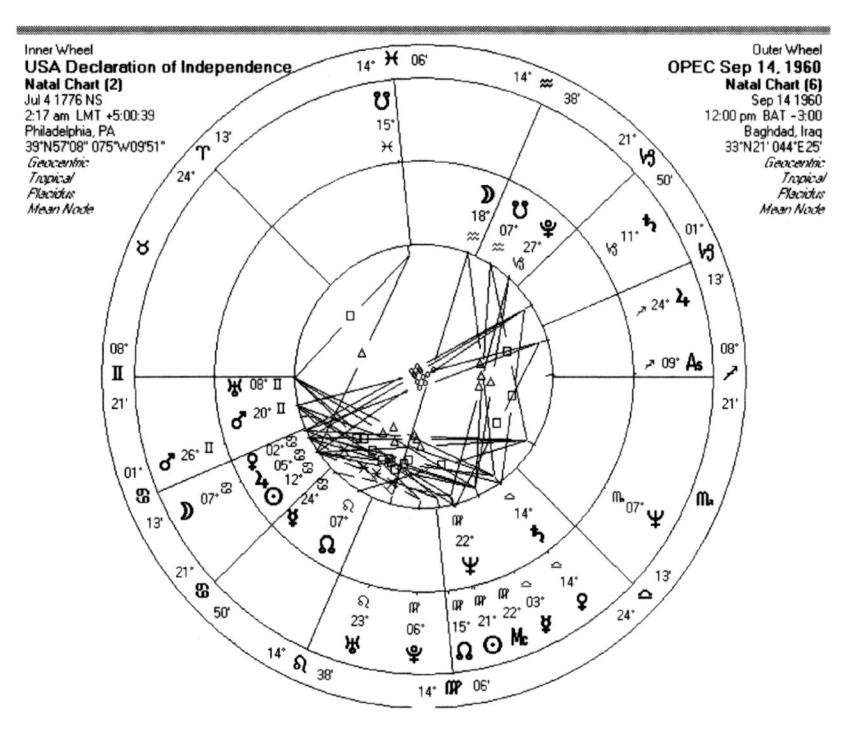

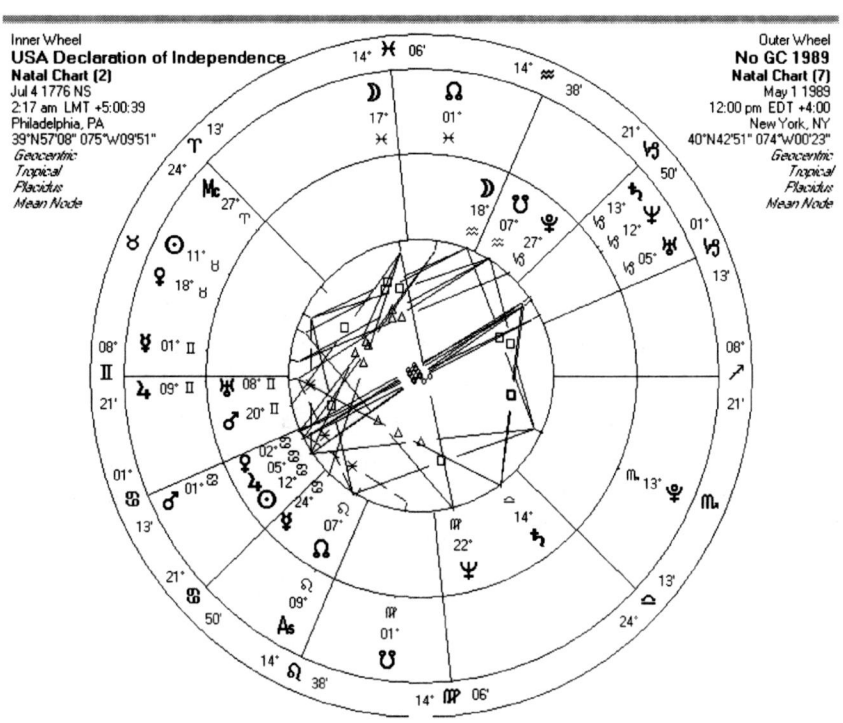

Robert Gover

Most notable in the third chart for May 1, 1989, is that Saturn, Neptune and Uranus are together in Capricorn opposite the US Sun—a rare conjunction of these three bodies—but with no outer planet in Aries, no great depression occurred. I've searched the table of daily planetary positions back to year 100 and found no other instance of these three simultaneously together in Capricorn. To find a previous instance, I suspect one would have to search back many millennia.

Economists who track the 30- and/or 60-year rhythm of great depressions were sure the 1990s would send the USA into another. Dr. Ravi Batra's book *The Great Depression of 1990* was a bestseller in the late 1980s. Saturn at 13 Capricorn is within one degree of a conjunction with Neptune at 12 Capricorn, and within 7 degrees of a conjunction with Uranus at 5 Capricorn. As Uranus moves faster than Neptune, they were soon to come exactly conjunct. So this time when Saturn moved opposite Uncle Sam's Sun, Uranus and Neptune joined Saturn in Capricorn. Note also that all three form a beneficent 60-degree sextile angle to Pluto at 13 Scorpio, which in turn forms a 120-degree harmonious trine aspect to the US Sun in Cancer.

No grand cross, no great depression.

Conjunctions of Uranus and Neptune occur once every 171 years. Uranus and Neptune had not come conjunct in Capricorn for the past thousand years at least.

"When a great conjunction like this happens, it means humanity has come to a 'fork in the road.' It is a chance to start over after the slate has been wiped clean—a moment of decision when we must choose a path of destruction or a path or renewal. This is the key to events of the 1990s. The end of the Cold War forced us to shift the direction of our lives and our society. Whether we move toward a peaceful, sustainable way of life that allows us to express our creative potential, or simply allow the destructive, depersonalizing corporate, military-industrial society to continue, is the great issue we confront in the years after this great conjunction." (*Horoscope for the New Millennium* by E. Alan Meece, Llewellyn Publications, 1997, page 84).

Uranus-Neptune Crossroads

The 1989 Uranus-Neptune crossroad brought us to the end of the Cold War, the reunification of Germany and the Tienamen Square protest in Beijing. The Berlin Wall came down November 9, 1989, marking a major turning point.

During the Uranus-Neptune conjunction of 1650, the Thirty Years War ended, marking an end to a protracted period of religious wars, and beginning another long period of wars between kingdoms and then nation-states. The Uranus-Neptune conjunction of 1821 coincided with the breakup of the Turkish Empire.

Later in the first decade of the 21st Century when Pluto and Uranus move into a square, we can expect abrupt, dramatic and unprecedented changes. A foreshadowing of the kind of events this will bring occurred September 11, 2001, when a Saturn-Pluto opposition afflicted, and terrorists hit the World Trade Center and Pentagon.

Neptunian Speculative Bubble

Economically, the end of the Cold War was followed by a record run-up of US stock prices during the 1990s. This was not as beneficial as it at first seemed, for it created a Neptunian speculative bubble, coupled with a foggily-perceived, widening gap between rich and poor—the two conditions which have always led to previous great depressions.

Would this bubble and gap bring another?

Not during the 1990s.

This roughly 20-year period of the '80s and '90s was called "the best economy in American history," but that Neptunian delusion confused the stock market with the overall economy. Only the wealthiest partook of the stock market's fabulous run-up. The media shouted that a new record number of jobs were created during this run-up, but that was another Neptunian delusion. In previous decades, one worker could support a spouse and their children, but by the mid-1980s it took two or more wage earners to keep most families afloat. Thus arose "the latchkey kids," children who came home from school to empty houses because both parents were working jobs that didn't pay either enough, in purchasing power, to hold a family together during this so-called "best economy in American history." Exacerbating the situation for working class Americans, many US-based companies moved overseas to obtain cheaper labor, abandoning workers, latchkey kids and towns. The migration of cheap laborers from Mexico further depressed wages for American workers. While the media focused on "protecting our borders," corporations focused on hiring Mexican workers cheap.

Economic Indicators

Two economic indicators which measure the economy's health—stock prices and unemployment figures—were dramatically good, so few economists noticed the plight of the working class. Also, by the late 1990s, many working class families had adjusted to the new two-job situation, and younger generations were coming of age never having known the single-worker household. Occasionally, someone such as Clinton Administration Secretary of Labor Robert Reich appeared on TV and mentioned the downward trend of working class wages in purchasing power, but such spokespersons were invariably sandwiched between pundits whose net worth were so expanding their prides, they would not hear a discouraging word about "the best economy in American history."

The Ominous Gap

"As it gets increasingly difficult for most Americans to make a living, it also becomes increasingly easier for a select handful to make a killing," wrote Morris Berman in *The Twilight of American Culture* (Norton, 2000, page 22). "According to the Census Bureau, the bottom 20 percent of US families in 1970 received 5.4 percent of the national income, while the top 5 percent received 15.6 percent. By 1994, the corresponding figures were 4.2 percent and 20.1 percent."

"This is what happens when irrationality shapes economic policy," said Ravi Batra (*The Great American Deception*, John Wiley and Sons, NY, 1966). "People suffer because the leaders trust the self-serving theories of established economists, most of whom are engaged in pleasing their affluent patrons," the wealthy few, the government and brokerage companies.

Economists who worked for governments and brokerage companies maintained their optimism through these two decades of the roaring bull stock market. A few dissented but were barely audible in the roar.

Monetarists and Keynesians

Monetarist or classical theory versus fiscal or Keynesian theory: this is the essential contention between economists.

Classical theory grew out of the works of Adam Smith, David Ricardo and J. B. Say, and was called supply-side economics during the Reagan Administration. "Supply creates its own demand" is the belief of supply-siders. The profits from production are distributed throughout the economy in the form of wages, rents, interest incomes and dividends: stimulate production and the whole economy will prosper—that's the belief of supply-siders, which included the Bush Administration's advisors.

Against supply-siders are Keynesians or fiscal economists. John Maynard Keynes turned "Say's Law" around and argued that demand creates supply. If demand shrinks, businesses are stuck with unsold goods, and thus layoffs and recession or worse ensues. Keynesians hold that the way to stimulate a contracting economy is to get purchasing power into the hands of consumers.

Who Gets How Much

Ravi Batra's complaint that people suffer because establishment economists are busy pleasing their most affluent clients is, I believe, correct. Supply-side economics is beloved by big corporations because it means government will favor them over workers/ consumers. Politics is how we decide who gets how much of the collective wealth.

If great depressions of the past have been brought on by new record disparities between the haves and have-nots and speculative bubbles, why had we not fallen into another great depression by year 2001? By any reckoning, we had seen a new record speculative bubble in the stock markets, concurrent with a loss of working class purchasing power, and a new record gap between the richest and poorest.

Astrologically, the answer is clear: no grand cross anchored by Saturn in mid-Capricorn square another heavy in mid-Aires has formed since the one that coincided with the last great depression, the 1930s. By 2001, the economy was in a recession, but by no measurement could it be called a great depression. Not yet.

Good News and Bad

As we moved into the new millennium, Saturn wasn't due to arrive opposite Sam's Sun till January 2019. That's the good news.

The bad news is we are not likely to make it to 2019 without suffering something like a combination of the 1930s, the 1960s and the Revolutionary War. This is because Pluto slowly transits opposite Sam's Uranus and Mars early in this new millennium, where it was for 911, then forms the Great Depression grand cross with Uranus in Aries.

The Uranus-Pluto square and grand cross will begin to take effect in 2008. Two grand crosses will occur. The first will involve the US Mars-Neptune square, the second will involve the US Sun-Saturn square. The first will take effect in 2008; the second will climax in 2015.

As predicted in the following chapter, the stock market crashed in 2008 as the Uranus-Pluto square began to form and Saturn opposed Uranus from Virgo. By later 2010, the official word was that the country was recovering from what pundits called "the great recession." But as the table below suggests, the worst was yet to come as the Uranus-Pluto square continued.

Uranus-Pluto Square Direct Hits

June 24, 2012	8 Aries to 8 Capricorn
Sept. 19, 2012	7 Aries to 7 Capricorn
May 20, 2013	11 Aries to 11 Capricorn
Nov. 1, 2013	9 Aries to 9 Capricorn
April 21, 2014	13 Aries to 13 Capricorn
Dec. 15, 2014	12 Aries to 12 Capricorn
March 16, 2015	15 Aries to 15 Capricorn

When this upcoming Uranus-Pluto square is most exact, it simultaneously makes its most exact oppositions to the US Sun-Saturn square—Uranus opposite US Saturn and Pluto opposite US Sun. At 8 Aries and 8 Capricorn, both Uranus and Pluto will be within orb of the grand cross to the US Sun-Saturn square. By 2014, at 13 Aries and 13 Capricorn, both will be within a degree of exact.

Based on the history of Uranus-Pluto squares, what we are likely to experience during the first two decades of the new millennium is something like the growing discontent between rulers and ruled which triggered the Revolutionary War the last time Uranus and Pluto moved through Aries and Capricorn.

Notice on the chart below for 2014 that Pluto at 13 Capricorn square Uranus at 14 Aries form the great depression grand cross with the US Sun-Saturn square. Jupiter and Mars are participating in this grand cross—Jupiter being found at 14 Cancer conjunct Sam's Sun, and Mars at 11 Libra conjunct Sam's Saturn.

Robert Gover

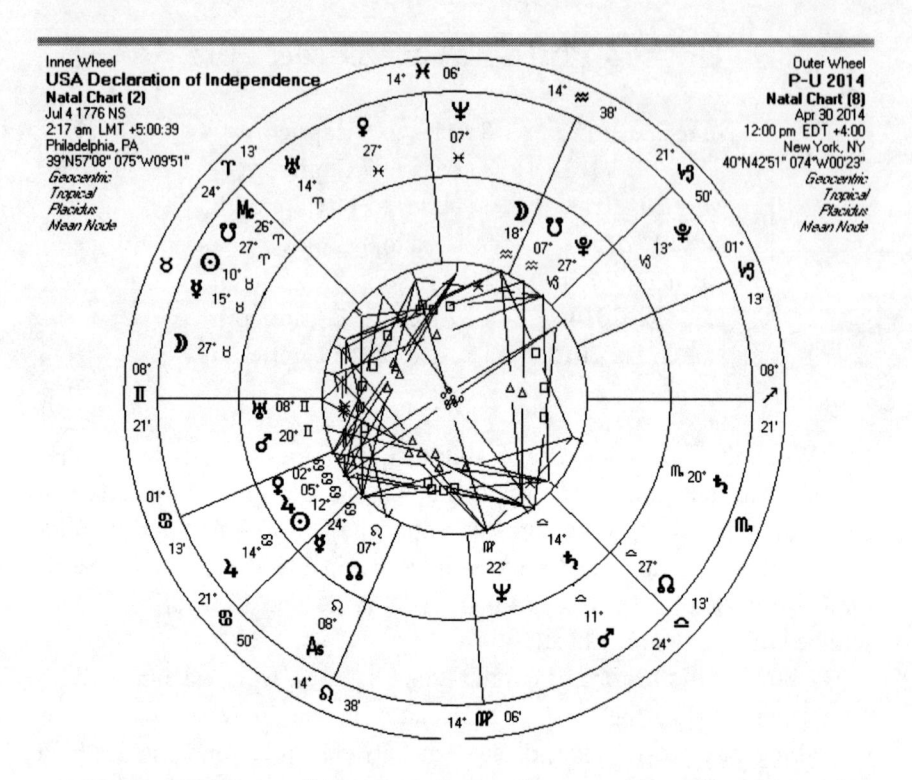

Before Pluto was discovered, Saturn was considered the energy that brought death and destruction. Tracing Pluto's history has shown it is well named for the god who rules the mystery from which we emerge at birth and into which we disappear at death.

Most amazing is that this upcoming Uranus-Pluto square is going to be within orb for most of the 11 years from 2008 to 2019. This will be the longest lasting Uranus-Pluto square going back to at least year 1. (I have not searched further back.)

Stock Market Panics

With one exception, every time there has been a stock market crash steep and abrupt enough to cause panic, the US natal Mars-square-Neptune has been afflicted by transiting planets forming oppositions, squares and/or conjunctions. Not every time this affliction has formed has there been a panic, however.

It's said that greed and fear drive the stock markets. Greed motivates people to rush in when stocks prices are rising, and fear demands they sell and run when stock prices are falling. Greed creates speculative bubbles; (Check the myth of Icarus flying too close to the Sun) and panic is the inevitable result. The Mars-Neptune square afflicted—to stay with the Icarus metaphor—is the investor lifted by the wings of Neptunian inspiration flying up, up and away to the inevitable consequences.

Another perspective: Mars in square aspect to Neptune suggests a combination of aggressive risk-taking (Mars) despite the unknown, mysterious future (Neptune). I think of this aspect in the USA's natal chart are symbolizing a loaded merchant ship crossing a vast sea. When the ship is structurally sound and the sea is calm, the journey is pleasant. If the ship encounters stormy seas or develops mechanical problems, the trip becomes nasty. Adverse aspects by transiting planets to Uncle Sam's Mars-square-Neptune seem to roil the sea or undermine the ship's structural integrity.

Raymond A. Merriman, in an article titled "The May 2000 Astrological Lineup and the Global Economy" (The Mountain Astrologer Magazine, Dec. 1999-Jan. 2000, page 19) noted that there are two ways to make astrological forecasts. "One is to choose certain classical astrological keywords for planets, signs and aspects involved at a given time, and combine these to create a prediction...

Robert Gover

"The other way...is to combine astrological keywords and arrive at certain mundane possibilities, and then go back and research historically what happened under similar signatures. See if, in fact, the type of events one might have expected, given the astrological principles in effect, did indeed occur...By going through this process, and relating past incidents to support one's forecasts, the astrologer adds immense credibility to the subject of astrology. It no longer becomes a question of 'faith in the messenger,' but rather an objective reporting of the facts, followed by an educated speculation about possibilities for the current and future time."

A Common Signature

That is how I arrived at the discovery that the stock market is in danger of crashing whenever the US Mars-square-Neptune is afflicted by oppositions, squares or conjunctions. I searched for a common signature and found no small number of possibilities. I found by reviewing the history of previous crashes that an affliction to Uncle Sam's Mars-Neptune square is the most reliable indicator. It's not 100 percent but when it comes to predicting stocks, no system is 100 percent.

These adverse aspects are found by "reading the transits" to Uncle Sam's birth chart. One of the amazing things about astrology is that one system of finding such danger times does not refute other ways. The celestial clock is amazingly complex and can be read in a variety of ways, from a variety of perspectives.

For instance, back in 1938, Louise McWhirter published her book *Astrology and Stock Market Forecasting* in which she revealed how to use the Moon's Nodes to know when the markets are likely to rise and fall. Her system isn't fail-safe, but in its day it was groundbreaking. Other astrologers have used a variety of other methods which have proven valid 85 percent or better.

I focused on crashes and panics because people lose the most money at such times. Most individual investors and fund managers can finesse cycles of weeks or months, but are liable to go down in flames in crashes so severe they cause panic. Such crashes almost inevitably follow boom periods, and almost invariably coincide with afflictions to the US Mars-Neptune square.

Panic of 1837

The Panic of May 10, 1837 is an exception to the rule of thumb that crashes occur when the US Mars-Neptune square is hit by adverse transits. This panic was preceded by a speculative bubble and triggered by President Jackson's sentiment against federalizing the banking industry; his administration sabotaged the Second Bank of the United States. From the web site "This Day in History on Wall Street" www.gnu.org, we get a cogent explanation.

"The battle over the Second Bank of the United States (SBUS), which pitted states' rights advocates against proponents of the federal financial institution, took its toll on the nation's economy on (May 10) in 1837. The Bank (battle) had ostensibly been settled a few years earlier, as...President Andrew Jackson marshaled his forces and effectively crushed the federal-based SBUS...In the wake of Jackson's putative victory, a number of legislators predicted that the demise of the bank would wreak havoc on America's fiscal health. These dire forecasts proved to be all too prescient: the absence of the SBUS...triggered a liquidity crisis that imperiled small banks..."

The Jackson Administration hatched its scheme during the Saturn-Pluto opposition of 1834, with Saturn at 13 Aries opposite and Pluto conjunct the US Saturn in Libra, forming a T square with the US Sun in Cancer. This was about a generation after the passage of the Constitution and Bill of Rights. Jackson's move was an effort to blunt the power of bankers, and was part of an ongoing conflict between those who wanted a privatized central bank and those who wanted a government independent of "the money powers." Bankers retaliated against Jackson's abolishing the SBUS by constricting credit.

"The panic (three years later) not only felled hundreds of banks, but it wiped out the scores small businesses and farmers who had heavily relied on the support of local fiscal institutions. Unemployment climbed to unprecedented peaks, while tension and anguish gripped good chunks of the country; in New York, the militia had to be called in to keep order on Wall Street. All told, the Panic of 1837 stretched on for seven long and painful years"—into what came to be called the great depression of the 1840s.

On May 10, 1837, the US Mars-Neptune square was not hit by any major transits. Instead, Pluto was opposite the US Saturn, square the US Sun. This panic was blamed on Jackson's actions three years previous but astrologically the culprit was Pluto. And Nicholas Biddle acting as Pluto's agent.

By May 8, 1842 when it was clear a great depression had taken hold, Saturn and Jupiter were conjunct in mid-Capricorn opposite the US Sun, and Mars and Pluto were conjunct in Aries opposite the US Saturn completing the grand cross which coincides with great depressions. So we might say that the Panic of 1837 was a Plutonian hint of worse to come.

Panic of 1857

In February 1857, the US natal Neptune was opposed by transiting Mars and Neptune in Pisces, putting this pair also square US natal Mars in Gemini. This T square pattern coincided with what is now called the Panic of 1857. "Economists attribute this panic to over development in the West and excessive railroad construction during this period." (McWhirter)

Black Friday, 1869

On what was called Black Friday, September 24, 1869, Saturn moved into an opposition to Sam's Mars, forming the T square with Sam's Neptune. This crash was a prelude to the great depression of the 1870s.

"This panic was mostly a Wall Street affair. Stocks had advanced to high levels from a long period of speculation since the Civil War and a reaction set in. Money rates were at their highest level since 1857 and 1860." (McWhirter)

There would be other "black" panics and crashes. The color black has a bad reputation. If you look up the word black in an Oxford English Dictionary and trace its meaning back to the 16th Century, you will gain

Time and Money

insight into this very important phenomenon in American culture. It's possible that there is no other word in the English language that conveys a more vile cargo of intimations.

Black Friday 1873

The next crash to be cursed with that fabulously evil word happened on Friday, September 19, 1873, when Mars at 13 Sagittarius widely but effectively formed an opposition to Sam's Mars-square-Neptune that created the T square, with Jupiter and Mercury together in Virgo conjunct Sam's Neptune.

This sunk the nation deeper into its third great depression, called at the time "The Secondary Post-War Depression." The New York Stock Exchange closed its doors for the first time in history on September 20, 1873. It remained closed for 10 days.

Panic of 1893

"The Panic of 1893," led to a depression but not a great depression. "The sharp and irregular depression of 1893 came at a time when prices were the lowest they had ever been in the economic history of this country. Crop failures both in 1893 and 1894 were numerous." (McWhirter). In the 1800s, when most Americans were what we now call "family farmers" (before the rise of agribusiness corporations), stock market panics and crashes often coincided with crop failures. Also in the 19th Century, what are now called "severe corrections" were called depressions. Economic language has since been refined. We now distinguish between panics, corrections, bear markets, recessions, depressions and great depressions.

Neptune, Venus, the Sun and Moon were the culprits in 1893. The T square includes the Moon in Sagittarius opposite Sam's Mars, which was simultaneously being conjoined by transiting Venus at 18 Gemini, Neptune at 11 Gemini, with help from the Sun at 9 Gemini, all thus tied into a square to Sam's Neptune in Virgo.

Robert Gover

Rich Man's Panic, 1903

This one found Sam's Mars-square-Neptune afflicted by five transiting planets: Uranus at 25 Sagittarius, Jupiter at 15 Pisces, Neptune and Venus in Gemini conjunct Sam's Mars, and T Mars at 27 Virgo conjunct Sam's Neptune. This was called The Rich Man's Panic because it affected newly enriched railroad and industrial investors. Rails dropped from 110 to 92 and industrials dropped from 64 to 47. I include a chart for this one because it shows Pluto opposite where it is as I write this.

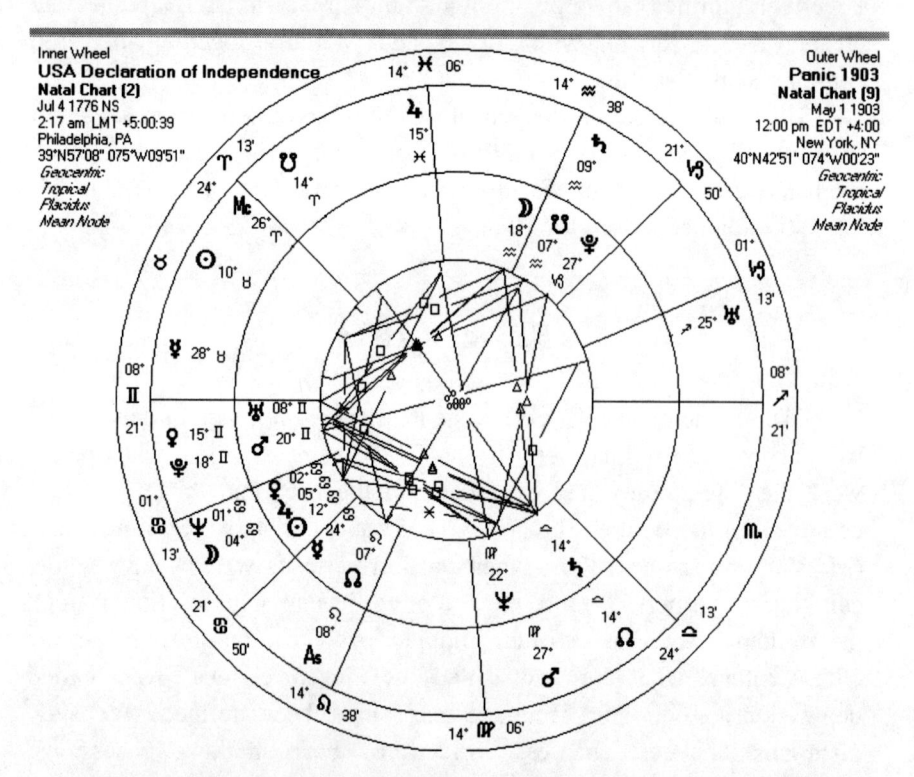

Notice that none of these afflicting planets—Uranus, Jupiter, Venus and Mars—are making exact squares or oppositions, but are within a 7 degree orbs of exact. The rule of thumb I use is that the orbs of transiting planets expand beyond 7 degrees when they are within orb of other transiting planets which in turn are within orb of oppositions, squares or conjunctions of natal planets.

Panic of 1907

The Panic of 1907 arrived when Saturn reached 22 Pisces, opposite Sam's Neptune and square Sam's Mars at 21 Gemini, which was simultaneously being hit by transiting Pluto at 24 Gemini, forming a T square.

This was a classic. It was not followed by a great depression (Saturn was in Pisces at this time and has always been in Capricorn for great depressions), but in terms of dollars lost, it was horrendous. It followed what is called The Corporate Prosperity period from 1905 to 1907, when corporate stocks rose dramatically. The primary economic measurement of those times, The Business Curve, dropped 26 points, to 18 points below normal.

Crash of 1920

This time the US natal Mars-square-Neptune was afflicted by Saturn conjunct Sam's Neptune in Virgo and transiting Mars opposite Sam's Mars. Another T square. This brought plunging stock and bond prices coupled with high interest rates. "The Business Curve dropped 26 points below the normal line. During most of the year of 1921 Saturn was in conjunction with Jupiter (in Virgo) and both planets were opposite Uranus." (McWhirter).

This period was called a depression, although its duration was brief and today economists might find the word *recession* more apt to describe it.

The Big Crash of '29

What kicked off the great depression of the 1930s was really a series of severe crashes. Prices roller-coastered down, down, and further down to eventually hit an unprecedented low by 1932. Picking October 24, 1929 as the day when panic first become palpable, the US natal Mars was caught between an opposition formed by Saturn at 26 Sagittarius and Jupiter at 15 Gemini to form another T square with Sam's natal Neptune in Virgo.

The transiting aspects would quickly become far worse, catching the US natal Sun-square-Saturn in a grand cross formed by Saturn in Capricorn, Uranus in Aries and Pluto in Cancer. However, the crash of '29 was kicked off by the US natal Mars being caught between Saturn in Sagittarius and Jupiter in Gemini.

Witchdoctors and Economists

There is nothing like the unknown to bring out the superstitious side of otherwise rational people. It has long been acknowledged that economics is not a "hard" science. A lead article in the June 15, 1958, issue of FORBES Magazine helps make the point:

"'If I were an anthropologist,' a highly successful but largely self-educated businessman recently remarked, 'I would say that modern business, as much as any primitive African tribe, has its own witch doctors and medicine men. I'm referring to economists. We businessmen call them in to read the future, rationalize the past and justify the present to us. And, like tribal medicine men, the economists don't have to produce results—only explanations and a kind of business cosmology.'"

More recently, Fred L. Block, a professor of sociology at the University of California at Davis, explored in more depth the mythical content of economics in his book *The Vampire State*. "If capital is seen as the lifeblood of the economy, then the Conventional Wisdom treats the state as a vampire who is regularly sapping the economy's strength... This imagery of a parasitic state is centuries old. It dates back from the long struggle of liberalism against absolute monarchies that were depicted as parasitic monsters preying on their societies. Ironically, those governments that were created as a consequence of democratic anti-monarchical revolutions inherited the same set of images."

The Power of Incantation

Economist John Kenneth Galbraith, in his classic *The Great Crash: 1929* (Houghton Mifflin), captures the superstition of that time (page 94): "In Wall Street, as elsewhere, there is deep faith in the power of incantation. When the market fell many Wall Street citizens immediately sensed the real danger, which was that the income and employment—prosperity in general—would be adversely affected. This had to be prevented. Preventive incantation required that as many important people as possible repeat as firmly as they could that it wouldn't happen. This they did."

Such incantation continues to be part of Wall Street culture. And it's understandable when you consider that most stock drops are explained logically after the fact, and then, as though in response to these explanations and incantations of optimism, equity prices usually rise again. Such incantations and rational explanations have appeared to do the trick since the crash of '29. The prevailing assumption as we approached the next millennium was that they would continue to work. There were even those who had such faith in the machinations of the Federal Reserve that they believed great depressions were a thing of the past and not possible in the future. Among these faithful were none who had actually lived through the irrationality of the 1930s.

Most economists believe astrology is superstition. Belief trumps evidence. An economist caught consulting astrology would be in big trouble with his colleagues, most of whom believe those sun-sign fortune-cookie blurbs in newspapers and magazines are all there is to astrology. This is unfortunate because astrology is a far more precise tool of economic prediction than economics.

It bears repeating that not every time the T square affliction to Sam's Mars-square-Neptune has formed have we had a stock market panic. During the 1960s, the T square formed without coinciding with a panic. Even though Pluto and Uranus were conjunct Sam's Neptune in Virgo and Saturn moved to opposite this position from Pisces, putting all three—Saturn, Pluto and Uranus—square Sam's Mars, stocks did not crash. Nor had there been a speculative bubble of "irrational exuberance." Instead, a bear market dip bottomed out in October of 1966, then the Dow met the bulls again. What else happened during a Uranus-Pluto conjunction opposite Saturn is now called The Sixties. Stocks held their own. It was the rest of society that went over the edge.

Black Monday 1987

On another Black Monday, October 19, 1987, Saturn and Uranus were in Sagittarius, opposite Sam's Mars, square Sam's Neptune, with the Moon this day conjunct Sam's Neptune. This was the most dramatic one-day drop to this point in history. Saturn by itself brings frustration and disappointment. Uranus conjunct Saturn adds surprise, drama, the unprecedented.

With Pluto at 9 Scorpio making a protective 120 degree angle to Sam's Sun in Cancer, this panic did not bring down the whole economy, thrilling though it was for investors. Important people recited the old incantation and, presto, prices rose almost as dramatically as they'd plunged. Deceptive Neptune at 5 Capricorn opposite Sam's Jupiter and Sun in Cancer suggested the old incantation was mere superstition, however, and lots of market-watchers believed this crash would lead to another great depression. Believers in "mass psychology" as the primary market mover were also baffled by the quick recovery. The last time transiting Uranus had moved opposite Uncle Sam's Mars, it had coincided with the Rich Man's Panic of 1903, one 84-year orbit of Uranus ago.

Time and Money

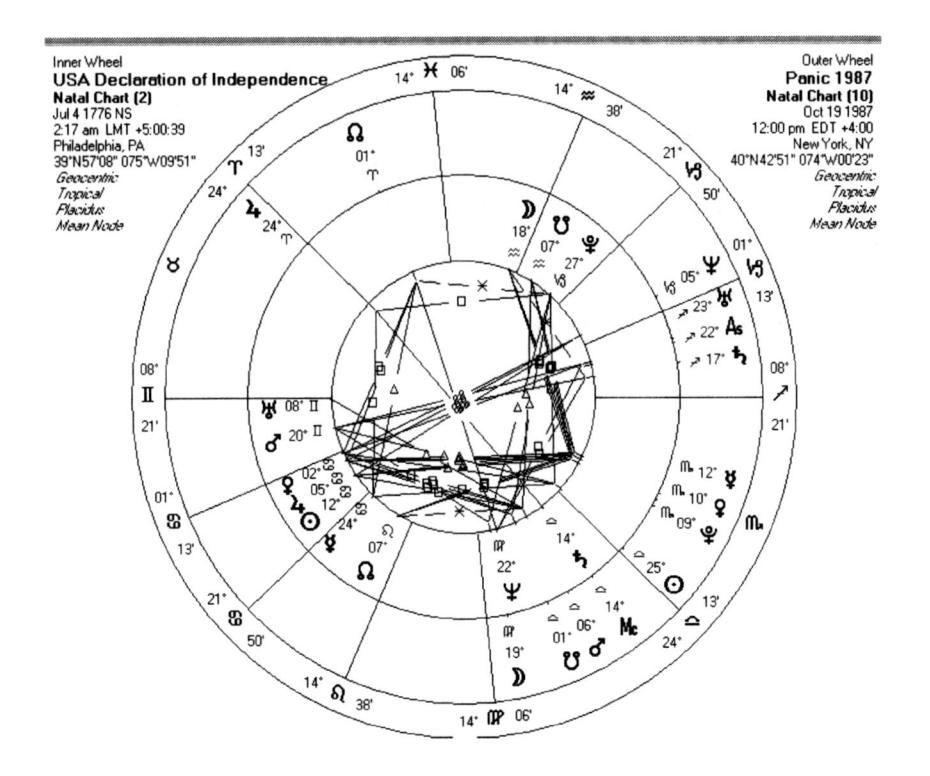

Scare of 1997

On October 27, 1997, transiting Mars was conjunct transiting Venus at 20 degrees of Sagittarius, opposite Sam's Mars-square-Neptune. And the Moon that day happened to be conjunct Sam's Neptune in Virgo, (as it had been for the fright of '87) just to keep things dicey. The biwheel chart for this event also shows transiting Saturn moving retrograde through Aries opposite Sam's natal Saturn in Libra and thus also square Sam's Sun: another T square. Some believed at the time that this was the end of the record-breaking run-up of the 1990s, but again the old incantations "proved" magical: emotional Moon conjunct delusional Neptune.

If we view the planets around us in our solar system as a huge celestial clock, the first thing history teaches us is that the celestial clock is not mechanically precise like our earthly clocks. Although we can discern from history when like economic events are due, clock-like precise prediction isn't possible. Certain planetary patterns create seasons when certain types of events can be expected. But the planets cannot tell us specifically how events will unfold, nor how we will respond. We know when winter is nigh but not how cold it will get. Some hurricane seasons bring great devastation, others are less severe. Planetary cycles repeat but always within an overall pattern which is unique. No two moments in celestial time are the same.

Record Highs

Astrology can tell us when another economic winter is nigh, but specifically how it will unfold, what proper nouns we'll use to describe it, and how the nation will respond cannot be predicted.

Still, knowing when inclement economic weather is due can be extremely helpful. In a sense, the industrial-age economy is a fishing expedition and the last thing it needs is to be surprised by "the perfect storm."

By the summer of '98, stocks continued to set new record highs. The pace of this rise was such that some doom-and-gloomers proclaimed it a speculative bubble destined to burst eventually, as all speculative bubbles in the past have done. Such pessimists were poo-pooed by the pundits. This dramatic run-up was happily called, at the time, "the dotcom phenomenon." The NASDAQ topped out at 5,048.62 on March 10, 2000.

NASDAQ Loses 78 Percent

As the longest bull market in US history began to peter out after the turn of the century; the Dow suddenly dropped 436 points on March 12, 2001.

Transiting Pluto and Mars in Sagittarius were opposite Uncle Sam's Mars in Gemini, while the Sun in Pisces was opposite Sam's Neptune in Virgo to form a grand cross pattern with Sam's Mars-Neptune square.

Time and Money

Two days later, when the Moon moved conjunct Mars in Sagittarius, the Dow and NASDAQ dropped again, and by week's end the doom-and-gloomers and the shorts were standing tall.

The NASDAQ bottomed on October 9, 2002, at 1,114, having lost 78 percent from its top in March 2000. Concurrently, Pluto was at 15 Sagittarius opposite the US Mars and square Neptune. Saturn was at 29 Gemini, conjunct the US Mars, and Mars and Mercury were conjunct the US Neptune.

The 1990s unfolded during one of Pluto's perihelion passages; after swinging so far into outer space it is more than twice the distance from the Sun as Neptune, Pluto swings back to spend twenty years inside Neptune's orbit. It "surfaced above the god of oceans" last in 1989, coinciding with the end of the Iron Curtain, with revolutions in Eastern Europe and the old Soviet Union, thus effectively ending the Cold War: another example of Pluto's transits leaving a wake of tremendous change.

By year 2020, people may look back on the first decade of the 21st Century as a dress rehearsal for the more dramatic events of the 2000-teens, when Pluto reaches 14 Capricorn where it was last when James Watt developed the first steam engine, launching the industrial revolution. The huge difference will be that this time Pluto in Capricorn will square Uranus in Aries and both will form a grand cross with the US natal Sun-square-Saturn. In 1768 when Watt made his breakthrough invention, Pluto was in a grand trine with Uranus-Mars conjunct in Taurus and Neptune in Virgo.

Pluto first inched into Sagittarius in 1995 and wouldn't move into Capricorn till 2008. Its effect on stock markets could be expected to begin to take hold when it reached 12 degrees of Sagittarius, which it did in December of 1999. We had no historic record of what Pluto's affliction to Uncle Sam's market-sensitive Mars-square-Neptune would be, however, because financial markets today are nothing like they were in the mid-1700s when Pluto was here last.

By early March 2001, the NASDAQ was down over 60 percent, so that by spring the "tech rally" was seen to have been a speculative bubble, vindicating the long-ignored doom-and-gloomers. Now the question on investors' minds was, "How low will it go?"

Robert Gover

As in 1929 and 1930, the incantation began, the prevailing belief being that a positive attitude begets positive results. But a positive attitude disconnected from reality is like sunbathing in a rain storm. The Wall Street shaman had their work cut out for them this time, because Mars was due to move forward and retrograde—conjunct transiting Pluto and opposite Sam's Mars—through the summer of 2001 and early September, while Saturn was in Gemini opposite Pluto.

9/11/01

Quickly following the attack on the World Trade Center and Pentagon September 11, 2001, the stock markets dropped decisively. Astrologically, the big news was the Saturn-Pluto opposition with Saturn at 14 Gemini between the US Uranus and Mars-square-Neptune. The biwheel for this day, found in chapter 2, indicates not only a danger zone for stocks but with Sun conjunct the US Neptune, the distinct possibility of illusions and delusions, miscalculations and deceit.

911 created two big questions: 1) what could the USA do to protect itself from multinational terrorist individuals and small groups, and 2) would the financial system survive Pluto's eight-year long opposition to the US Mars-square-Neptune? Chaos historically precedes Pluto's more dramatically transformative effects. Opposite Saturn with both afflicting the US Mars-Neptune square, something transformative was promised for the financial system. With this in mind, Enron, Worldcom and the rash of other corporate sandals could be seen as Pluto's sprites of chaos leading the parade up Constitution Avenue in DC, with Lord Pluto somewhere back there, we can't be sure where exactly. We'll know his whereabouts when his works manifest.

By September 2002, assuming Pluto's impact on financials, the indications were that the process would be gradual, punctuated by scandals. There had been by 2002 bull market rallies within the context of an overall bear market, but no sustained recovery. Pluto is famous for dredging up corruption, and by January 2002, Enron became the first of a growing list to come to public attention, slowly eroding confidence in US markets.

Time and Money

This exposure of corporate malfeasance is reminiscent of what happened when Pluto was 180 degrees opposite, traveling through Gemini at the end of the 19th Century, leading to the Trust Busting of President Teddy Roosevelt and culminating in 1913 with the creation of the Federal Reserve, America's central bank.

By the eve of the 2004 election, the hoped-for recovery had faltered. My expectation was that the financial markets and the overall economy would not crash definitively as happened in 1929-30 but that the overall direction would be down to a bottom around 2014-15.

The crash of '29 and '30 resembled Niagara Falls; the first decade of the new millennium would resemble the Snake River's white water rapids.

Before we move on, a recap of the worst panics show that the outer planets are usually involved, and that Mars and the Moon often trigger. The Signs to be aware of when searching for future danger times for stocks are Pisces and Sagittarius (oppositions and squares) and Gemini and Virgo (conjunctions and squares).

Summary of Past Panics

1857: Neptune and Mars in Pisces.
1869: Saturn in Sagittarius.
1873: Mars in Sagittarius; Sun, Mercury, Jupiter in Virgo.
1893: Pluto, Neptune, Sun, Venus in Gemini.
1903: Pluto and Venus in Gemini; Uranus in Sagittarius; Jupiter in Pisces.
1907: Pluto in Gemini; Saturn in Pisces.
1920: Saturn in Virgo; Mars in Sagittarius.
1929: Saturn in Sagittarius; Jupiter in Gemini.
1987: Saturn and Uranus in Sagittarius; Moons Nodes in Pisces and Virgo.
1997: Mars and Venus in Sagittarius; Moon's Nodes in Pisces and Virgo.
5/15/2001: Pluto, Mars and Moon in Sagittarius; Sun in Pisces.
9/11/2001: Pluto, Chiron in Sagittarius; Saturn, Moon in Gemini; Sun in Virgo.
10/9/2002: Pluto in Sagittarius, Saturn in Gemini; Mars and Mercury in Virgo.

Rule of thumb*: a hard angle formed to the US Mars-Neptune square from an outer planet alone isn't likely to bring a crash or panic. It's when one or more of the outer planets afflict the US Mars-Neptune square that panics are likely.*

Looking Ahead

Looking ahead with that in mind, on May 5, 2007, Pluto, Jupiter and the Moon in Sagittarius will square Uranus and Mars in Pisces, with added oomph from the Moon's Nodes in Pisces-Virgo, and Venus in Gemini. Uranus at 17 Pisces will be applying to a square with Pluto at 28 Sagittarius—not yet within orb but too close for comfort. And with the square formed by Mars and Uranus in Pisces to the Moon in Sagittarius, Pluto's effects cannot be discounted. Pluto's wake often manifests the most obvious plutonian events. Also on May 5, 2007, Saturn in Leo will be opposite Neptune in Aquarius, with both forming beneficent angles to the US Mars. We will be moving into a danger zone for the financial markets during 2007, with the danger intensifying as this year unfolds.

Another time for investors to watch out for is the summer of 2008, when Uranus and Pluto are within orb of a square, with Uranus at 22 Pisces precisely opposite the US Neptune and square the US Mars. The Moon and Mercury will be conjunct the US Mars on July 1, 2008: the most likely date of a panic.

Second Edition Update

The crash of 2008 began in late 2007. On September 16, 2007, financial institutions bumped into trouble in the form of collapsing subprime loans and credit default swaps. Astrologically, there are remarkable similarities between this period and the 1930s: a Saturn-Uranus-Pluto T square characterized both.

As shown on the biwheel for this September 16, 2007 when the downturn began, the US Mars-Neptune square was afflicted by a grand cross formed by Pluto at 26 Sagittarius, Mars at 23 Gemini, Uranus at 16 Pisces and the Sun at 23 Virgo.

Time and Money

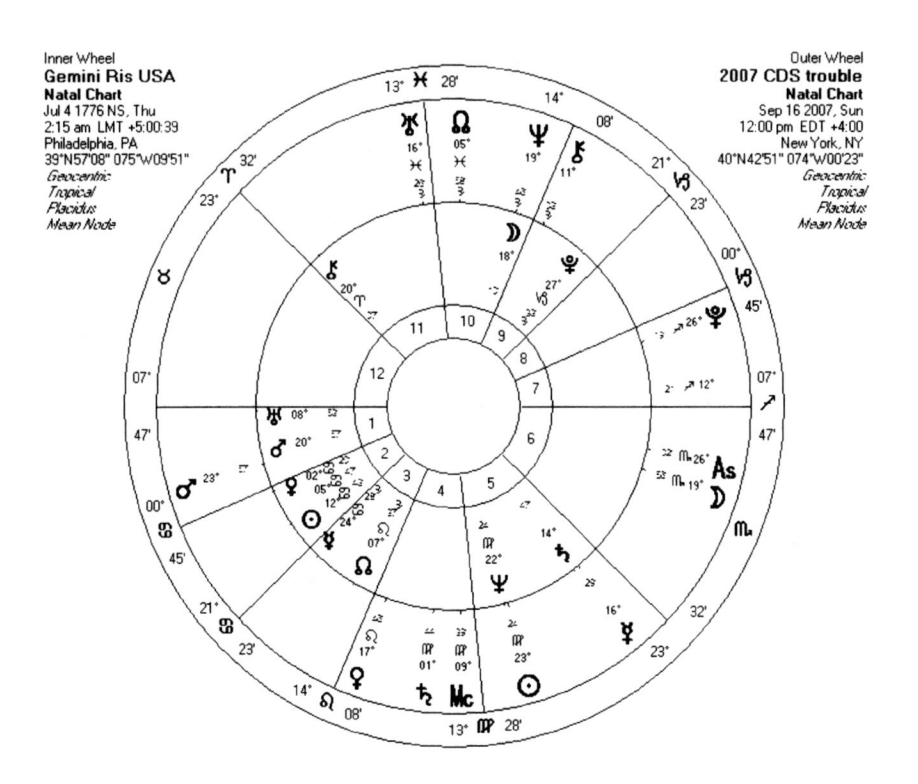

By the following September 2008, the Full Moon was conjunct and opposite the US Neptune square Pluto at 28 Sagittarius, and also opposite Uranus at 20 Pisces. By October 7, 2008 when the Dow dropped 508 points, the Saturn-Uranus opposition was tightening with Saturn conjunct the US Neptune and Uranus opposite, and Pluto lingering at 28 Sagittarius, opposite the US Mars and square the US Neptune. During eight trading days in October 2008, the Dow lost a total of 2,399 points or 22.11%.

According to Wikipedia: "The decline of 20% by mid-2008 was in tandem with other stock markets across the globe. On September 29, 2008, the DJIA had a record-breaking drop of 777.68 with a close at 10,365.45. The DJIA hit a market low of 6,443.27 on March 6, 2009."

By this time, Pluto had moved into the first degrees of Capricorn but the Saturn-Uranus opposition continued to be conjunct and opposite the

Robert Gover

US Neptune, with the Sun conjunct Uranus and all forming a T square with the US Mars.

After the low in March 2009, stock markets turned bullish but the overall economy continued to sink as unemployment rose. Astrologically, the problem for the overall economy was that a lingering Saturn-Uranus-Pluto T square would eventually evolve into an affliction to the USA's economically sensitive Sun-Saturn square by the summer of 2012. By June 24, 2012, Uranus and Pluto would be within 1 degree of a precise square at 8 Aries and 8 Capricorn, putting both within orb of a grand cross with the USA's Sun-Saturn square—the "great depression grand cross" except that this one has Pluto in Capricorn instead of Saturn.

Pluto's previous sojourn through Capricorn coincided with the American and French Revolutionary years, and the time before that, the early 1500s, with the pandemic that swept through the Caribbean and South America when millions of Native Americans died from diseases brought over from Europe by newly arrived conquistadors and priests. During both those previous periods, concentrations of wealth seemed to migrate—from the New World to Europe in the 1500s and then into the newly formed USA following the Revolutionary War.

Money was "migrating" again by 2010, this time from the USA and European Union to Southeast Asia, especially China. And what had begun as a financial sector crisis in 2007 was worsening with unemployment continuing high. This time it didn't seem to be happening as suddenly as it had during the 1930s. This time it felt more like white water rafting down the Snake River. Astrologically, this difference was due to Pluto being in Capricorn rather than Saturn. If the past is prologue, Pluto in Capricorn promises huge, cultural-transforming change that endures till the next sojourn of Pluto through Capricorn.

The Maya Calendar

The Winter Solstice 2012 is famous because that's when the Mayan Calendar "ends"—at least as far as records left undestroyed by Spanish explorers and priests indicate. At dawn on this day, our Sun will be conjunct a rift in the Milky Way which the Maya symbolized as the Creative Mother's vagina. This will be symbolic, not astronomically accurate because of the Precession of the Equinoxes, the apparent backward movement of our constellations. It's become another "end of the world" tale. Given the accuracy of so many other Maya predictions, my surmise is that this day will mark a turning point in human affairs. That is, as the years following this day unfold, we'll realize our attitudes toward our situation on planet Earth have changed.

Concurrent with the Winter Solstice 2012 will be the tightening of the Uranus-Pluto square, moving within orb of a grand cross with the US Sun-Saturn square. This is another instance of two different astrological traditions, using different techniques, arriving at virtually the same predicttion. End-of-world predictions for roughly this time period come from a variety of ancient traditions, from the Christian to the Tibetan. What history suggests is that "The World" (our Earth) does not drastically change—what transforms is our perception of our human reality.

Uranus, Pluto, and Revolution

When a conjunction or square of Uranus and Pluto have simultaneously formed T squares or grand crosses with Uncle Sam's natal planets in Gemini or Cancer—even when it's a waning square—historic turning points have occurred in US history: Bacon's Rebellion in the 1670s, the French and Indian War in the 1750-60s, the years leading up to the American Revolutionary War, the Great Depression of the 1930s, and the latest, the 1960s conjunction and 911 during the forming of the waxing square.

The upcoming waxing square between Uranus in Aries and Pluto in Capricorn, will form a grand cross with Uncle Sam's Sun-square-Saturn, and follows the Uranus-Pluto conjunction of the 1960s. The sixties Uranus-Pluto conjunction was simultaneously conjunct the US Neptune and square the US Mars in Gemini, which was opposite Saturn in Pisces.

Uranus will arrive opposite the US Neptune in Virgo by January 1, 2008, and simultaneously square transiting Pluto at 29 Sagittarius. This suggests the upcoming square of the 2000-teens (Uranus in Aries and Pluto in Capricorn) will manifest a new phase of revolutionary changes begun in the 1960s.

This upcoming Uranus-Pluto square from Aries to Capricorn during the 2000-teens is exceedingly rare. For an indication of how rare, you'd have to search the Ephemeris back before the time of Christ. In year 295, during the Roman Empire, Pluto was in Capricorn square Uranus, but at that time Uranus was in Libra, opposite Aries.

The last time Uranus was in Aries it sunk the economy into the great depression of the 1930s, and did so with suddenness and unprecedented surprises. The last time Pluto was in late Sagittarius and early Capricorn, the American Revolution was in the making.

Time and Money

Bacon's Rebellion

The second and most unprecedented thing about the 2000-teens is that no Uranus-Pluto square in the past 2,000 years—and perhaps the past five millennia—has lasted as long as this upcoming square will last. If we read astrology as "God's Newsletter," the news is that we face a lengthy, rare, fiery time of unpredictable events leading to huge, fundamental changes. Out of aspect with key points in the US natal chart, Uranus-Pluto squares have brought abrupt changes; forming a grand cross with the US Sun-Saturn square, this upcoming period portends the most dramatic events so far in US history.

During the 1670s, Uranus and Pluto formed a square that would resemble the square formed during the great depression of the 1930s: Uranus in Aires, Pluto in Cancer. An event called Bacon's Rebellion broke out in the Virginia Colony in July of 1676.

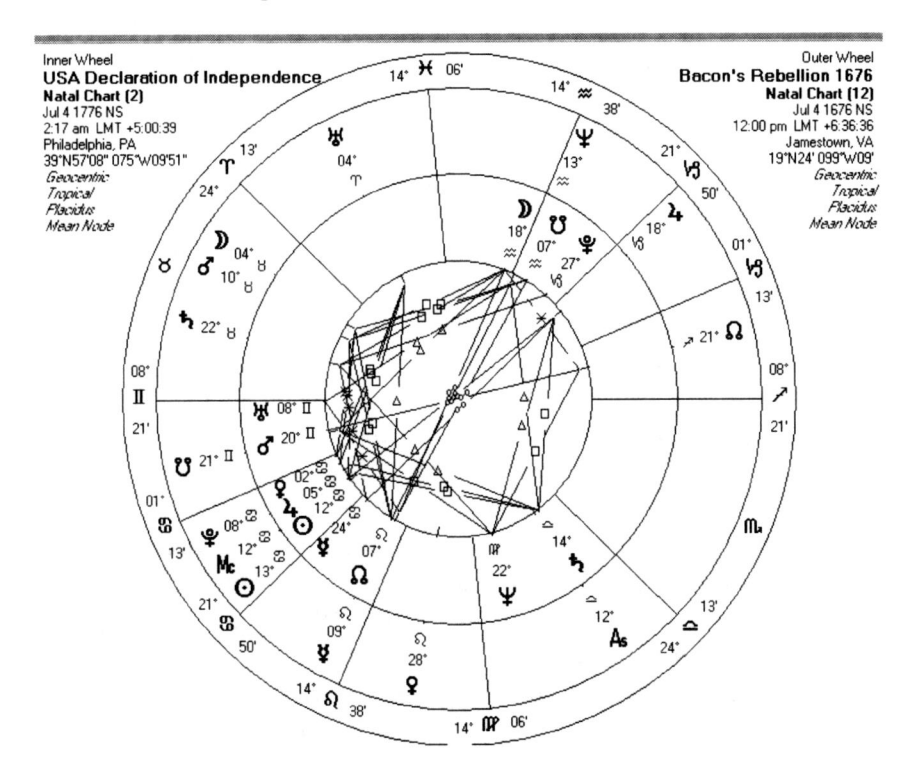

Robert Gover

Without Precedent

In the chart above for Bacon's Rebellion, Pluto at 8 Cancer (conjunct the US Jupiter, Venus and Sun) squares Uranus at 4 Aries. This same configuration was to repeat 254 years later during the great depression of the 1930s. During both periods, the quarrel between haves and have-nots erupted into open conflict. The threat to the rich posed in the time of Bacon's Rebellion was called "leveling," and during the great depression of the 1930s it was called socialism or communism. By whatever name, the have-nots demanded a greater share of the collective wealth their labor had helped create.

If one were to chart the growth of democracy in the broadest, most comprehensive meaning of the word, the trend line would show sharp turns in 1676, 1776, 1930 and 1965, all coinciding with Uranus-Pluto squares or conjunctions afflicting key points in Sam's chart. What this tells us is that when these key points of the Uranus-Pluto cycle hit key points in the US natal chart, major historic turning points are reached. And this has been so since before the USA was "born."

When African slaves first arrived in Virginia in 1619, most were housed with English indentured servants. At first, their masters made little or no distinction between servants and slaves, but mixed offspring soon posed a problem. Were such children servants or slaves? At first this question wasn't crucial because both servants and slaves were "rewarded" with freedom in old age. The outcome of Bacon's Rebellion was the passage of laws color-coding the American lower class into Black and White, and the punishing of race mixing.

Bacon's Rebellion arose as an alliance of English servants and African slaves led by one Nathaniel Bacon, and was to jolt the upper class into taking steps to prevent poor Whites and Blacks from uniting again—until the 1960s when Uranus and Pluto came conjunct over Uncle Sam's natal Neptune in Virgo about 300 years later, when a few Whites joined Blacks agitating for civil rights, then White and Black together protested the Vietnam War.

Bacon's Rebellion, not emphasized in American high school history classes, is confusing; it began as a movement to kill Indians, then morphed into an uprising against the ruling class. It seems Bacon wanted to kill Indians but his troops (servants and slaves) were thirsty for the blood of their masters.

Nathaniel Bacon was landed gentry. The aristocracy who controlled Virginia had pushed immigrating frontiersmen westward into Indian territory as a buffer between themselves and their "savages." Being intruders into Indian lands, these immigrants were constantly threatened by Indians. Howard Zinn describes the situation thus:

"It was a complex chain of oppression in Virginia. The Indians were plundered by White frontiersmen, who were taxed and controlled by the Jamestown elite. And the whole colony was being exploited by England...In the 1600s and 1700s, by forced exile, by lures, promises, and lies, by kidnapping, by their urgent need to escape the living conditions of the home country, poor people wanting to go to America became commodities of profit for merchants, traders, ship captains, and eventually their masters in America." (*A Peoples History of the United States*, by Howard Zinn, HarperPerenial, page 42-43).

Many of these frontiersmen were former indentured servants, who'd been bought and sold just as slaves were. Masters had the legal right to mistreat and whip both servants and slaves. Rape of servant and slave women was common and unpunished by the law of that time.

Seeds of Class War

A planned uprising of indentured servants in 1661 (with Pluto afflicting where Uncle Sam's natal Mars would be in 1776) was foiled by an informer being rewarded with his freedom and 5,000 pounds of tobacco. Four plotters were executed. Discontent continued.

Bacon's Rebellion grew directly out of a chain of events in 1675. Referring to Edmund Morgan's *American Slavery, American Freedom*, "In July, 1675, a group of Doegs, who were apparently trading in Stafford County, Virginia, took some hogs belonging to Thomas Matthew, alleging that he had failed to pay for goods he had bought from them. Matthew and his men pursued them, recovered the hogs, and killed or beat several Indians. The Doegs retaliated with a raid in which they killed one of Matthew's servants."

Virginia Colony's British-appointed Governor Berkeley deemed some tribes friendly, others not. Some Virginia settlers could distinguish one tribe from another; others could not. George Mason got himself in trouble with Governor Berkeley when he and his antique prototype of the modern SWAT team killed 14 Susquehannas "before discovering they had the wrong Indians."

Indian Tribes Upset

The new immigrants had upset traditional relations among Indian tribes, compounding this confusion with death from disease brought from Europe. The Susquehannas had just been driven from their site at the head of the Chesapeake Bay by an invasion of displaced Senecas, and had taken refuge with their friends the Piscataways. After George Mason's assault, they conducted retaliatory raids on Virginia settlers. In response, the settlers laid siege to the Indians. Five chiefs offered to negotiate for peace. They were killed. The Indians then killed 10 settlers and moved west into the forests.

On March 7, 1675, Governor Berkeley added political grievances to the settlers' anxieties about the Indians by proposing five forts be built at the head of each local river, to be defended by soldiers, who were to be paid 1,500 pounds of tobacco, "more than a frontier farmer was likely to make in a year." In other words, "To the people...the act that was supposed to end the Indian menace looked like a prescription for profiteering." (Morgan) Further complicating the situation were orders from the distant and unknowing Mother Country concerning how the governor was to handle the Indians, who, knowing the terrain, could strike at will and disappear before a military response could be organized.

Time and Money

A Certain Disdain

Into this situation stepped newly-arrived Nathaniel Bacon, feeling "a certain disdain for wealthy Virginians who had reached their positions from 'vile' beginnings or 'whose tottering fortunes have bin repared and supported at the Publique chardg.'" Not a populist by temperament, Bacon "harbored something of the scorn of the wellborn Englishman for the provincial (newly rich) among whom he found himself." Commiserating with the locals, Bacon soon came to the conclusion that not just some Indians should be killed, but all Indians.

To abbreviate the story, Bacon attracted the overwhelming majority of the local slaves and servants by his charm (and free rum), and asked Governor Berkeley for a commission to carry out attacks on Indians. Berkeley refused. He had treaties with some tribes.

The clash between Governor Berkeley and Rebel Bacon becomes a fascinating story within the overall story: Bacon calls for a new election of the House of Burgesses, giving all Virginians the opportunity to have their views made law in an anomaly of the times, a popular election. Thus elected to the House of Burgesses, Bacon showed up in Jamestown on a sloop with 50 armed men. But by the time the burgesses assembled, Bacon had been outwitted by Berkeley—it's not clear how, exactly. Berkeley then presented Bacon, subdued and on his knees, to the assembly of burgesses.

Kill All or Kill Some

Berkeley, triumphant, then showed his magnanimity: he pardoned Bacon the rebel, restored him to his seat on the burgesses, and promised him the Indian-fighting commission he'd sought. A promise he soon withdrew as debate continued over whether to kill some Indians or all Indians, the decision finally being to kill "any who left their towns without English permission." Such "disobedient" Indians would forfeit their lands. Men recruited to deal with them were to be paid 1,500 pounds of tobacco for foot soldiers and 2,250 pounds for horsemen, plus the plunder of Indian possessions and the capture of Indian slaves.

This did not satisfy Bacon. On July 30, 1676, with Uranus square Pluto, Bacon issued a "Declaration of the People" which denounced Berkeley's "crowd of placeholders" and upheld the frontiersmen's right to "not only ruine and extricate all Indians in generall but all Manner of Trade and Commerce with them." Governor Berkeley wanted to continue commerce with some Indians at taxpayers expense; Bacon and his followers saw this as a rip-off of taxpayers. Uranus and Pluto square indicates the unprecedented at a crossroads with great transformations. "It was time," in Morgan's words, "to redistribute some of their (the planters) ill-gotten wealth, time to plunder the estates of a few upstart grandees as well as time to plunder the Indians."

Slaves and Servants United

Rebel Bacon foiled Governor Berkeley by offering freedom to all slaves and servants who joined his cause. His militia then captured 45 peaceful Pamunkeys and paraded them through Jamestown. Governor Berkeley and friends fled the unruly mob across Chesapeake Bay to the Eastern Shore, now known as the Delmarva Peninsula. Bacon's militia of servants and slaves then burned Jamestown to the ground, demonstrating that their anger was focused on their masters, not Indians.

Howard Zinn: A member of the Governor's Council "noted that Bacon's Rebellion had started over Indian policy. But the 'zealous inclination of the multitude' to support Bacon was due, he said, to 'hopes of leveling.' (eliminating the difference between rich and poor)."

Bacon, at age 39, fell sick and died from "swarmes of Veremyn that bred in his body." Dysentery. A minister loyal to the aristocracy wrote his epitaph: "Bacon is Dead and I am sorry at my heart, That lice and flux should take the hangman's part."

23 Rebel Leaders Hanged

Then a British ship armed with 30 guns, cruising the York River, came upon a contingent of Bacon's rebels, "armed Englishmen and

Time and Money

Negroes, a mixture of free men, servants and slaves." The ship captain promised to pardon everyone and to free the slaves and servants if they'd surrender their arms and disperse. Most did. "Eighty Negroes and twenty English who insisted on keeping their arms" were promised by the ship captain safe passage down river, "but when they got into the boat, he trained his big guns on them, disarmed them, and eventually delivered the slaves and servants to their masters. The remaining garrisons were overcome one by one. Twenty-three rebel leaders were hanged." (Zinn, page 41.)

The Virginia Legislature gave amnesty to White servants who had rebelled, but not to Black slaves, who were no longer permitted to carry any weapons. English servants, finishing their terms of indenture, would get muskets in addition to their allotment of corn and cash. Thus, the longer lasting effect of Bacon's Rebellion was to add racial distinction to economic class, color-coding the lower class for centuries to come.

Another complication in the social mix of the 1600s was that English servants and African slaves often escaped to the frontier, joined Indian tribes or established new enclaves. Those who joined tribes or became friendly with the natives, discovered that Indian society was economically democratic—something these runaways had never before experienced. A chief maintained his position as long as he served the will of the people. Sharing food, shelter and clothing was taken for granted. Women and men were equal, and although the sexes had different duties, status was not based on wealth. Native American aristocracy was based on moral intelligence as demonstrated by an ability to maintain economic justice and peace.

Rights and Freedoms

Along the coast of North America, the new immigrants White and Black found "from Virginia southward, fairly advanced tribes whose semi-hereditary rulers depended upon the acquiescence of their people for the continuance of their rule. The explorers and first settlers (perceived) these rulers as kings, their people as subjects. They found that even the commonest subjects were endowed with many rights and freedoms, that nobility was fluid, and that commoners existed in a state of remarkable equality." (Oliver La Farge, "Myths that Hide the American Indian," *Historical Viewpoints*, Harper and Row, 1987.)

The discovery that people could live in economic democracy, plus the abundance of game, fish, garden vegetables, fruits, wild nuts and berries, was mind-altering to English and Africans who had friendly contact with the Indians. Conversely, it is easy to understand why the ruling class preferred the myth of the crazed, nearly-naked, blood-thirsty savages—or, later, the war-bonneted, diseased and starving Plains Indians depicted in photos of the late 1800s.

Seeding Revolutions

Uranus-Pluto conjunctions, squares or oppositions—some forming no major aspects to Uncle Sam's natal planets—have coincided with the seeding of other revolutions. The one in 1711 saw the incendiary works of Voltaire come to light in France. The conjunction of 1850 on the cusp of Aries-Taurus marked the works of Karl Marx. In 1966, the Red Guard mounted a cultural revolution in China while the US was rocked by massive protests against war and in favor of civil rights for descendants of African slaves. A worldwide student movement sent violent ripples through France and Czechoslovakia. John Lennon's song "Give Peace a Chance" became a kind of anthem that endures today.

A century after Bacon's Rebellion, the Uranus-Pluto square of the French and Indian War quickly gave way to a series of beneficent trines leading into and through the Revolutionary War. It should be noted, again, that Pluto's orbit is extremely erratic. Like the god of death Pluto is named for, its influence in human affairs often begins as unexpected tragedy and only later manifests as the new and heroic.

The French and Indian War was fought for domination of North America, the primary contenders being the monarchies of Britain and France. But caught up in this struggle were American colonists and Indians, especially Iroquois in the Ohio Valley. And although this war

Time and Money

began in North America, it expanded into Europe, 1756 to 1763, where it was called the Seven Years War, and then into Asia as the Third Caryatid War.

The first chart in this set shows that Pluto at 11 Sagittarius was exactly square to Uranus at 11 Pisces for the French and Indian War. The Lord of the Netherworld and Master of the Unprecedented were at a crossroads, with neither having a green light or stop sign.

Notice on the chart below that Uranus is at 11 Pisces exactly square Pluto at 11 Sagittarius, thus applying to a grand cross pattern with the US Mars-Neptune square. Note, too, that Saturn at 14 Capricorn is exactly opposite the US Sun and square the US Saturn.

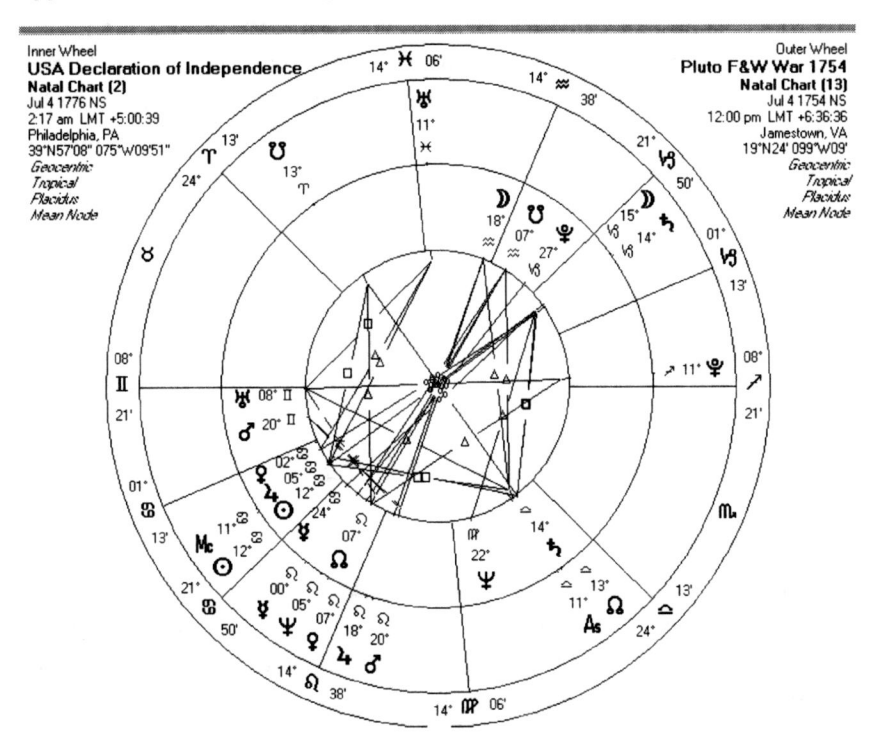

The French and Indian War began when the appointed governor of Virginia assembled an armed force under the command of a young George Washington. Washington's mission was to expel the French from Fort Necessity at the confluence of the Allegheny and Monongahela rivers, where the city of Pittsburgh now is. The French and their Indian allies defeated Washington's troops on July 3-4, 1754.

In 1755, British General Edward Braddock was sent by the English King to take Fort Duquesne. His militia was badly beaten by a French and Indian force. The British continued to suffer defeats till 1757 when William Pitt rose to political power in England and made victory in North America his top priority. By this time, Pluto had gone retrograde (appeared to be moving backwards around the Zodiac) lessening its influence, even though it continued to maintain its 90-degree square to transiting Uranus at 22 Pisces.

The indigenous peoples of North America had no animosity toward the French, for they perceived the French as having come to trade, not colonize. The Indians resented British colonists, who had uprooted tribes and scattered indigenous peoples hither and yon. English colonists were interested only in pushing the Indians further west and had little interest in subordinating themselves to British officers, who treated the colonists as second-class citizens. The major change Pitt made was to treat American colonists as allies rather than subordinates.

Thereafter the tide of war changed as combined British and colonial forces seized French forts, and under General James Wolfe defeated France's main army at Quebec in 1759.

English Language and Culture

According to Microsoft Encarta's pithy summary: "The Treaty of Paris (1763) ended French control of Canada, which went to Great Britain. France also ceded all its territories east of the Mississippi given by France to Spain a year earlier in a secret treaty. Spain had to give Florida to the British."

Time and Money

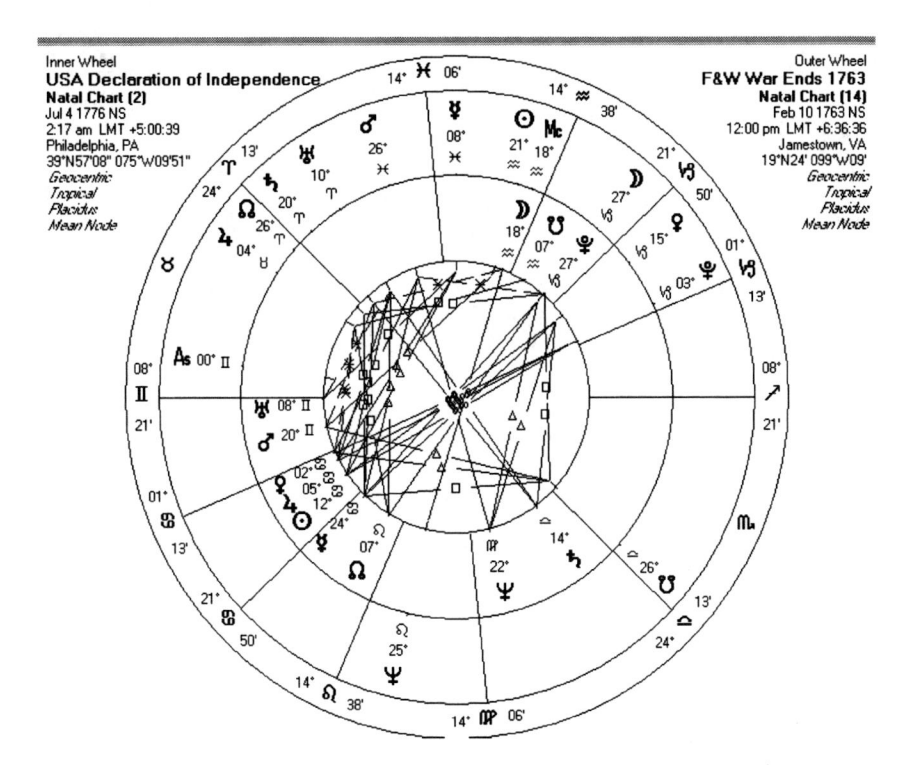

Thus the British Colony in North America was greatly expanded, and English rather than French language and culture would henceforth dominate.

At the time of the Paris treaty, the Uranus-Pluto square was no more. Pluto was at 3 Capricorn and Uranus at 8 Pisces, forming a separating sextile. Peace and rationality returned.

Robert Gover

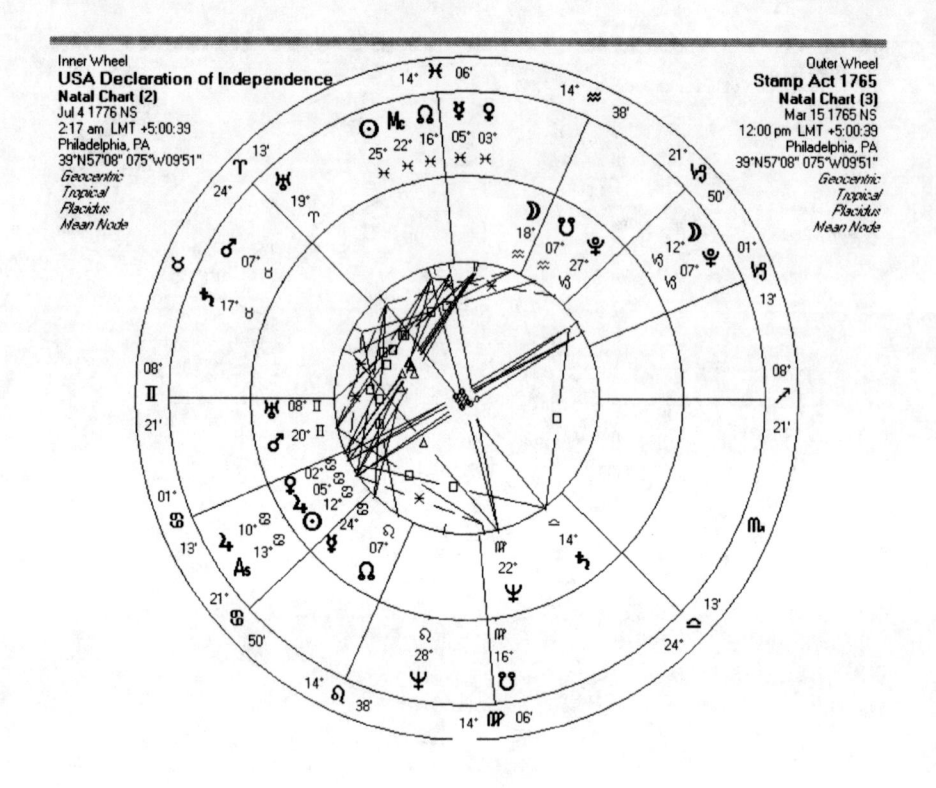

The Stamp Act

In March, 1765, Parliament passed the Stamp Act to raise revenue in the American Colonies in order to repay the Bank of England for this costly war. All colonial documents were to be taxed—deeds, mortgages, newspapers, pamphlets—and those who refused to pay were to be prosecuted by a military court without jurors. The Moon was conjunct Pluto at 7 Capricorn with both separating from a square to Uranus in Aries, and both forming a beneficial trine to Mars and Saturn in Taurus.

With Pluto in the first 10 degrees of Sagittarius in the 1760s, a rift began to grow between King George and the American colonists. The next time Pluto arrived in this area was 2000 when another rift would begin to develop between the American people and an increasingly corporatized US government, led by President George Bush.

"Sons of Liberty"

To the American colonists of 1765, the Stamp Act was a violation of their rights and soon the slogan "No taxation without representation" rang through the land. The Uranus-Pluto square, although separating, still created a militant mood. Riots organized by the "Sons of Liberty" erupted in colonial port cities, blocking British-appointed stamp distributors. Assemblies of American colonists passed resolutions denouncing the Stamp Act. Colonial merchants banded together to boycott British goods.

Since Bacon's Rebellion in 1676 to the end of the French and Indian War in 1763 there had been 18 recorded attempts to overthrow colonial governments, 6 recorded slave rebellions and 40 events called "riots" from South Carolina to New York. Given that many uprisings went unrecorded and unreported, and that news traveled by sailing ship or horse and buggy, it's a safe surmise that this was a century of rising rage and conflict between colonial masters and slaves or servants. The war between Britain and France over control of North America had not been popular with the working class of the colonies.

"The American leadership was less in need of English rule, the English more in need of colonial wealth... The war had brought glory to the generals, death to the privates, wealth to the merchants, unemployment to the poor." (Zinn, page 60).

The population of New York City had swelled from 7,000 in 1720 to 25,000 by the end of the French and Indian War. "A newspaper editor wrote about the growing number of 'Beggars and wandering Poor' in the streets of the city. Letters in the papers questioned the distribution of wealth: 'How often have our streets been covered with Thousands of Barrels of Flour for trade, while our near Neighbors can hardly procure enough to make a Dumplin to satisfy hunger?'" (Zinn, page 60)

Hostilities Escalate

Chaos continued to mount when British merchants, impacted by the colonial boycott, urged Parliament to give in to the American settlers and repeal the Stamp Act. Parliament, still in need of a way to pay for British wars, then enacted the Townsend Acts, imposing taxes on colonial imports of lead, glass, tea, paint and paper. Hostilities between the mother country and its American offspring escalated, along with growing class conflict in the 13 American colonies. James Otis, speaking against the conservative rulers of Massachusetts in 1762, said, "I am forced to get my living by the labour of my hand; and the sweat of my brow, as most of you are, and obliged to go thro' good report and evil report, for bitter bread, earned under the frowns of some who have no natural or divine right to be above me, and entirely owe their grandeur and honor to grinding the faces of the poor."

The Boston Massacre

Zinn points to this as the first instance of a phenomenon now of long standing in American history: the mobilizing of the lower classes for the purposes of the aristocracy and political leaders. The Boston Tea Party and The Boston Massacre soon followed the Townsend Act. By the time of the latter, a trine between Uranus and Neptune tied Pluto into a grand trine; Pluto was within orb of a trine to Neptune, and Neptune within orb of a trine to Uranus, stretching the Uranus-Pluto orb a degree or two.

The Boston Massacre in 1770 ocurred when Pluto had made another of its erratic moves, as seen from Earth, and suddenly and swiftly was now found at 17 Capricorn, opposite the US Sun and transiting Saturn at 25 Cancer, forming a beneficent 120-degree trine aspect to transiting Neptune in Virgo. If we stretch the orb a degree or two, Pluto, Neptune and Uranus formed the extremely beneficent grand trine. But Pluto was still opposite the US Sun, where it will next be in 2014-2015.

Revolutionary Fervor

Pluto's dance around the Sun is extreme at times, as we earthlings observe it from our perspective. Pluto wasn't discovered till 1930, but astronomers have been able to map its past orbits. Astrologically, what's

Time and Money

amazing is that even though Pluto is the smallest and the most distant body from the Sun, its impact is culture-altering.

The important point is that Pluto, Uranus and Neptune formed a grand trine as revolutionary fervor mounted in the American Colonies and James Watt created a breakthrough design for the steam engine, leading to the near-simultaneous birth of both the USA and the Industrial Revolution. Watt was not the original inventor of the steam engine, but his innovation made it practical for factory use, and later led to its use to power railroad locomotives. With steam-powered ships and trains, migrations were revolutionized, bringing millions from Europe and Asia to the Americas.

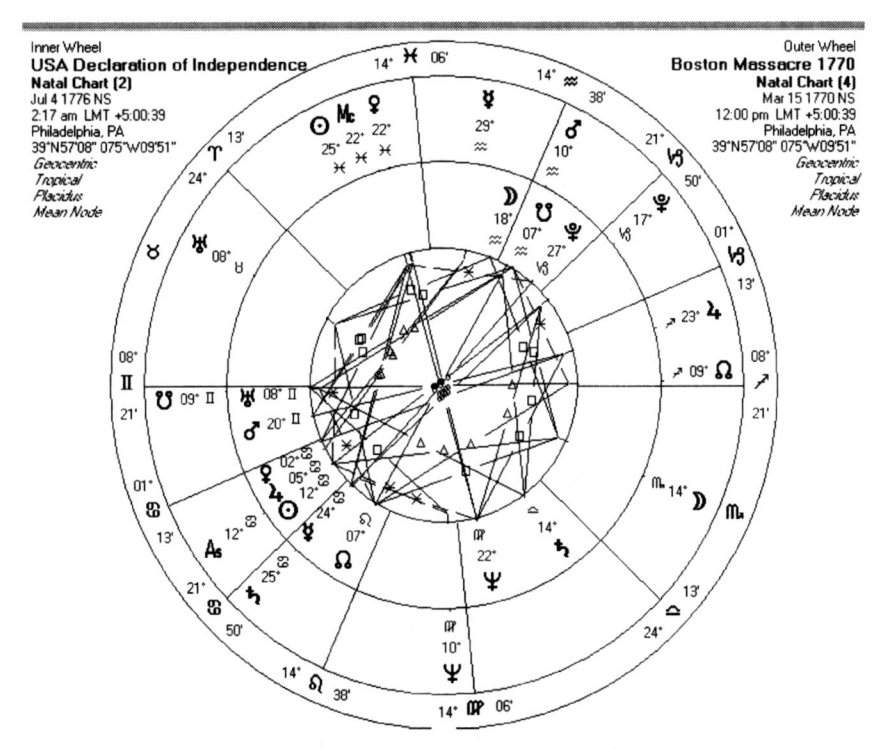

By the time the first Continental Congress convened in 1774, this very fortunate grand trine had tightened its orb, plus added the cluster of planets in Virgo—Mercury, the Moon's North Node, Neptune, Sun and Saturn. The Lord of the Netherworld, in a sense, had rallied his troops in the cause of the next new thing, creating a very contentious time.

Would the servants and slaves rebel against their colonial masters? Or would the masters enlist their servants and slaves in their fight against Britain? History indicates it hardly matters whether Uranus and Pluto trine or square—either trine or square coincides with historic turning points if either forms major aspects to key positions in the USA's natal chart. Whether beneficent of malefic, Pluto is powerful when combined with Uranus. Much depends on which belief or cause has the most momentum.

Uranus-Pluto Trine

"Patrick Henry's oratory in Virginia pointed a way to relieve class tension between upper and lower classes and form a bond against the British. This was to find language inspiring to all classes, specific enough in its listing of grievances to charge people with anger against the British, vague enough to avoid class conflict among the rebels, and stirring enough to build patriotic feeling for the resistance movement." (Zinn, page 69.)

Through the first armed clash between British troops and Colonial Minutemen at Concord, Massachusetts, April 19, 1775, the Uranus-Pluto trine shined good fortune on the Colonial cause. This is when a silversmith named Paul Revere, a member of the Committee of Safety, rode his horse through the countryside to warn that British troops were approaching. Eight Minutemen were killed and the British continued marching toward Concord, not realizing what they were marching into. Soon British troops were being sniped at from behind trees and hedges and buildings, and were falling into disarray.

About 200 years later, with Pluto conjunct Uranus, American troops would confront similar problems from the Viet Cong whose cause was independence; 40 years later with Pluto square its 1960s position, US troops would be likewise involved in Iraq. About one cycle of Pluto in Sagittarius later, the king's empire of the 1700s has morphed into the American global empire of today and its US military backup, and again rebellious sentiment is rising, this time worldwide.

Paine's Immortal Essay

Thomas Paine's immortal essay "Common Sense" appeared on January 1, 1776, asserting that American colonists received no advantage from Britain, which was intent only on exploiting them, and thus "every consideration of common sense" called for the colonies to become independent of Great Britain and establish a government of their own. Pluto ends beliefs that have outlasted their usefulness, and Paine in this instance spoke as though possessed by Pluto in Capricorn. He articulated the spirit of the times, put words to the feelings growing in the colonies, and did so in a way that echoed down through time and around the world.

"The cause of America is in a great measure the cause of all mankind. Many circumstances hath, and will arise, which are not local, but universal, and through which the principles of all Lovers of Mankind are affected, and in the Event of which, their Affections are interested. The laying a Country desolate with Fire and Sword, declaring War against the natural rights of all Mankind, and extirpating the Defenders thereof from the Face of the Earth, is the Concern of every Man to whom Nature hath given the Power of feeling; of which Class, regardless of Party Censure, is the AUTHOR."

Divinity and Common Sense

As for the divine right of kings, Paine described the origin of the British monarchy this way: "A French bastard (William the Conqueror) landing with an armed Banditti and establishing himself king of England against the consent of the natives, is in plain terms a very paltry rascally original. It certainly hath no divinity in it." "Common Sense" went through 25 editions in 1776 and was the most dramatic bestseller of its time. It appealed to a broad spectrum of colonialists, coalesced public opinion, articulated the popular aims of the American Revolution. It also caused fear among aristocrats. John Adams, although he was with the patriot cause against the British, feared democracy. Adams denounced

Paine's idea for a single body of popularly elected representatives as "so democratical, without any restraint or even an attempt at any equilibrium or counter-poise, that it must produce confusion and every evil work." Paine trusted the public will; Adams feared a misinformed and malleable public. Adam's idea of balance was between the ruling aristocracy and the roiling working class. Paine believed that workers were entitled to the fruits of their labors.

A previous essay by Paine had denounced slavery, and most of the Founding Fathers owned slaves. Paine was for universal suffrage, against property ownership as a requirement for voting. "There is an extent of riches, as well as an extreme of poverty, which, by harrowing the circles of man's acquaintance, lessens his opportunities of general knowledge." Paine articulated Pluto's influence at this time, enlisting revolutionary momentum in the democratic cause.

Cohesion

The colonial ruling class fought back with a rumor campaign against Paine, depicting him as an impotent drunk and social misfit. But Paine's feat as a pioneer thinker suggests that he had scant time for anything but his writing. "Common Sense" brought cohesion to revolutionary sentiments and became the basis for the Declaration of Independence, which was written by Thomas Jefferson seven months later and clearly expresses the thrust of Paine's thinking, although Jefferson's anti-slavery clause was later deleted by other founders. Paine "lent himself perfectly to the myth of the Revolution—that it was on behalf of a united people...The Declaration of Independence brought that myth to its peak of eloquence." (Zinn, page 70-71)

Time and Money

Most remarkable is that Paine's essays are still vilified and suppressed by rightwing conservatives, two hundred and some years after "Common Sense" appeared. Then, as now, the wealthy regarded those of the lower economic classes, such as Paine, not as intelligent or worthy in God's eyes as themselves. Since the dominant corporate executives of our day are would-be heirs to the aristocracy of Paine's day, the arguments of his essays continue to disturb the powerful and inspire the oppressed.

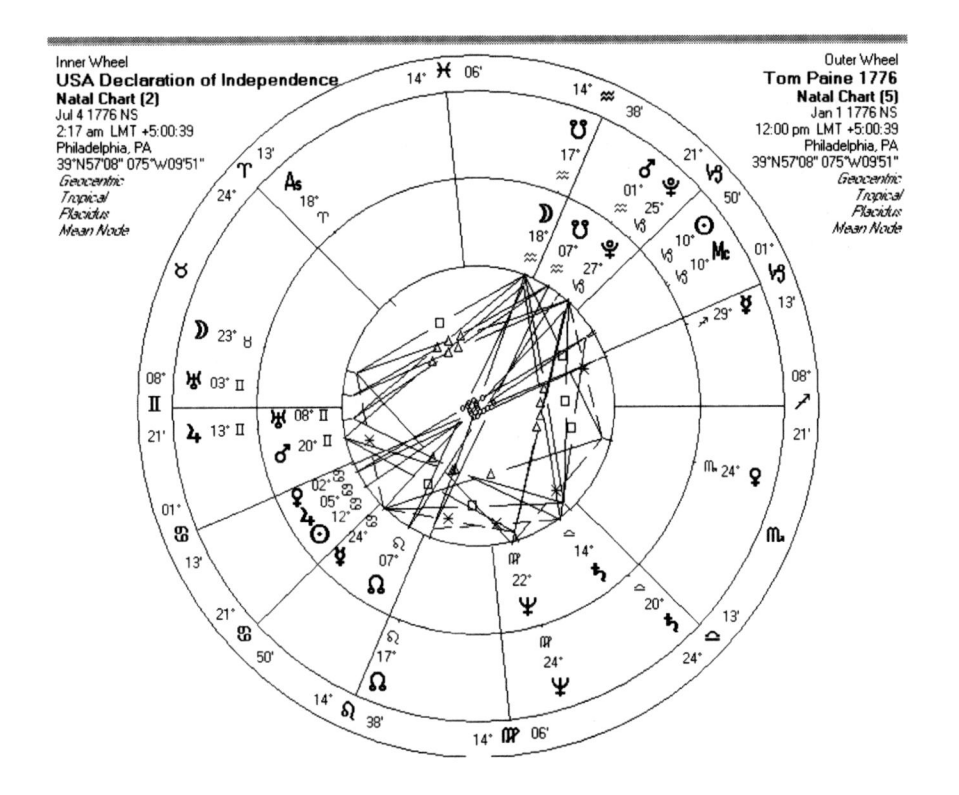

Tom Paine's Uranus

When "Common Sense" appeared, Uranus was applying to a conjunction of the US natal Uranus and Gemini Ascendant. Pluto at 25 Capricorn made a grand trine to Neptune at 24 Virgo and the Moon at 22 Taurus. The two most powerful war influences, Mars and Uranus, were also in trine aspect, with Mars within conjunction of Pluto and Uranus 120 degrees away at 3 Gemini. This combination of aspects could hardly be better for militant revolutionaries.

Pluto is the essence of revolution—the most transformative events in anyone's life being birth and death—while Uranus and Mars are the two most militant and war-making influences in the Solar community. Whenever Pluto and Uranus form a major aspect, whether malefic or beneficent, protectors of the status quo are in trouble. Two hundred years after the American Revolution, in the late 1980s and early 1990s, with Pluto in Scorpio trine the US Sun and sextile the conjunction in Capricorn of Saturn, Uranus and Neptune, the American business community would undergo a rash of mergers, acquisitions and massive layoffs of workers. This wasn't called a revolution by the US media, but its effect was to sabotage American democracy and strengthen corporate control of governance.

American and French Revolutions

The Revolutionary War, as it grew after July 4, 1776, became extremely difficult for General Washington's troops. Notice that in the USA's birth chart, Pluto at 27 Capricorn is trine Neptune at 23 Virgo, but out of aspect with Uranus at 9 Gemini, but Uranus here is conjunct its natal position. Uranus and Pluto had formed major aspects—squares and trines—leading up to the war, but were out of major aspect as the war began. Information in those times traveled at the speed of sailing ships: it took about 2 months to get from Philadelphia to London. A belligerent Uranus-Pluto square mood had fomented revolution; by the time war was officially declared, the mood had changed and was focused more on finances, how to pay for the troops and supplies needed to resist what was then the mightiest military the world had eve known.

The revolution was on hold by the winter of 1778. Pluto was opposite the US natal Mercury. Uranus had moved out of major aspect with Pluto. Transiting Mercury was marooned at 14 Aquarius square Saturn in Scorpio. Communications and the movement of money were at a standstill.

Robert Gover

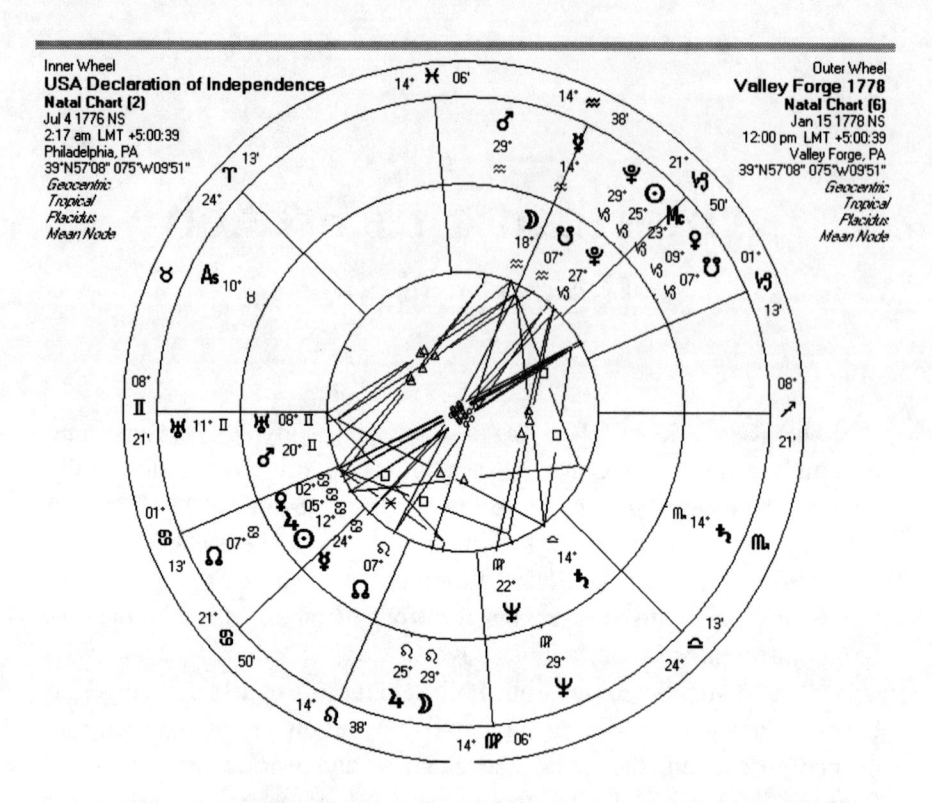

"The Continental Army's encampment at Valley Forge in Pennsylvania during the winter of 1777-1778 was the bleakest time of the American struggle for independence. Hunger and disease compounded the problems of inadequate shelter and lack of adequate winter clothing. More than 2500 men died of typhus, dysentery, and pneumonia. Washington made repeated appeals for aid and supplies, but the Congress was unable to move the states to provide them. (Encarta, 1998 Edition.)

Enemy of My Enemy

The French eventually came to the rescue of the struggling new nation: "The enemy of my enemy is my friend." When the British surrendered at Yorktown, Virginia, on October 19, 1783, Pluto had moved to 7 Aquarius and into a trine with the new nation's natal Uranus

Time and Money

at 9 Gemini, a harmonious flow of these two most "bull headed" of the heavenly influences. Transiting Uranus had moved out of major aspect to Pluto by reaching 11 Cancer, where it was conjunct the US natal Sun and opposite transiting Saturn at 7 Capricorn. As Mars moved opposite the US Saturn, a grand cross formed afflicting the US Sun-Saturn square, and the new nation fell into its first great depression.

An entity with Uranus prominent, on a point of the horizontal/perpendicular cross in an astrological chart, is perceived as being eccentric and unpredictable, and there are indications that the British leaders thought the Americans quite mad. A kind of mad genius, by turns euphoric and grumpy, had joined the community of nations—with the help of the French, who took this opportunity to avenge their defeat by the British a decade previous.

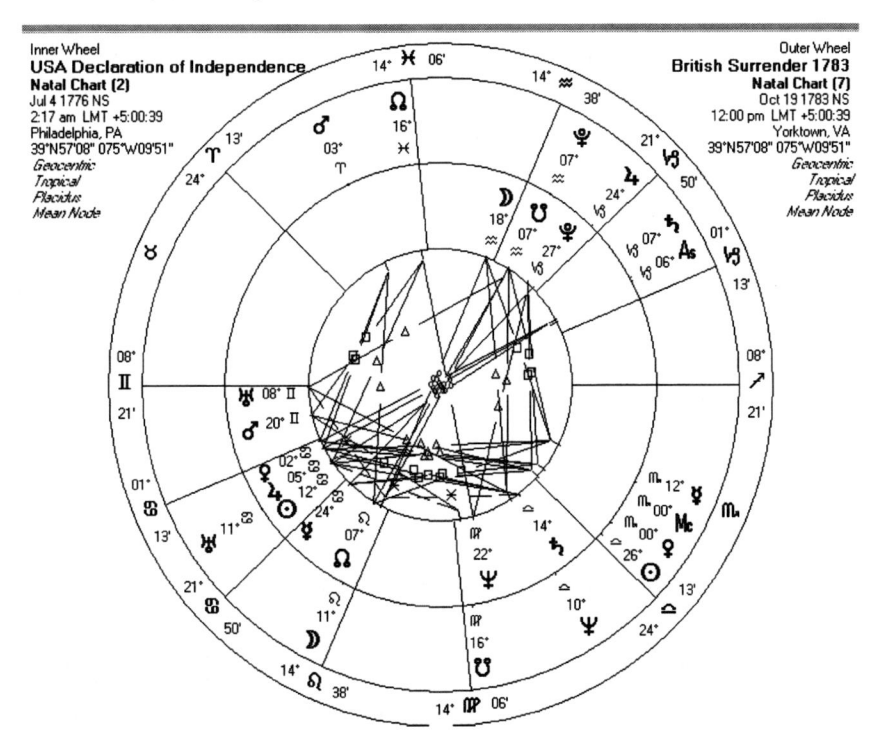

Victory and Great Depression

We see the beginning of the great-depression grand cross forming at this time, 1783. Saturn, Mars, Uranus and Neptune are part of this grand cross affliction to the US Sun-square-Saturn.

The Yorktown victory was won—with the help of the French Navy—when the new nation was falling into its first great depression. Aristocrats were fleeing to Canada. Revolutionary soldiers were discovering the paper money they'd been paid was worthless. African Americans who had fled their masters and fought for General Washington found themselves, a hundred years after Bacon's Rebellion, plagued by racial discrimination. Remnants of the colonial aristocracy were debating the pros and cons of democracy. Conservatives of this time were adamantly against "mob rule." Thomas Jefferson's foxy wording of the Bill of Rights was destined to prolong that debate through the next two centuries and into the future.

But by the end of the Revolutionary War, Americans had their Declaration of Independence, and would soon have their Bill of Rights, creating a mood of bravely moving into uncharted waters. James Watt's steam engine was about to revolutionize industry and travel. Adam Smith's *The Wealth of Nations* was about to revolutionize economics.

The American Revolution ended with the surrender of British troops on October 19, 1781. American and French land forces under General George Washington, collaborating with a French fleet commanded by Admiral François Joseph Paul, comte de Grasse, surrounded the British under Lieutenant General Charles Cornwallis. The siege lasted 20 days.

Star-Crossed Lovers

Cornwallis's surrender resulted in the resignation of British Prime Minister Lord Frederick North. His successor accepted the terms of the Treaty of Paris, signed on September 3, 1783, which officially ended the war.

Time and Money

It was during the American Revolution that the US and France began a unique relationship which has endured ever since. A comparison of the birth charts of these two nations speaks to this relationship. If the two were human lovers, we'd say they can't keep their hands off each other yet can't get along, are continually snipping at each other.

It's often difficult to agree on the day of a nation's "birth." Germany, for instance, is not the same nation it was before World War II. Should we erect charts for both West German and East Germany following World War II? Or should we go back centuries to the original formation of Germany from tribal groups during the Roman Empire? Like Germany, France went through major political transformations during the 20th Century, but unlike Germany, France made a decisive break with its feudalistic past on what continues to be celebrated as Bastille Day, July 14, 1789, a decade after the revolution against the British monarchy and six years after the British formally relinquished control of its North American colonies at the Treaty of Paris.

The newly formed USA probably could not have defeated Britain were it not for the help of the French military. The Founders were inspired by French philosophers, and the French in turn were inspired by the American Revolution to mount their own, now known as Bastille Day. The Statue of Liberty, perceived worldwide as the symbol of American freedom, was a gift from France. The USA came to the aid of France when it was invaded by Germany in World War I, and then again in World War II. But in 2003 when France refused to participate in the invasion of Iraq by joining the so-called "coalition of the willing," the Brush Administration bad-mouthed French wines, renamed French fried potatoes "freedom fries" and in other ways had a petulant temper tantrum.

Robert Gover

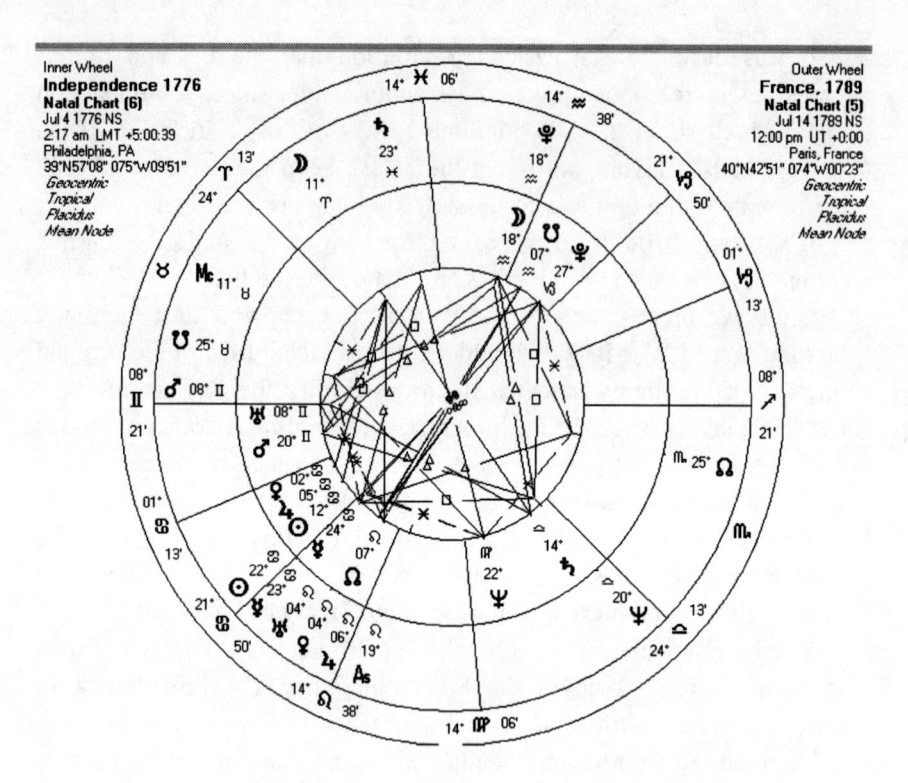

This love/hate relationship is indicated by a comparison of the two birth charts. The French Saturn is opposite the US Neptune and square the US Mars, indicating the US often feels financially curtailed or frustrated by French attitudes and actions. The French Uranus is opposite the US Pluto, climaxing the cycle which began with the Uranus-Pluto conjunction of 1710. And the French Pluto is conjunct the US Moon: the American public finds things French somewhat exotic, sometimes dangerous, and decidedly erotic. With a conjunction of Uranus, Venus and Jupiter in Leo, the French are expansively and innovatively erotic. The French Mars conjunct the US Gemini Ascendant and Uranus is saved from being aggressive toward the US by the US Mars-Saturn-Moon grand trine, which includes the French Neptune and Pluto. During the 1960s Uranus-Pluto conjunction, both nations experienced social upheavals and student revolts.

Time and Money

France in 2015

All in all, this is a difficult relationship, by turns inspiringly adoring and emotionally wounding. Since the last cycle of Pluto through Sagittarius and Capricorn, though, both nations have progressed democratically along separate but parallel tracks. And by 2015, when we can expect revolutionary changes to be peaking in the USA, they will be doing much the same in France.

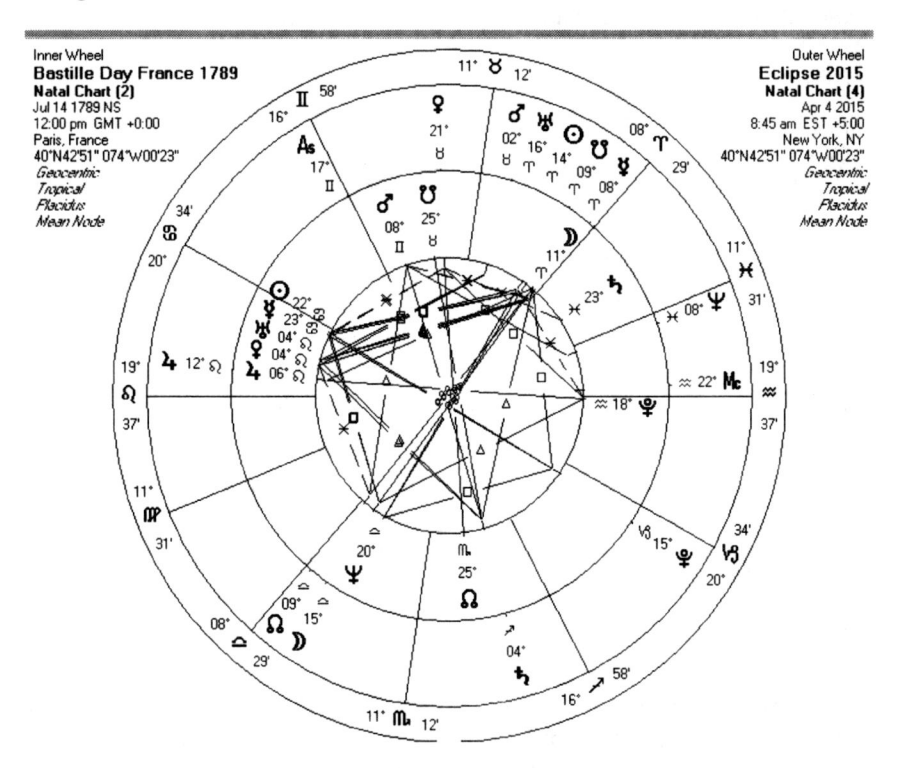

Notice that the Uranus-Pluto square of 2015 forms a grand cross with France's Sun-Mercury, Moon and Neptune. What this portends is that France will be more amenable to change, since its natal Saturn (protector of the status quo) is not involved in this grand cross, and transiting Saturn is part of a grand trine to France's Moon and Uranus-Venus-Jupiter conjunction. The 2000-teens will by no means be an easy period for France. But because of the grand trine anchored by transiting

Saturn, the clash between protectors of the status quo and agitators for change is not likely to become as violent as it is likely to become in the USA. America has a history of making war, and/or mounting militant efforts on everything from building highways to prohibiting alcoholic beverages and, when that failed, mounting a "war on drugs," meaning every mind- or mood-altering substance that is not produced by the corporatized alcohol and pharmaceutical industries. It follows that American protectors of the status quo will resort to war in some form when threatened by radical changes occurring rapidly.

Pluto and Adam Smith

It was during this rare post-war period that Smith's economic theories were spreading. Smith said, among other things surprising at the time, that labor creates capital, and that wage labor is more profitable than slave labor because wage-earners buy food and pay rent, expanding the economy, while slaves are fed and housed. By this time, African Americans had been in North America for a century and a half. Slavery had been institutionalized in the colonies. Both free Blacks and slaves had fought in the Revolutionary War but many, if not most, European Whites were unable to break out of their box of xenophobic beliefs about people described by that awesome adjective Black.

Today, one cycle of Pluto after the volatile years of working class rebellions leading up to the Revolutionary War, communications are practically instantaneous. And a new corporate aristocracy has arisen, backed by what is now the mightiest military the world has ever known. Since this new corporatized empire is now global, the American working class is one of many exploited populations which are ripe to rebel. There has also been a major change in money—what it is, how it is employed—which were explained in a previous chapter.

Given that the upcoming Uranus-Pluto square will be the longest in many a millennia, and will simultaneously impact those sensitive points in the USA's natal pattern, the combination of instantaneous communications and global working class discontent compares to the 1760s like a fire cracker to a nuclear bomb.

Drumbeats of Civilization

Twice a millennium, about every 496 years, Pluto's 248-year orbit and Neptune's 164-year orbit bring them conjunct by Latitude. They are usually within orb of each conjunction for a decade or more. These two most distant planets are "the base notes of the cosmic symphony, and the drumbeat of all civilization." (*Horoscope for the New Millennia* by E. Alan Meece, page 37)

Feudalism was transplanted to the New World from Europe, and developed into so-called "free-market" capitalism. In this chapter, we go in search of the cultural origins which underlie today's economic beliefs, and manifest as the corporatized global empire.

These half-millennium conjunctions mark changes in cultural tides. Such changes may go unnoticed for a century and be appreciated only in retrospect. Or, if the Neptune-Pluto conjunction forms a major aspect to Uranus, (as when the Roman Empire crumbled) change becomes evident within a decade or two.

The Neptune-Pluto conjunctions do not mark definitive boundaries between old and new cultural assumptions. I have come to think of the conjunctions as low tides and the oppositions as marking high tides, when whatever was seeded at low tide, climaxes or culminates. This historical skim will be Euro-centric to show the roots of our current Americanized 21st Century culture.

During the past 2000 years, Pluto and Neptune have come conjunct four times. The following brief list is for the first exact hit of each of those conjunctions and succeeding oppositions.

Robert Gover

Conj. 6/30/411 at 23 Taurus
 Opp. 1/13/657 at 26 Scorpio
Conj. 5/22/905 at 28 Taurus
 Opp. 12/28/1150 at 29 Scorpio
Conj. 6/23/1398 at 3 Gemini
 Opp. 1/16/1644 at 3 Sagittarius
Conj. 8/2/1891 at 8 Gemini
 Opp. 1/29/2137 at 7 Sagittarius

In the four biwheel charts below, I have again used the USA's birth chart as the astro-clock's stationary face to help show what time it was for each of these four latest Neptune-Pluto conjunctions, even though three of them occurred long before the USA existed as a nation.

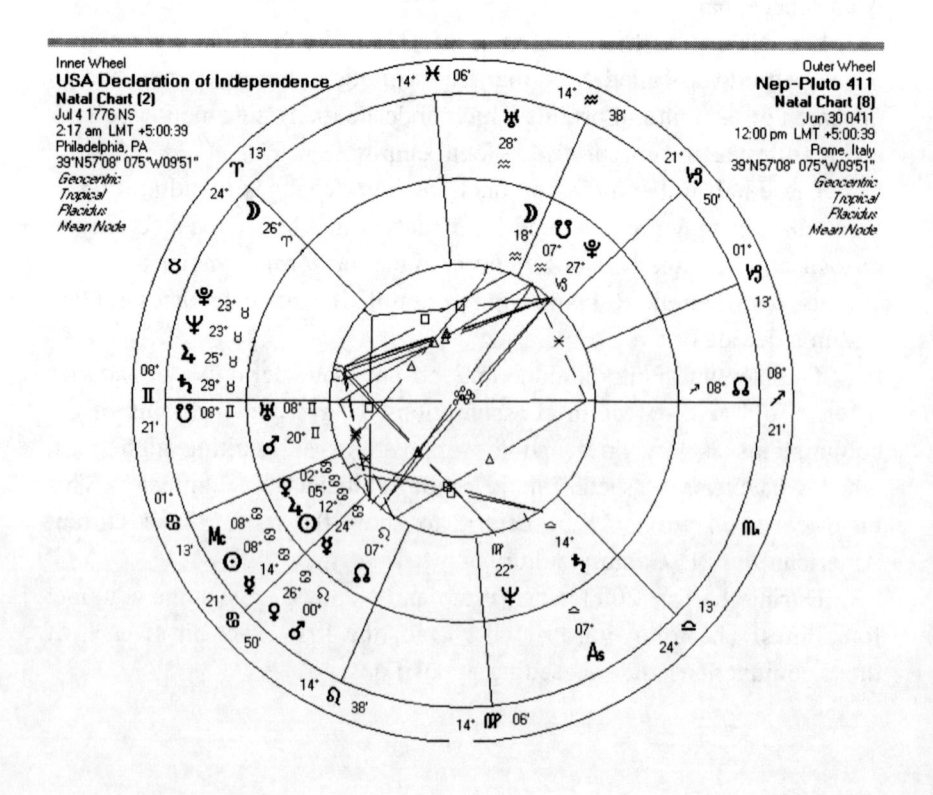

Time and Money

Notice on the outer wheel of the chart for 411 that Uranus at 28 Aquarius formed a square with the Neptune-Pluto conjunction at 23 Taurus, coinciding with the end of the Roman Empire. Neptune and Pluto are also conjunct Jupiter and Saturn, so Uranus at 28 Aquarius squared all four—an extremely rare configuration.

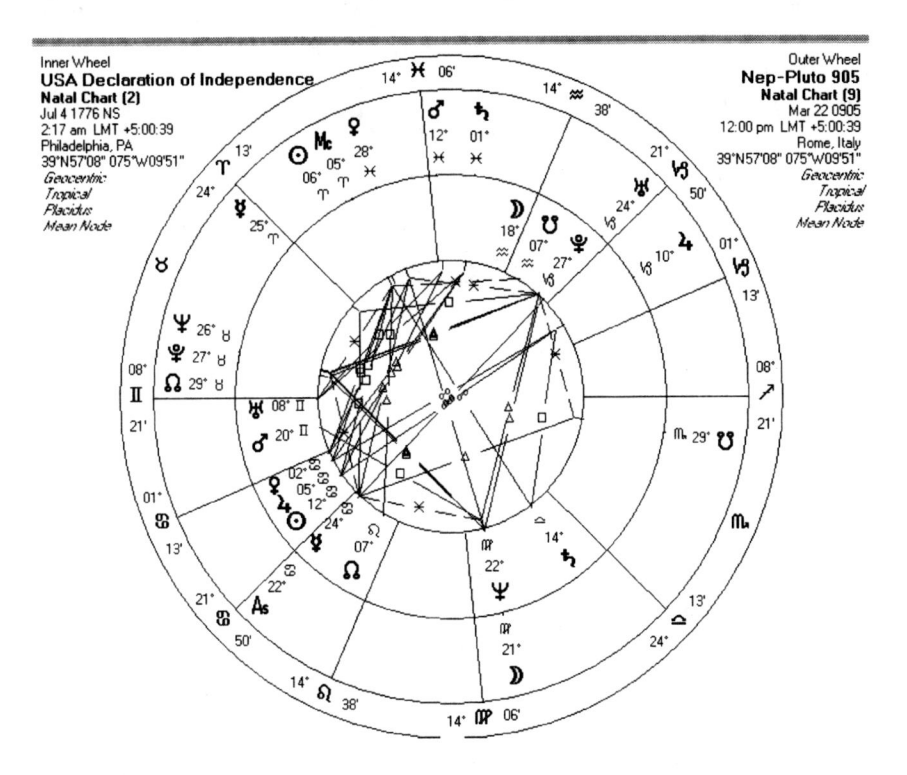

The Neptune-Pluto conjunction of 905 formed a beneficent 120 degree trine to Uranus at 24 Capricorn. The disintegration of the Roman Empire was complete and the Dark Ages was beginning. European Crusaders were soon to invade the Holy Land to slaughter "infidels," retaliating against Muslims who had previously occupied parts of Europe.

Robert Gover

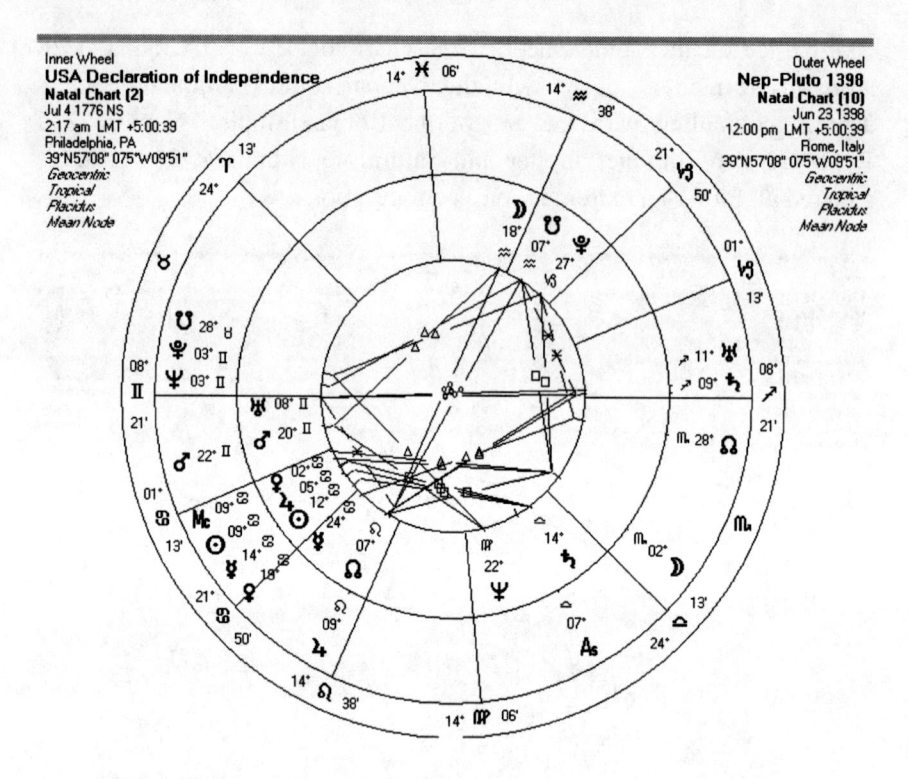

As the Dark Ages were morphing into an age of exploration, the Neptune-Pluto conjunction of 1398 was opposite Uranus and Saturn in Sagittarius (shown on the outer wheel). Fiefdoms were forming into kingdoms, which would soon send companies sailing the high seas in search of new wealth.

Europeans are said to be Arians, ruled by Mars. The most positive of Mars' influence is a pioneering spirit. During this period, Europeans explored philosophically, artistically, scientifically as well as geographically. A Yoruba myth has it that Mercury, god of luck good and bad, often plays tricks on Mars. When pioneering explorer Columbus ran aground in the Bahamas, he thought he'd found a shortcut to India. Note Saturn's opposition to the Uranus-Pluto conjunction, from Sagittarius to Gemini, much like the Saturn-Pluto opposition extant on September 11, 2001, marking major turning points.

Mars is also depicted as the good, honest, dedicated policeman. Europeans of this period believed their creation of national boundaries

Time and Money

was so beneficial, they imposed this innovation on the rest of humanity. Now, even though maps show distinct national boundaries, the peoples of Central and South America, Sub-Saharan Africa and many parts of Southeast Asia move across such political borders like they don't exist. Billions of humans have never adopted the Arian idea of national borders.

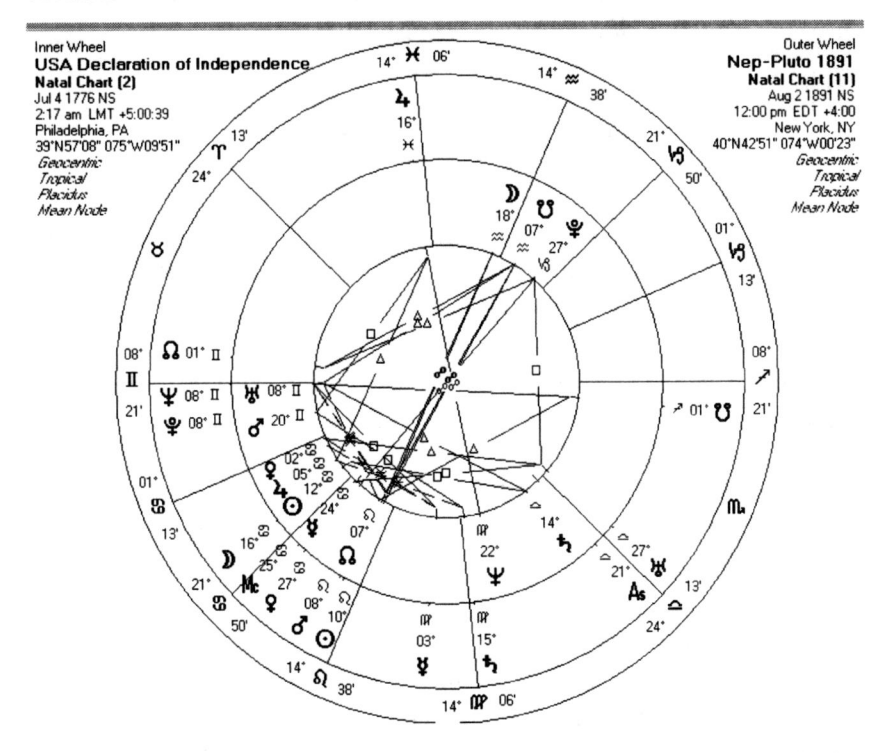

[Astrological chart: Inner Wheel — USA Declaration of Independence, Natal Chart (2), Jul 4 1776 NS, 2:17 am LMT +5:00:39, Philadelphia, PA, 39°N57'08" 075°W09'51", Geocentric, Tropical, Placidus, Mean Node. Outer Wheel — Nep-Pluto 1891, Natal Chart (11), Aug 2 1891 NS, 12:00 pm EDT +4:00, New York, NY, 40°N42'51" 074°W00'23", Geocentric, Tropical, Placidus, Mean Node.]

Most remarkable about the latest Neptune-Pluto conjunction is that it fell conjunct the US natal Uranus in Gemini, on the Ascendant, one's interface with the world.

One of the reasons I prefer the Gemini Rising chart is that, following its formation as a nation state, the USA rapidly arose to world prominence, verifying the astrological expectation of an entity with Uranus in Gemini Rising. This "spectacular entrance" is also foretold by the Neptune-Pluto conjunction being conjunct the US Uranus-in-Gemini Rising, simultaneously forming a T square with an opposition of Jupiter (16 Pisces) and Saturn (15 Virgo). With Sagittarius Rising, the entity would be more expansively philosophical, much less aggressively innovative.

During the preceding 500 year cycle, Portugal, Spain, France, Holland, and Great Britain took turns dominating the world as they knew it, creating colonies far and wide, spreading the European concept of nation states, and profiting on the resources of lands they found, and exploiting the labor of people within those lands.

Zionism and Terrorism

Also launched during the conjunction of the 1890s was the Zionist Movement that would lead to the creation of the state of Israel; this ongoing conflict involved Western European and American governments, exacerbating a rift between Christians and Muslims. This creation of Israel by Western colonialists was at least one ingredient in the stew of motivations of the 19 Arabs who carried out the kamikaze attack on the World Trade Center and Pentagon September 11, 2001.

Religious movements marked previous conjunctions, but following the latest, technology was also dramatically revolutionized. By the end of the 20th Century, there were still some old-timers around who could remember when the main means of transportation was the horse and buggy, and homes were lit at night by candles or oil lamps; when there were no telephones, radios, TVs, computers or telecommunications of any kind. Such old-timers lived through more transformations of the physical landscape than any other generation in history. The night is still dark in some third world cities, however, indicating the growing disparity between the Have Gots and the Have Nots.

Phases

Each approximately 500-year period between Neptune-Pluto conjunctions can be parsed into phases, much like the phases of the Moon except that the Neptune-Pluto phases are measured in centuries rather than days. During the first phase of the conjunction of the 1390s, Columbus "discovered" America and was followed by millions of migrants from Europe. Gold was shipped back to Spain by the ton, greatly transforming all of Europe. Meanwhile, Native Americans, having no immunity to diseases brought over from Europe, perished in large numbers. Whether those numbers were thousands or millions of hundreds of millions depends on which version of history one believes.

Revolutions: American, French, Industrial

Between the conjunctions of the 1390s and the 1890s, Pluto and Neptune formed a beneficent 120-degree trine aspect for an especially long period during the 1700s. This trine first became exact on May 8, 1704. It continued to be within orb till the 1750s, when these two planets formed a square till the end of the French and Indian War, then moved back into trine aspect till the 1780s. Neptune and Pluto were in beneficent trine aspect for the American and French Revolutions and the Industrial Revolution, among many other important transformative events.

Pluto's orbit around the Sun is so erratic, it takes huge swings into space that, viewed from Earth, sometimes break the rhythm of its relationship with Neptune temporarily, before it swings back. Pluto and Neptune formed a 90-degree square aspect from 1568 to 1572, or (adding the allowable orb) from about 1555 to 1580. This was an interesting time in the development of authoritarian bodies presuming the right to legislate which sexual behaviors are moral and which are immoral, what books and ideas are permissible, and what books and ideas are not. This was epitomized by what came to be called the Inquisition.

The Inquisition

Pope Paul IV in 1555 "...approved and published the first Index of Forbidden Books... Although later popes tempered the zeal of the Roman Inquisition, they began to see it as the customary instrument of papal government for regulating church order and doctrinal orthodoxy; for example, it tried and condemned Galileo in 1633. In 1965 (when Uranus and Pluto came conjunct) Pope Paul VI, responding to complaints, reorganized the Holy Office and renamed it the Congregation for the Doctrine of the Faith." (Inquisition, Microsoft Encarta.)

Pluto and Neptune were moving opposite each other from roughly 1810 to 1825, before completing their cycle by coming conjunct again in the 1890s. What is seeded during Neptune-Pluto conjunctions, matures during oppositions. The conjunction marks the end of the familiar, the cusp of a new world as yet unformed. Of course it's not the material world that ends; what these conjunctions mark are transformations of culture—the complex of beliefs and assumptions societies live within. Cultural change then leads to changes in the landscape. Or a clash between two cultures, two opposing perspectives, may result in a war catastrophic to one or both.

Fall of Rome

The first Neptune-Pluto conjunction after the year 1 coincides with the disintegration of the Roman Empire and the onset of the Dark Ages. The two conjunctions during the Dark Ages coincide with major religious changes during that long period, culminating in the Renaissance and the migration of millions of Europeans to the Americas. The last conjunction, exactly conjunct Uncle Sam's natal Uranus in Gemini, indicated that the USA would be most immediately and strongly impacted by this latest major sea-change of cultural assumptions.

Symbolic of this last Neptune-Pluto conjunction was that henceforth democracy, government by consent of the governed, flowered—not yet as a reality but as an ideal spreading worldwide. The USA's matrix for democratic governance provided for continuing control by a wealthy ruling class, even though the ideal became pure democracy, "one man, one vote," suggesting economic equality, since politics is how we divvy up the collective wealth.

The USA's Declaration of Independence and Bill of Rights caught on around the world like hit songs. During the 20th Century, the USA rose to prominence and assumed world dominance in a dramatic turnover from rule by royalty to rule by the ruled. In one form or another, the "will of the people" became the new assumption about how governments should govern, even if it's not yet the reality. Old habits die hard.

Changing Religious Beliefs

From around year 400 to 1400 in Europe, these 500-year conjunctions of Neptune and Pluto coincided primarily with changes in religious beliefs. Many call this period of approximately 1,000 to 1,200 years the Middle Ages or Medieval Age. But it was not the middle of our development as human beings, and the word medieval conjures images of everything from exotic art to bloody Inquisitions. I prefer the term Dark Age, or Ages, for in retrospect it seemed a kind of long night of irrationality before the light of reason returned with the Age of Enlightenment.

After the conjunction of 905 came invading Vikings, Saracens and Magyars to terrorize people on continental Europe. Alfred the Great and his son founded what we now call England. Royal dynasties were also established in France, Czechoslovakia, Hungary and Russia. The Byzantine Empire began a second flowering. In China the once all-powerful Tang Dynasty collapsed, and in Mesoamerica the Maya civilization seems to have mysteriously disappeared.

Economic Democracy

A tribal form of economic democracy prevailed in the Americas when Columbus arrived. From written accounts by early European explorers, most native tribes were peaceful, pleasure-oriented and philosophical. This is not to say that Native Americans had not engaged in national or tribal wars, but that most had evolved out of warfare into economic interdependencies. What later came to be called the Iroquois Confederacy was one example. Native Americans were also pantheists, a belief system that corresponds to astrology in that it poses a central god (the Sun) and a pantheon (the planets). Every pantheistic "cult" I've studied had correspondences between their gods and the seven visible planets.

Robert Gover

Old Gods Obliterated

After the 411 Neptune-Pluto conjunction, Europeans had undergone a thousand years of Christianization, during which pantheistic gods and spirits were forcefully obliterated. This was reminiscent of what had occurred in Egypt during the reign of Akhenaton, about five Neptune-Pluto conjunctions previous. Microsoft's Encarta is a handy source for innocuous summaries about this historic turn in ancient Egypt.

"Beginning with the Middle Kingdom (2134-1668 BC) Ra worship acquired the status of a state religion, and the god was gradually fused with Amon during the Theban dynasties, becoming the supreme god Amon-Ra. During the 18th Dynasty the pharaoh Amenhotep III renamed the sun god Aton, an ancient term for the physical solar force. Amenhotep's son and successor, Amenhotep IV, instituted a revolution in Egyptian religion by proclaiming Aton the true and only god. He changed his own name to Akhenaton, meaning 'Aton is satisfied.' This first great monotheist was so iconoclastic that he had the plural word gods deleted from monuments, and he relentlessly persecuted the priests of Amon. Akhenaton's sun religion failed to survive, although it exerted a great influence on the art and thinking of his time, and Egypt returned to the ancient, labyrinthine religion of polytheism after Akhenaton's death."

Change the proper nouns in the above description to European Christian and pantheistic nouns and it comes close to describing the transformation from pantheism to monotheism which Europe underwent. How did Christianity, derived from the Middle East, evolve into the monotheistic belief system that would grow after 411 to dominate Europe and then the Americas? Encarta's version of this is not so simple. Yet it's possible to discern in the following similarities with the Egyptian Middle Kingdom.

St. Augustine

"Some (European) theologians sought to protect (Christ's) holiness by denying that his humanity was like that of other human beings; others sought to protect the monotheistic faith by making Christ a lesser divine being than God the Father...In response to both of these tendencies, early creeds began the process of specifying the divine in Christ, both in relation to the divine in the Father and in relation to the human in Christ. The definitive formulations of these relations came in a series of official church councils during the 4th and 5th centuries—notably the one at Nicaea in 325 and the one at Chalcedon in 451—which stated the doctrines of the Trinity and of the two natures of Christ in the form still accepted by most Christians. To arrive at these formulations, Christianity had to refine its thought and language, creating in the process a philosophical theology, both in Greek and in Latin, that was to be the dominant intellectual system of Europe for more than a thousand years. The principal architect of Western theology was St. Augustine of Hippo, whose literary output, including the classic *Confessions* and *The City of God*, did more than any other body of writings, except for the Bible itself, to shape that system."

Jesus: God or Human?

In other words, during the first Neptune-Pluto conjunction after the year 1, academicians got together and squabbled over whether Jesus was a human or a god. The pantheistic beliefs of Europeans were then transformed into a monotheism extracted from Hebrew religious tradition and the authoritarian Roman Empire, and this new amalgamated theology spread to the Americas via the printing press and Bible, sailing ship and gun.

Saint Augustine wrote his culture-changing religious tracts during the Neptune-Pluto conjunction which became exact in 411. Neptune and Pluto, the most distant two planets in our Solar System, are astrologically symbolized by those most remote, mysterious and fearful kingdoms ruled (in Greek mythology) by Poseidon and Hades: gods of the great mystery we live with from womb to tomb. Their conjunction in year 411 at 23 Taurus formed a square with Uranus at 28 Aquarius: invasions creating a mood of insecurity, nervousness and contention brought chaos to Europe. In retrospect, it seems this chaos created an urge for a more certain, even dogmatic religious belief.

Robert Gover

20th Century

The Neptune-Pluto conjunction of the 1890s occurred at a point which in 1965 was squared by the Uranus-Pluto conjunction opposite Saturn during the Vietnam War years. A variety of beliefs, including religious, were questioned during this time. Then followed, in 1989-1992, the Uranus-Neptune conjunction in Saturn-ruled Capricorn, opposite Uncle Sam's planets in Cancer, and trine Pluto "at home" in Scorpio. The mood this time focused on the economy, setting off a rash of aggressive corporate restructurings, mergers and acquisitions. The American working class was "downsized." Two or more working class wage-earners were henceforth needed to support a family, which previously had relied on only one wage-earner.

But these were seeds of radical transformations to come, holding battles waged by protectors of the Medieval feudal status quo, dressed up in the three-piece suit. And since the latest Neptune-Pluto conjunction had occurred conjunct Uncle Sam's Uranus, it seems the USA will pioneer whatever this latest conjunction will bring. We have hints. To cite just a couple: the anti-establishment protests of the 1930s that almost rewrote the cultural script; the overthrow of some cultural assumptions in the 1960s, and in the 1990s a conservative reaction to this threat to democratic governance controlled by the wealthy—an accelerated expansion of corporations from national to international. The rise of unions and the rash of socially beneficial laws passed during the 1930s and 1940s met new resistance. Corporate public relations efforts convinced most Americans that "the company creates jobs" and "free market economies thrive in democratic societies." This buried Adam Smith's assertion that "labor creates capital" and blurred the fact that free-market capitalism is autocratic, not democratic. "Capitalistic democracy" is an oxymoron. Capitalism fights a holding battle; democracy has momentum.

Although we like to think of religion and economics as two separate and different things, both are so closely interwoven into the whole cultural fabric that they are practically one and the same. Pantheists and monotheists tend to organize themselves differently economically. Monotheists build authoritarian nation-states and autocratic corporations, the bigger the better. Polytheists prefer communal tribes, villages, towns.

Spiritual Knowledge Lost

Technological breakthroughs made during the Roman Empire were not lost during the Dark Ages. It was moral and spiritual knowledge which was lost or transformed. The notion of a Heaven and Hell gained ascendancy in European consciousness over the ancient belief in reincarnation. Polytheistic paganism was swept away, replaced by monotheistic Christianity: one god, one king, one same ideal for all.

Prior to the onset of the Dark Ages, the peoples of Western Europe believed in one supreme being as the source of all—and this one god's "children," the gods and goddesses and spirits of ancestors. The one creator god of the pantheists had spiritual offspring, and its spirit imbued all and everything. The new god of Christianity was a singular Being, a divine son of the Hebrew patriarchal god, replacing the so-called "nature sprites" of the pantheists. The Christian god was remote, not alive in humans, plants, animals, mountains and seas.

During the Dark Ages, the Roman Catholic Church arose like a phoenix from the ashes of the Roman Empire. Acceptance of many concepts of the great creator gave way to a single concept—as had happened in ancient Egypt—this new one propagated by the Roman Catholic Church. Saint Augustine wrote 22 books, 10 of which were polemics against pantheism.

Evil Redefined

During pantheistic times, evil was defined as harmfulness. With the rise of Christianity, sexual pleasure became an evil when enjoyed for itself; reproduction became a duty. (Fortunately, people continued to "sin" passionately despite this new dictate "from God.") Dante's *Inferno*, written in the 13th Century, vividly describes a hell where the souls of the sinful were destined to reside forever after death. This new belief shaped the lives of Medieval Europeans, then was exported to the Americas, as capitalism and then state-run communism arose from the ashes of feudalism, serfdom and slavery—and as new, more efficient and expansive ways were developed to create wealth for kings, aristocracies and then corporations.

We habitually move into the future with an eye on the memory-mirror of our mythical past, so we don't appreciate the magnitude of such changes until later. Historians tell us the Dark Ages lasted from the 4th or 5th Century to the 15th or 16th Century, depending on which historians you consult. So the conjunction of Neptune and Pluto in the year 411 coincides with the last years of the Roman Empire and the beginning of the Dark Ages.

Culmination of Trends

The Encarta account says this: "No one definitive event marks the end of antiquity and the beginning of the Middle Ages. Neither the sack of Rome by the Goths under Alaric I in 410 nor the deposition in 476 of Romulus Augustulus, the last Roman emperor in the West, impressed their contemporaries as epoch-making catastrophes. Rather, by the end of the 5th century the culmination of several long-term trends, including a severe economic dislocation and the invasions and settlement of Germanic peoples within the borders of the Western Empire, had changed the face of Europe. For the next 300 years western Europe remained essentially a primitive culture, albeit one uniquely superimposed on the complex, elaborate culture of the Roman Empire, which was never entirely lost or forgotten."

Invasions Then and Now

Visualize what "invasion" meant in the 5th century and you have something akin to modern migrations. No single army suddenly rode into Europe and took over. Rather, there was a gradual influx of migrants, some violent, others peaceful. Back in the 1500s, American Indians had no idea how many immigrants they were to welcome, and after another few hundred years, the Indian as a race would have been through the worst "germ warfare" holocaust in known history.

Time and Money

What gradually arose in Europe during the disintegration of the Roman Empire were smaller empires, known now as feudal manors, fiefdoms or kingdoms. Masses of people became dependent upon landlords for protection from violence brought by roving gangs. Chaos reigned while scholars valiantly wrestled with St. Augustine's theological concepts of Christianity.

Of the Neptune and Pluto conjunction during the middle of the Dark Ages in 905, Encarta says: "The early Middle Ages drew to a close in the 10th Century with new migrations and invasions—the coming of the Vikings from the north and the Magyars from the Asian steppes—and the weakening of all forces of European unity and expansion. The resulting violence and dislocation caused lands to be withdrawn from cultivation, population to decline..."

The key words: weakening of unity.

Onset of Dark Ages

We are now ending the first fifth of the latest Neptune-Pluto cycle. The economist Lester Thurow has many insightful things to say in his book *The Future of Capitalism* about then and now, these two Neptune-Pluto conjunctions which were both sharply aspected by Uranus.

"Consider the slide from the peak of the Roman Empire to the bottom of the Dark Ages. With the onset of the Dark Ages...real per capita incomes fell dramatically from their imperial Roman peak. The technologies that allowed the Roman Empire to have such high levels of productivity did not disappear. No malevolent god forced man to forget during the following eight centuries of uninterrupted decline. The rate of invention was actually up from the Roman era. Output was down despite those new and old inventions. The devil appeared in the form of social disorganization and disintegration. Ideology, not technology, began the long downward slide. Humans gradually threw away what they knew over a relatively short period of time. Once they had thrown it away, they could not recapture their old standard of living for more than twelve hundred years." (Page 261).

Humpty Dumpty could not be put back together again.

Robert Gover

Today, most Americans and others from wealthy nations ignore, as much as possible, the plight of the starving millions worldwide, and the disappearing middle class in the USA. The affluent say, in effect, it's not our fault the poor are poor; the poor have always been with us; there's nothing we can do about it except protect ourselves from the poor. History suggests that this attitude is so short-sighted as to be self-destructive. After the fall of Rome, "Even the mightiest of the feudal barons had standards of living far below those enjoyed by the average citizen of Rome. Without safety from roving robbers and good transportation systems, many of the goods that had been widely available in Rome became unavailable even to the rich." (*The Future of Capitalism*, by Lester Thurow, Morrow & Co., March 1996, page 262).

Astrologically, it's interesting to note that Pluto moved through mid-Libra, conjunct Uncle Sam's Saturn, during the late 1970s into the early 1980s, simultaneously squaring Uncle Sam's Sun. This was not an explosively eventful period, such as the 1960s, for Pluto was not then afflicted by the other era-shaping planets, Neptune, Uranus, or Saturn. Rather, it was the seeding of a new mindless greed which sprouted in the 1990s when Uranus and Neptune accompanied Saturn through Capricorn, sextile Pluto in Scorpio. It's astrologically logical to expect this will bear fruit in the 2000-teens when Pluto moves through Capricorn, square Uranus in Aires, with both forming a grand cross with Uncle Sam's Sun-Saturn square.

Parallels

"Consider the parallels between then and now," Thurow continues. "Immigrants are flooding into the industrial world but no one is willing to incur the costs that will make them into first-world citizens. Both the Soviet empire and the American alliances have broken apart. Weak nations are succumbing to feudal lords (Somalia, Afghanistan, Yugoslavia, Chechnya, Congo) and even strong ones are giving up their powers to local leaders. If one takes the 'Contract with America' seriously, the federal American government will give up all of its powers except defense to local leaders. Over time local leaders will cement these powers into their portfolios and the national government will essentially lose its power to act, as governments did in the Dark Ages." (Thurow, Page 263).

The "Contract with America" was a Republican Congressional agenda led by House Speaker Newt Gingrich in the 1980s. Among other things, these conservatives sought to make environmentalists pay the cost of pollution control, deny welfare payments to children of unwed mothers, end health and safety regulations and funding for the arts, cut funding for Medicare, cut taxes for the rich, and increase military spending and other forms of corporate welfare. It was launched with fanfare on January 2, 1995, as Mars turned retrograde in Virgo. It fizzled at that time for a lack of Martian energy and it helped reelect President Bill Clinton for a second term. It did not disappear from the consciousness of conservatives, however.

Bribery Institutionalized

By the middle 1990s most Americans realized that those elected to the US Congress, as well as to state assemblies, had already lost their traditional powers and abilities to act. Most national and state politicians were beholden to whoever had funded their campaigns, much as some argued otherwise. Bribery was by no means new in American governance, but this time it was unmitigated and pure. Politicians were expressing concern that fewer and fewer of their constituents were voting, while consumer-oriented groups pointed out that the political system had become thoroughly corrupted. Americans en mass increasingly felt un-represented and powerless to change this frustrating state of affairs. Politics being how we decide who gets how much of the collective wealth, the powerful few had grown dramatically wealthier, creating an ever-widening gap between themselves and the majority of their countrymen.

Thurow: "The (onset of the Dark Ages) began with falling incomes at the bottom of the social ladder and gradually spread up the social ladder. Today (the early 1990s) total productivity is still rising but real wages have begun to fall for 80 percent of the population...In the Dark Ages the public (good) was squeezed out by the private. Banditry became widespread and was seen as a revenge upon the defenders of the political and social order (hence the legend of Robin Hood). Unwalled cities and free citizens were replaced by walled manor houses and serfs...Graffiti dominated the walls of the early Middle Ages—just as it does the walls of modern cities...In 1970 twice as much money was spent on public policemen as on private policemen. By 1990 the reverse was true...Almost by definition feudalism is public power in private hands." (Pages 264-265).

Lawyers and Inquisitors

Returning to the metaphor of Neptune-Pluto conjunctions marking low tides, we are still in the first phase of this latest cyclic conjunction and it is not preordained that we will repeat the pattern of events manifested after the cyclical conjunction of 411. Such planetary cycles repeat with rhythmic regularity but always at different points in an ever-changing Solar System, and with the other bodies of that system arranged differently. History repeats but does not duplicate. Just as we can prepare for and prosper during seasonal winters, so we can prepare for and prosper during economic winters. If, that is, we understand our situation within the larger, Solar System context. Will we learn from the past, or are we doomed to repeat the mistakes of the past?

In modern America and spreading around the world, corporations have all the rights of individual citizens but few to none of the legal responsibilities, and armies of lawyers who, like the Inquisitors of the Dark Ages, are poised to zap anyone who protests this situation. The rich are united, the middle class and poor in competition with each other. The fact that the rich are few underlines the power of union but does not deter the growing chaos.

One indication of this chaos is that children have become economic liabilities, especially for middle and lower class families; only a few generations ago, children were economic assets. It's wonderful that virtually everyone in the First World is far better off than their ancestors

Time and Money

previous to the latest Neptune-Pluto conjunction. Yet it seems the solution to one economic problem has created unintended consequences, the plight of children in industrialized societies being a prime example.

By the Neptune-Pluto conjunction of 905, the era of migrations into Europe had come to a close and (quoting Encarta): "Europe experienced the continuity and dynamic growth of a settled population." That is, the Roman Empire was gone and in its stead was a new fundamentalist religious dictate. Encarta strives to be "non-controversial." Much of this "settled population" happened during what we now call the Inquisition. This was an era when religion and militancy merged and Europeans sent armies to invade the Muslim areas. The first Crusade sacked Jerusalem on July 15, 1099, when Neptune had moved on to trine Pluto, and Saturn was opposite Pluto. As the chart below shows, Pluto in Aries at this time formed a T square with Saturn in Libra and Mars and Mercury conjunct in Cancer.

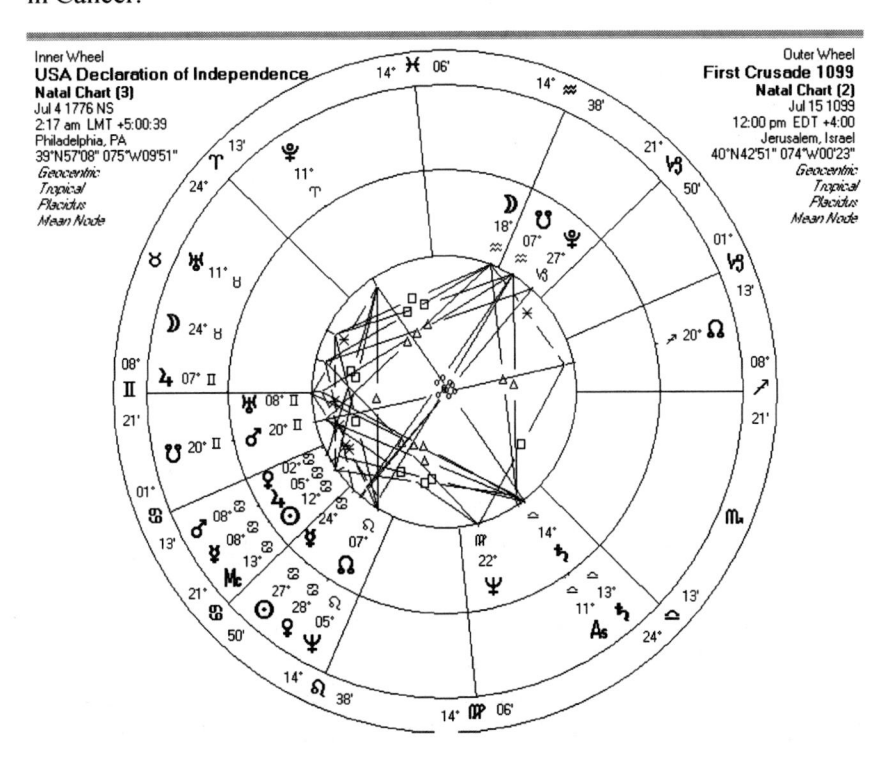

Neptune pertains to religions (also illusions, delusions, inspirations) and Pluto (death of the old, birth of the new) coincides with disintegration of old social and economic organizations and the manifestation of new. The Roman Empire had died and from its ashes the Roman Catholic Church arisen. The planet Pluto is symbolized as the mythic phoenix bird rising from its own ashes. It is sometimes depicted, too, as a masked saboteur blowing up a distant target. Both the sacking of Jerusalem in 1099 and the leveling of the World Trade Center in 2001 happened during Saturn-Pluto oppositions.

Change Or Be Changed

One way to phrase the impact of an affliction from the planet Pluto is: "The entity will either change or be changed." The conjunction of Neptune and Pluto in 905 coincided with a period of religious upheaval. "Late medieval spirituality was characterized by an intense search for the direct experience of God, whether through the private, interior ecstasy of mystical illumination, or through the personal scrutiny of God's word in the Bible," Encarta says. Then came a long period (1095 to about 1633) encompassing the Crusades, which in effect brought the Inquisition to the "infidels" of Arabia, during a stretch of fanaticism which didn't wind down till the condemnation of Galileo, about 200 years after the so-called discovery of America. Galileo had the gall to assert something the Catholic clergy denied: that the Earth orbited the Sun. There are those who assert that pre-Catholic Europeans knew this, as did Arabs, Mesoamericans, Chinese, Polynesians, Africans and other "star gazers." Yet even today, American text books tell children that before Galileo, no one knew the Sun was the center of our Solar System.

Thurow compares the religious upheavals of the Dark Ages with the world in the 1990s (Page 232-233):

"Historically, periods of uncertainly have always seen a rise in religious fundamentalism. Human beings don't like uncertainty and many retreat into religious fundamentalism whenever the uncertainties of the physical world become too great. It happened in the Middle Ages and is happening now. Individuals escape the economic uncertainty of their real world by retreating into the certainty of a religious world where they are told that if they follow the prescribed rules they will certainly be saved." Arab suicide bombers, as devout Muslims, have a clearly envisioned paradise as their eternal reward. American patriotism (loyalty to government) has grown into something akin to a religious belief.

Interesting Similarity

There is this interesting similarity between the charts for the first Crusade in 1099 and the bombing of the World Trade Center and Pentagon in 2001: Pluto and Saturn were opposite each other on both occasions. When the Crusaders brought the wrath of their religion to the Arabs in 1099, Pluto at 11 Aries opposite Saturn at 13 Libra both formed a T square with Mars at 8 Cancer, adding determined aggression. When Islamic fundamentalists brought shock and awe to America, Pluto at 12 Sagittarius opposite Saturn at 14 Gemini both formed a T square with the Sun at 18 Virgo, conjunct the US Neptune, adding confusion. Most Americans had no idea why they'd been attacked in 2001.

Both clashes also epitomize the old saying, "The road to hell is paved with good intentions." In 1099, Christian attackers believed their cause to be inspired by their god; in 2001 Muslim attackers believed their cause to be inspired by their god.

Unintended Consequences

It was during the Neptune-Pluto conjunction of the 1890s that another road of good intentions was being paved. Theodor Herzl of Vienna wrote a book, *The Jewish State*, in which he proposed that a Jewish homeland be established in either Palestine or Argentina. And thus the Zionist Movement was seeded.

At this time, Palestine was part of the Ottoman Empire. By 1903, the first wave of 25,000 Zionist immigrants had gone to Palestine, coming mainly from Eastern Europe. Baron Edmond de Rothschild lent financial backing to these early pioneers. For centuries, Jews had been persecuted in Europe, so this migration to the Biblical holy land was widely seen in Europe as the solution to a seemingly intractable problem.

By 1914, a second wave of Jewish immigrants had increased the Jewish population to 6 percent of Palestine's total. World War I freed Palestine from Ottoman rule at a time when the nation-state was a European concept; most Arabs saw themselves as part of an Islamic world. Imperial Britain had acquired control of Palestine because of its strategic importance. The Balfour Declaration on November 2, 1917 radically changed the status of the Zionist Movement by adding Britain's support.

In 1922, a British Mandate endorsed the concept of Palestine as the Jewish Homeland, and it won backing from the US and most European powers. By this point, Palestine was 78 percent Muslim, 11 percent Jewish and 9.6 percent Christian Arab. For the next 80 years, there occurred events akin to what had happened in the Americas after the arrival of Columbus: the indigenous population was removed to make way for more and more immigrant settlers.

Arabs and Indians

The US became Israel's primary financial and military backer in the 1930s, taking over from the British. What most Americans don't know is that millions of Arabs have been impacted by the killing or removal of native Palestinians. Being Muslims, most Arabs do not see Palestine as the homeland of the Jews, and thus perceive the situation as an invasion backed by European Christians, another Crusade, now led by the Americans.

Jews and their European allies launched this migration motivated by the best of intentions. The aim was to end the persecution of Jews. Arabs, like the American Indians, were viewed as in need of the civilizing influence of Europeans. After all, Christ had arisen among Jews in this area of the Middle East, so it seemed utterly right and logical to Christians that Jews should "return" to Palestine, escaping persecution in Europe and elsewhere. This belief had a growing complexity of consequences yet to be resolved.

Columbus Runs Aground

Howard Zinn begins *A People's History of the United States* by imagining the arrival of Columbus:

"Arawak men and women, naked, tawny, and full of wonder, emerged from their villages onto the island beaches and swam out to get a closer look at the strange big boat. When Columbus and his sailors came ashore, carrying swords, speaking oddly, Arawaks ran to greet them, brought them food, water, gifts... These Arawaks of the Bahaman Islands were much like Indians on the mainland, who were remarkable (European observers were to say again and again) for their hospitality, their belief in sharing."

These events befell the indigenous people of the Americas almost one hundred years after the conjunction of Neptune and Pluto in 1399. Columbus did not come to "make nice." What the Spanish Crown had sent him to find was a shortcut to India, where profitable trade, gold and slaves were to be obtained. He was to learn the world, though round, was a lot larger than he'd estimated, for he'd sailed only about one third of the way to India when he'd bumped into the Americas. He was soon to learn there was scant gold to be found in the Caribbean, where he and his people first set to work digging, and also that these indigenous people prized personal freedom. A friend of Columbus, Peter Martyrs, wrote in the early 1500s that the natives encountered "seem to live in that golden world of which old writers speak so much, wherein men lived simply and innocently without enforcement of laws, without quarreling, judges and libels, content only to satisfy nature."

Robert Gover

Christians and Cannibals

As Columbus and his crews continued to explore the Caribbean Islands, they encountered other Indians who, they said, "relished the taste of human flesh; for them it was a gourmet's revenge on an enemy." ("America: Illusion and Reality" by J. H. Plumb in *Historical Viewpoints*, Harper and Row, 1987, page 37.) It is possible word had gone out that these newcomers from the East had come to enslave and plunder, and that they brought diseases, especially small pox, to which native people had no immunity.

The chief source of written information about early Spanish-Indian contact on Cuba and other Caribbean islands is Bartolome de Las Casas. He estimated that from 1494 to 1508, over three million natives of one island died. "Who in future generations will believe this? I myself writing it as a knowledgeable eyewitness can hardly believe it."

The Neptune-Pluto conjunction of 1399 occurred at 3 degrees of Gemini, indicating inspiring and/or confusing new discoveries and expanded communications, a turning point in human cultures. The economic system of the Native Americans aimed at a balance between the people's needs and the provisions of Mother Earth. Both their culture and that of the European was to be transformed by the migration which soon followed Columbus's first voyage.

Freedom From State Rule

Las Casas described the Indians as largely nonviolent, saying they "fight when they are individually moved to do so because of some grievance, not on the orders of captains or kings." He also noted that "Marriage laws are nonexistent: men and women alike choose their mates and leave them as they please, without offense, jealousy or anger." It was this freedom from autocratic rule that characterized Indians, a freedom Europeans of the time found astounding, baffling, and in need of "civilizing."

"But our work," Las Casas continued, "was to exasperate, ravage, kill, mangle and destroy; small wonder, then, if they tried to kill one of us now and then." The Spanish quickly subjugated these confused native peoples and "thought nothing of killing Indians by the tens and twenties and of cutting slices off them to test the sharpness of their blades." Las Casas describes how one day two Spaniards met two Indian boys carrying parrots, and "they took the parrots and for fun beheaded the boys."

Ponce de Leon Finds Florida

Ponce de Leon was born in Santervas, Spain, in 1460, fought Muslims as a soldier in 1490, and sailed with Columbus' second expedition in 1493. Ponce de Leon was named governor of the province of Higuey in what is now the Dominican Republic before conquering Puerto Rico; because of his extreme brutality to native Americans, he was removed in 1511 but given the right to search for a legendary fountain said to bestow eternal youth and health. This search landed him in what is now St. Augustine, Florida, on April 2. 1513, Palm Sunday. He named this land "Pascua de Florida" (feast of flowers) and claimed it for Spain.

Pluto was at 25 Sagittarius (where it would be again in January 2006) forming a grand cross (to what would become the US Mars-Neptune square) with Mercury at 27 Pisces and the Moon's Nodes in Pisces and Virgo. By August 31, 2006, Pluto will again form a grand cross with the US Mars-Neptune square, this time with Mars conjunct the US Neptune and the Moon's Nodes again in Pisces and Virgo.

With Pluto moving through the last 10 degrees of Sagittarius and into early Capricorn, rapid, long-lasting changes occurred in the Americas during the years just following Columbus' first voyage, and one cycle later, the years leading up to the American Revolution. Going back to the previous time Pluto was here, we find the Barons' Revolt and Battle of Evesham in England and the first convening of the English Parliament.

Culture Clash

In 1519 when Cortez invaded Mexico, the Aztec had a "prophesy about the return of Quetzalcoatl, a legendary god-king who was light skinned and bearded..." (Encarta, Cortez). European myth interprets the Aztec prophesy to mean that the Indians perceived Hernado Cortez as a physical god-king. But from the Indian perspective, a man may be possessed by a god force and not even know it. Being pantheists, the Aztec made a distinction between Cortez the physical man and the horrendous spirit force which he brought in 1519 to their principle city of Tenochtitlan, now Mexico City. Mexico had a population of 20 million when Cortez and his troops arrived in 1519; by 1608 the population was 1 million.

Aztec Astrologers

Since the Aztec were expert astrologers, it's possible their prophesy concerned the planetary pattern of this time, 1517 to 1520, when Saturn and Pluto came conjunct in Capricorn. This put both opposite where Uncle Sam's Sun would be found about 240 years later during the French and Indian War; Pluto will arrive in mid-Capricorn next in 2012-15. Although the planet Pluto would not be seen by telescope till the 1930s, it's possible that Mesoamerican astrologers had tracked the 33.8 year rhythm of the effects of Saturn-Pluto conjunctions, and attributed these to other celestial cycles.

Again using the US birth chart as the stationary clock face, we see that at the height of this slaughter Saturn and Pluto were conjunct in Capricorn, within opposition to Cancer. Uranus at 4 Taurus was forming a harmonious trine to Pluto and Saturn. Mars at 18 Capricorn could be seen as tied into the US Sun-Pluto/Saturn opposition too—a ripe time for death of the old, birth of the new.

Time and Money

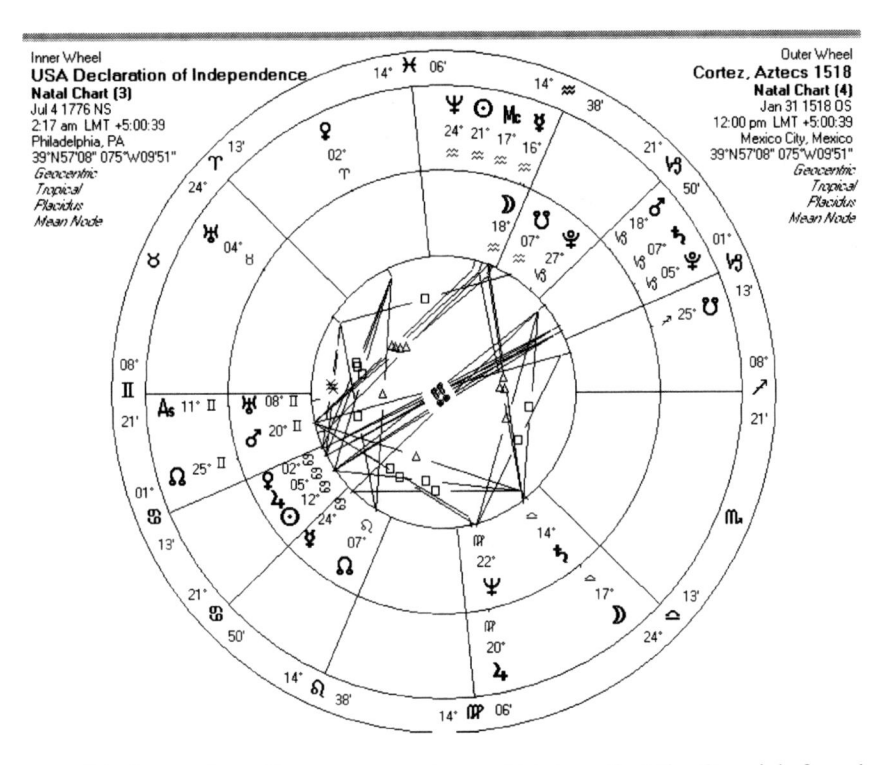

We know from European versions of history that the Spanish found the Aztec exotic, colorful, strange. To the Indian, the mindless cruelty of these hairy psychopaths from the East would be a plague through the next five hundred years. No one knows for sure how many millions of Indians perished as a result of European immigration. Uncounted others died by acts of random murder perpetrated by Europeans educated to believe it was their God-ordained duty to conquer what they called the "New World" and confiscate its riches. They were also coming from the Inquisition: "infidels" were to be converted or killed.

English Clothes

The experience of the Spanish in the New World did not go unnoticed by the English, also lusting for plunder, who believed they could bring freedom from Spanish tyranny and their "gentle" governance to the Indians, and that peaceful Indians would welcome them gladly once they realized the benefits of Anglican Christianity. The English were baffled when their early colonies were first welcomed by Indians, and then attacked.

Howard Zinn points out that official history is almost invariably written by such confiscators of humanity's collective wealth as conquerors, kings, statesmen—those Caesars of the Christian era. One reason I choose Zinn's history over others is contained in the following quote (Page 9):

"My viewpoint in telling the history of the United States is...that we must not accept the memory of (nation) states as our own...The history of any country, presented as the history of a family, conceals fierce conflicts of interest (sometimes exploding, most often repressed) between conquerors and conquered, masters and slaves, capitalists and workers, dominators and dominated in race and sex. And in such a world of conflict, a world of victims and executioners, it is the job of thinking people...not to be on the side of the executioners."

In the Long Run

Zinn states his motives most succinctly when he says, "In the long run, the oppressor is also a victim. In the short run...the victims, themselves desperate and tainted with the culture that oppresses them, turn on other victims...I will not try to overlook the cruelties that victims inflict on one another as they are jammed together in the boxcars of the system. I don't want to romanticize them. But I do remember (in rough paraphrase) a statement I once read: 'The cry of the poor is not always just, but if you don't listen to it, you will never know what justice is.'"

The contrast between European and Indian concepts of wealth pertains here. Wallace C. Peterson in *Silent Depression* (Simon and Schuster, 1994) offers one rooted in European culture:

"Wealth can be likened to the amount of water in a reservoir at any moment, income to the flow of water into the reservoir...If we spend less than our income, our wealth will grow...A nation gets 'wealthy' by merely not using up—spending—all of its income...the actual goods and services produced by its citizens." (Page 97)

By contrast, the Indian sought a balance between human need and nature's seemingly unending abundance. Mother Earth shared her wealth with the people and they shared with each other.

Old World and New World concepts of real estate clashed too. In 1584, Sir Walter Raleigh dispatched an expedition to claim the 2,000 mile east coast of what is now the USA. When this expedition landed on what is now Roanoke Island, North Carolina, they were met by Indians described by Arthur Barlow. "We were entertained with love and kindness and with as much bounty, after their manner, as they could possible devise. We found the people most gentle, loving and faithful, void of all guile and treason, and such as lived after the manner of the Golden Rule."

By August 7, 1590, the first baby born in the new English colony together with about 100 settlers had vanished. The only clue to what had befallen them was the word "Croatoan," carved on a post at the entrance of the empty palisade. It was the name of the local Indian tribe.

Welcoming Then Slaughtering

From the perspective of English nobility, these English colonists came in "good faith" to claim land and employ Indians for the greater glory of their queen. No evidence that they actually died on Roanoke was ever found. One widely held belief is that they joined the Croatoan, since some people of Croatoan ancestry now living in the North Carolina hill country have English names. They may have been blown away by a hurricane or starved during one of the worst droughts in 800 years. Or the Indians may have killed some and taken others prisoner. A pattern of Indians first welcoming and then slaughtering English settlers was to repeat up and down the east coast during the coming decades. And uncounted numbers of English indentured servants and, later, African slaves were to run away and join Indian tribes during the 1600s and 1700s.

Robert Gover

In the following chart for the disappearance of the Roanoke Island colony, Uranus in Pisces is square Saturn in Gemini, Pluto in Aries is opposite Jupiter, and opposite the point in Libra where Saturn would be when the USA was born almost 200 years later.

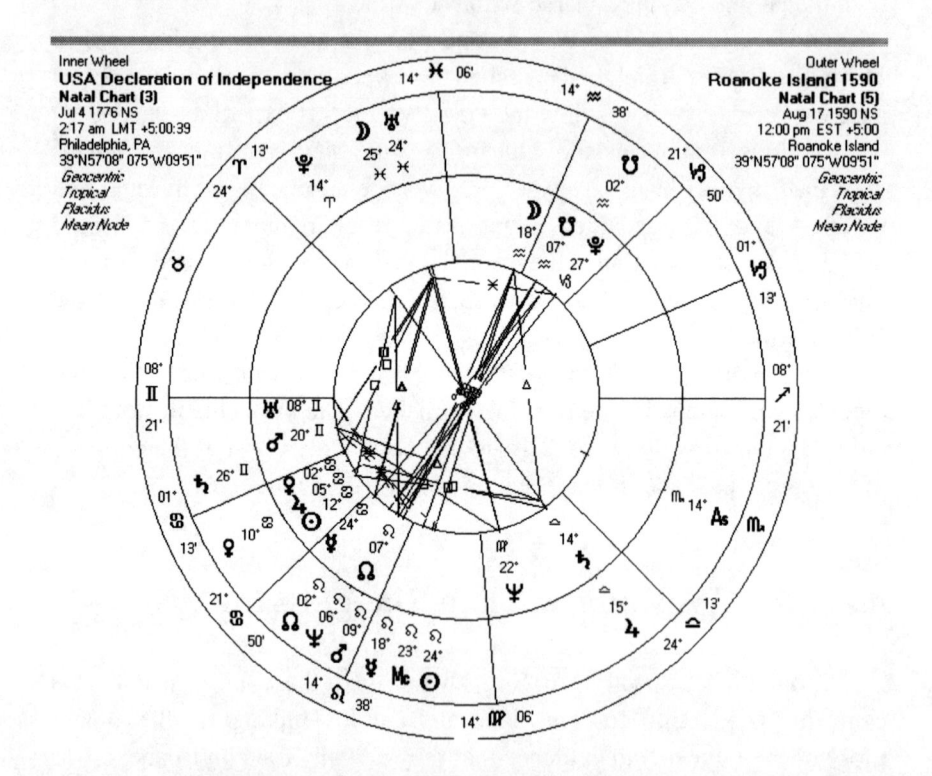

The Jupiter-Pluto opposition marks many a proselytizer for religious, social or political causes, and we know that the English version of Christianity had a strong streak of missionary zeal. Another Jupiter-Pluto opposition was extant in 1602 when advertisements urged English, Dutch and other Europeans to sail to the New World and bring salvation to the Indians as well as seek their fortunes. Another had formed for the American Civil War when both sides believed God was on their side. The most recent Jupiter-Pluto opposition coincided with the series of stock crashes in 2000 to 2001, puncturing the speculative bubble of the 1990s, and bringing President George Bush to the White House with his faith-based policies.

"He Who is Rich"

In 1584, when Raleigh's contingent of Englishmen reached Roanoke on the outer banks of what is now North Carolina, they found the people living in small towns of a hundred or two, each with a chief called a "werowance," meaning "he who is rich."

"The tribe's goods...all flowed into the hands of the chief, but his role was redistributing, so that all shared the bounty. If he had tried to control the wealth, he would have lost his people's respect...(for he) led by moral authority." (Karen Ordahl Kupperman, "Roanoke: The Lost Colony," *Historical Viewpoints*.) Such behavior was disorienting to Europeans, coming from a culture of dominance and submission. Saturn and Pluto were conjunct in early Aries.

In 1607 when the Jamestown Colony was founded, the planet Saturn had arrived at 12 Capricorn to be opposite where Uncle Sam's Sun would be on July 4, 1776. Reading: "You are trying to resolve your personal insecurity so that you can get on with the business of making a place for yourself." (*Planets in Aspect* by Robert Pelletier, Para Research, Inc., 1974.)

Worse yet, Uranus up there in the sky was within orb of a conjunction of 8 Gemini, Uncle Sam's natal Uranus placement. I've mentioned that Uranus's 84-year arrival in Gemini has never failed to coincide with wars in US history: the Revolution, Civil War, World War II. Another coincidence is that even before the USA was born, Uranus in this area coincided with historic conflicts. First was the one frightened colonists in Jamestown waged against the native people they encountered in the early 1600s, and 84 years later when Uranus returned to Gemini, in the 1690s, American colonists were caught up in a series of wars—King George's War, King William's War, Queen Anne's War—which would not be finally settled until the French and Indian War swept through in the 1750s. The 1690s also coincided with the famous trials of witches in Salem, Massachusetts, capping the Inquisition.

Successful Ad Campaign

First and foremost, Jamestown: From the World Wide Web: tobacco.org/history/jamestown we learn that in 1606 "America and advertising begin to grow together. One of the first products heavily marketed is America itself. Richard Hofstadter called the Virginia Company's recruitment effort for its new colony, 'one of the first concerted and sustained advertising campaigns in the history of the modern world.' The out-of-place, out-of-work 'gentlemen' in an overpopulated England were sold quite a bill of goods about the bountiful land and riches to be had in the New World. Daniel J. Boorstin has mused whether "there was a kind of natural selection here of those people who were willing to believe in advertising.""

King James I gave the colonists three objectives: find gold, find a route to the "South Seas," and find the Lost Colony of Roanoke. After adverse winds held the first shipments of Jamestown immigrants near England for 6 weeks, seriously depleting their food reserves, 45 died on the Atlantic crossing but 101 men and 4 boys made land (Cape Henry on the Chesapeake Bay, April 26, 1607).

Jamestown Joys and Sorrows

Zinn: "Jamestown itself was set up inside the territory of an Indian confederacy...Chief Powhatan watched the English settle on his people's land, but did not attack, maintaining a posture of coolness." Declared John Smith: "Heaven and earth never agreed better to frame a place for man's habitation."

But that assessment would soon change. The Internet: "Then came blistering heat, swarms of insects spawned in the nearby wetlands, typhus, unfit water supplies, starvation, fierce winters, Indian attacks, shiploads of inappropriately-prepared Colonists sent from a changing England that had no other place for them, and even a period of tyrannical martial law when missing church 3 times was a capital offense...(these early colonists were) often lesser scions of nobility with no future in overpopulated England, who were lured by the Virginia Company with promises of land and wealth, (but) these 'prospectors' didn't know how to farm, didn't know how to hunt...and were not known for their spirit of cooperation either among themselves or with the local Indians of the Powhatan Confederacy."

The first Indians to encounter arriving Europeans must have viewed them as alien humanoids from another dimension of reality. These newcomers grew hair on their faces, beards, while Indians grew little or no body hair. The newcomers rarely bathed; Indians bathed daily. Indian visitors brought and received gifts; the newcomers accepted gifts but rarely reciprocated. The Europeans were coming from a culture of scarcity; the Indians lived in a culture of abundance.

Indians and Runaways

Zinn: "When the English were going through their 'starving time' in the winter of 1610, some of them ran off to join the Indians. When the summer came, the governor of the colony sent a messenger to ask Powhatan to return the runaways, whereupon Powhatan, according to the English account, replied with 'noe other than prowde and disdayneful Answers.' Soldiers were therefore sent 'to take Revendge.' They fell upon an Indian settlement, killed fifteen or sixteen Indians, burned the houses, cut down the corn growing around the village, took the queen of the tribe and her children into boats, then ended up throwing the children overboard 'and shoteinge owtt their Braynes in the water.' The queen was later taken off and stabbed to death." Uranus and Jupiter were conjunct in early Gemini, with both conjunct what would become the position of natal Uranus in the USA's natal chart in 1776. Uranus here has brought the USA's most devastating wars, beginning with the "Starving Time" in Jamestown and the conflict with Indians following it.

It took the Indians 12 years to mount an organized retaliation. It had never been their way to mount wars at the behest of chieftains, or in large, organized armies. The North American Indians were not organized into authoritarian nation-states; chiefs were seers, not soldiers or lawyers, and were elevated to their positions by popular consensus. The chief's main duty was to make sure everyone prospered, that human greed did not get out of hand. In 1622, the Powhatan wiped out 347 men, women and children in the Jamestown colony.

Hurricanes

It should be remarked that besides being dependent on a supplyline stretching back to England, faced with Indians who did not take to English governance, and unprepared to survive in their new wilderness home, these earliest settlers encountered another element unprecedented in their experience: hurricanes. "They did extensive crop damage, destroyed many structures, uprooted thousands of trees, altered shorelines and courses of rivers, and caused extensive damage to shipping..." (*Everyday Life in Colonial America* by Dale Taylor, Writers Digest Books, 1997.) By some accounts, the earliest colonists experienced several hurricanes which would be described today as "the storm of the century."

Saturn next moved, in 1636, opposite what would become the US natal Sun placement. No grand cross formed; no great depression occurred. Harvard College was founded that year, and the Puritans of New England decided their usurpation of Indian land was based on the Bible. Although the Indians had a "natural right" to their land, the Puritans decided, they did not have a "civil right." The Puritans quoted Romans 13:2: "Whosoever therefore resisteth the power, resisteth the ordinance of God: and they that resist shall receive to themselves damnation."

Duty to God and King

The Puritans had intended to land near the mouth of the Hudson River, which was then part of the Virginia Colony, but by an accident of navigation, put ashore at Plymouth Rock. Finding themselves beyond English law, on November 11, 1620, they created the Mayflower Compact, becoming the first self-governing British colony in North

Time and Money

America. And promptly decided that their duty to God and king demanded they deliver damnation to the "heathen savages."

As an English expedition neared the first Pequot village to deliver some damnation, according to one of the officers of that expedition, the Indians ran down to the water's edge and are quoted as joyfully crying, "What cheer, Englishmen, what cheer, what do you come for?" Thus the Pequots had their consciousness altered. Soon massacres were being perpetrated in what is now New England by both Indians and Englishmen. What humans, as distinct from other life forms on planet Earth, seem to do best is the wholesale slaughter of their own kind.

The following charts show Uncle Sam's birth positions on the inner wheel and two of Saturn's four "returns" to Capricorn on the outer wheel during the 1600s. Even though the USA was not yet born as a new nation, it's interesting to note that Saturn's sojourn through Capricorn—later to anchor great depression grand cross patterns—marked turning points in American history a century and a half before the USA was born as an independent nation.

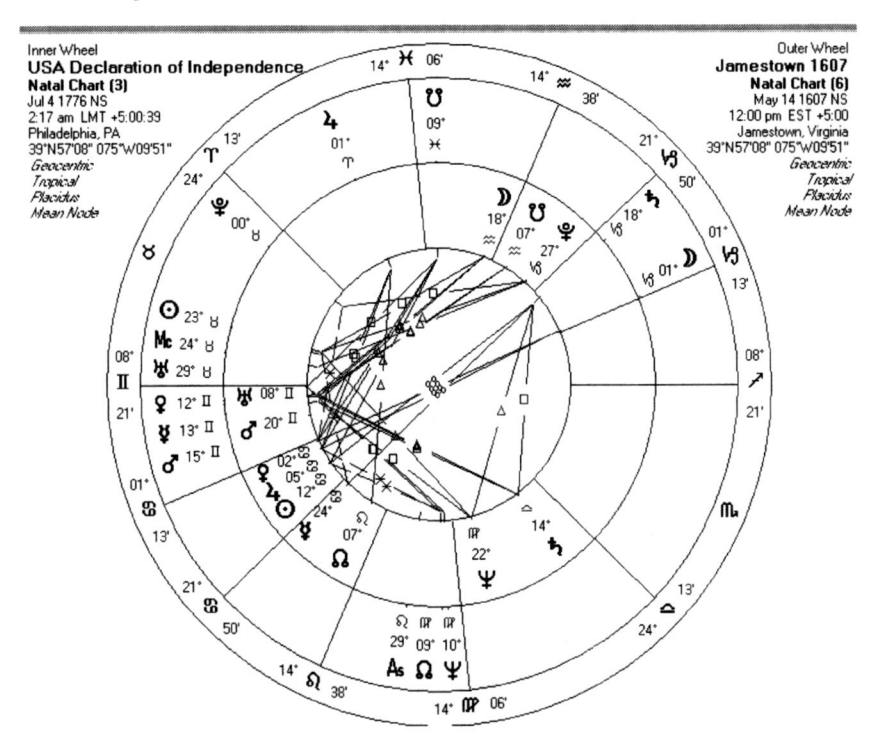

Robert Gover

In the chart for the landing at what would become Jamestown in 1607, note that Saturn is within orb of an opposition to where Uncle Sam's natal Sun would be in 1776. Uranus and Mars were conjunct what would become Sam's Gemini Ascendant and Uranus, and it was simultaneously being squared by Neptune in Virgo (six o'clock). Mars and Uranus afflictions bring violent conflict, and that's what was happening between the newly arrived English and indigenous people.

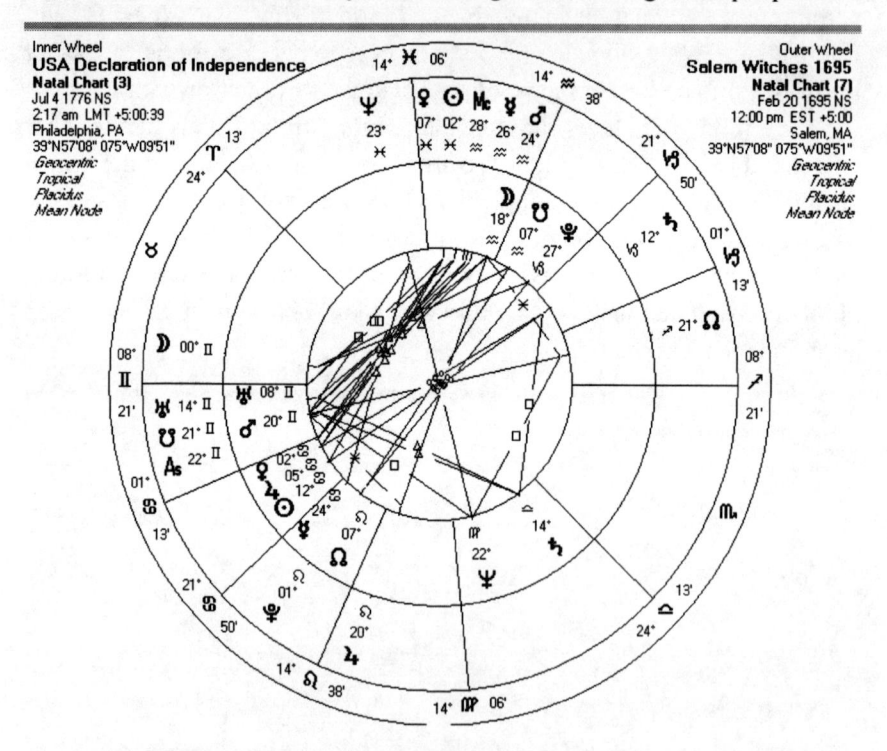

When Saturn returned to Capricorn in the 1690s, the now-famous Salem Witch Trials were climaxing the Dark Ages. As shown on the biwheel chart for this time, transiting Neptune (around 12 o'clock) was opposite Sam's natal Neptune with both widely square transiting Uranus conjunct both Sam's war-making Uranus and Mars (around 8:30). Neptune pertains to the deeper mind, the realm of religions as well as delusions, illusions, inspirations. Reading: a clash of religious beliefs.

Time and Money

Witches

"A single shocking episode—the Salem 'hysteria' of 1692—has dominated the lore of this subject...Yet the Salem trials were distinctive only in a quantitative sense—that is, in the sheer numbers of the accused. Between the late 1630s and 1700 dozens of New England towns supported proceedings against witchcraft; some did so on repeated occasions. The total cases were over a hundred (and this includes only actual trials from which some record survives today). At least forty of the defendants were put to death; the rest were acquitted or convicted of a lesser charge...'Witches' were suspected, accused informally, and condemned in unofficial ways. Gossip and rumor about such people constituted a staple part of the local culture." "(Witchcraft in Colonial New England" by John Demos, *Historical Viewpoints*.)

To go back on the timeline a bit, in 1656, England and Spain were at war, fighting over the spoils taken from the Indians, and a second stage of colonization was in progress. Zinn asks, "Who were these people who came out on the beach and swam to bring presents to Columbus and his crew, who watched Cortez and Pizzaro ride through their countryside, who peered out of forests at the first settlers of Virginia and Massachusetts? Columbus called them Indians because he miscalculated the size of the earth. In this book we call them Indians, with some reluctance, because it happens too often that people are saddled with names given them by their conquerors."

All the Gold

As for gold, the reason why Europeans sailed West in the first place, Zinn quotes Hans Koning's book *Columbus: His Enterprise*.

"...All the gold and silver stolen and shipped to Spain did not make the Spanish people richer. It gave their kings an edge in the balance of power for a time, a chance to hire more mercenary soldiers for their wars. They ended up losing those wars anyway, and all that was left was a deadly inflation, a starving population, the rich richer, the poor poorer, and a ruined peasant class."

Besides gold, Europeans found something in the Americas far more sustaining: maize (corn) and a variety of fruits, tomatoes, potatoes, peanuts and chocolate. In exchange they would bring to their New World a culture of rich and poor, male heads of families, factories and plantations, and large armies organized under single autocrats, sworn to subdue whatever "savages" might question their mission as they sought gold on the vast landmasses of North and South America.

By contrast, practically all Indian groups shared goods with each other, just as they perceived nature shared with them. Indian children were taught to think independently, each to discover his or her uniqueness; women were equal to men and both had functions in tribal councils. Invading Europeans perceived these natives as uncivilized, since they didn't behave like Europeans or worship Christ but were, instead, pagan infidels, to be converted or killed.

Pleasures and Philosophies

A Jesuit priest in the 1650s was astounded to find that the "savage" Iroquois were kind, humble and courteous, and that this "not only makes them liberal with what they have, but causes them to possess hardly anything except in common." After providing for their food, shelter and clothing, Indians had abundant leisure time to devote to various pleasures and philosophy.

By the 1660s, one cycle of Neptune after the first Europeans arrived in the Americas, the plunder, Christianizing and annihilation of Native Americans was well underway, and slavery institutionalized. Zinn quotes J. Sanders Redding's description of a ship that arrived in Jamestown, 1619.

20 African Slaves

"Sails furled, flag drooping at her founded stern, she rode the tide in from the sea. She was a strange ship, indeed, by all accounts, a frightening ship, a ship of mystery. Whether she was trader, privateer, or

Time and Money

man-of-war no one knows. Through her bulwarks black-mouthed cannon yawned. The flag she flew was Dutch; her crew a motley. Her port of call, an English settlement, Jamestown, in the colony of Virginia. She came, she traded, and shortly afterwards was gone. Probably no ship in modern history has carried a more portentous freight. Her cargo? Twenty African slaves."

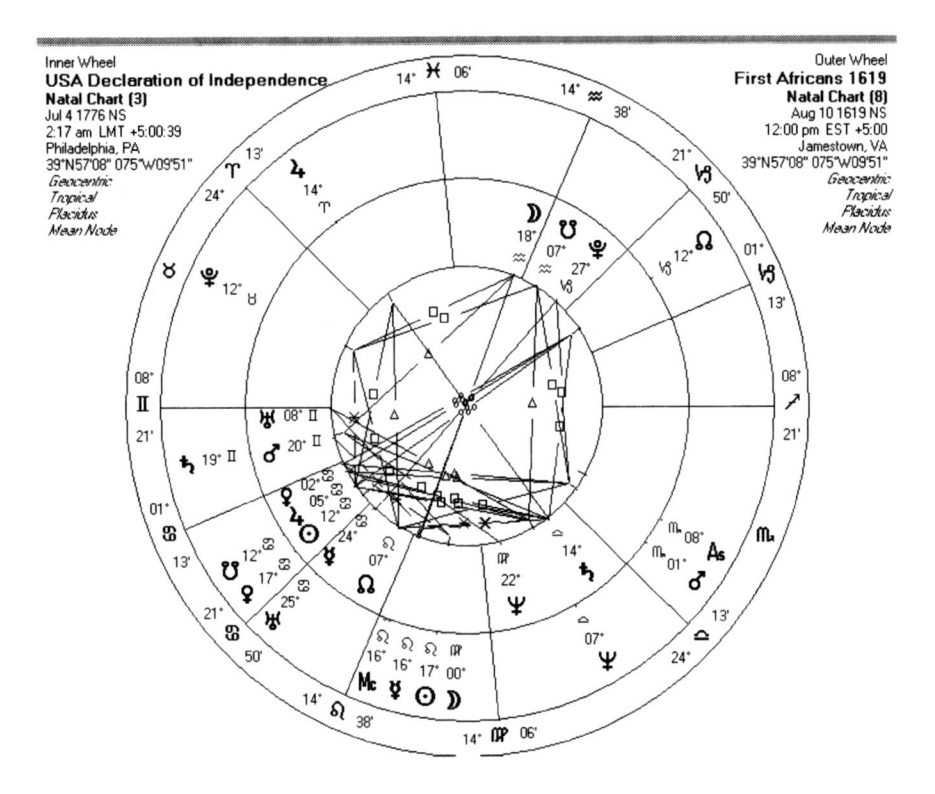

Note that transiting Jupiter is opposite the US Saturn, while it was conjunct Saturn for the Roanoke Island settlement's disappearance. It again squares Venus, which is conjunct Sam's Sun, to form another T square. Uranus would soon move on to square Pluto, and Neptune is forming a 120-degree beneficent trine to the US natal Uranus. In individual charts, Uranus trine Neptune is considered an indication of intuition, psychic ability. The Africans brought a powerful tradition of intuition, the marriage of instinct and intellect.

Cost-Effective Labor

The first African slaves to Jamestown were viewed as indentured servants when they landed, as there was no law pro or anti slavery in Virginia then. Most English indentured servants at this time died before they'd served their time and were freed. Planters didn't want to pay more for a slave whose life expectancy was so brief, and thus few slaves were imported to Virginia for the first two or three decades of Jamestown's existence.

By around 1640 the newcomers had learned to survive in the colonies and African slaves were in demand by planters in Virginia and other colonies. It was in 1713 that the British South Sea Company obtained the exclusive right to supply African slaves. As we shall see in the following chapter, the South Sea Company, along with John Law's financial innovations, would soon become a precursor of that modern stock market phenomenon known as the speculative bubble.

John Law's Long Shadow

Speculative bubbles have been repeating since before the famous Tulip Mania in Holland in 1637, when—could you have guessed it?—Neptune in Scorpio opposed Pluto in Taurus. Neptunian delusions before the advent of paper money were tame compared to those after paper money became ubiquitous. Neptune would be in Taurus opposite Saturn in Scorpio when two panics hit in 1720.

The innovation called paper money takes us back to the early 1700s when a gentleman named John Law rose to prominence in Paris. His downfall would come about the same time as the South Sea Bubble burst in England, 1720, and be caused by the same assumptions about price and value. His legacy lives on.

In the 1700-teens, Europeans with money, in the form of metal coins or bonds bought with coins, were especially fascinated by the investment possibilities offered. "'To Make Salt Water Fresh—For Building of Hospitals for Bastard Children—For building of ships against Pirates—For importing a Number of large Jack Asses from Spain...For a Wheel of Perpetual Motion,'" to cite a representative list of promotions at the time of the South Sea Bubble." (*The Great Crash*, Galbraith, page 51.)

Promotions Then and Now

Galbraith goes on to compare the investment trusts of the 1720s with those of the 1920s (both comparable to the mutual funds of today): "Historians have told with wonder of one of the promotions at the time (1700s)...It was 'For an Undertaking which shall in due time be revealed.' The stock is said to have sold exceedingly well. As promotions, the investment trusts (of the 1920s) were, on the record, more wonderful. They were undertakings the nature of which was never to be revealed, and their stock also sold exceedingly well."

On March 24, 1720, banks closed in Paris and panic swept London and Paris in the wake of an orgy of speculation, the likes of which would not arise again till the Florida Land Boom of the 1920s and the Dotcom Boom of the 1990s. Back in the early 1700s, it was the South Sea Company in London (which had a franchise on shipping slaves to the American colonies, among other ventures) that wrecked English investors.

The economic genius of the 1720s was John Law, a Scottish exile who had conned the French Regent, the Duc d'Orleans. Law created a paper money system in France then launched a company that bought shares in land far across the Atlantic Ocean along the Mississippi River. That inspired Englishman Robert Harley of the South Sea Company to encourage investors to buy South Sea Company stock. In six months South Sea shares rose from 150 to 1,000. Soon hundreds of other companies had formed to fulfill a variety of missions: "to drain bogs in Ireland, to get gold from sea water, to collect hair for wig-making, to organize funerals" and so forth.

Money As Value Itself

What is so phenomenal about the speculative bubble is that, even though it's happened repeatedly before, it continues to happen, as witness the Dotcom mania of the 1990s, and the credit default swaps of 2008.

"In 1720, England had enjoyed a long period of prosperity, enhanced in part by war expenditures, and during this time private savings are believed to have grown at an unprecedented rate." (Galbraith, page 175).

Although bubbles are by nature a Neptunian delusion, Saturn also has been involved in bubble bursts. Tulipmania crashed in 1637 with Saturn square Uranus; John Law's and the South Sea bubbles popped in 1720 with Saturn opposite Neptune; the crash of 1929 occurred with

Time and Money

Saturn square Uranus; the Japanese Bubble burst in 1990 with Saturn conjunct Neptune and Uranus; the Crash of March 2001 found Saturn square Uranus and the Crash of 2008 found Saturn opposite Uranus.

What makes John Law so intriguing was how fervently he believed and how passionately he espoused the idea that money isn't just symbolic of value but value itself.

Although this financial panic was remote from the American colonies, I use Uncle Sam's birth chart again as the stationary clock face to see what relationships show up. Notice, first, Saturn around 4 o'clock opposite Neptune near 10 o'clock.

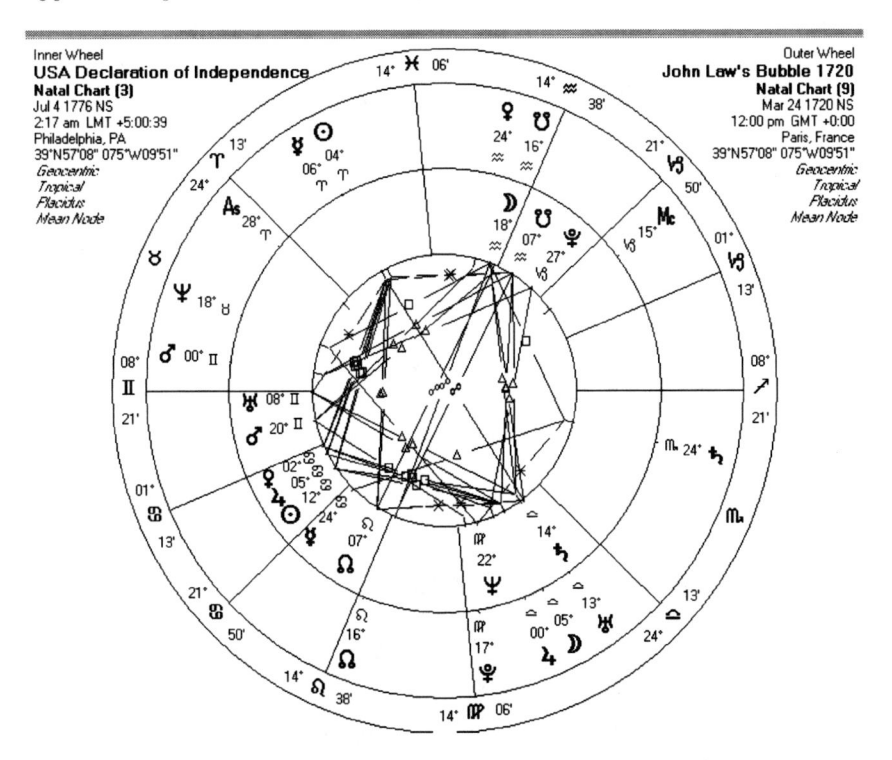

What also appears in the biwheel is that Pluto in 1720 is conjunct the US natal Neptune in Virgo, while Uranus is conjunct the US Saturn in Libra. Both Sam's economically sensitive Sun-Saturn square and his financially sensitive Mars-Neptune square are hit. As we have seen, every panic in US history since 1857 has involved afflictions to Sam's

Mars-square-Neptune. So the planetary pattern of 1720 is a kind of foreshadowing of investment bubbles to come.

Repeatedly Forgotten

John Law's monetarist thinking has cast a long shadow from the 1720s through the American Revolution and into the 20th Century. In retrospect, it's easy to see that his notion was flawed, but not so easy to see this same flaw at work in today's financial markets. Today's electronic transfers of billions does not seem, on the surface of it, to be anything like John Law's selling of shares in land along a wide river about a month's sail from the Paris of his day. But what is the same is the belief that more money, by itself, equals more wealth, forgetting that money must be based on something of real value to denote real value itself. It's a fact that repeatedly gets lost in the excitement of boom times.

Today, trillions of "e-dollars" wire-transferred around the Earth each trading day are increased or decreased by the momentary ratio of one currency to another. Nothing of value is produced in these transactions. There is a big difference between profits made by price changes and profits made by producing goods and services of real value. This is the lesson John Law inadvertently taught, and which has yet to be fully comprehended.

Speculations Useful and Foolish

This lesson in the speculation on price changes is not to be confused with speculations on commodities futures contracts, which serve the useful purpose of enabling farmers to minimize risks; those futures contracts are indeed valuable to our economic well-being; they stabilize prices, facilitating trade. Nothing of real value is gained by speculations on currency ratio changes minute by minute, although huge dollar profits are derived. Such "derivatives" have derived far from economic reality.

John Law was born in Edenborough, Scotland, on April 21, 1671, educated at the University of Edenborough, studied banking in

Time and Money

Amsterdam, and had found his way to France by 1717. It's not clear how he came to the attention of the French king, but in Paris, through the patronage of the monarch, he founded the first French central bank, then printed and issued bank notes, paper money, and exchanged them for metal coins which, by royal decree, his paper money could be used to pay taxes. This was a tremendous innovation in those times.

His formal contribution to economics came in 1720 when he wrote *Money and Trade Considered With a Proposal for Supplying the Nation with Money*, in which he explained this bright idea which is very much with us today: Money is wealth; therefore the more money people have, the wealthier they are. It thus follows that the state will prosper by increasing the amount of money in circulation.

Wilderness Speculations

Law "test marketed" this idea in 1717. After creating his bank and issuing paper money in exchange for coins, he established a company which controlled tracts of land along the Mississippi River in what was then France's Louisiana Territory. He acquired exclusive rights to trade in this territory for 25 years, and proceeded to sell shares to investors, speculating that prices were sure to rise on those wilderness sites.

What's going on here? John Law gets hold of a printing press, prints IOUs and trades them for metal coins, and gets the French government to accept his paper money for tax payments. That was radical enough in 1717, but Law then tops himself with this other innovation, selling shares in land along a distant river to Frenchmen in Paris, who pay John Law for their shares with paper money printed by John Law.

Do we recognize here the prototype of today's Federal Reserve System and the central banks of other nations? And even the more recently-created World Bank?

No wonder his company was such a success that it soon absorbed its rival East India and China Company, while his *Banque Generale* became the official French government bank. France rewarded John Law by making him its Councilor of State and Comptroller General of Finance.

John Law's bright idea went over so well that coined money disappeared and the prices of his paper money shares rose astronomically. Indians living along the Mississippi River had no idea their homeland was being sold out from under them, but to Europeans the Indians were "ignorant heathen savages" so there was no reason to believe they'd appreciate this get-rich-quick scheme.

Prices to Great Heights

"When the public was invited to invest in shares in the Mississippi venture," Encarta tells us, "a great wave of speculation drove the prices of shares to great heights. At the same time the country was being flooded with paper money from Law's bank."

So dramatic was the rise in the price of these shares that by royal decree in 1720, the government was forced to abruptly cut their price by 50 percent. Thereafter: "The shares in Law's company, which had been amalgamated with his bank, sank in price as rapidly as they had risen, and the bank suspended payments," Encarta says dryly. In other words, John Law's Mississippi Bubble was structured the same as the British South Sea Bubble in 1720, and this phenomenon would repeat again and again—most recently in the Great Crash of 1929, the NASDAQ crash of 2001, and the Real Estate Derivatives Crash of 2008. As long as demand (money) is balanced against supply (goods and services) the system works. Balance is lost when speculations are mistaken for real goods and services—when price is mistaken for value.

Price and Value

Law found a popular way to create wealth and made a lot of people "king for a day," but had been mistaken about one very important thing. Money is not real wealth itself; money is a symbolic measure of wealth; the money price of something may or may not represent its true value. The value of a home today is the same as it has always been even though the prices of homes have gone through horrendous ups and downs over the centuries.

Time and Money

Law's genius flowered again during the American Revolution when Continental Army soldiers—the first in history to fight for a political ideal—were paid in paper money which, by the end of the war, had become worthless. This was primarily because the British had sabotaged the Continental by printing wagonloads of them and distributing them throughout the colonies—too much money for the supply of goods and services available resulted after the war.

Money is mysterious stuff. Today, measures of American money are categorized as M1, M2, M3 and L, but essentially money is created out of thin air as though by magic: (*Secrets of the Temple* by William Greider, page 59): "A bank officer authorizes a $100,000 loan to a small businessman—a judgment that the businessman's future earnings will be sufficient to repay the loan." The banker does not hand over the $100,000 in dollar bills. He writes a check or, more likely, enters a credit in the businessman's bank account for $100,000. "Either way, money has been created by a simple entry in a ledger."

Money From Thin Air

This is, as Greider points out, something everyone accepts, assumes, takes for granted—even though most are unaware of its audacity. The borrower spends in actual dollars whatever sum was created by the lending banker, based on the banker's estimate of the future value to be created. The loan is not collateralized by any existing thing of measurable value; it is based on something to be created of an estimated value. It is based on trust. As long as members of a society trust each other and their currency, money created out of thin air (and/or the fancies of bankers) can be used to build things of real value. Cash money then moves around in the system as people pay and get paid real dollars in exchange for real goods and services.

Greider uses an image of oil pumped through a system of complicated machinery, with these different classifications of money—M1, M2, M3 and L—symbolized as different viscosities of oil keeping the machine running. That's a fine analogy but...

Robert Gover

Piracy and Business As Usual

Consider two people in contemporary America: a counter worker at a fast food outlet and the parent corporation's CEO. The worker earns around $6 per hour while the CEO, asleep or awake during the same hour, earns around $600 or over $5 million a year. The counter worker provided goods and services; the CEO supposedly oversaw the entire operation of the chain, although in reality he may have merely been sleeping, or golfing or sharing a cocktail with his congressman. Viewed from the perspective of real value, the CEO makes Black Beard the Pirate look inept. By funding the campaigns of politicians, our CEO strongly influences a system that creates the growing and increasingly dangerous divide between haves and have-nots, and concurrently between money as value itself and money as based on goods and services of value.

Astrologically, afflictions from Saturn coincide with feelings of frustration and fear, worry, distrust. In the 1780s, when Saturn came opposite the US Sun, during and following the American Revolutionary victory, paper money turned worthless, exacerbating the dramatic disparity between rich and poor, leading to a great depression and a rash of revolts typified by Shays Rebellion.

"We the People"

Four groups were not included as "we the people." They were Indians, African slaves, White men without property and all women—the overwhelming majority of the American population at that time. The "people" the Founders had designated were themselves and their aristocratic friends. Most of the Founders assumed the vast majority would do as they were told. This is how the economy of their European mother country had functioned, so why wouldn't it continue to function this way when transplanted to North America? The class system was believed to be God-ordained. Moreover, the new nation had not yet created its own monetary system, which exacerbated the wealth disparity of this period.

Time and Money

Economic trouble began as early as February, 1782, when transiting Saturn reached 29 Sagittarius opposite transiting Uranus at 29 Gemini, conjunct Sam's Mars-square-Neptune. (Saturn would be within 3 degrees of this placement 147 years later for the big crash of 1929.) An angry crowd blocked the door of the courthouse in Pittsfield in the Berkshires. "A court that did not sit could not process foreclosures, pass judgments on debts, or confiscate property for defaulted taxes." ("Shays Rebellion" by Alden T. Vaughan, *Historical Viewpoints*, page 198.)

During this time, former clergyman Samuel Ely led an attack on judges in Connecticut, and urged the crowd to "go to the woodpile and get clubs enough, and knock the grey wigs off, and send them out of the world in an instant." When Ely was arrested and imprisoned in Springfield, an angry crowd freed him. Thus, even during the Revolutionary War, poor Americans were rebelling against rich Americans, whose only "crime" was adhering to the transplanted cultural script, again illustrating that belief trumps evidence.

"Greatly Abused"

"Illegal conventions began to assemble in some of the western counties (of Massachusetts) to organize opposition to the legislature," Zinn notes (page 91). "At one of these a man named Plough Jogger spoke his mind: 'I have been greatly abused, have been obliged to do more than my part in the war; been loaded with class rates, town rates, province rates, Continental rates and all rates...been pulled and hauled by sheriffs, constables, and collectors, and had my cattle sold for less than they were worth...The great men are going to get all we have and I think it is time for us to rise and put a stop to it, and have no more courts, nor sheriffs, nor lawyers.'"

The same sentiments were being expressed in most of the other 13 original states by this time, 1786 when Mars and Uranus came conjunct over the US Sun. In Massachusetts some of these events were recorded. Veterans of the Continental Army, who upon discharge had been paid with paper money that quickly became worthless, began to organize farmers into squads and companies. One of these veterans was Luke Day, who arrived the morning of his court hearing with a fife-and-drum corps, "still angry with the memory of being locked up in debtors' prison in the heat of the previous summer...The sheriff looked to the local militia to defend the court...but most of the militia was with Luke Day." (Zinn page 91.)

Armed Farmers

While waiting for the judges, who were waiting for an armed guard to escort them to the court house, Luke Day read a petition, "asserting the people's constitutional right to protest the unconstitutional acts of the General Court, asking the judges to adjourn until the General Court could act on behalf of the farmers. Standing with Luke Day were fifteen hundred armed farmers. The judges adjourned."

Both protesters and judges were locked into the same cultural beliefs and economic system. Instead of attacking the system, they attacked each other.

Another veteran of the Revolutionary War, John Shattuck, led a caravan of carts, wagons, horses and oxen onto another village green with a message for another judge: "The voice of the people of this county is such that the court shall not enter this courthouse until such time as the People shall have redress of the grievances they labor under at present."

At Great Barrington, MA, another confrontation between militia and judges climaxed when "the crowd went back to the square, broke open the county jail, and set free the debtors. The chief justice, a country doctor, said, 'I have never heard anybody point out a better way to have their grievances redressed than the people have taken.'" (Zinn page 92).

Rebellious Lower Class

Pluto is famous for bringing chaotic social disintegration as a prelude to change. The new nation's ruling class, which had managed to direct a rebellious lower class into fighting the British, had no response

Time and Money

to the situation than to adhere to the inherited cultural script. It was within this context that one Daniel Shays arose.

"A poor farm hand when the revolution broke out, he joined the Continental Army, fought at Lexington, Bunker Hill, and Saratoga, and was wounded in action. In 1780, not being paid, he resigned from the army, went home, and soon found himself in court for nonpayment of debts. He also saw what was happening to others: a sick woman, unable to pay, had her bed taken from under her." (Zinn page 92).

While the Supreme Judicial Court waited to hear and indict Luke Day, it met in Worcester and indicted 11 leaders of rebellions, including 3 of Daniel Shays' friends, as "disorderly, riotous and seditious persons... (who) unlawfully and by force of arms (prevented) the execution of justice and the laws of the commonwealth." The name "commonwealth" given some states, and the phrase, "We the people" in the Declaration of Independence are indicative of a split among the Founders over how much democracy should be established, a split in opinion that continues to this day, as witness how President George W. Bush was appointed by the Supreme Court's snarled logic.

Shays organized 700 men and went to Springfield for another court hearing. They were met by 900 soldiers and a cannon; Shays asked the general of this contingent for permission to parade. As his men marched with drums banging and fiefs blowing, some of the soldiers joined them and reinforcements came in from the countryside. The judges postponed the hearings.

Sam Adams Reads Riot Act

The duly constituted authorities of the state, recent rebels against the British Crown, now attempted to put down this new rebellion against themselves. Samuel Adams helped write a Riot Act suspending habeas corpus so that people could be held in jail without trial. Some concessions were made to the farmers by the state legislature, allowing certain taxes to be paid in goods instead of money, but it was too little too late. Confrontations between farmers and militia multiplied. The reading of Sam Adams' Riot Act did not help. At one gathering, as a sheriff harangued the crowd with threats of hanging, someone came up behind him and decorated his hat with a sprig of poisonous hemlock.

Shays marched with a thousand men toward Boston, but a blizzard forced them to retreat, and one of his men froze to death. As the winter grew worse, the rebels were outnumbered and on the run as soldiers employed by the state were at least fed, and battles were apparently quite disorganized, for in one a soldier lost both arms to his own cannon. A general's horse was slaughtered, barns burned, a government solider was killed in a strange collision of two sleights at night. When six rebels were caught and three sentenced to death, the sheriff of Pittsfield found a note on his door that could have been written by the god of Hades:

"Your Life or Mine"

"I understand that there is a number of my countrymen condemned to die because they fought for justice. I pray have a care that you assist not in the execution of so horrid a crime, for by all that is above, he that condemns and he that executes shall share alike...Prepare for death with speed, for your life or mine is short. When the woods are covered with leaves, I shall return and pay you a short visit."

Six more rebels were sentenced to die. An argument over the merits of such action brought these words from Sam Adams, speaking for the new American establishment: "In monarchy the crime of treason may admit of being pardoned or lightly punished, but the man who dares rebel against the laws of a republic ought to suffer death."

Shays fled to Vermont. He was pardoned in 1788, returned to Massachusetts and died, "poor and obscure," in 1825. Yet the idea of "leveling," which powered Bacon's Rebellion during the Uranus-Pluto square of 1676 had resurfaced during the series of Uranus-Pluto squares and trines of the 1750s through the 1770s.

Planets and Revolution

Astrologically, it is interesting to note the positions and movements of our economically significant planets during this first great depression and series of post-revolutionary revolts. In 1783, Saturn was exactly opposite Uncle Sam's Sun-square-Saturn, with Uranus conjunct Sam's Sun, Neptune conjunct Sam's Saturn, and Mars in Aries opposite Sam's Saturn. Pluto at 7 Aquarius was trine Uncle Sam's natal Uranus. As the celestial clock moved on through time:

Saturn would next be found in mid-Capricorn coinciding with the great depression of the 1840s.

Uranus would next arrive in Gemini (where it had been during the American Revolution and popular uprisings) to coincide with the Civil War's worst battles.

Neptune would next arrive in mid-Libra during the climax of World War II, around 165 years after Shays Rebellion and the Post-Revolutionary War Depression.

The effects of the square between Uncle Sam's Sun at 13 Cancer and his Saturn at 15 Libra speak astrologically of this unresolved confusion and conflict over who "we the people" are, and what economic justice is. In the history of the US, justice has meant one thing for the rich and something else for the poor. The thrust of the law has been to protect the haves from the have-nots, and "individual freedom" has been interpreted one way for the haves, another way for the have-nots. Yet the have-nots have gained greatly by literal interpretations of law designed for the rich, owing mainly to Thomas Jefferson's foxy phrase, "We, the people..." which he was able to salvage even after his words against slavery had been removed by less liberal Founders. Jefferson meant all the people, making him a traitor to his class in his time, while giving the Declaration of Independence resonance into the foreseeable future.

Savages and Democracy

Little-known information about the influence of Native American forms of government on Founding Fathers Ben Franklin and Tom

Jefferson can be accessed by referring to *Forgotten Founders* by Bruce E. Johansen, published first by The Harvard Common's Press in 1982 and since then reprinted by others. There are some sources that also show a connection between Rousseau and Native American thinkers. That these "heathen savages" might have something valuable to contribute was naturally a tough sell for Ben and Tom back then, so they referred instead to the classical Greeks of antiquity, highly esteemed by European Americans. But there is some evidence (for those disposed to look for it) that they managed to slip in some Indian ideas that subtlely sabotaged the cultural script transplanted from Europe.

If Uncle Sam were a single human being, we might say that his Sun-square-Saturn manifests in his proclivity to say one thing but do another. His Cancer Sun inclines him to be sensitive and caring of the less fortunate, but his Saturnian square to Sun and prominent Uranus compel him to react much like Ebenezer Scrooge, miserly and overly protective of his wealth, paranoid about those he imagines might wrest it from him, as he wrested it from others.

Common Property of All

General Henry Knox, writing to George Washington in late 1786 about this rebellious period, expressed one perspective on this underlying split in the American psyche: "The people who are the insurgents have never paid any, or but very little taxes, but they see the weakness of government; they feel at once their own poverty, compared with the opulent, and their own force, and they are determined to make use of the latter, in order to remedy the former. Their creed is, 'That the property of the United States has been protected from the confiscation of Britain by the joint exertions of all, and therefore ought to be the common property of all. And he that attempts in opposition to this creed is an enemy to equality and justice and ought to be swept off the face of the earth.'" General Knox spoke from Uncle Sam's Sun in Cancer, and expressed a perspective that was part of the Native American cultural script.

"Impudence of Democracy"

Alexander Hamilton, speaking from Uncle Sam's Saturnian side, saw the divide between rich and poor differently: "The (poor) people are turbulent and changing; they seldom judge or determine right. Give therefore to the first class (the rich) a distinct permanent share in the government...Nothing but a permanent body can check the impudence of democracy."

It's easy to see Hamilton's point when, today, the media manipulates public opinion so adroitly. My personal objection to Hamilton's qualms is that it's not the rich who should rule, but the wise. Wealth does not confer wisdom, and there is abundant evidence that it engenders brain-damaging hubris.

Howard Zinn, writing with the benefit of hindsight from the 20th Century, gives us another perspective:

"The problem of democracy in the post-Revolutionary society was not...the Constitutional limitations on voting. It lay deeper, beyond the Constitution, in the division of society into rich and poor. For if some people had great wealth and great influence, if they had the land, the money, the newspapers, the church, the educational system—how could voting, however broad, cut into such power?" This question continues to plague American society.

Bill of Rights

It was Shays Rebellion and other uprisings following the Revolutionary War which led to the drafting of the Constitution by the convention which gathered in Philadelphia from May 25 to September 17, 1787, followed by the first ten amendments to this document, called the Bill of Rights, adopted in 1791.

From an astrological perspective, this remarkable period (from the French and Indian War to the ratification of the Bill of Rights) demonstrates the transformative effects attributed to the planet Pluto. Pluto transited opposite Uncle Sam's Gemini Uranus, then opposite his

Sun in Cancer and his Mercury in Cancer during these decades. And during this period, the assumption that power naturally flowed from God to king and aristocracy was transformed into its antithesis: that power flows from the will of the people. Pluto was not to repeat its journey through this area of the heavens again until the first two decades of the 21st Century, when the idealism of the Founders had been lost but not forgotten.

What was to actually emerge as the US evolved from 13 colonies into a nation and then an empire was a unique custom: the rich would cultivate a buffer class between themselves and the poor, giving this middle class just enough rights and liberties to ensure popular support, and entrusting this buffer class with the task of preserving the cultural script. A first step in this evolution was a tacit agreement between Northern industrialists and Southern slave owners: both would get a large national market for their products in return for allowing slavery to continue.

Inefficiency of Slavery

An interesting sidelight on this period is that Adam Smith's now-biblical-like treatise, *The Wealth of Nations*, appeared as the American Revolution occurred, and in it Smith said, among many other things startling at the time, that slavery was a less efficient use of labor than manufacturing; factory workers must pay for their own food and rent. Eventually Southern landowners would get this message and increase their profits by converting to what has come to be called the sharecropper system—the freed slaves given a share of the products they grew and harvested, but obliged to pay for food and rent. A sharecropper's share was rarely, if ever, enough to cover food and rent, so slavery merely changed form, not content, and expanded to include poor White sharecroppers as well. The development of true democracy thus took about two steps forward and one back.

The newly formed nation was struggling through its first great depression when the Constitution was enacted September 17, 1787. Pluto was in Aquarius trine Neptune in Libra (conjunct the US Saturn) trine the US Mars in Gemini, with Jupiter conjunct Sam's Mars. A very favorable configuration, covered in more detail in the next chapter.

However, on December 15, 1791 when the Bill of Rights and first ten amendments were added to the Constitution, Saturn was at 12 Aries, opposite the US natal Saturn and square the US Second House Sun, Jupiter and (by tie-in) Venus. This formed a very difficult T square to that area of the US natal chart which has shown itself to be the most sensitive to the overall economy. Note that Pluto is conjunct the US Moon (public) and opposite Uranus. This comparison chart speaks to the question, what's the economy for? The enrichment of the already rich, or the betterment of all Americans? The rights of the people versus the rich would have a hard row to hoe.

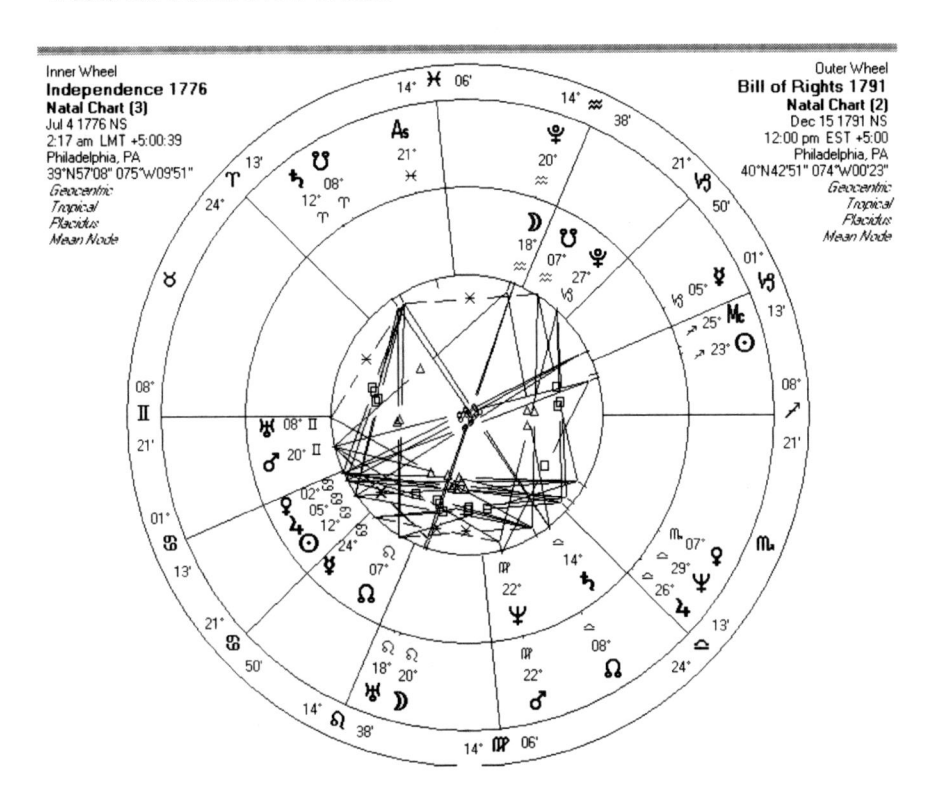

Robert Gover

"The Constitution became even more acceptable to the public at large after the first Congress, responding to criticism, passed a series of amendments known as the Bill of Rights...What was not made clear...was the shakiness of anyone's liberty when entrusted to a government of the rich and powerful." (Zinn page 99).

During the following decades, benefits to the people would usually come as the result of crises, verifying the T square of the Bill of Rights date. On the other hand, the wealthy were to face little difficulty obtaining their aims, except during times of crisis. Old cultural habits die hard.

Gold and the Dollar

We humans are a comparatively recent species on planet Earth. Snakes, sharks and other ancient creatures worked out their "economies" millennia ago; by that I mean they have fit themselves into the planet's ecology in a way that enables them to survive and prosper.

From as far back as 700 BC, human societies have been held together by language and money. Money is defined as "a medium of exchange." Many things have been used as money down through time, from seeds to stones, although metal coins arose as the form of money most preferred.

Of the metals, gold became the most popular and ubiquitous. It had the qualities needed: it was scarce, durable, portable; it could be standardized; it could be weighted for larger or smaller amounts.

For something to work well as money it must have another quality: in economics this thing is called "intrinsic value." But that's a misnomer. No thing under the Sun actually has intrinsic value strictly defined as meaning value in and of itself, independent of anything else. And just about any thing under the Sun can be imbued, by common agreement, with intrinsic value. It's our perception that gives gold or any other form of money "intrinsic value." The more accurate term would be *perceived value*.

Over millennia, gold proved it had another rare quality that set it apart from other forms of money: it's "immutable." It cannot be transformed it into something else, and as the alchemists found during Medieval times, no other thing can be transformed into gold. Thus gold was considered the most universally accepted form of money from about 700 BC till 1970, about 2,670 years.

When the first paper form of money arose is not clear; some say it was used in ancient China, others that it was first tried in Sweden. The printing press was developed around 1500. Since the early 1700s, paper IOU's exchangeable for gold or silver or other mental coins gradually came more into use, as the story of John Law suggests. Paper money is lighter to carry around, and can be denominated more flexibly. Moreover, with enough optimism, one ounce of gold can become the basis for any amount of paper money.

"to regulate the value thereof"

By 1787 when the US Constitution was passed by the first Congress, it had been decided that the federal government would control America's money. The colonists had been dealing with money controlled by monarchies and their aristocrats. The Founders wanted to leave feudalism behind by breaking this control of money by plutocrats and spread it more democratically throughout the whole society.

Section 8 of the Constitution states: *"The Congress shall have power ...to coin Money, regulate the Value thereof, and of foreign Coin, and fix the Standard of Weights and Measures."*

Astrologically, all systems were go for the creation of American money at this time. Some of the Founders were Masons and aware of astrology but not yet aware of the influences of the outermost three planets. Jupiter was then seen as the primary influence of prosperity, and it was found conjunct the US Mars. Mars was conjunct the US Venus. A more fortunate combination is hard to find.

Time and Money

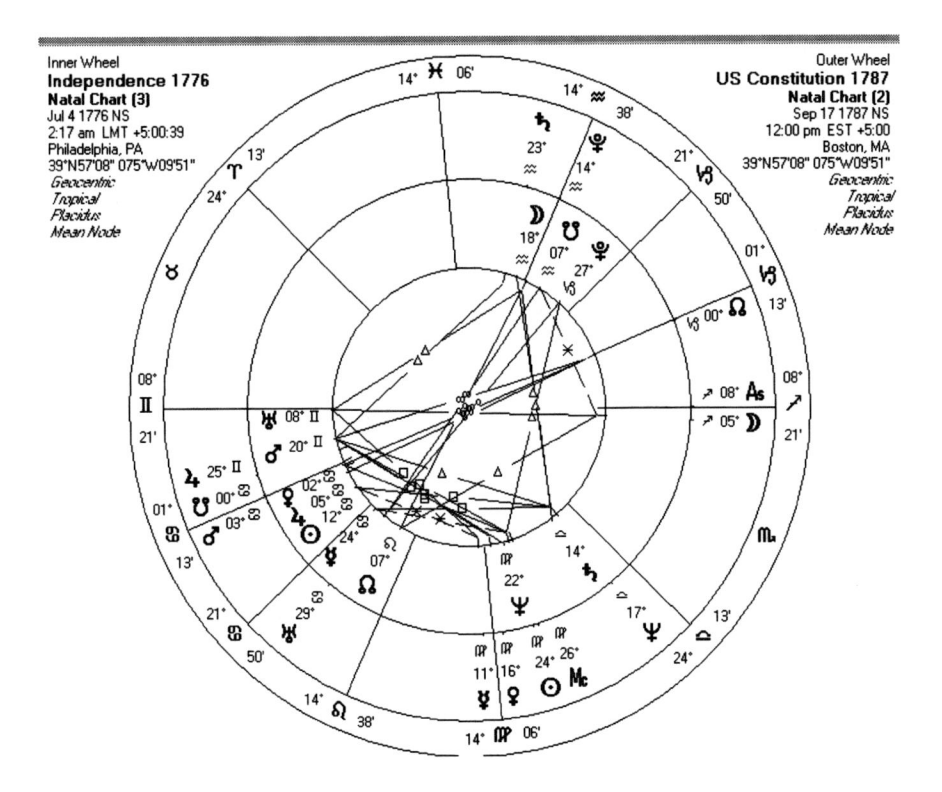

[Astrological chart: Inner Wheel — Independence 1776, Natal Chart (3), Jul 4 1776 NS, 2:17 am LMT +5:00:39, Philadelphia, PA, 39°N57'08" 075°W09'51", Geocentric, Tropical, Placidus, Mean Node. Outer Wheel — US Constitution 1787, Natal Chart (2), Sep 17 1787 NS, 12:00 pm EST +5:00, Boston, MA, 39°N57'08" 075°W09'51", Geocentric, Tropical, Placidus, Mean Node.]

Invisible to the Founders was Pluto, influence of long-range change, at 14 Aquarius forming a grand trine to a spot midway between the US Uranus and Mars in Gemini, and to the US natal Saturn at 14 Libra.

Saturn was at 23 Aquarius trine the US Mars at 21 Gemini, and if we use a generous orb, Saturn was also forming a grand trine with the US Saturn at 15 Libra.

Also unknown to the Founders was Uranus at 29 Cancer transiting opposite the US Pluto at 27 Capricorn—by itself a discordance. However, the only major aspect to this opposition was the US Pluto's trine to the US Neptune in Virgo. So, all in all, this was a most providential time for the passage of the document that would guide the new nation for the next two centuries.

Until the first US Congress took control of America's money, many and various things were used as money in the original 13 colonies, including a variety of other nations' coins, IOU notes, and wampum. The new nation wanted to standardize its means of exchange and keep its money under the control of representatives of the people. Even though the Founders were wealthy, most wanted to sow the seeds of an expanding economy, and this they did.

There were two attempts to establish privately-held national banks, Hamilton's First Bank and Nicholas Biddle's Second Bank of the United States. Both were given 20-year charters by the Federal Government, and both were discontinued at the end of those 20 years.

Rise of the Bankers

US money did well controlled by Congress for the next 126 years. The new nation rapidly grew economically. But also growing was a conflict between bankers on one hand, and small merchants, artisans and working class people the other hand: the sellers of money versus the users of money.

By 1900, the wealthy were feeling threatened by the ideas of Karl Marx, and by such panics as those of 1903 and 1907. Rough patches loosely called depressions were occurring just about every decade; there were two great depressions during the 1800s. Workers were blaming the rich and the rich were blaming the government.

In 1913 Congress created the Federal Reserve System, America's central bank. In effect, Congress got out of the money-creating business by handing it over to the bankers.

The astrological prognostication for the Fed was not as upbeat as the Constitution's. Saturn was conjunct the US Uranus and Mars in Gemini, tying it into a square to the US Neptune in Virgo, a negative indicator for financials. A grand cross was formed by the Moon's Nodes with Saturn and the US Neptune, and Mercury and Venus in Sagittarius. Pluto was conjunct the US Mercury opposite the US Pluto. Uranus and Jupiter were conjunct the US Pluto. Another negative indicator was Mars conjunct the US Sun, square the US Saturn. The positions of Saturn and Pluto, by themselves, would be enough to indicate difficult times ahead for the newly formed Fed.

Time and Money

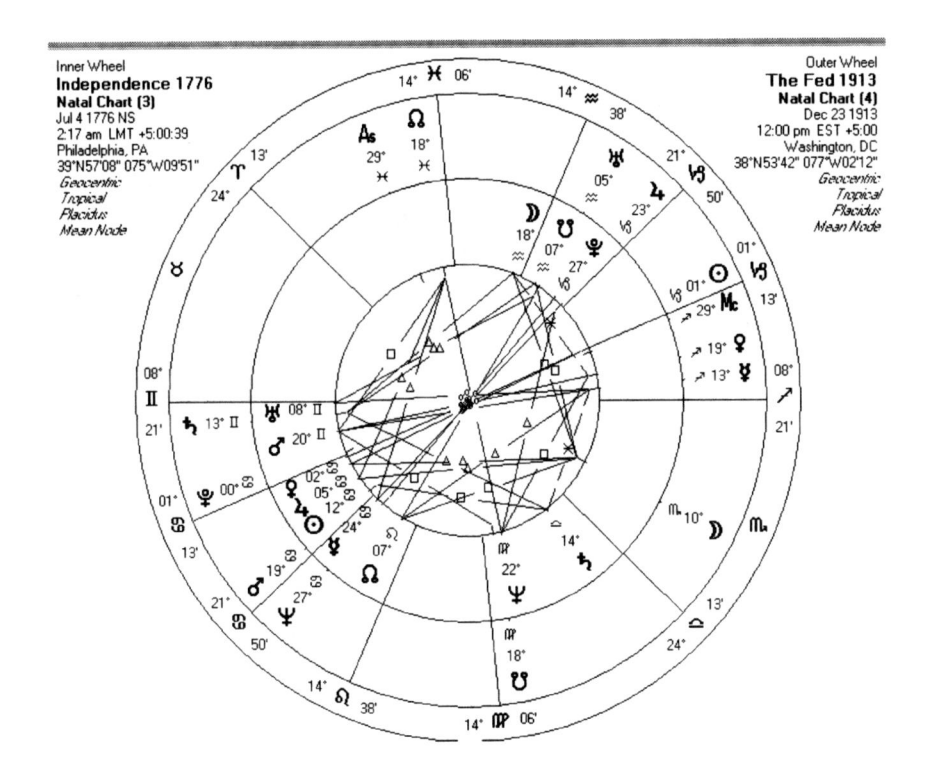

A Major Restructuring

The creation of the Fed was a major restructuring, as indicated by the heavy aspects to the US Saturn, ruler of structures and restructuring. Removing money from the control of Congress and putting it under the control of bankers was not seen by all as a good idea. Some argued that it was regressive. By this time, bankers were replacing the old British aristocracy, from whom the Founders had originally removed control of money. The goal of Congress, as democratically elected representatives of the people, was to make money as viable as possible; the goal of bankers, as the sellers of money, was to charge as much interest as possible. Exactly how much money bankers contributed to politicians to grease this de-democratization of money is unknown.

Then came the crash of '29 and the great depression of the 1930s, and on April 5, 1933, President Roosevelt invoked authority given him by Congress to outlaw owning or holding gold coins or bullion. Soon thereafter, Roosevelt devalued the dollar from $20.67 per one troy ounce of Gold to $35.00.

The Treasury, now the possessors of all the nation's gold (theoretically, at least), saw the value of their holdings increase by $2.81 billion worth of gold bullion. No one else inside the US was allowed to own gold except by the expressed permission of the Treasury. This was done to avoid a catastrophic run on banks to exchange paper money for gold. There probably wasn't enough gold in the world to redeem all the dollars in circulation by this point.

Mercury-Pluto Opposition

What emerges from a study of the three biwheel charts to this point in time, 1933, is that the USA's natal opposition between Mercury and Pluto is involved in creating and developing the USA's money. At each of these times of major change in US money, one of the outermost planets has been in late Cancer, conjunct the US Mercury and opposite the US Pluto. In 1787, it was Uranus; in 1913 it was Neptune; in 1933 it was Pluto conjunct the US Mercury opposite the US Pluto. Mercury rules communications of all kinds, including business; Pluto here speaks to the plutocrats operating behind the scenes.

At the pits of the great depression, Saturn was in Capricorn square Uranus in Aries creating the grand cross pattern with the US Sun-Saturn square. By 1933, Saturn had moved on to 14 Aquarius, forming a beneficent trine to a point about midway between the US Uranus and Mars in Gemini, and completing a grand trine with the US Saturn at 14 Libra.

The major negative aspect in 1933 was Jupiter applying to a conjunction of the US Neptune-square-Mars, with Mercury moving opposite the US Neptune, completing a T square affliction. But a T square formed by Jupiter and Mercury is nowhere near as difficult to deal with as one formed by Saturn, Uranus, Neptune or Pluto.

Time and Money

In July 1944, this new ratio of $35 to an ounce of gold was made the world's Reserve Currency. The World Bank and International Monetary Fund were established in 1947, and this $35 per ounce of gold was to endure till 1971.

These decades between the end of World War II till the social upheavals and Vietnam War of the 1960s were, by most measurements, the best for the US economy in the 20th Century. Not by all measurements, however, for the nation was still overcoming the lingering effects of the great depression of the 1930s; young men were still being drafted, this time to fight a war called a "police action" in Korea; the McCarthy Committee was holding forth, searching for communists in seemingly every nook and cranny of the nation; and the military-industrial complex, having discovered the magnificent profits to be made in war, was propagandizing for what came to be called "the Cold War" with the Soviet Union, the USA's military ally in World War II but economic competitor before and after that war. With the dollar consistently backed by $35 per ounce of gold, however, plus the Roosevelt Administration's socially beneficial programs, the overall economy steadily expanded to build a huge middle class. This was an ideal situation for the overall economy but not believed to be such by the banks' favorite clients, big corporations, whose mission was to maximize profits.

Gold Abandoned

On August 15, 1971, the world departed from its 2,760-year reliance on gold as the most basic and universal form of money and "entered the first era in its history in which no circulating paper anywhere was redeemable in gold by anyone." (The Privateer Market Newsletter, 2001.) "On that date, US President Richard Nixon 'closed the gold window.'"

Thereafter, gold was "just another commodity," not the basis of paper money. Officially, that is. Actually, people still perceived gold as the most basic form of "intrinsic value" money.

Robert Gover

At this time, there was an opposition hitting the US Ascendant and Uranus formed by Saturn at 5 Gemini within orb of 180 degrees from Neptune and Jupiter in Sagittarius. Pluto was in a separating conjunction with the US Neptune-square-Mars, with the Moon conjunct the US Mars, and Uranus applying to conjunction of the US Saturn, square US Sun.

Uranus and Pluto's positions suggested surprising, innovative and transformative financial events were in the offing. The 2760-year tradition of imbuing gold with the "intrinsic value" of humanity's most basic form of money had been broken by political decree. All nations' paper currencies "floated free," changing their ratios to each other monthly, weekly, then daily, hourly and with new instantaneous communications, in nanoseconds.

John Law would have loved this to pieces. It created the kind of financial system he had passionately advocated: money is wealth, therefore the more money there is, the wealthier a nation (or world) is. The amount of gold is limited but the Fed could print electronically as many dollars as it pleased.

Not Everyone Convinced

Outlawing the gold standard and converting gold to a commodity like soybeans and pork bellies did not convince everyone. By the end of 1974, gold had soared from $35 to $195 an ounce. Paper money had a history of creating financial crises. The USA was mired in the Vietnam War, civil rights for African Americans, an increasingly virulent antiwar movement, and a counter-culture movement, to name the most publicized. President Nixon left the White House instead of facing impeachment because of the Watergate scandal. The US government was increasingly being corporatized, and the US military was the mightiest in the world. Big corporations were lobbying Congress to lower or abolish tariffs on imports. Wages for working class people were slowly sinking.

To hold down the price of gold by official means, in August 1976 gold auctions were tried. By October 1978, the dollar had lost 25 percent of its value against a basket of other currencies. By February 1979 gold was at $250 an ounce, and then at $300. It hit $400 in October 1979.

Time and Money

President Carter's Fed Chairman Paul Volcker took a momentous step with gold at $850 in January 1980. He announced on January 28 that the Fed was switching its policy from controlling interest rates to controlling the money supply. Since the dollar had replaced gold as the world's most basic form of money, this was something like saying that instead of controlling the price of gold, Volcker would control the mining and refining of gold.

The US prime rate hit 20 percent in April 1980 and stayed there (with a brief dive in mid-1980) until the end of 1981. There was a rush out of gold and back to dollars.

To quote the Privateer Newsletter again: "In early 1980, Mr. Volcker's new Fed policy began to bite. US interest rates began to skyrocket. As they rose, the dollar first slowed its descent, then stopped falling, and then began to rise. Both the public and the investment community which had stampeded into gold were lured back into paper by this huge rise in interest rates—and by the prospect of a higher US dollar. The threat of financial meltdown was averted, but at a cost. The US Prime Rate hit 20 percent in April 1980 and stayed there (with a brief dive in mid-1980) until the end of 1981. There was a rush out of Gold and back to dollars."

Where were our astro-economic indicators at this time? On January 20, 1980, Neptune was at 21 Sagittarius, opposite the US Mars, square the US Neptune: inspiration, religion, idealism on the positive side, and deception, delusion, illusion on the negative side. And since 1980, the dollar as the world's basic form of money has been inspirational to some, delusional to others, and both inspirational and delusional by turns to many.

Pluto was conjunct the US Saturn, square US Sun, and Saturn and Mars were conjunct the US Neptune, square US Mars. This combination did not bode well for the long-range future of the dollar as the world's basic money. Uranus was trine the US Mercury and sextile the US Pluto. There were some electrifying, unprecedented, pleasant surprises in store for big business and the super rich, indicated by the US Pluto's position sextile Uranus.

After Volcker's decree, the price of stocks took off. The Dow rose from 776 to nearly 1100 between August 1982 and late January 1983.

Volcker had produced more dollars. People needed somewhere to invest them. But gold had been the basic money for so many centuries, people were loathe to abandon it; gold rose too, from $296 in June 1982 to $510 by January 1993.

Two Views of Inflation

There are two perceptions of inflation: too much money chasing too few goods, and no shortage of goods but rising prices. In effect, Volcker shouted "Let's roll" to the foreman of the Fed's money printing press. A long bull market in stocks, and a long stagnation of gold, had begun.

And of course the federal government rolled, too. When Nixon closed the gold window in 1971, Congress had a permanent debt ceiling of $400 billion. By late 1982, US debt had tripled to $1.25 trillion. By 2010 the national debt would be $13 trillion, Congress changed its "permanent" debt ceiling to "temporary."

With the dollar having replaced gold as the world's "reserve," the road was paved for an explosion of debt and credit, and for the creation of speculative bubbles in stocks and real estate at home and abroad.

"Derivatives" were first developed in the 1980s, greatly expanding the amount of employable dollars. Definition: "securities that derive their value from another physical asset, also known as synthetics, i.e. futures and options." Alfred Steinherr's book *The Wild Beast of Finance* published by Wiley in 1998 cautioned that the explosion in derivatives trading could destabilize the global financial market. Derivatives are a prime example of what I mean by investing dollars to make more dollars without producing anything but profits.

Back in the bad old days, people borrowed against gold stocks held in banks. After 1971 people borrowed on dollar reserves, providing more leverage for more aggressive trading, and greatly expanding the amount of money in circulation without increasing the Fed's money supply. This was a neat fiscal trick and, surprisingly, it caused a slowdown in inflation (defined as rising prices). The amount of paper money in circulation did not increase, it was the amount of "derivatives" borrowed on paper money that grew explosively.

Production and Profits

In gold standard days, production was the measurement of how much profit was made from the manufacture and sale of goods and the providing of services. In the post-gold-standard world, record profits could be produced without making anything for sale. Dollar profits ballooned "production" by derivatives trading. Little or no paper money had to change hands to produce this John-Law form of wealth, as credit card numbers and computerized "e-money" whizzed through the planet's electromagnetic field like swarms of e-locusts. This development coincided with a rare conjunction of Uranus (ruler of electricity), Neptune (ruler of delusions) and Saturn (structures and restructuring) in 1989-90.

By the 1990s, NAFTA and the WTO and the new high-tech industries in Silicon Valley were as popular as John Law's real estate along the Mississippi in 1720. By 2000, the outcome would be similar. Beyond 2000, Enron and other corporate scandals waited in the wings of history.

But the worst downside of this revival of John Law's fiscal theory was that the pyramid of wealth distribution became more like an Eiffel Tower reaching to the moon with a broadening base—unlike the ancient Egyptian pyramid proportions. The wealth of the rich skyrocketed while the middle class and poor sank.

Hit "Enter"

The World Bank and International Monetary Fund sold huge amounts of money to poorer countries at juicy interest rates—ostensibly so they could upgrade their infrastructures and join the wealthy nations, but in reality so the big US corporations could create a global empire. Which they did. When bankers lend money they do not count out and hand over the paper currency, they hit "enter" and transfer numbers from one account to another. Halliburton needs $7 billion to rebuild bombed out Iraq? Tap, tap, tap, enter and presto, $7 billion has been added to the amount of dollars in circulation without the Fed having increased the cash money supply; Hallitburton gets to work and the people of Iraq are stuck with repaying this loan. Theoretically, they do this by selling oil to American consumers, using the dollars earned to pay down the loan. Actually, that's not how it really works.

Does this mean the corporatocracy is also plundering the American middle class? Indeed it does.

"By the beginning of 2003 the United States' national debt exceeded a staggering $6 trillion and was projected to reach $7 trillion before the end of the year—roughly $24,000 for each US citizen." (Perkins, page 212.) By 2010 it was pushing $50,000 per citizen.

American Taxpayer-Owned

This humongous national debt is to be repaid by American consumers/taxpayers for generations. The American working class thus capitalizes the empire, buys its foreign-made products, then pays interest earned by foreign elites investing US taxpayer-derived dollars in government securities—this John-Law-like system has expanded dramatically for the past few decades.

"However, if another currency should come along to replace the dollar, and if some of the United States' creditors (foreign elites)...should decide to call in their debts, the situation would change drastically. The United States would suddenly find itself in a most precarious situation." (Perkins, page 212.)

"A decision by OPEC to substitute the euro for the dollar as its standard currency would shake the empire to its very foundations. If that were to happen, and if one or two major creditors were to demand that we repay our debts in euros, the impact would be enormous." (Page 213.)

Would the American and foreign elites who used this magical money making system to conquer the world's poor with debt—would the beneficiaries of this system be stuck with the bill?

No, it would be the American taxpayer who would be tapped to make up the shortfall in US government debt. The famous "full faith and credit" of Treasury securities is based on the government's ability to collect taxes from the American working class—whose wages have been dropping in terms of purchasing power since the mid-1970s, and whose jobs have been being shipped overseas or replaced by cheaper labor migrating north from south of the border.

Who's to Blame?

"It would be great if we could just blame it all on a conspiracy, but we cannot," continues Perkins. "The empire depends on the efficacy of big banks, corporations, and governments—the corporatocracy—but it is not a conspiracy. This corporatocracy is ourselves—we make it happen—which, of course, is why most of us find it difficult to stand up and oppose it. We would rather glimpse conspirators lurking in the shadows, because most of us work for one of those banks, corporations, or governments, or in some way are dependent on them for the goods and services they produce and market. We cannot bring ourselves to bite the hand of the master who feeds us." (Page 217.)

A Zero-Sum Game

Even if the dollar corporatocracy is replaced by a euro corporatocracy, the system wouldn't change. It's inadvertently designed to make more and more money profit for less and less people. Eventually, that becomes a zero-sum game. The elites eventually devour the goose that laid their golden eggs. But this is the system which has developed from Medieval feudalistic times and it's as faith-based as the immaculate conception. Belief trumps evidence. The overwhelming evidence is that this system creates huge amounts of money (paper and computerized numbers) while destroying what money must be based upon to be valid: real wealth. When gold was the basis for the creation of paper and e-currencies, money was rooted in material reality. The "genius" of Richard Nixon was to delink money from material reality.

Robert Gover

To some, the moral of Nixon's world financial revolution may be this: Do not abandon gold as the basis for paper money when happily expansive Jupiter is conjunct deceptive Neptune and both are opposed by the celestial task master Saturn. But, although Nixon delinked the dollar from gold, circumstances replaced gold with "black gold," oil. Neptune "rules" oil as well as such deceptions as creating paper money out of bankers' fancies.

The burgeoning need for oil by industrialized nations seems to guarantee that this magical money making machine is infallible, but that's another Neptunian delusion because oil is used, burned up, and the supply of oil is finite. Nixon's delinking of the dollar from the gold standard was inadvertently based on John Law's thesis. In turn, this inadvertently led to oil becoming the new basis for paper currencies. But oil is rapidly being transformed into the stuff that brings us global warming and all the horrors that promises in the not-too-distant future.

Gold, being immutable, cannot be transformed into anything else, nor can anything else be transformed into gold.

Which brings us back to this: "From the perspective of the ancient Mayan astrologers, the abstracting of money from Mother Nature means our modern world's financial system is ripe for radical change around 2012, change more revolutionary than any known in recorded history." (See page 4 of this book.)

We humans like to tell ourselves scary end-of-the-world stories. None have come to pass. We're still here. And if by "world," we mean the Earth, there's no reason to believe the Earth will not endure. It may give some mighty geophysical shrugs and bathe itself of what we humans experience as catastrophic weather events, however.

The whole world will undergo something hugely dramatic around this time, although precisely what is not predictable. Astrology enables the prediction of good periods and difficult periods—it's how we humans respond to these ever-changing conditions that determine the historic details. By 2010, what seemed ripe for transformation were the privatized money system and a cycle of increasingly more dramatic weather events such as floods, droughts, earthquakes and tsunamis. Since it takes big expenditures of government funds to deal with such weather events, the two are linked.

Time and Money

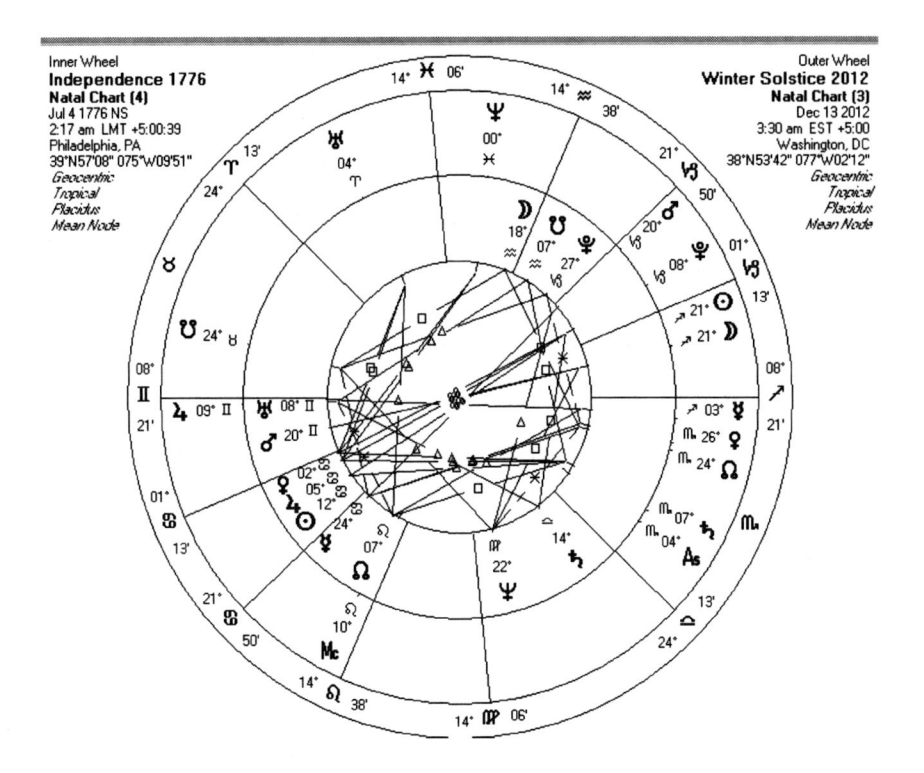

How Uncle Sam will react may be foretold by Jupiter, Uranus and Neptune. Jupiter is conjunct the US Ascendant and Uranus, expanding the USA's proclivity for volatile, headstrong, temperamental reactions. Neptune at 0 Pisces is within orb of a trine to the US Ascendant, adding illusion, delusion and/or inspiration, depending on the wisdom of our political leaders at this time.

Suggesting how our political leaders are likely to react is Uranus at 4 Aries square the US Jupiter and Venus at 2 and 5 Cancer. In a synastry chart for two lovers, we could say that this pattern means "opposites attract." Those who have been made destitute by the American global corporatocracy do have a kind of love-hate attitude toward Americans: they love the joy of life and music of the American people yet at the same time hate how the corporatocracy has removed, impoverished and discarded them and destroyed the ecosystems they once lived harmoniously within.

Robert Gover

The Lunation opposite the US Mars suggests violence, as does Mars at 20 Capricorn opposite the US Mercury and applying to a conjunction of the US Pluto. All these aspects combined with the domestic and worldwide situation suggests that the corporatocracy faces swelling resistance and/or a worldwide revolt around this time.

Pluto's previous sojourn through this area of the heavens coincided with the American and French revolutions; its next is more likely to coincide with a worldwide revolution. Those previous revolutions freed us from monarchies but did not trash the feudalistic cultural script. A moneyed mercantile ruling class arose, changing the names of the roles but not the functions of the role-players. Although we call the form of governance we now have "democracy," we are in fact ruled by autocratic oligarchs who function today as the feudal kings functioned before 1776. Consequently, a clash is brewing between the forces of real democracy and these leftovers of feudalism.

The Institutionalized Oxymoron

Strictly speaking, capitalistic democracy is an oxymoron. The aim of capitalism is to make the owners of capital richer; the aim of democracy is to distribute wealth as evenly as possible; the essential purpose of politics is to decide who gets how much of the collective wealth. It follows that if the USA were really a democracy, wealth would be more evenly distributed. In the early decades of the new nation's existence, wealth was spread more evenly. But the gap between rich and poor, by 2000, was at an all-time record.

Among contemporary thinkers who grapple with this big oxymoron, capitalistic democracy, there are some huge disagreements. Most of these disagreements are based on two contradictory assumptions: 1) that global capitalism must prevail, and 2) that global poverty must be eliminated in order for global capitalism to prevail.

There are periods of time when aggressive capitalism has dominated, creating wondrous wealth but new speculative bubbles and new record gaps between rich and poor, thus leading (when the relevant grand cross forms) to great depressions. Since the industrial revolution began with the steam engine, capitalism has developed parallel to modern democracy's development, which also began around 1776 with the American Revolution. Both capitalism and democracy have been gradually transforming since the late 1700s, and both are due to change dramatically when the next Uranus-Pluto square is in effect from 2008 to 2019.

Capitalism seems the best way to generate the most wealth; democracy seems the best way for societies to spread the wealth and govern themselves. Can we have both simultaneously?

Forms of Democracy

One problem is that there are various forms of both capitalism and democracy. The word democracy means governance by the people, but beyond that essential definition, things get gnarly. Does democracy mean governance directly by all the people, or representatives elected by the people? Should everyone have the right to vote, or should the vote be allowed to only those qualified? Who should decide who qualifies? Is a vote necessary to determine the will of the people? Must the will of a democratic majority usurp the rights of minorities and unique individuals? How can democracy achieve a wise consensus? Are elected representatives necessary? Or should the people be polled to settle each political question? Most importantly, whose version of information should inform the public and thus create public opinion?

Veneer of Democracy

For any form of democracy to work, an informed public is needed. Public opinions are shaped by information. Leaving aside ethnocentric beliefs for the moment, if the information people receive is controlled, perverted or restricted, democracy is crippled. Today's corporate media, owned by ideological capitalists, restricts information and propagates disinformation. This has given rise to the brain-snarling oxymoron, "capitalistic democracy." And to politicians owned and controlled by the wealthy few, so that we have governance of, by and for the rich only. Behind a veneer of democracy, we have reverted to autocracy, the antithesis of democracy.

Which brings up the question to be resolved during the up-coming long Uranus-Pluto square: What form of governance will emerge dominant: corporate autocracy, or economic democracy?

Until the expansion of the multinational corporate combines, representative democracy appeared able to stand between the rights of citizens and the profit-making zeal of corporations. But by the 1980s it had become glaringly evident that too many democratically elected representatives had prostituted themselves to the wealthy owners of capital. With enough campaign money, a politician can buy public relations manipulations of voters. And, given the religious-like belief in corporate profits, it seemed natural that the wealthy owners of capital should fund campaigns. Thus America's politicians joined the world's oldest profession and Congress came to house the best-dressed whores in the world, who virtually sold to campaign contributors the right to plunder the American public. I have dubbed this system "plutocracy masquerading as democracy." It has rapidly spread around the world.

Capitalist Delusions

Meanwhile, the delusion that "free-market" capitalism promotes democracy was propagated. Capitalism was likened to a small farm or business; if run intelligently it prospers. This is another delusion, for clearly the mega corporations that dominate food, energy and other industries bear little resemblance to the family farm or small business. The traditional farmers markets of developing countries still operate in a democratic way in that their "profits" are really wages, spent for necessities. A big corporation's profit is what's left after all expenses have been paid. Thus the profits of big corporations are a kind of tax levied on the public, and then invested for the further enrichment of the wealthy few, creating the imbalance that brings economic disaster.

During the great depression of the 1930s, the wealth imbalance in America was addressed by socially beneficial legislation to refurbish and expand infrastructure, public schools, unemployment insurance, Social Security, etc. These "socialistic" programs enabled a new round of capitalistic expansion.

By year 2000, however, every right of citizenship was under assault by the forces of "free market capitalism," whose profits (derived from consumers/workers) was needed by politicians seeking election to positions enabling them to collect and spend taxes from those same consumers/workers, and perpetuate the economic class system of the Dark Ages.

Robert Gover

"Bribe-ocracy"

Given current projections, the politicians in this "bribe-ocracy" will give corporations worldwide control of farming and food distribution, public schools, Social Security, health care, child care, municipal construction, sewage, sanitation, police, and drinking water.

There is an ancient Chinese proverb which says, in effect, that without a supply of drinkable water, there is no community. Water is capital in its most basic form. Without drinkable water, there is no production of goods and services. Given current projections, the multinationals will acquire ownership of humanity's water sources by essentially the same rationale Columbus used to acquire ownership of whatever land he put his feet upon.

Free Market Tyranny

Even George Soros, whose Quantum Fund has been called the best performing investment fund in history, expressed concern about this. "One of the great defects of the global capitalist system is that it has allowed the market mechanism and the profit motive to penetrate into fields of activity where they do not properly belong." (*The Crisis of Global Capitalism*, Public Affairs, NY, 1999). "To put the matter simply, market forces, if they are given complete authority even in the purely economic and financial arenas, produce chaos...The owners of capital...left to their own devices would continue to accumulate capital until the situation became unbalanced. Marx and Engels gave a very good analysis of the capitalist system 150 years ago, better in some ways, I must say, than the equilibrium theory of classical economics. The remedy they prescribed—communism—was worse than the disease. But the main reason why their dire predictions did not come true was because of countervailing political interventions in democratic countries."

As Soros sees it, the wealth-generating genius of capitalism must work for the benefit of society, and the way to achieve this is through democratic governance. But for democracy to flourish, a strict separation of wealth-acquiring capitalists and democratic politicians must exist.

Christianity and Democracy

Robert D. Kaplan makes a strong case for the demise of true democracy in his essay "Was Democracy Just a Moment?" (*The Coming Anarchy*, Random House, 2000, page 59):

"In the fourth century A.D. Christianity's conquest of Europe and the Mediterranean world gave rise to the belief that a peaceful era in world politics was at hand, now that a consensus had formed around an ideology that stressed the sanctity of the individual. But Christianity was, of course, not static. It kept evolving, into rites, sects, and 'heresies' that were in turn influenced by the geography and cultures of the places where it took root. Meanwhile, the church founded by Saint Peter became a ritualistic and hierarchical organization guilty of long periods of violence and bigotry. This is to say nothing of the evils perpetrated by the Orthodox churches in the East. Christianity made the world not more peaceful or, in practice, more moral but only more complex. Democracy, which is now overtaking the world as Christianity once did, may do the same...

"I submit that the democracy we are encouraging in many poor parts of the world is an integral part of a transformation toward new forms of authoritarianism; that democracy in the United States is at greater risk than ever before, and from obscure sources..."

Another Perspective

Kaplan apparently assumes free-market capitalism will continue to prosper and sweep the world. In effect, he says that since there is no alternative visible on the horizon, democracy will be subservient to this economic system, which, together with other social forces, is very likely to end or radically alter our experiment with governance by the governed.

Noam Chomsky approaches the big oxymoron from a different perspective. "I think it is hard to find a time in American history when policy has been so radically opposed to public opinion on issue after issue," said Chomsky in *Class Warfare*, Interviews with David Barsamian, (Common Courage Press, 1996, page 137). Chomsky sees the same erosion of democracy since 1970 as Kaplan sees but Chomsky is much more specific about the "obscure sources" involved.

Public Relations

Chomsky revealed that according to polls in the mid-1990s, 82 percent of the American population believes that the economic system is inherently unfair, that government is run for the benefit of the few. That statistic is amazing in light of another fact of American life. "We have a fantastic propaganda system in this country. There's been nothing like it in history. It's the whole public relations industry and the entertainment industry...And it is dedicated to certain principles. It wants to destroy democracy. That's its main goal. That means destroy every form of organization and association that might lead to democracy. So you have to demonize unions. And you have to isolate people and atomize them and separate them and make them hate and fear one another and create illusions about where power is."

Help the Poor, Kill Welfare

While 80 percent of the population thinks the government has a responsibility to help the poor, there is great opposition to government welfare programs designed to help the poor. Corporate/government propaganda has led people to believe that welfare is the biggest item in the federal budget when in reality it's miniscule. Propaganda also has the general population believing that huge corporations such as manufacturers of military hardware become rich because they understand "market forces." In reality, poor and middleclass taxpayers make the big corporations rich because the government funnels tax money to those corporations, then funnels more tax money to foreign governments to buy what those corporations produce.

Reforms and Threats

Propaganda has convinced the public that the Republican Party is pressing for "reforms." Chomsky points out that the word reform "has a nice feel about it" but "we don't call what Hitler did reform..." Newscasts proclaim that "you may not like what the Republicans are doing, but they're fulfilling their promise to the American people. If I say I'm going to beat you to a pulp, and I do it, that's not a promise. I didn't promise to do it. I threatened to do it. So what they ought to say is, the Republicans are keeping their threat to the American people. Especially when we know how the American people feel about it. These are not reforms, any more than we'd say Stalin and Hitler instituted reforms. These are changes."

"Provide Jobs"

In contemporary propaganda lingo, there are profit-making corporations which "provide jobs," and they are deemed good. And there are non-profit organizations which help the poor and elderly, and they "have agendas." Having an agenda, as compared to making a profit, is bad and should be "defunded."

"The big story," says Chomsky, "is the increasing concentration of tyrannical power in private, unaccountable hands..." Rightwing conservatives and liberals are together in the passionate drive to dismantle democracy whenever and wherever they can. Why? The social upheavals of the Sixties frightened conservatives and liberals alike. "There was this 'crisis of democracy.' People were getting involved in the public arena." Conservative and liberal protectors of the status quo had to "drive them back to their preferred apathy and ignorance...That led to a big attack on universities, on independent thought, on independent media, just about everything (independent) across the spectrum."

Free Thought and Kiddy Porn

Since those words by Chomsky in the mid-1990s, the Internet has arisen as a new and, for a time, uncontrolled, democratic media. People were communicating all manner of facts and disinformation via the Internet. Now there are attempts to control the Internet, beginning with a campaign against child pornography. If the public can be aroused to support a corporate/government crack down on "corrupters of children," independent thought can be thrown out with the kiddy porn.

A good argument can be made that the reason why industrialized nations, led by the USA, have such high rates of murder and sexual violence is that this is the only outlet of the oppressed. Isolate a society from common-sense solutions to everyday problems and illogical, perverse, violent non-solutions will arise. The divided and conquered take to dividing and conquering each other.

What it boils down to is this: those who control information, control opinions and a lot more. The public forms its opinions based on the information or disinformation it gets from its media. Information creates how people relate to each other, as well as how they relate to their rulers.

Doing God's Work

This is not to say that Columbus or his progeny of Books-Brothers-suited capitalists are motivated by evil. Many believe they are doing God's work. And individually, they are no better or worse than any other collection of humans. The problem is the religious-like belief that motivates them. In this regard they are the reconstituted priests of the Dark Ages who mounted the Inquisition against those they believed to be infidels.

But the larger Solar System context we Earthlings live within abhors imbalance. The end effect of such planetary patterns as Uranus-Pluto afflictions is to restore balance. Going into great depressions, there have always been new record gaps between the richest and poorest. By the end of those great depressions, those gaps have been narrowed, restoring better balance between rich and poor.

Hate Socialism, Love Social Security

The aim of democratic socialism, as demonstrated by such modern nation states as Norway, Finland, Sweden and Denmark, is a more equitable distribution of the collective wealth. Propaganda has conditioned Americans to hate the word socialism yet love Social Security, public schools, public parks, and other manifestations of democratic socialism. The masterminds of this amazing propaganda campaign aren't evil or greedy or anti-social. On the contrary, they believe their version of freedom (to amass family fortunes) is good for everyone, for all society. The freedom to amass personal fortunes is as sacred today as it was when Columbus arrived.

Even the Congress persons who voted to give media corporations something the government did not own and therefore did not have the right to give away—control of the public airwaves—do not see themselves as evil. The word democracy has morphed its meaning from government by all the people to government by the wealthy few whose fervent mission is to amass ever-larger fortunes from whatever resources they can find to exploit, including the trillions of dollars now confiscated from taxpayers. The politicians, caught up in the same religious-type fervor for capitalism, are acting on the same rock-solid belief: to "make money" is a sacred right. To those on the other side of the American class war, it's a baffling situation, for they too are steeped in the inherited faith, but are born without the means of amassing fortunes; instead, they are the means to the fortunes of others.

Ongoing Class War

This antagonism between the rich minority and the general population has been a fact of life since the original 13 colonies were established in the 1600s. The conflict between the aim of capitalism and the aim of democracy is now ripe to be resolved. And, although the form of democracy established by the Founders has been expanded during the past two centuries as suffrage was extended to all White males without property, then to women, and finally to African Americans, a wealthy elite has simultaneously managed to foil the true mission of democracy, and run the country to enrich itself—many in the belief that what's good for them is good for all.

Major turning points in this ongoing national saga have occurred when Uranus and Pluto have formed major aspects at points in the Zodiac where important planets were when the USA was born.

Every 110 to 130 Years

It takes Uranus 84 years to circle the Sun and Pluto 248 years, on the average. Uranus-Pluto conjunctions occur every 110 to 130 years, or 127 years on the average. To quote E. Alan Meece (*Horoscope for the New Millennium*, Llewellyn, 1996): "This is a loud signal to humanity that an earth-shaking, revolutionary transformation has begun...when these two planets come together, a great revolution begins that not only topples governments, but starts a whole movement, one which shapes the goals of all subsequent revolutions. Whenever Uranus and Pluto join forces, the status quo is seriously threatened. People jump ahead decades or even centuries and boldly experiment with radically different ways of being and living together. Afterward, they are brought 'back to reality' to gradually try to make the new ideas work under existing conditions."

The most recent Uranus-Pluto conjunction occurred during the 1960s in Virgo (conjunct the US natal Neptune and, for a time, opposite transiting Saturn). The Sixties was certainly a time of revolutionary passions. It left few Americans, no matter what their sentiments, unchanged.

Before USA Was Born

When Uranus-Pluto conjunctions, oppositions or squares occur in areas where important US planets were found in July 1776, America has been impacted, going back to years before the USA was formed as a nation state. No one has discovered a scientific cause-effect reason for this, but history verifies it as a cyclically repeating phenomenon.

Time and Money

The square formed during the time of Bacon's Rebellion in 1676 repeated during the great depression of the 1930s. The square formed in the 1750s and 1760s coincided with the French and Indian War, the outcome of which was to establish English language and culture in what is now the USA, and the rise of revolutionary fervor leading to the American Revolution.

During the 1820s and 1870s, Uranus-Pluto squares formed but did not directly conjunct, oppose or square those important points in the USA's natal chart. Both were tempestuous periods, however. In 1876-77, with Uranus 24 Leo and Pluto 24 Taurus, the bitterly contested election of Rutherford B. Hayes to the presidency unfolded, followed by violent outbreaks, as the following quote from the web site **WSWS:History** describes:

In the summer of 1877 a massive railroad strike erupted, the most violent outbreak of class conflict in the United States to that date. General strikes paralyzed Chicago and St. Louis. In Pittsburgh crowds of angry workers, responding to the shooting of 20 strikers by militia, set fire to the railroad yards and destroyed 100 locomotives. Hayes redeployed some of the very same federal troops that had been used previously to uphold the rights of blacks in the South to Northern industrial centers to suppress *striking workers...The events of 1876-77 brought to a definitive close the period where the political representatives of American capitalism could play a progressive role. From that date on the Republican Party, the main party of Northern industrial capital, shifted rapidly to the right, abandoning its egalitarian pretenses and operating more and more openly as the representative of the wealthiest layers of society.*

Women's Right to Vote

By 2005, democracy was thoughtlessly defined as "the right to vote." If Iraqis had the right to vote, Iraq was a democracy, even if the corporatocracy controlled the candidates Iraqis had a right to vote for. This shallow definition of democracy arose from the USA's history with the right to vote.

Robert Gover

When the USA was founded, the only people who had a right to vote were White men with property. That left out White men without property, all Blacks, all Indians and all women. Although the Fourteenth Amendment, passed in 1866, bestowed full citizenship upon ex-slaves and other African Americans, most Blacks were prevented from voting by various local Jim Crow laws and customs. Over time, it was to be corporations which benefited most from the Fourteenth Amendment, for they were able to twist the meaning of the amendment to redefine corporations as having all the rights of individuals. (More about this later.)

Some Indians, having mixed with Whites since the mid-1500s, were plantation owners by the time of the Civil War (google the history of the Chickasaw for more information about this), and were classified as propertied Whites. Women had mounted a long struggle to win suffrage dating back to 1848 and before. Suffragettes and suffragists including Susan B. Anthony, Elizabeth Cady Stanton, the Pankhursts, Mathilda Jocelyn Gage, and many others struggled long and hard to obtain this right. (The word suffrage, incidentally, comes from the Latin *suffragium*, meaning vote. Americans use Roman and Greek words to create the impression of authority.)

On August 18, 1920, American women finally achieved *suffragium*. That was the day the Nineteenth Amendment was ratified by Congress after a struggle dating back before passage of the Fourteenth Amendment declaring African Americans full persons with all the rights of White male citizens. The Nineteenth Amendment stated, "The right of citizens of the United States to vote shall not be denied or abridged by the United States or by any State on account of sex."

Notice that on August 18, 1920, Uranus at 4 Pisces was forming a very beneficent 120-degree trine angle with Pluto at 8 Cancer, conjunct the US Jupiter, indicating a revolutionary expansiveness. In the coming decades, women voters and women politicians were to play increasingly more active roles in American political and economic life. Saturn, this day, was forming a square to Uncle Sam's macho Uranus and Mars in Gemini, in effect throwing a wet blanket on the male chauvinism which had frustrated the drive for women to vote for about a century. It's worth noting that Indian women, before the arrival of Columbus, were active in tribal and national governments going back centuries.

Time and Money

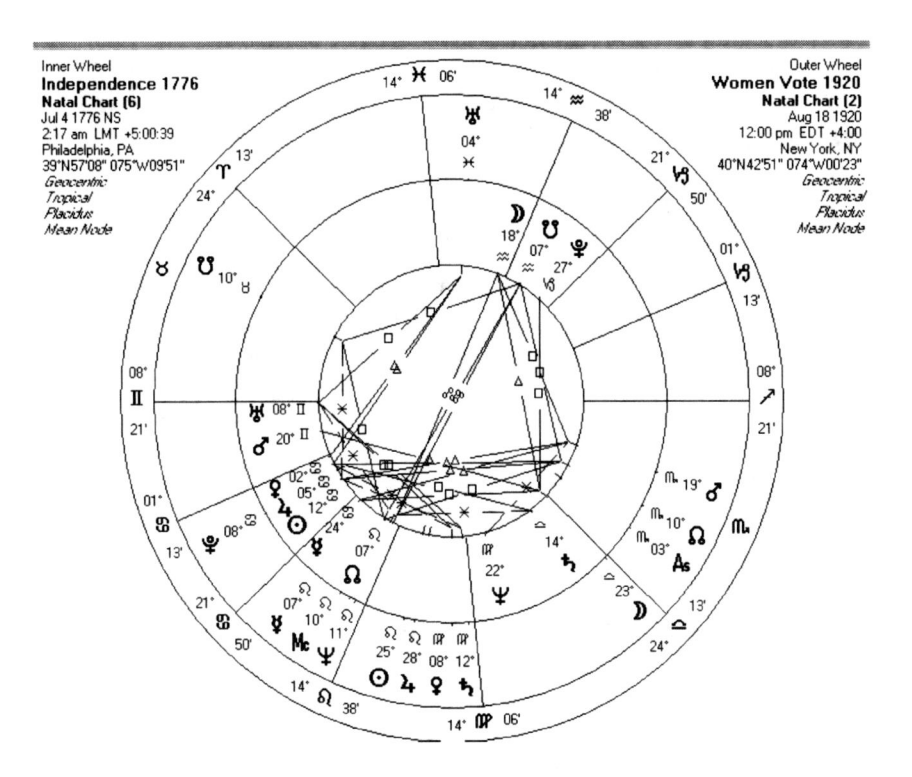

American women were granted by the US Government their God-given rights less than three years after the Russian Revolution of 1917, following World War I, and about six week before the stock market crash of Oct. 1, 1920.

What astrological signature accounts for this period of upsetting the status quo in both Russia and the USA? Pluto's transit through Cancer, conjunct the US natal 2nd house Jupiter, Venus and Sun. With Uranus trine Pluto, both the women's vote and the new economic system soon to dominate the USSR had a psychological impact on conservative investors in capitalistic countries. So when Mars moved from where it was for the passage of the Fourteenth Amendment (in Scorpio trine the US Sun and Mercury) to Pisces where it opposed Saturn and both afflicted the US Mars-Neptune square, stock markets were ripe to crash.

The fears of investors ripened the markets for crash; Mars and Saturn afflicting the US Mars-Neptune square brought what investors feared. Those who say, "The planets do not cause stock market panics"

205

Robert Gover

are correct. That's why astrologers do not posit a cause-effect relationship, but rather concordance, correlation, coincidence. Even the attempt to discover and catalogue all the zillions of greater and lesser strings of cause-effect happenings in an ocean wave would jam computers and breakdown brain cells.

In the 1960s, the conjunction of Uranus and Pluto coincided with a rash of rebellions to achieve civil rights for blacks and end military conscription—two big steps toward a more refined democracy. The waxing Uranus-Pluto square is due to arrive within orb in 2008.

Changes and the Masses

Uranus, bringer of unforeseeable surprises, wasn't discovered till the time of the American Revolution, which coincided with the French and Industrial revolutions. Pluto was discovered as the great depression of the 1930s was taking hold; its history shows that it has to do with masses of people and transformations which eventually impact all mankind. At hard angles, these two heavenly bodies have correlated with a long list of revolutions and innovations which have changed humanity's situation on Planet Earth, going back as far as astronomical calculations and historic records can take us. Thus, there is every reason to believe it will do so again.

Pluto and Class Conflict

Pluto in 2001 was roughly opposite where it was in 1905, when it previously afflicted Uncle Sam's financially sensitive Mars-square-Neptune. At that time the Industrial Workers of the World was formed in Chicago by unionists from all over the United States. Howard Zinn tells us that "Big Bill Haywood, a leader of the Western Federation of Miners...picked up a piece of board that lay on the platform and used it for a gavel to open the convention: 'Fellow workers...This is the Continental Congress of the working-class. We are here to confederate the workers of this country into a working-class movement that shall have for its purpose the emancipation of the working-class from the slave bondage of capitalism...The aims and objects of this organization shall be to put the working-class in possession of the economic power, the means of life, in control of the machinery of production and distribution, without regard to the capitalist masters.'" (Zinn Page 322).

The capitalist system was also under attack from some of the nation's leading novelists: Upton Sinclair, Jack London, Theodore Dreiser, Frank Norris. One of the strongest indictments of the system was found in Jack London's *The Iron Heel*: "In the face of the facts that modern man lives more wretchedly than the caveman, and that his producing power is a thousand times greater than that of the caveman, no other conclusion is possible than that the capitalist class has mismanaged... criminally and selfishly mismanaged."

Muckrakers and Plutocrats

This was the decade of the "Muckrakers," magazine writers and other journalists busy exposing the underbelly of the economic system, which was rapidly being consolidated by J. P. Morgan and John D. Rockefeller. If capital could safely be monopolized and workers made to function as interchangeable parts in the machinery of profit production, plutocracy would take a giant step forward. In 1907, the Carnegie steel plants of Western Pennsylvania employed 14,359 common laborers, 11,694 of which were newly arrived immigrants from Eastern Europe—a labor force not likely to communicate with each other, much less unite. Nevertheless, a new round in the class war want forward.

"It was a time," Howard Zinn writes, "of public investigations aimed at soothing protest. In 1913 the Pujo Committee in Congress studied the concentration of power in the banking industry, and the Commission on Industrial Relations of the Senate held hearings on labor-management conflict... The system was rich, productive, complex; it could give enough of a share of its riches to enough of the working class to create a protective shield between the bottom and the top of the society."

A Thrill for Investors

The "Progressive Movement," however, was largely an attempt to stabilize the boom-bust cycles of capitalism by encouraging greater centralized authority. The Panic of 1907 gave investors a roller coaster thrill by dropping the Business Curve from about 8 points above normal to 18 points below, a sudden, steep plunge. A biwheel chart for this market event shows Pluto conjunct Sam's Mars in Gemini, square Sam's Neptune in Virgo. Saturn at 22 Pisces is square Pluto and the US Mars, and simultaneously opposite the US Neptune in Virgo. As we have seen from our inspection of other stock market panics in US history, it's been when Sam's Mars-square-Neptune has been afflicted that such panics have occurred. If at the same time Sam's Sun has also been afflicted, the panic has been intensified. The one in 1907 coincided with Uranus in Capricorn opposite Neptune in Cancer, both afflicting Sam's Sun-square-Saturn. With all four outermost planets involved in harsh aspects to the USA's natal placements, this crash was among the worst in US history.

Trust Buster Teddy

From this astrological perspective of the US economy, it could be surmised that the nation was not in danger of another great depression in 1907 because, although Uranus afflicted Sam's Sun-square-Saturn, Saturn was in Pisces, not in Capricorn square another of the outer planets in Aries. No grand cross, no great depression. Instead, we had the waning Saturn-Pluto square. It was believed by the haves that ways should be explored to ease—if not entirely eliminate—stock market panics. And also such frightening events as the growing anger of labor. It was a Pluto-effect turning point in the ongoing class war which has marked American history since the Jamestown colony.

Under "Trust Buster" Teddy Roosevelt, Congress passed the Meat Inspection Act, the Hepburn Act to regulate railroads and pipelines, a Pure Food and Drug Act, and under William Taft, the Mann-Elkins Act; telephone and telegraph systems were brought under the Interstate Commerce Commission. The Federal Trade Commission was created to control the growth of monopolies; the Sixth Amendment to the Constitution enabled the creation of a graduated income tax; and the Seventh Amendment ended the election of US senators by state legislators—henceforth senators would be elected by the people.

The Fed

Of all these and other reforms, the one that would have the most influence over time was the creation of a central bank, known as the Federal Reserve System, designed to regulate the nation's money and banking system. To say that the Fed is simply another central bank, however, is to miss the point of its creation in America. A clearer way of perceiving it is presented in *Secrets of the Temple* by William Greider, (Simon and Schuster, 1987, page 11):

"The American system depended upon deeper transactions than elections. It provided another mechanism in government, beyond the reach of the popular vote, one that managed the continuing conflicts of democratic capitalism, the natural tension between those two words, 'democracy' and 'capitalism.' It was part of the national government, yet deliberately set outside the electoral process, insulated from the control of mere politicians. Indeed, it had the power to resist the random passions of popular will and even to discipline the society at large. This other structure of American governance coexisted with the elected one, shared power with Congress and the President, and collaborated with them. In some circumstances, it opposed and thwarted them."

Saturn, which had been in mid-Capricorn in 1901, in Pisces in 1907, was found at this time, 1913, conjunct Sam's Ascendant and his fiery Uranus. This has the effect of dampening the nation's tempestuous tendencies. Notice that Pluto, Mars and Neptune are strung out through Sam's Second House of money, spilling over into his Third House of intellect and commerce. These astro-economic indicators are positioned where anyone in favor of a central bank for the USA would prefer they be, especially with the Moon in Scorpio forming a beneficial trine to the US natal Sun. However, Pluto at 0 Gemini opposite the Sun at 1 Capricorn was destined to put the Fed through some kind of transformation after 2008 when Pluto moved into Capricorn.

Auspicious Timing

Also notice that Uranus, at about 2 o'clock on the outer wheel, is forming a 120 degree trine to Uncle Sam's Ascendant, and by tie-in effect, also to Saturn, tying harmoniously Uranian innovations to Saturnian systems and problem solving. This mix of positive and negative influences nevertheless bode well for the launch of an institution charged with the task of steering the ship of state through the roiled waters of economic storms.

This is not to say the Fed would enjoy smooth sailing. After Pluto moved over Sam's Sun in the 1930s to become part of the grand cross formed by Saturn in Capricorn and Uranus in Aries, the nation found itself in the great depression of the 1930s and the Fed was unable to turn the economy around as was supposed it would do. Yet as an instrument of the Hamiltonian outlook on what America should be, how it should conduct its business and employ capital to create wealth and defend the nation militarily, the Fed showed it was paramount among the world's central banks. Its only major problem is that it stands as a wall protecting capitalistic autocracy from political democracy.

Greider: "Political tension existed inevitably between Wall Street and Washington. They were separate capitols, in a sense, representing two different sources of power in the American society. One spoke for capital, the accumulated financial wealth generated by private enterprise. The other spoke for popular democracy, the collective desires of the voting population, rich and poor, owners and workers. The two constituencies were overlapping, of course, and in harmony on many issues. But the two centers of power were often in conflict on the most fundamental questions, particularly in the one area where they both exercised authority, the management of the American economy."

The Fed's Mission

If its mission were to function like an Indian chief and distribute the nation's wealth evenly to all the people, it would fit the democratic mold. As guardian of an economic system that benefits the few at the expense of the many, the Fed's goal is not the well-being of the population, but the perpetuation of assumptions inherited from Medieval Europe. The Fed was conceived by the interpenetrating interests of democracy and capitalism, but essentially it was Mother Wall Street's baby.

Greider notes that the Fed is more secretive and autonomous than the CIA, and that Henry Ford quipped, "It is well that the people of the nation do not understand our banking and monetary system for, if they did, I believe there would be a revolution before tomorrow morning." Richard Syron, assistant to Fed Chairman Paul Volcker during the 1970s, compared the Fed to the Catholic Church. "It's got a pope, the chairman; and a college of cardinals, the governors and bank presidents; and a curia, the senior staff. The equivalent of the laity is the commercial banks."

Robert Gover

People and Wealth

In other words, the federal government delegated the power to create and control money to a kind of Medieval sovereign Pope John Law, who ruled by something close to divine right. This separated governance by and for the people from control of the collective wealth, the source of true governmental power. In effect, the people have their government and the ruling 1 percent have theirs, and theirs protects and perpetuates the economic system that made them wealthy.

Just as John Law's first central bank in France of 1720 had the power to transmute coinage into paper money, so does the Fed. However, the creators and managers of paper money had learned a thing or two since John Law's Mississippi Swindle, and it had learned "crowd control" from the Roman Catholic Church, for it gives the impression that it knows things about money and the economy that lesser mortals are not able to comprehend.

Money Defined

Which brings up the question, what exactly is money? Greider has some interesting comments, delivered in the past tense, as though inspecting an institution that was but is no more. "Above all, money was a function of faith. It required an implicit and universal social consent that was indeed mysterious. To create money and use it, each one must believe and everyone must believe. Only then did worthless pieces of paper take on value. When a society lost faith in money, it was implicitly losing faith in itself...the money process...required a deep, unacknowledged act of faith, so mysterious that it could easily be classified with divine powers." (Page 53).

That's why early Hebrews did their banking in temples, noted The Wall Street Journal, and why later Americans and Europeans built banks that looked like temples.

And why Mark Twain satirized capitalism as Tom Sawyer tricking his friends into whitewashing his auntie's fence for him.

Time and Money

Bankers Are Human

"Bankers, however, could be dangerous," Greider (page 600). "They were human, after all. Left to their own impulses, they might be tempted to expand their loans and create new money infinitely—collecting more and more interest income, the main source of bank profits, until eventually the system collapsed of its own greed. They were restrained from doing so by the Federal Reserve."

In other words, the Fed was created to be a kind of intermediary between lesser mortals and the mysteries of money, and between capitalist greed and common sense. And the creation of the Fed came at a time (not long after a bi-millennial conjunction of Neptune and Pluto conjunct Uncle Sam's Ascendant and natal Uranus) when a long tug-of-war between the new forces of modern democracy and the old forces of Dark Age autocracy was growing in intensity.

Exporting the Oxymoron

During the 20th Century, the USA was to bring this tug-of-war to the world. Led by President Teddy Roosevelt, America had gotten deeper into the Old World game of colonialism by the time the Fed was created. As the 20th Century unfolded, the USA would use its other gift, political democracy, in a bait-and-switch to sell Old World capitalism. In order to accomplish this feat, America's ruling class would use its media to promote the notion that capitalism and democracy are harmonious, not contradictory.

This was a delicate balancing act. The aim of democracy (one person, one vote) is to share power equitably. Money is power. The aim of the classical capitalist is to manufacture for less money and sell for more money. To turn invested capital into profits, cheap labor and able consumers are needed. The Fed's job was to act as an intermediary between the interests of capital and the American people. Its mission was to create the image that the USA was a nation of stable money, prosperous markets and economic justice. To accomplish its mission, it would have to control the economy by predicting the future so it could anticipate and avoid the worst.

Self-Fulfilling Prophecy

The Fed's "estimates of the future are calculated by scientific reasoning, but the function closely resembles the prophetic role of the ancient temple priests who were given divine license to look into the future and foretell whether lean or abundant years lay ahead. The Federal Reserve governors make prophecy; and they have the ability to make their predictions come true," Greider reminds us.

Ah ha! The Fed has the ability of self-fulfilling prophecy! Thus it pilots the economy through the stormy seas of uncertainty. If a Fed board or chairman becomes convinced that it should add more money to the system, or raise interest rates, or discipline certain regional banks for certain types of loans, or loans to certain types of people—the Fed Chairman has the divine-like powers of a Roman Catholic Pope to order this.

The actions of the Fed, it may be assumed by the rational, has thus resulted in the landscape of early 21st Century America: inner cities that appear ravaged by war, and palatial corporate headquarters; the stark contrast in Washington, DC, of corporate-managed governmental opulence side by side with poverty, depression and escape into drug addiction found in the surrounding streets of the nation's capitol. The Fed is operated, after all, by people who adhere to the cultural script inherited from Old Europe, what I call "the Columbus mission."

Divining the Future

Astrologically, this can be read as the two major squares in Uncle Sam's chart: the square between Sam's Sun in the Second House of money and Sam's Saturn in the House of creativity; and the square between Mars in Sam's First House of personality and Neptune in his House of conscious thought and busyness.

As the Fed first set about divining the future by "scientific calculations," World War I erupted, involving the US when Uranus moved to 22 Aquarius and thus into a 120 degree trine with Uncle Sam's Mars at 20 Gemini, a positive omen for victory. At the same time, however, Saturn had moved to 23 Cancer where it was conjunct Sam's

Mercury (expression, communications, business, news, etc.) which is opposite Sam's natal Pluto. A reading of this last aspect is that the people would feel oppressed by the media (Mercury) and used by the plutocrats (Pluto). The result was a popular disenchantment with foreign involvement and the military.

In 1914, the larger worry for the wealthy was the growth of socialism. "The IWW (Industrial Workers of the World) seemed to be everywhere. Class conflict was intense." (Greider, page 350). Senator James Wadsworth of New York lamented that "these people of ours shall be divided into classes." He had the solution: "We must let our young men know that they owe some responsibility to this country." By country, the senator did not mean the terra firma, of course, for most of the land was owned by the rich and the government; he meant that working class young men owed responsibility to the rich and their government, which was soon to conscript them and send them "Over there," as a popular tune of the day jauntily sang out.

Over There

Over there was France, where 10 million were to die on the battle field; 20 million more people of hunger and war-related diseases, as governments controlled by capitalists fought over national boundaries, colonies, spheres of influence, for Alsace-Lorraine, the Balkans, Africa, the Middle East. But weapons technology had far outpaced military thinking. Soldiers were ordered forward into the fray as though they were still using muskets and horse-drawn cannon rather than howitzers and tanks. An attack launched by a British battalion of 800 left 84 alive. German attacks and British and French counterattacks along the Seine River cost 600,000 lives. British General Douglas Haig ordered eleven divisions of English soldiers to climb out of their trenches and attack. Four hundred thousand were killed. Another 300,000 were dead or wounded after a German attack on the Somme. Mutinies were occurring in the French army. Out of 112 divisions, 68 would mutiny; 629 men would be tried and condemned, 50 shot by firing squads. It was, in a sense, an orgasm of hubris-caused brain-damaged capitalism.

"The Greater Good"

Into this pit of death and deception came the United States, in the spring of 1917. President Woodrow Wilson had promised the US would remain neutral, but since the Americans were shipping great amounts of war material to Germany's enemies, German submarines were attacking US shipping, and when the Lusitania, a British liner, went down with 1,198 on board, 124 of them Americans, Wilson had the excuse he needed to break his promise, and the "greater good" of capitalistic opportunity to uphold.

Richard Hofstadter (*The American Political Tradition*) noted that "this was rationalization of the finest sort." In 1914, although there was no great depression, there was what is now called "a serious recession." J. P. Morgan would later put it this way: "The war opened during a period of hard times...Business throughout the country was depressed, farm prices were deflated, unemployment was serious, the heavy industries were working far below capacity and bank clearings were off." War orders stimulated the American economy. By April 1917 $2 billion worth of goods were sold to the European allies. "America became bound up with the Allies in a fateful union of war and prosperity." (Greider)

Artificial Community

W. E. B. Dubois saw deeper into the situation: this was a war for the plunder of what is now called the third world, but, he added, "It is no longer simply the merchant prince, or the aristocratic monopoly, or even the employing class that is exploiting the world: it is the nation, a new democratic nation composed of united capital and labor."

Howard Zinn puts it another way: "American capitalism needed international rivalry—and periodic war—to create an artificial community of interest between rich and poor, supplanting the genuine community of interest among the poor that showed itself in sporadic movements. How conscious of this were individual entrepreneurs and statesmen? This is hard to know. But their actions, even if half-conscious instinctive drives to survive, matched such a scheme. And in 1917, this demanded a national consensus for war."

Anti-democratic forces had a field day. Congress passed the Espionage Act, used to imprison any American who spoke or wrote against the government's wisdom in entering this war. The Supreme Court upheld it in a case against Charles Schenck of Philadelphia, who distributed 15,000 leaflets protesting the new draft law and the war itself, based on the 13th Amendment's provision against involuntary servitude. The Espionage Act remained on the books through World War I, World War II, the Korean War, and was even dusted off during the Vietnam War in a failed attempt to use it against American journalists who wrote critical articles about the American-created puppet governments of South Vietnam. It blossomed again in 2003 when George Bush II invaded Iraq.

Conscription

The IWW newspaper, The Industrial Worker, objected to World War I: "Capitalists of America, we will fight against you, not for you! Conscription! There is not a power in the world that can make the working class fight if they refuse." By 2003 conscription had been replaced by the unctuous skills of corporate public relations to rally "patriotic" Americans to Bush's cause.

As would happen again during the Uranus-Pluto conjunction of the 1960s, tens of thousands of draft protesters resisted; thousands were imprisoned, and the war went on as planned. When it ended in November 1918, 50,000 American soldiers had died, "and it did not take long, even in the case of patriots, for bitterness and disillusion to spread through the country." (Zinn, page 365). Anti-war sentiment became so prevalent that, by the time World War II arrived a couple of decades later, American military officers were forced to buy their own uniforms and were regarded by most people as colorfully costumed oddballs.

As for the newly established Federal Reserve, there was not much it could do about this public opinion defeat except keep Congress in check so it didn't pass any laws restricting the powers of the richest families, many of whom had increased their share of the collective American wealth during the "war to end all wars," as World War I was called. Another positive residual for the plutocratic system is that the American media could brag, "We have never lost a war!"

Russian Revolution

Such was the belief when Saturn next arrived in Capricorn and America suffered through the great depression of the 1930s. But there was to be another major event prior to this great depression which would impact American society, even though it occurred on the other side of the planet: the rise of the Soviet Union, instigated by a revolt of the working class in Russia.

The Russian Revolution was a series of conflicts in Imperialist Russia, leading to the overthrow of the aristocracy which had ruled Russia. The single most dramatic event—the one that would eventually seal the doom of Russia's old ruling class—came November 7, 1917. This armed uprising supposedly brought about a change in all economic, political and social relationships in Russian society. Russia and its satellite countries, which had been acquired by the Imperialist government, would thereafter embark upon a huge social experiment aimed at establishing the kind of economic justice envisioned by Karl Marx: "From each according to his ability, to each according to his needs." This ideal would eventually run aground on the shoals of deeply embedded cultural assumptions. Seems the Russians changed the names of the roles (i.e., Czar to Premier) but not the script's basic storyline.

Around the time of the Neptune-Pluto conjunction in the 1890s, other nations had experienced a stepped-up interest in democracy along the lines promulgated by the American Declaration of Independence of 1776. Not only had the seeds of anti-colonialist movements been spawned, but Marxist socialism as an economic system was being hotly debated in all the capitols of Europe. It seemed, at first to some, a natural outgrowth of American democracy.

"Enemy of My Enemy"

So this event on November 7, 1917, frightened the ruling class of America and other European nations. The US, in a too-little too-late attempt to put down the Bolshevik Revolution, sent troops to Russia. The fate of these Americans is not something that is prominent in official American history books, and about 20 years later, Uncle Sam would unite with this enemy, the Soviet Union, against "the enemy of my enemy," Nazi Germany.

Following World War II, Uncle Sam would revert to his pre-war stance against communism, bringing us to the Cold War years, which fired up America's anti-Communist passions, fomenting Keynesian investment in military preparedness. By the end of the 20th Century fear of communism would have dominated the American psyche for seven of the 20th Century's ten decades.

Unexpected Effects

At the end of World War II, fear of communism was to have unexpected effects. The GI Bill of Rights was created out of fear that returning veterans, if merely dumped back into society jobless and hopeless, would rebel against the ruling minority. Passed in 1944, the GI Bill provided veterans of all classes—male and female, White and Black—college educations, unemployment compensation and help with home loans. In effect, it gave a whole generation of working class people a taste of economic democracy, which resulted in a ballooning affluent middle class, creating the foundation for the best economic years in American history, expanding American potential in practically all endeavors. Because the American ruling class feared Soviet Communism, economic democracy took a great leap forward. There was more for every American. The share going to the richest 5 percent dropped from around a third to about 12 percent of the whole, but even the richest had more in total amount than before the 1930s' great depression as the whole economic pie expanded.

Robert Gover

State-Run Capitalism

Some argue, me among them, that the Soviets never really tried Marxist communism at all, but rather instituted state-run capitalism. Ironically, corporate capitalistic societies thrived by socially-beneficial programs creating a more equitable distribution of wealth than their communist neighbors. But by the mid-1990s, corporate financial interests were dealing with another communist (state capitalist) regime, Red China's, which had the classic capitalistic advantages of slave labor, authoritarian management, no real democracy. Meanwhile Uncle Sam chose to ignore the more democratic socialist societies of Scandinavia and make economic war on autocratic socialist Cuba.

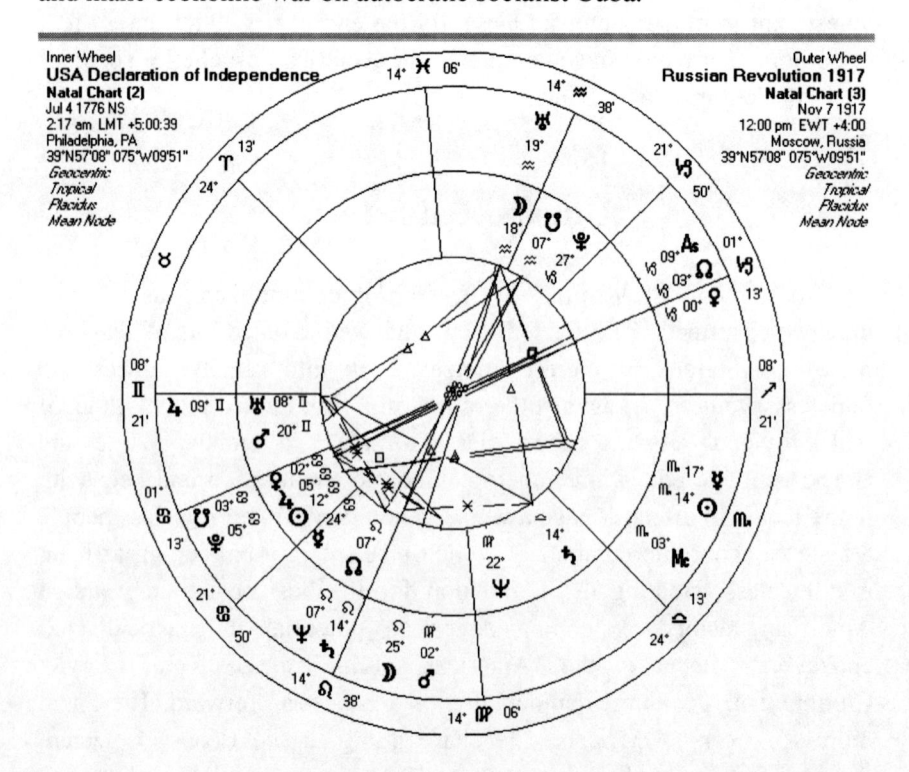

The next chart shows the planets at the time of the Russian November Revolution on the outer wheel and Uncle Sam's birth positions on the inner wheel. Given the kind of impact this event would have on the USA, we look first to the positions of Mars and Uranus at this time, the birth of the Soviet Union.

The USSR's Uranus is found at 19 Aquarius (near 1 o'clock), forming a 120 trine to Uncle Sam's Mars at 20 Gemini, which in turn makes it part of Uncle Sam's grand trine (Uranus-Mars trine Saturn trine Moon-Pluto). For most Americans, the Russian Revolution was a curiosity. To the American rulers of wealth, it was a horror, as described by the opposition from Saturn to Uranus with both hitting the US Moon in Aquarius.

The Soviet Pluto

The USSR's Sun-Mercury conjunction in Scorpio is square its Saturn-Neptune conjunction in Leo, indicating a tendency to narrow-mindedness, oppression, dishonesty, pessimism and economic delusions. The US Sun trines the Soviet Sun and Mercury (compatibility) but this is offset by the Soviet Jupiter conjunct the US Uranus, expanding Uncle Sam's militant independence. Adding to the angst was a square formed by the Soviet Jupiter and Mars. Above all, the Soviet Pluto conjunct Sam's Jupiter and cluster of planets in the Second House of Money, square the US natal Saturn, engendered deep distrust.

Down and Down and Down

The point of this skimming of history is to show that the US (as well as every other nation and each individual) has its being within a larger Solar System context. If we come to understand this larger context, it can save us a lot of pain and suffering. The history of economic astrology strongly suggests that this larger context abhors economic imbalance.

"Until 1929," writes Ravi Batra in *The Great Depression of 1990*, "the fateful year of the 'Great Crash,' a name coined by John Kenneth Galbraith, few economists were interested in the question of unemployment. They had been reared in the classical tradition and regarded business downturns and the attendant loss of jobs as temporary phenomena, to be replaced by prosperity and boom within one or two years."

Concentrations of Wealth

Then, as now, conventional economists focused on statistics and data having to do with the stock market and corporate goals. Workers were paid as little as possible and, as consumers, charged as much as possible. A poor and hungry work force was considered a great benefit to the economy.

"My argument," Batra continues, "is that depressions, as distinct from recessions, are caused by an extreme concentration of wealth. However, the subject of wealth disparity is more or less a taboo subject among established economists and those in power. Just look into the top ten economic journals over the past fifty years and you will find less than one percent of space devoted to this question. This is really unfortunate, because faulty economic thought frequently leads to economic disasters."

The problem is, among economists there is no universal agreement about which thoughts are faulty. There was no such agreement then, and there is no such agreement now.

Insatiable Wants

In 1929, prior to the crash, President Herbert Hoover's Committee on Recent Economic Changes, published a report that gladdened the hearts of supply-side thinkers, politicians and businessmen alike: "The survey has proved conclusively what has long been held theoretically to be true, that wants are insatiable; that one want satisfied makes way for another. The conclusion is that economically we have a boundless field before us; that there are new wants which will make way endlessly for newer wants as fast as they are satisfied...By advertising and other promotional devices...a measurable pull on production has been created..." (Jeremy Rifkin in *The End of Work*, Tarcher/Putnam, 1996, page 23).

In other words, supply creates demand: that was the fervent belief back in the 1920s, (and would return as the faith by the 1980s). "If we advertise it, they will buy it." Corporate bottom lines could be endlessly fattened by marketing campaigns.

"Unfortunately," writes Jeremy Rifkin, "the income of wage earners was not rising fast enough to keep up with the increases in productivity and output. Most employers preferred to pocket the extra profit realized from productivity gains rather than pass the savings along to the workers in the form of higher wages." Henry Ford's advice that workers be paid enough to buy the products America's companies were producing was ignored. "By displacing workers with labor-saving technologies, American companies increased productivity, but at the expense of creating larger numbers of unemployed and underemployed workers who lacked the purchasing power to buy their goods." (Page 24).

A More Awesome Panic

In the autumn of 1929 when there suddenly occurred a stock market panic more awesome than any other in US history, no one had an acceptable explanation, including the experts. John Kenneth Galbraith, premier among independent economists, captures the shock in the Federal Reserve at the time, and a whole nation depending on their prescience and prognostications:

"First there is the question of why economic activity turned down in 1929. Second there is the vastly more important question of why, having started down, on this unhappy occasion it went down and down and down and remained low for a full decade."

Astrologically, the explanation is that when Saturn reached mid-Capricorn, it formed a grand cross with Uranus in Aries and an opposition to Pluto conjunct Sam's Sun in Cancer, square the US Saturn in Libra. This was the fourth time a grand cross anchored by Saturn coincided with a great depression. Faulty economic thought greatly exacerbated the situation.

"Even during the depression years," Rifkin points out, (page 24), "productivity gains continued to result in labor displacement, greater unemployment, and a further depression of the economy...The economic system seemed caught in a terrible and ironic contradiction from which there appeared no escape. Trapped by an ever-worsening depression, many companies continued to cut costs by substituting machines for workers, hoping to boost productivity—only to add fuel to the fire."

Economic Catch 22

What amazes is that those "ignorant savages" who greeted Columbus when he ran aground back in 1492 never would have gotten into such an economic catch 22; the idea of profit was alien to them, as was a society in which some were ridiculously rich while others were desperately poor. The goal of practically all Indian economies was balance and harmony with Mother Earth.

Time and Money

The American economy, by the 1920s, was as successfully capitalist, if not more so, than its European counterparts, and thus subject to the same industrial-age booms and busts. This is not to imply that cycles of human abundance and scarcity do not impact non-industrialized peoples. They do. The cycles of economic highs and lows are "persistent," as Ravi Batra puts it, "in their longevity and antiquity." These cycles have persisted down through recorded time, and there has been no discernible, rational reason for them, only the observation that economies, industrial and agrarian, go through cyclical ups and downs. There is evidence that the ancient Egyptians, Maya and other peoples, millennia before the invention of the steam engine, were aware of economic-planetary cyclical correlations. However, the booms and busts of industrialized societies are exaggerations of these ancient cycles, and far more devastating.

Earthbound Time

If we refuse to consider the possibility that life on our planet exists within the larger context of our Solar System, we are like blind people groping for reasons why prosperous times and times of want occur in cycles, and why these cycles are irregular according to our earthbound measure of Time. Modern science, unable or unwilling to verify much ancient knowledge, has led us to the notion that modern knowledge is valid, while ancient knowledge is interesting but, like ancient ruins, not viable. My argument is that ancient astrology—the study of correlations between types of earthly events and planetary cycles and aspects—is in need of modernizing, because it is the key to our most excruciating economic problem: how to know when the next season of economic hardship is due and thus prepare for it. As more and more residents of Planet Earth are brought into the money (or post-industrial) society, this need becomes more and more acute.

Louise McWhirter, in the second paragraph of her book: "The way conditions exist today, man is the victim of the business cycle. With detailed charts and graphs, he can tell you when business began to pick up, and when a recession started, but he cannot tell you these factors in advance, with all his statistical research, because he has no time factor."

Forecasting Economic Conditions

McWhirter devised her method of forecasting business conditions based on the following: "It is a well known fact that certain countries are 'ruled' by certain signs of the Zodiac. That is, from observation and research, it has been found that a planet passing through a certain sign has a very definite bearing on the fortunes of a particular country. For example, the United States is strongly under the influence of the signs Gemini and Cancer and planets passing through these two signs, or forming major aspects to them, have a very definite effect upon the business conditions of this country, depending of course on the nature of the planet. The same is true of war conditions, crop conditions, booms, recessions, etc., the angular relation of the planetary bodies forecasting the conditions."

McWhirter found that it was the Moon's North Node's 18.6 year cycle which most closely correlates with the business cycle (as distinct from longer-lasting 30-to-60-year cycles which correlate with great depressions). "The word 'node' is the name for the points in the orbit of a planet where it crosses the Ecliptic, or Sun's path. The point where it crosses from south to north is the North Node; the point where it crosses from north to south is the South Node."

McWhirter's System

In her system, the Moon's North Node indicates the basic trend of business activity and volume. "Planetary aspects and angels to the North Node and to each other form the secondary trend."

Exceptions to her theory are primarily due to the angles formed by Saturn and Uranus, Neptune and Pluto.

My purpose is to keep the focus on those longer, more intense periods called great depressions which impact the whole economy, while noting wars and stock market panics, and those even longer-range

Time and Money

changes in human consciousness signaled by the twice-a-millennium Neptune-Pluto conjunction. And for this purpose, it's Saturn, Uranus, Neptune and Pluto we must look to, for it is their rhythmic dance around the Zodiac which correlates with great depressions and revolutions.

The Missing Time Factor

My premise is simple: based on certain past planetary configurations which coincided with drastic economic conditions, we have a key to unlock the mystery of when another drastic economic time will arrive. In other words, we have what we need to provide that time factor that's been missing in modern economics.

This astrological system does not correlate with Greenwich Mean Time; does not correlate with our clocks. To grasp this larger sense of time, we must send our minds out into the universe, as the ancient astrologers must have done. Out there among the distant galaxies, as we imagine looking down on our Solar System and see how tiny our Earth is in relation to the other planets, it's easier to appreciate how our well-being here on Earth is linked to the movements and angles of these huge heavenly bodies in the big molecule.

Reading the Stars

Those who have not studied astrology may wonder why two different systems of astrological prediction work—McWhirter's and mine, for instance. The answer is this: McWhirter's aim was to track the cycles of the business curve's ups and downs; mine is to locate those drastic times when great depressions and wars have brought major upheavals. I learned from McWhirter's research that her system was greatly affected by angles from Saturn, Uranus, Neptune or Pluto. She used a chart for the establishment of the New York Stock Exchange. Both her system and mine work because the New York Stock Exchange is part of the corpus that composes this entity, the USA, Uncle Sam, born on the forth of July in 1776. Sam's birth is the constant moment in time

Robert Gover

which I am using to track how great depressions and wars correlate with angles formed by Saturn, Uranus, Neptune and Pluto.

McWhirter died not long after the on-set of the Great Depression. Since it's the only great depression recent enough to have been personally experienced by some still alive today, it is known now as *The Great Depression*. If we take a centuries-long view of the economy, it may have been the worst depression in US history, but certainly not the worst humanity has ever endured. To compare it to pre-industrial age depressions is somewhere between difficult and impossible, however, because before industrialization, great depressions had to do with severe-weather-caused famines, floods, or other natural catastrophes. Modern great depressions have correlated with such natural catastrophes, too, but are also exacerbated by the decisions made by those who control large financial and industrial interests. Pre-industrial people could store food in good times to get them through bad times.

Finger of Blame

Much has been written by economists and others about how, and more importantly why, the stock market crash of October 26, 1929, seemingly precipitated this catastrophe we now refer to as The Great Depression. During and since the 1930s, pointing the finger of blame became something of a sport: the government was to blame; the industrialists were; the unions were, or the Federal Reserve System. In retrospect, Monetarists blame Keynesians, and vice versa. McWhirter offers this explanation:

"The lunation, or New Moon, occurred October 2, 1929 in 8 degrees Libra, exactly opposition aspect (180 degrees) to the chaotic and epoch-making planet Uranus which was posited in the mid-heaven of the New York Stock Exchange Chart (and/or in mid-Aries)."

(I should add a reminder here that astrologers do not believe the "stars control destiny." The astrological belief is that when planetary angles become harsh, whatever earthly things need to be put back into balance will be put back into balance—hopefully with the cooperation of the affected entity, but without it if necessary.)

Time and Money

Great Depression Reviewed

In my system, the New Moon of October 2 at 8 Libra occurred within 7-degree orb of a conjunction with Sam's economically sensitive Saturn at 15 Libra, both opposite transiting Uranus at 8 Aries, square Sam's Sun at 14 Cancer, which was conjoined at the time by Pluto, opposite transiting Saturn, creating a grand cross pattern to Sam's Sun-Saturn square.

I've included three charts for the great depression of the '30s to show how the grand cross tightened.

When the "big crash" began in late October 1929, Saturn was 26 Sagittarius, creating a T square to the US Mars-Neptune square.

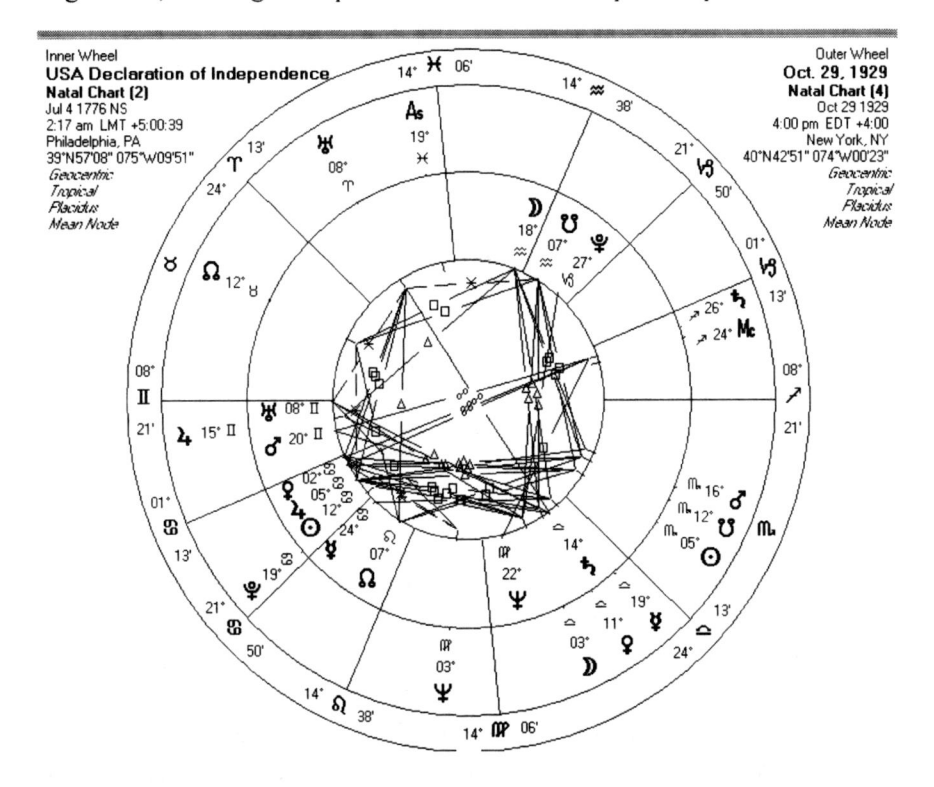

By January 1, 1930, Saturn had moved to 13 Capricorn, opposite the US Sun and square Uranus at 7 Aries, within orb of an opposition to Sam's Saturn.

Robert Gover

By September 22, 1931, at the point some consider the pits of the crash, Saturn at 16 Capricorn and Uranus at 18 Aries had tightened their square and also the grand cross pattern formed with the US Sun-Saturn square. Pluto in Cancer conjunct the US Sun and square transiting Uranus foreshadowed major changes in the USA's Sun "I Am" sense of itself.

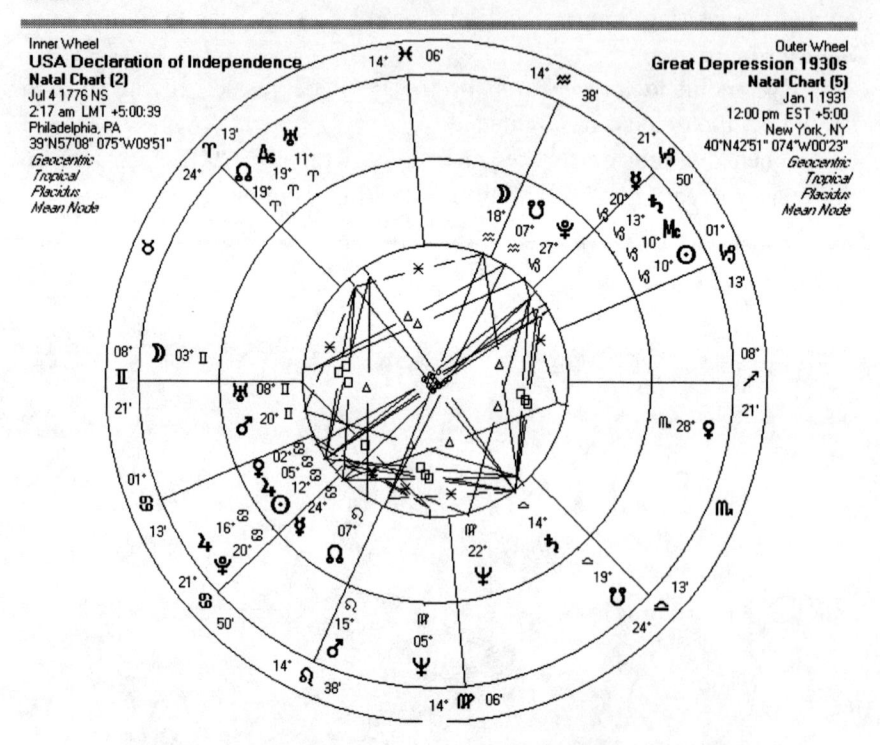

As I pointed out previously, exactly when this great depression hit bottom is debatable. Saturn had gone retrograde for months during 1931 and stock prices ticked upward—till September 22, 1931 when Saturn turned direct again, and signs of a stock market and overall economic recovery vanished. Notice that in 1931 Pluto at 21 Cancer continues to be very much a part of this grand cross pattern. Because Pluto would linger so long in late Cancer, this grand cross didn't really separate till February of 1932, when Saturn moved from Capricorn into Aquarius. Uranus and Pluto were to maintain their square till mid-1936, when

Time and Money

Uranus moved on through Taurus while Pluto continued to linger in late Cancer, fomenting World War II. This is especially pertinent because during the 2000-teens, Pluto will linger opposite Cancer in Capricorn, square Uranus again in Aries.

Astrologically, the point is this: the stock market crashed when Saturn afflicted Sam's Mars-Neptune square, and the economy then went into its fourth great depression when Saturn, Uranus and Pluto formed a grand cross to the US Sun-Saturn square.

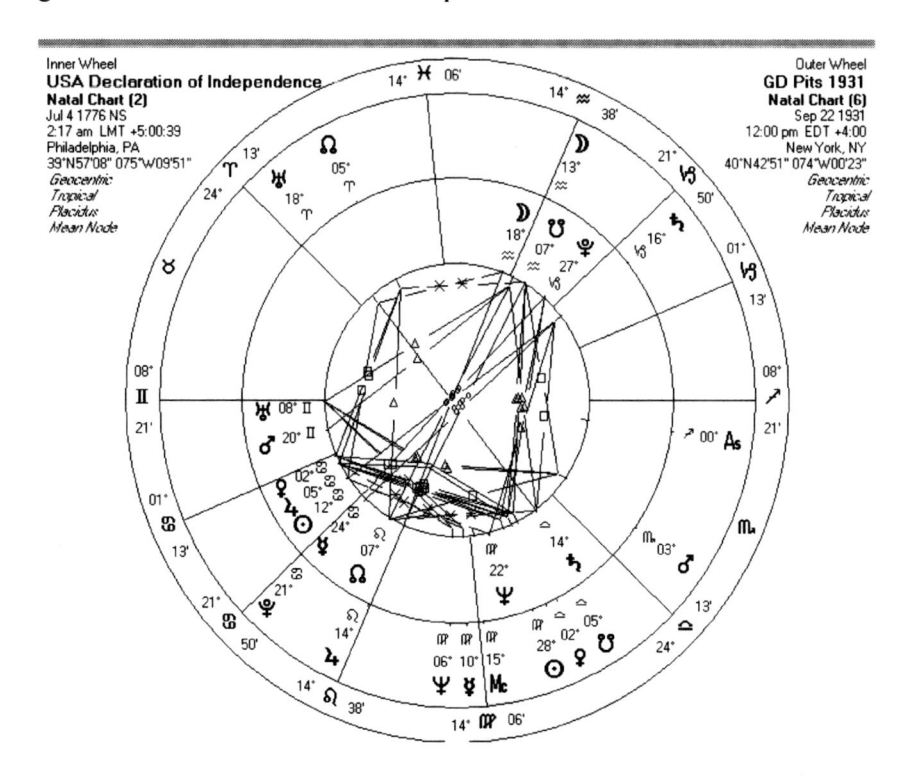

Stocks and Overall Economy

During the worst of this great depression, all four of the astro-economic indicators were in malefic aspect to sensitive points in Uncle Sam's birth chart. They were likewise to McWhirter's transit chart for the New York Stock Exchange, so both her system and mine show this

Robert Gover

planetary correlation to the Great Crash of '29, even though hers focuses on the Moon's Nodes and the stock market, and mine on the outermost planets and the overall economy.

But McWhirter was also aware of the outermost planets, for these are what upset the rhythmic cycles of the Nodes: "From October through December 1929 the Business Curve dropped 16 points. Saturn moved into Capricorn November 30, and came within an orb of an unfavorable aspect (90 degrees) to Uranus (in Aries)."

At the depths of this catastrophe, Saturn was in mid-Capricorn, she noted, and Uranus was in mid-Aries, "in unfavorable aspect to Pluto and Jupiter." If we juxtapose this configuration over Sam's birth chart, we get the grand cross pattern shown in my charts for this period.

McWhirter: "Uranus has the most unusual, revolutionary, unexpected and epoch-making effects upon conditions, and surely this final crash, for which Uranus was responsible, was epoch-making. It caught most traders unaware of danger, and then wiped them out. This panic, which saw industrial averages plummet from a high of 381 to a low of 198 by the middle of November, and Rail averages drop from a high of 189 to a low of 128 in the same length of time, marked the beginning of a period, the effects of which have dominated the 1930s."

With the Dow-Jones Average around 10,000, a comparable drop would show the Dow around 5,200. As was the case in 1929, this would mean that heavily leveraged investors would be immediately wiped out, unless the Dow rebounded quickly as it did on Black Monday, October 19, 1987. No grand cross formed in 1987. No grand cross, no great depression. Just a stock market panic, notable for a one-day stock drop, 508 points, about 22 percent, and how quickly prices rebounded.

For this second edition, here is a quote from Wikipedia about the Crash of 2008 to the low of March 2009:

"On October 9, 2007, the Dow Jones Industrial Average closed at the record level of 14,164.53. Two days later on October 11, the Dow would trade at its highest intra-day level ever, at the 14,198.10 mark...On September 15, 2008...The DJIA lost more than 500 points for only the sixth time in history, returning to its mid-July lows below the 11,000 level. A series of bailout packages... did not prevent further losses. After two months of extreme volatility during which the Dow experienced its largest one day point loss, largest daily point gain, and largest intra-day range (more than 1,000 points), the index closed at a new twelve-year low of 6,547.05 on March 9, 2009 (after an intra-day low of 6,469.95 during the March 6 session), its lowest close since April 1997, and had lost 20% of its value in only six weeks" (and 4,728 points from its high in 2007).

Astrologically, this 19-month plunge coincided with a Saturn-Uranus opposition hitting the US Mars-Neptune square—Saturn conjunct and Uranus opposite the US Neptune, square US Mars.

Contrast: 1929 and 1987

By contrast, between September 1929 and June 1932 stock prices fell 86.2 percent. Note, too, that coinciding with the 1987 panic was an opposition affliction to Sam's Mars from Saturn and Uranus in Sagittarius. With no "heavy" opposite Sam's Saturn from Aries, the Crash of '87 was a stock market event, not the prelude to another great depression.

To help clarify what a stock market crash without a rebound would mean in the late 1990s, let's consider a hypothetical situation: Joe Blow has $500,000 invested in stocks, 50 percent of that ($250,000) borrowed—considered a very smart move because he is thus able to take advantage of record-breaking run-ups of tech stocks, which occurred during the roaring bull market of the 1990s. Suddenly he is faced with a market crash that wipes out 50 percent his portfolio. He's forced to sell to repay the $250,000 he owes. This removes him entirely from the stock market. He owns a house worth $250,000, let's say, and has a good job. Because of the market crash, his company is forced to declare bankruptcy and Joe loses his job. He tries desperately to trim back on expenses and find a new job, but competition for the reduced number of jobs is cutthroat—a lot of people are in Joe's situation. He takes his kids out of private school, his wife finds work as a waitress but makes far from enough to make ends meet, so eventually he's unable to save his house: the bank repossesses it. Thus Joe goes from prosperity to poverty—at which point he probably reconsiders his grandfather's "irrational fear" of stock market investing.

Grim Scenarios

Theoretically, if the market in the 1990s had dropped 82 percent as it did in the 1930s, Joe's $500,000 would have plummeted to $90,000, leaving him $160,000 in debt to his lender; he'd be totally wiped out and in debt.

For those wealthier than Joe, those not leveraged and able to stay in the equities markets come hell or high water, a drop comparable to the 1929-1932 plunge of 82 percent would mean a portfolio worth $50 million would wind up worth around $9 million. And of course there were those who surfed the plunge with put options, creating huge fortunes as the Dow fell. The money lost in the crash did not evaporate, it wound up with those who sold short.

As I write this in April 2001, the NASDAQ has brought carnage to its heaviest investors, having dropped over 60 percent, with no bottom in sight. Someone focused on the high-tech bull market of the late 1990s, and leveraged 50 percent, could have seen $10 million reduced to $4 million. And if half that $10 million had been borrowed, he might have a debt of $1 million, depending on when he'd bought into the NASDAQ rally and when he'd bailed out.

If Pluto's slow sojourn through Sagittarius continues to impact stock markets during the first decade of the 21st Century, as I expect it will, and if the battle cry of the average investor continues to be "Buy on the dips," there could be a virtual Super Bowl Blame Game by 2008.

In 1929, rational, scientifically-oriented economists tried mightily to figure out the whys and hows. "Each generation, it seems," says Greider (Page 90), "discovered new truths from its own experience and discarded competing truths from the past." From the astrological perspective, this is like deducing from the conditions this winter what conditions will be like every winter, and thus what must be done every winter to cope—when in reality each winter is different.

After the Crash

"After the crash," writes Zinn on page 378, "the economy was stunned, barely moving. Over five thousand banks closed and huge numbers of businesses, unable to get money, closed too. Those that continued, laid off employees and cut the wages of those who remained, again and again. Industrial production fell by 50 percent, and by 1933 perhaps 15 million (no one knows exactly)—one-fourth or one-third of the labor force—were out of work. The Ford Motor Company, which in the spring of 1929 had employed 128,000 workers, was down to 37,000 by August of 1931."

Not long before the crash, President Herbert Hoover had said, "We in America today are nearer the final triumph over poverty than ever before in the history of any land." After the crash, former President Calvin Coolidge said, "When more and more people are thrown out of work, unemployment results"—in case anyone was wondering. He added to that gem by saying, "This country is not in good condition." Presidents usually understate economic bad news unless, as President George Bush did in 2001, they blame it on a predecessor.

Overcoming Common Sense

Given a different corpus of cultural and economic assumptions, there are indications that the nation could have weathered this economic "storm of the century" much easier, for there was plenty of food being grown and the stock market crash had not diminished the housing stock. But farmers, faced with loses after transporting and selling their produce, destroyed much of it. "There were lots of houses but they stayed empty because people couldn't pay the rent, had been evicted, and now lived in shacks in quickly formed 'Hoovervilles' built on garbage dumps." (Zinn page 378).

In *The Grapes of Wrath*, John Steinbeck's novel about the depression, we get a stronger feel of these times:

And a homeless hungry man, driving the road with his wife beside him and his thin children in the back seat, could look at the fallow fields which might produce food but not profit, and that man could know how a fallow field is a sin and the unused land a crime against the thin children...

And in the south he saw the golden oranges hanging on the trees, the little golden oranges on the dark green trees; and guards with shotguns patrolling the lines so a man might not pick an orange for a thin child, oranges to be dumped if the price was too low...

Store Invaders

In pre-industrial times, ripening fruit would be for eating; now it was for profit and could not be eaten till it had been sold. This tended to make otherwise peaceful people dangerous.

"England, Arkansas, January 3, 1931. The long drought that ruined hundreds of Arkansas farms last summer had a dramatic sequel late today when some 500 farmers, most of them White men and many of them armed, marched on the business section of this town... Shouting that they must have food for themselves and their families, the invaders announced their intention to take it from the stores unless it were provided from some other source without cost."

In Detroit, a mounted policeman was knocked off his horse by a stone to the head when 2,000 men and women met in Grand Circus Park in defiance of police orders. In Chicago, 500 school children marched on the Board of Education to demand food; in Boston 25 hungry children raided a buffet luncheon set up for Spanish American War veterans and "two automobile-loads of police were called to drive them away." In Seattle, 5,000 unemployed besieged the County-City Building for two days before police managed to evict them.

The Bonus Army

In the spring and summer of 1932, World War I veterans formed the Bonus Army and marched on Washington, demanding immediately payment by Congress of bonuses due years in the future. Eventually, more than 20,000 camped across the Potomac River from the Capitol on Anacostia Flats. Four troops of cavalry, four companies of infantry, a machine gun squadron and six tanks were assembled to drive the vets out. When the tear gas had cleared, the whole encampment was ablaze, two veterans had been shot to death, an 11-week-old baby had died, two policemen had fractured skulls and a thousand veterans had been injured by gas.

The song, "Brother, Can You Spare A Dime" became popular; years later its writer would tell Studs Terkel:

"In the song the man is really saying: 'I made an investment in this country. Where the hell are my dividends?' It's more than just a bit of pathos. It doesn't reduce him to a beggar. It makes him a dignified human, asking questions—and a bit outraged, too, as he should be."

People Help Themselves

By the time Franklin Delano Roosevelt took office in 1932, desperate people were not waiting for government help, they were helping themselves. Some walked into stores and walked out with food, using guns if necessary. "All over the country people organized to stop evictions...when word spread that someone was being evicted, a crowd would gather; the police would remove the furniture from the house, put it out on the street, and the crowd would bring the furniture back." (Zinn page 385)

"In Seattle, the fisherman's union caught fish and exchanged them with people who picked fruit and vegetables, and those who cut wood exchanged that. There were twenty-two locals, each with a commissary where food and firewood were exchanged for other goods and services: barbers, seamstresses, and doctors gave of their skills in return for other things. By the end of 1932, there were 330 self-help organizations in 37 states with over 300,000 members. By early 1933, they seem to have collapsed; they were attempting too big a job in an economy that was more and more a shambles." (Zinn, page 385).

Robert Gover

Juries Refuse to Convict

In Pennsylvania, unemployed coal miners snuck onto company property and mined coal, trucked it to cities, sold it below the commercial rate. By 1934, 5 million tons of this bootleg coal were produced by 20,000 men. When some were arrested, juries would not convict and jailers would not imprison.

It was during this time that the Communist Party USA swelled its membership, throwing a real scare into the ruling elite and their chattering buffer class. What if communist party organizers and others of a socialist persuasion were able to unite the people? Visions of the kind of violence which had swept Russia about 30 years previous danced in their minds as the depression worsened. Conservatives hated FDR with a blood-thirsty passion, fearing the new president was "class conscious" (sympathetic to the poor) and would turn the people against them. When the Wagner-Connery Bill was introduced in Congress to provide for the election of union representatives and the settlement of grievances, some thought this a violation of the American Way, destroying the "individuality" of workers. The ruling elite was united by family and business ties.

A lot happened quickly during the early 1930s. I'll name just a few. Japanese troops occupied Shanghai. The US Congress voted, over President Hoover's objections, to free the Philippine Islands. "The Lone Ranger" show made its debut on radio. An attempt was made in Miami to assassinate the new president, Franklin D. Roosevelt. FDR declared "a bank holiday," freezing all financial transactions, gave the first of his "fireside chat" radio talks ("The only thing we have to fear is fear itself"), created the Tennessee Valley Authority, pushed through the Federal Securities Act and Federal Trade Commission, and launched the Civil Works Administration putting 4 million to work building the nation's infrastructure. Dust storms in the West swept valuable topsoil away. Pacifist Gandhi was sentenced to prison in India. In Germany, a one-day boycott of Jewish businesses was organized by the Nazi Party.

Adolph Hitler was first seen as a charismatic presence and spellbinding orator. The military-industrial complex his regime cultivated pulled Germany out of their economic crisis of the 1930s and,

Time and Money

at its height, controlled most of Europe. The havoc his regime created is legendary. Hitler and the Nazis moved swiftly. On January 30, 1933 he was appointed Chancellor of Germany. A month later, Germany's parliament building in Berlin, the *Reichstag*, was torched. On March 5, Hitler's National Socialist Party won a 43.9 percent majority of the vote. On March 22, the first of many Nazi concentration and extermination camps, Dachau, was opened.

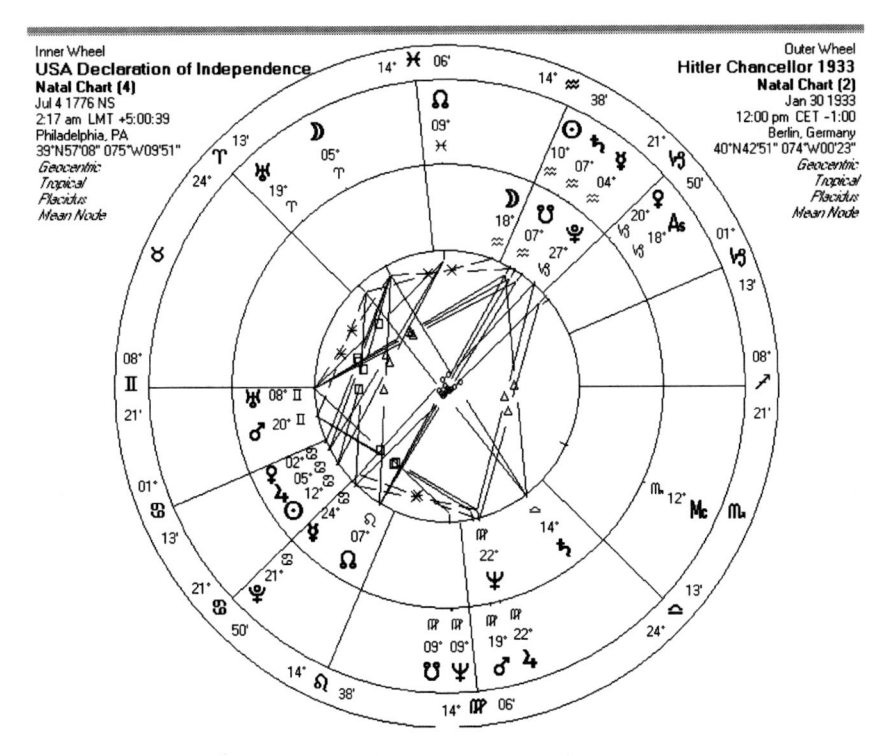

The day Hitler rose to power, Pluto was at 21 Cancer conjunct the US Mercury, opposite the US Pluto, which was conjoined this day by Saturn and Mercury. Uranus was opposite the US Saturn. Mars and Jupiter were conjunct the US Neptune, square US Mars.

Belief trumps evidence: In the USA, FDR's regime was busy pushing through socially beneficial legislation; in Germany, Hitler and the Nazis were busy building the mightiest military the world had ever before seen. Rightwing conservatives on both sides of the Atlantic adored Hitler and loathed FDR.

Robert Gover

Inherited Script

In 1934, a million and a half American workers in different industries went out on strike. When West Coast longshoremen struck, other unions cooperated by refusing to truck cargo; when police killed two strikers by gunfire in San Francisco, a general strike was called and 130,000 workers immobilized the city. Five hundred "special police" were quickly sworn in and 4,500 National Guardsmen assembled. The Los Angeles Times called this event "an insurrection, a Communist-inspired and led revolt against organized government. There is but one thing to be done—put down the revolt with any force necessary." The longshoremen accepted a compromise but the potential for national rebellion was palpable.

Flying Squadrons

Howard Zinn tells us that "in the fall of that same year, 1934, came the largest strike of all—325,000 textile workers in the South. They left the mills and set up flying squadrons in trucks and autos to move through the strike areas, picketing, battling guards, entering the mills, unbelting machinery. Here too, as in the other cases, the strike impetus came from the rank and file, against a reluctant union leadership...The New York Times said: 'The grave danger of the situation is that it will get completely out of the hands of the leaders.'"

Sharecroppers, Black and White, tentatively began to join forces. The Southern Tenant Farmers Union started in Arkansas and spread. By 1935, of 6,800,000 farmers, 2,800,00 were tenant farmers, sharecroppers; their average income was $312 a year; migrant farm laborers made about $300 a year.

Leaders Lose Control

By 1936, union leaders had indeed lost control. In Akron, Ohio, workers at the Firestone rubber plant, their wages already too low to pay for food and rent, were faced with another wage cut. Several union men were fired. Workers then began to sit down on the job. This new strike weapon spread and in two days, two of Firestone's plants were shut down. A court issued an injunction; 150 deputies were sworn in, but they soon faced 10,000 workers from all over Akron. The sit-down strike method spread quickly.

"The sit-downs were especially dangerous to the system because they were not controlled by the regular union leadership," notes Zinn, page 391. "It was to stabilize the system that the Wagner Act of 1935, setting up the National labor Relations Board, had been passed."

On Memorial Day, 1937, police fired on a mass picket line of people striking Republic Steel, killing 10. Autopsies showed they'd been shot in the back as they were fleeing. This has come to be called "The Memorial Day Massacre." Corporation executives, faced with a choice between sit-down strikes and factory takeovers on the one hand, and organized labor on the other, realized organized labor was their only hope. Unions could be controlled.

War Means Jobs

Then, suddenly, came the Japanese attack on Pearl Harbor and the US was thrust into World War II. Labor militancy gradually relaxed because the war economy created millions of new jobs at higher wages. Roosevelt's New Deal had succeeded in reducing the official unemployment figure from 13 million to 9 million. The war not only put the full labor force back to work, it called forth a unity of all classes against a common enemy: Fascism, German, Italian and Japanese rightwing dictatorships. It took this horrendous economic catastrophe to reprise the obvious: that wealth is created by cooperation, not competition. A truce was called in the American class war while everyone pulled together for the common cause.

During the great depression of the 1930s, the New Deal brought forth by President Roosevelt did bring millions of people together to solve common problems and devote themselves to common undertakings. The Tennessee Valley Authority brought cheap electricity to millions; roads and bridges were built, parks upgraded, and the Social Security System born. Federal theaters, writer's projects, and art projects were formed. Murals were painted on public buildings, plays produced for working class people, and books and pamphlets helpful to the poor written and published. People working to benefit other people were happy, and worked harder than they'd ever worked for corporate profits.

Capitalism Survives

"When the New Deal was over," writes Zinn, (page 394), "capitalism remained intact. The rich still controlled the nation's wealth, as well as its laws, courts, police, newspapers, churches, colleges. Enough help had been given to enough people to make Roosevelt a hero to millions, but the same system that had brought depression and crisis—the system of waste, of inequality, of concern for profit over human need—remained."

Yet much had changed. Out of this great depression arose the Keynesians, advocates of public works investments, according to its original proponent, John Maynard Keynes. In *The General Theory of Employment, Interest and Money*, Keynes presented what was then a startling notion: "We are being afflicted with a new disease of which some readers may not yet have heard the name, but of which they will hear a great deal in the years to come—namely 'technological unemployment.' This means unemployment due to our discovery of means of economizing the use of labor outrunning the pace at which we can find new uses for labor."

Human Labor Replaced

Karl Marx, writing in 1867, had foreseen this turn of events. "(He) believed that the ongoing effort by producers to continue to replace human labor with machines would prove self-defeating in the end. By directly eliminating human labor from the production process and by creating a reserve army of unemployed workers whose wages could be bid down lower and lower, the capitalists were inevitably digging their own grave, as there would be fewer and fewer consumers with sufficient purchasing power to buy their products." (Rifkin, page 17).

But, new theory being considered superior to old, along came Milton Friedman's opus in the 1960s, given glitter by his Nobel Prize in the 1970s; he said that Keynes had been wrong, and that it was really the Federal Reserve's failure to provide an adequate money supply, M1, that brought on and exacerbated the great depression of the 1930s. (Remember John Law?)

The debate continues. Trying to revive the economy by expanding the money supply, say modern Keynesians, is like "pushing on a string." Friedman's position is summarized by his believers in two words: "money matters."

Uranus and Keynesians

Keynesian economics would be given its way when Uranus returned to its natal position in Uncle Sam's birth chart, conjunct Sam's Ascendant. As noted, the 84-year cycle of Uranus has coincided with the Revolutionary War, then the Civil War, and now it was to coincide with World War II. Keynes' theory of economic stimulation, it seemed, worked to pull the US out of the great depression of the 1930s—but mainly because it was applied to public investment in weaponry. Modern bankers cannot seem to find a red cent for social programs but can conjure up billions of dollars for wars. World War II became the greatest public works program America had ever embarked upon—not the kind of public works Keynes had in mind, of course. He'd originally proposed investing in such real wealth-creating projects as roads, bridges, railroads, schools, etc., and the Roosevelt Administration had done some of that. But it seemed better suited to Uncle Sam's temperament to more passionately apply the Keynesian approach to military spending. Military spending does not create real and lasting wealth, since military products are either destroyed or become obsolete. But it is capitalized by taxpayers and puts big bucks in the pockets of people who, in turn,

Robert Gover

finance political campaigns, and it is part of the long tradition going back to feudalism, and to John Law's thesis: that money is the source of wealth; ergo, the more money a society has, the wealthier it is. This continues to be the argument of those who advocate evermore military spending to stimulate the economy, confusing money and what money represents: wealth, a word rooted in well-being.

In the three charts below, notice how Uranus travels into and through its 84-year return to where it was when the USA was born on July 4, 1776.

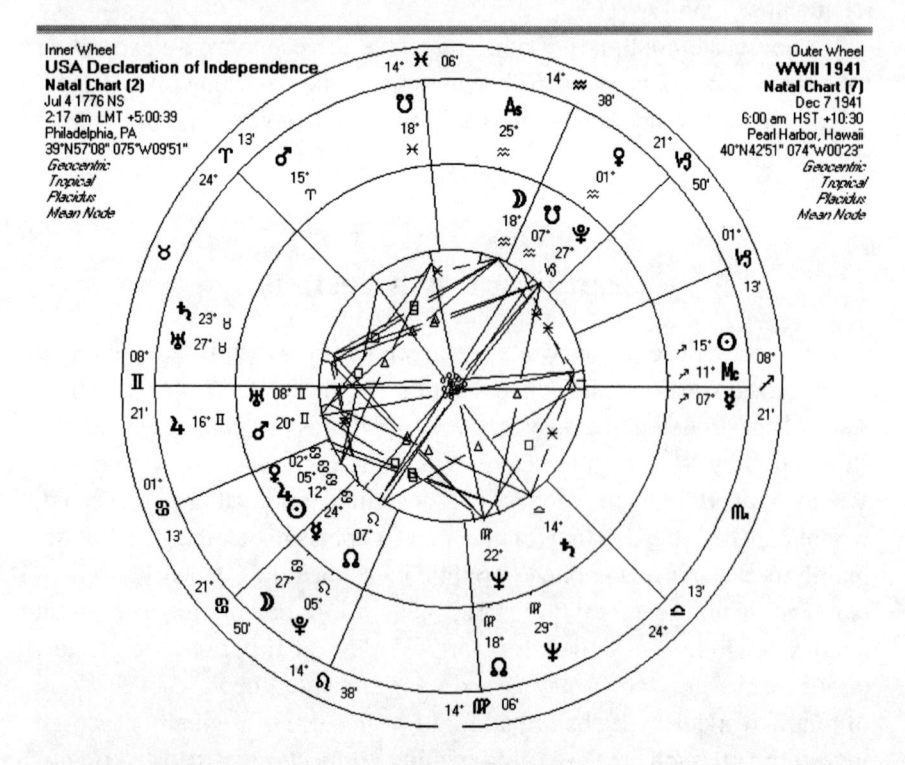

When Pearl Harbor was attacked on December 7, 1941, Uranus and Saturn were conjunct in late Taurus, applying to a conjunction with Sam's natal Uranus at 8 Gemini, but already tied into that conjunction by the opposition of Mercury and Sun in Sagittarius and Jupiter at 16 Gemini, between the US Uranus and Mars.

Time and Money

Also on Pearl Harbor Day, Pluto at 3 Leo was within sextile of Sam's Ascendant, but also within opposition of its natal position at 27 Capricorn. A dicey mix astrologically. There were some who wondered if Americans could put aside class antagonisms and cooperate, and others who felt America should side with Nazi Germany, get rid of Jews and send African Americans back to Africa.

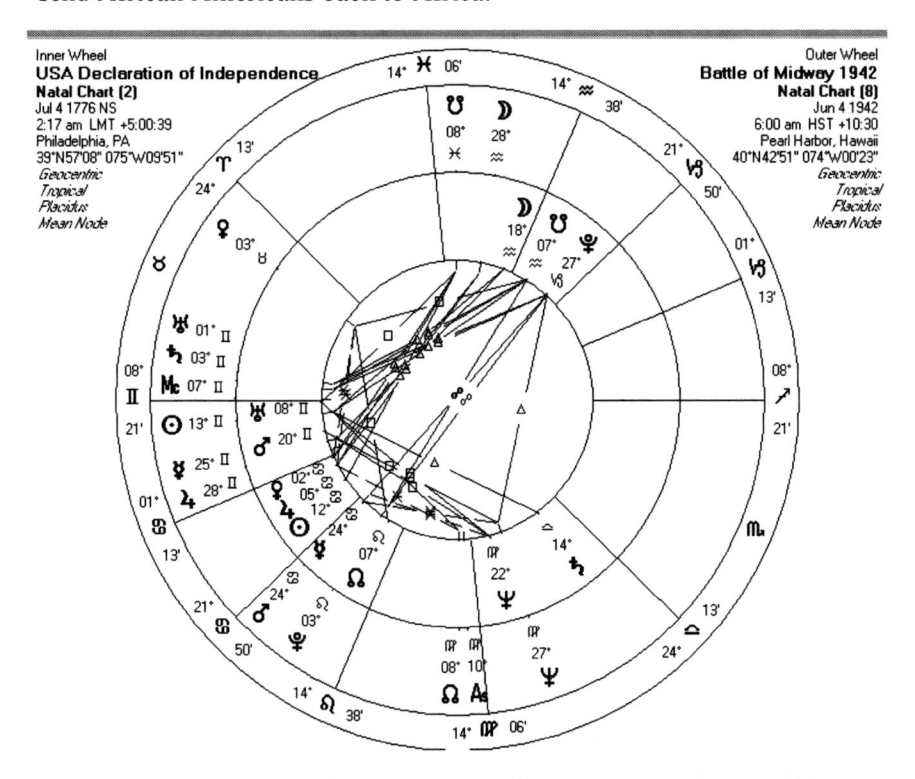

Uncle Sam's Gemini Ascendant and natal Uranus were crowded by the time of the Battle of Midway, a climactic event which turned the tide of the war with Japan. Transiting Uranus, Saturn and the Sun were within conjunction of Sam's Uranus, with natal Mars hit by Mercury and Jupiter.

By the time the atomic bomb was dropped on Hiroshima, changing war for ever more, Uranus had moved through it's conjunction with Sam's natal Uranus. Mars and Uranus were conjunct Uncle Sam's natal Uranus and Mars in Gemini, creating one horrendous gathering of war-

245

making energies. Pluto at 9 Leo formed a 60-degree beneficent sextile to Mars at 9 Gemini: this event was hugely transformative.

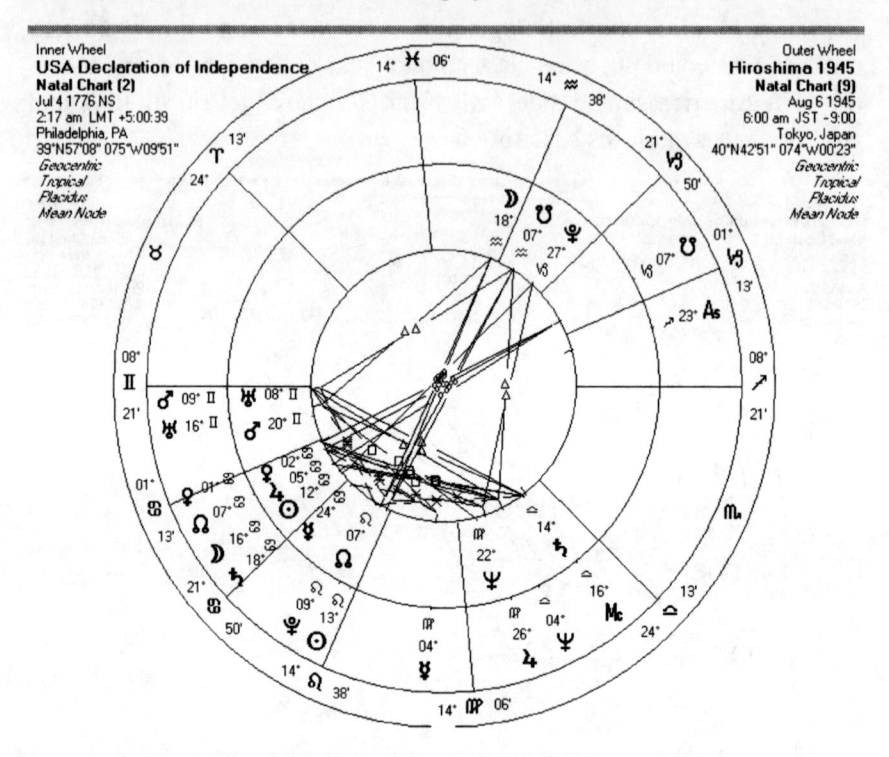

Targeting Civilians

Before World War II, industrial age wars had not specifically targeted civilian populations. Since then, civilians have been repeatedly attacked, although none has been as horrendously devastating as when the atom bombs were dropped on Hiroshima and Nagasaki, leading to Japan's surrender. This incredibly intense reaction to Japan's attack on Pearl Harbor argues for the Scorpio Rising US birth chart, since Scorpios are notoriously vengeful.

Usually, after major wars, the US economy had gone into a slump or worse, a great depression, as in the 1780s following the American Revolution and in the 1870s following the Civil War. It had come to seem almost a fact of nature that the larger, more intense and costlier a war, the more devastating would be the depression which followed. After World War II, however, the Keynesian philosophy of public spending to stimulate economic growth was continued through the Korean War, the Vietnam War, the Cold War, the Gulf War and beyond, into President Bush's invasion of Afghanistan and Iraq.

"After World War II," Greider notes, (page 102) "the US economy never actually returned to a peacetime footing. It demobilized briefly but quickly rearmed for global struggle. For the next three decades, driven by fear of conflict with the Soviets, the United States prepared for war. This was unlike any prior era of peacetime in American history."

Theories and New Realities

And it worked quite well, it seemed, through the '40s, '50s and most of the '60s. It began to be more widely and seriously questioned when, after the Uranus-Pluto conjunction in the 1960s, the Consumer Price Index jumped to the steepest inflation rate since the end of World War II. And by the middle '70s, Keynes' theory bumped into a time of both high inflation and high unemployment, two aggravations which were hitherto not believed to occur simultaneously.

As we shall see, "The Sixties" ushered in many events which were not supposed to occur at all.

"Break on Through to the Other Side"

That line from a song by The Doors rock group captures the essence of this period called The Sixties. There was an almost palpable feeling in the air, a sense that what could never happen had just happened or was about to happen.

By 1960 the US economy had grown by 25 percent during the 1950s. Real wages of workers in manufacturing had doubled since 1940. An interstate highway system had been built. The Federal budget was in balance. Unions were stronger than ever. Large numbers of families had moved from crowded inner cities to new, sprawling suburbs. African Americans in the South had launched a peaceful movement to break the grip of Jim Crow and obtain full civil rights.

As the Sixties unfolded and Uranus and Pluto tightened their conjunction in Virgo, with both conjunct the US Neptune, square the US Uranus and Mars, events would become very volatile.

Overshadowing the economic progress of the 1950s was the Cold War and the possibility that everyone was doomed by a "Dr. Strangelove" launching mutually assured destruction. The generation coming of age had had their intelligence insulted by being ordered as children to crawl under school desks—"duck and cover"—to survive nuclear holocaust. Many of this generation cared less about the spread of communism, the obsession of the ruling class, than about ending social inequality and sexual hypocrisy. It tacitly assumed there was more than enough for everyone so advocated "make love, not war."

As the Vietnam War heated up, resistance to being drafted to fight this war grew. By the mid-1960s, the American establishment was faced with antiwar demonstrators chanting slogans like, "Hey hey, LBJ, how

Time and Money

many kids did you kill today." Bobby Dylan sang, "The times they are a-changing," and millions of young people were breaking customs that bound them to the past. The Sixties was fast becoming the stormiest decade since the Civil War, with Uranus square where it had been for that bloodiest of American conflicts.

The Doors lead singer and poet Jim Morrison spoke for the Uranus-Pluto conjunction when he jarred audiences with the line, "No one here gets out alive." Death is the only certainty so let's enjoy life while we can. The words used most frequently to describe The Sixties would become *surprising*, *unprecedented* and *revolutionary*, words which describe the rare conjunction of Uranus and Pluto, especially when it squares an entity's natal Uranus, as it did Uncle Sam's through much of this decade.

Uncanny Unexpectedness

The Sixties were to become famous for eruptions of violent events both sudden (Uranus) and unfathomable (Pluto). The cause of, and the goal to be achieved by the Vietnam War were unfathomable to most Americans, and it returned beloved young men in body bags with uncanny unexpectedness. Since the government and its people had not yet become estranged, people asked each other, "Why are *we* in Vietnam?" By the end of this period, people spoke of their government as "they," and government officials referred to the people as "they." The Sixties revealed the split between the people and the government. Before this period called The Sixties could be said to have ended, the Pentagon Papers would reveal the hidden reasons why "we" were in Vietnam, and President Richard Nixon would resign to avoid impeachment proceedings.

Protests against this war pitted family members against each other as people tried to sort out the difference between loyalty to country and blind obedience to government. Was it patriotic to blindly obey government? Or was it patriotic to question government when it became autocratic and harmful? The culture of blind obedience to church and state was deeply ingrained. But now, millions were asking what rights and obligations individuals have to decide what is morally right and what is reprehensible. Democracy had reached another historic turning point.

A Mystifying Time

The Civil Rights Movement and conservative attempts to maintain segregation brought a new kind of war to US soil, and pitted otherwise friendly people, White and Black, against each other. And there was the sudden, unexpected and unprecedented (Uranus) rash of assassinations (Pluto) creating hot disagreements over who did these killings, and what motivated the killers, with no explanation satisfactory to everyone, adding up to a lingering mystery seemingly incapable of solution—Pluto's realm. Pluto and Uranus were both conjunct Uncle Sam's Neptune for most of this mystifying time. The Vietnam War, on a primal level, was another assault on a pantheistic people according to the monotheistic cultural script inherited from the Dark Ages. According to this script, people who lived simply and close to nature could not possibly be worthy, intelligent human beings. If they were intelligent, they'd be like "us." They were called "savages" in the 1500s and "chinks" in the 1900s. Like crazy Captain Ahab's obsession to kill the great white whale Moby Dick, symbolizing the awesome power and mystery of nature, Uncle Sam became obsessed with "communists." In Southeast Asia, these were people who organized to provide food, clothing and shelter for themselves without regard for any colonial power's capture of spoils or any corporation's disbursement to shareholders.

Riots and Love-ins

The Sixties really spanned about a decade and a half, from 1960 to the resignation of President Richard Nixon in 1974, and was composed of two ongoing, related streams of conflict which changed the country dramatically: the battle over the natural human rights of African Americans erupting as "race riots" in cities across the land, and the rising tide of anti-conservative protest erupting in such explosive events as the clash of antiwar demonstrators with Chicago police and National Guardsmen during the Democratic Convention in 1968—the legions of Caesar against the rabble again, this time with TV cameras rolling and the crowd chanting, "The whole world is watching."

When the dust settled, African Americans had legally acquired rights automatically assumed by others, and the Vietnam War had come to be regarded by most Americans as at best a mistake, and at worst a horror so vast it seemed impossible to comprehend. The seed of a surprising (Uranus) transformation (Pluto) had been sown.

Again, as in Bacon's Rebellion 100 years before the American Revolution, the deepest unspoken fear of the ruling class—and of its greatly expanded chattering buffer class—was that poor Whites and Blacks would analyze their common problem with clarity, unite and come up with a common solution. Fortunately for the ruling class, this was not yet ripe to happen.

Drugs, Radicals, Informants

LSD and other mind-bending drugs helped to scuttle such an analysis. There remain those who do not believe that the injection of such distracting drugs into urban centers was purely an act of Fate. Undercover cops and paid informants seemed everywhere "radicals" might gather, and often it was these disguised protectors of the status quo who dispensed the drugs.

The conjunction of Uranus and Pluto in Virgo began square Uncle Sam's Gemini Ascendant, natal Uranus and Mars. By itself, this aspect could be expected to bring a combination of explosive events of mysterious origins, leading eventually to long-lasting change. The question during The Sixties, as it had been since colonial times, concerned whose will would prevail: the democratic will of the populace, or the autocratic will of the wealthy?

Robert Gover

Ten years later it was clear that the wealthy had won this battle of the ongoing class war. The news media, now owned by large corporations, cooperated to re-frame the Sixties, effectively rewriting American history. The official version of what had happened did not erase the personal memory of participants, however.

An affliction from Pluto often makes the entity affected search out enemies, real or imagined, and the war in Vietnam began with the slogan, "Stop Communism in Southeast Asia." This assumed an idea could be stopped by bombs and guns, and that the Vietnamese people would become communists unless they were "protected," and their villages decimated into "pacification." The difference between what the government said it was doing and what it was actually doing became starkly obvious in "the first televised war," as Vietnam was called.

The Domino Theory

The news media was full of such notions as the "Domino Theory," which supposed that if the countries of Southeast Asia installed communist governments, a falling domino effect would cause more nations to fall, and eventually bring communism to Santa Monica, then Eastward to the "God-fearing" of America's Heartland.

Those of a more cynical bent perceived a bonanza for the military-industrial complex, or what would later be thought of as an ongoing Keynesian stimulation package for the Pentagon and its corporate contractors. Whether by design or national proclivity, the US government had gotten its foot in the door of this conflict by bankrolling French colonialists who were being driven out of Vietnam by a popular uprising. Uncle Sam then deluded himself into believing he could bring "peace and freedom" to Vietnam by carpet-bombing and napalm.

Zinn, page 460: "From 1964 to 1972, the wealthiest and most powerful nation in the history of the world made a maximum military effort, with everything short of atomic bombs, to defeat a nationalist revolutionary movement in a tiny, peasant country—and failed. When the United States fought in Vietnam, it was organized modern technology versus organized human beings, and the human beings won..."

Time and Money

Mekong and Mississippi

"In the course of that war," Zinn continues, "there developed in the United States the greatest anti-war movement the nation had ever experienced, a movement that played a critical part in bringing the war to an end. In was said that the US lost the war in both the Mekong Delta and the Mississippi Delta, where many of the most dramatic demonstrations demanding full citizenship for African Americans occurred."

The seeds of the social volatility now conveyed by the words The Sixties were planted during the 1950s with Uranus traveling through Cancer square Neptune in Libra. Rosa Parks, who commuted to and from her job by bus, was arrested for sitting in the front of a bus instead of moving to the "Black section" in the rear. This act led to the Montgomery Bus Boycott and the rise of Dr. Martin Luther King, Jr., as leader of a broad-based movement for African Americans to be legally allowed their natural-born human rights. On December 1, 1955 when Rosa Parks was arrested, Pluto and Jupiter were conjunct on the Leo-Virgo cusp, and Neptune and Mars were conjunct the Libra-Scorpio cusp. The nation entered a transitional period that would climax in the mid-1960s with the Uranus-Pluto conjunction in Virgo, with both conjunct the US Neptune, opposition T Saturn moving through Pisces, all square the US Mars in Gemini.

Lunch Counter Warriors

"On February 1, 1960, four freshmen at a Negro college in Greensboro, North Carolina, decided to sit down at the Woolworth's lunch counter downtown, where only Whites ate. They were refused service, and when they would not leave, the lunch counter was closed for the day." (Zinn, page 444).

During the early Sixties, African Americans arose in rebellion against laws and customs designed to keep them "inferior," which had been instituted since around the time of Bacon's Rebellion in the 1600s to prevent lower class Whites and Blacks from uniting to threaten the ruling class. By the end of the 1960s—after the assassinations of Martin Luther King, John F. Kennedy, Robert Kennedy, Malcolm X, and unknown numbers of less famous political activists—civil rights protests had turned violent and American cities had been torched in "race riots," as they were called by the media, and "police raids" as they were called in inner cities.

In brief, The Sixties was a major turning point in US history. Even presidents discovered their vulnerability to the popular will, as first Lyndon Johnson and then Richard Nixon left the Oval Office in disgrace—Johnson for his prosecution of the war, Nixon for a variety of autocratic acts. The military-industrial complex, with seemingly miraculous good fortune, would survive the rising tide of democratic forces that marked The Sixties; perhaps because of its Keynesian Cold War economic stimulation program, which "created jobs." A popular song of the time touted "Faster horses, stronger whiskey, younger women and mooooore money!" Indeed, transferring billions of tax dollars to corporations in the name of "defense" created more and more money, without producing anything of real economic value. Unless, that is, you believe military domination of other nations will continue to be as economically valuable in the future as it was in the time of Columbus.

Beginning, Middle, and End

I include three charts below. The first is for Saturn's return to mid-Capricorn as the Civil Rights Movement was developing. The second marks an intensification of the Vietnam War and anti-war protests in the US, and the third marks both the end of the Vietnam War and the resignation of President Richard Nixon after a series of revelations of corruption, known as "Watergate."

Time and Money

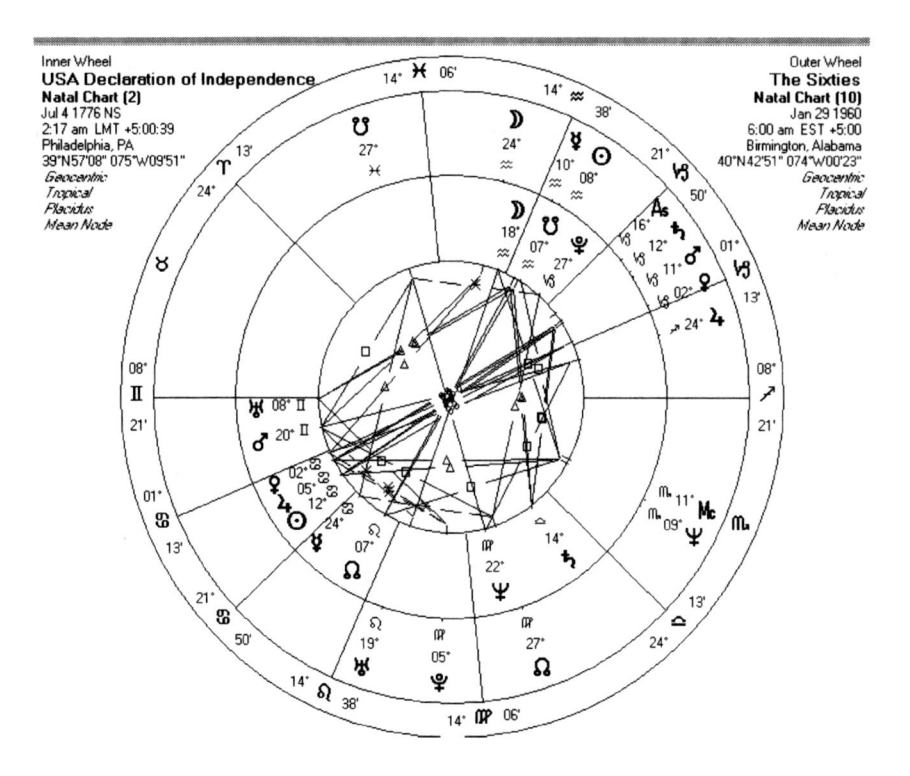

Notice that although Saturn has returned to its most historically dangerous position for the US economy, and is at this time conjunct Mars, no grand cross is formed in combination with Uranus, Neptune or Pluto in Aries. Uranus was at 19 Leo, forming a beneficent 60 degree sextile with Sam's natal Mars at 20 Gemini. Neptune was at 9 Scorpio, forming an even more beneficent 120 degree trine to Uncle Sam's Sun at 13 Cancer. No grand cross, no great depression.

However, the great transformer Pluto at 5 Virgo was square Uncle Sam's natal Uranus in 1960. An affliction from Pluto to Uranus brings large alterations in whatever area of an entity's life is indicated by the square, and before this decade ended, Uncle Sam's persona (signified by the Ascendant) would be greatly altered, as would the government's relations with the American people (signified by the nadir or 6 o'clock position in a chart).

Also notice that Uranus at 19 Leo was opposite the US Moon in Aquarius. By Sign, Neptune in Scorpio formed a T square with Uranus and the US Moon. The American public was about to be swept up into an unprecedented decade.

Coupled with the Saturn-Mars opposition to Uncle Sam's Sun in early 1960, this return of Saturn, rather than bring an economic downturn, was to prove upsetting to the whole American culture, as the conjunction of Uranus and Pluto and natal Neptune formed in the mid-1960s, with all three square Sam's natal Uranus and then Mars.

On the outer wheel of the combined chart for 1965, Uranus had caught up to Pluto at 17 Virgo, putting both 90 degrees square a spot between Sam's natal Uranus and Mars in Gemini. Not many believed back in the early Sixties that what was at first called a "limited involvement to stop communism in Indochina" would change the way Americans would think of war. Uranian surprise combined with mysterious Plutonian transformation impacted Sam's warrior persona signified by the Uranus-Mars pair in the First House.

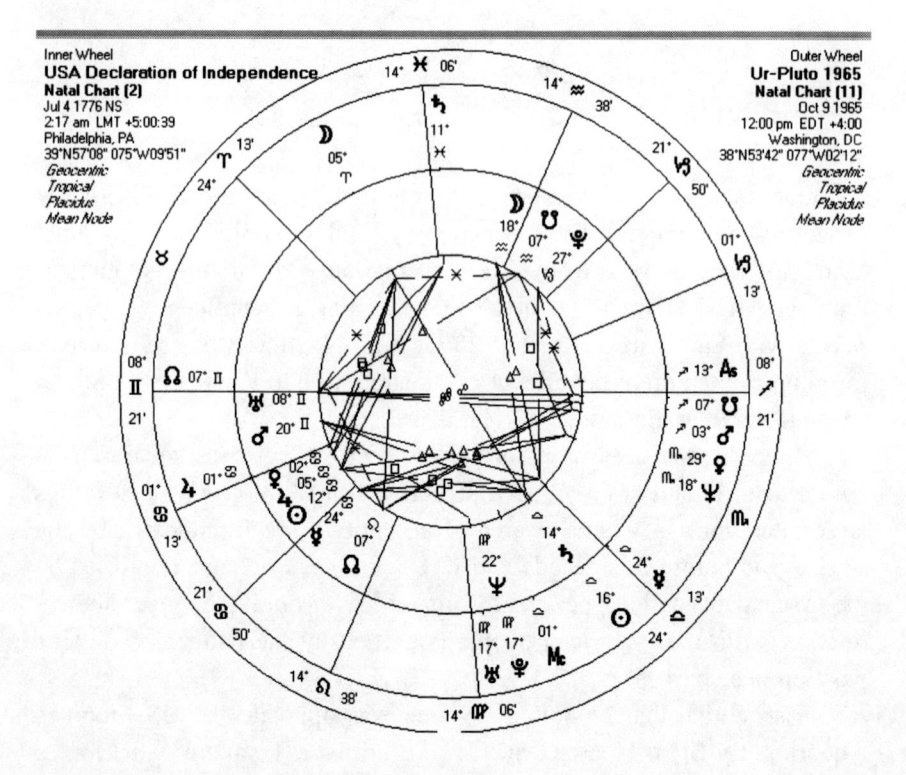

Time and Money

The American population would henceforth make a clear distinction between "necessary" wars such as World War II, and military-industrial profiteering such as the Vietnam War. (Even some 30 years later when the military had become "a good career" for volunteers, it was hard to imagine American troops occupying Iraq as they had occupied Vietnam without the general population quickly rising in protest. Improved public relations and censorship enabled the government to discourage dissent.)

Most notable in 1965 is that the conjunction of Uranus and Pluto came exact just as Saturn (around noon) moved into opposition, and Mars (about 3:30) moved toward an opposition with Uncle Sam's Ascendant and natal Uranus, which would form another grand cross during the last two months of that year. Unlike the grand cross patterns which have coincided with great depressions, this grand cross afflicts Uncle Sam's Ascendant and natal Uranus and Mars, the warriors of the Solar System.

Pelletier says of this rare conjunction of Uranus and Pluto: "You are offered two alternatives: either to turn your back on the decaying quality of life or make some effort to restore order to the chaos that man's insensitivity has produced." Of Uranus square the Ascendant: "You feel you have a right to do anything you want without adhering to any rules and regulations." And of Pluto square the Ascendant: "...you feel you are destined to have a powerful influence on the lives of the people you contact. Overly impressed with your righteousness, you feel that you alone can properly control their affairs." Add these feelings together and mix thoroughly and you have the psychological climate of The Sixties.

The resignation of President Richard Nixon ended the atmosphere of The Sixties and led into a new phase. Note Saturn conjunct the US Sun, Uranus at 24 Libra square the US Mercury-Pluto opposition, and Neptune opposite the US Ascendant and Uranus. Pluto at 4 Libra was square the US Jupiter and 2nd house of money. The most telling aspect at this time was the T square formed by Uranus to the US Mercury-Pluto opposition, I feel; Nixon had taken the nation off the gold standard so that the dollar now "floated free."

The American government, during the Sixties, made unprecedented efforts to restore the status quo. Rightwing conservatives banded together to establish their ideal America, while millions of middle Americans,

Robert Gover

mostly in their late teens and early twenties, made unprecedented efforts to bring about a very different idea of social harmony and peace. The result was that two diametrically opposed concepts of justice met head-on in the Civil Rights Movement, and then in the Anti-War Movement: the forces of democracy against the forces of plutocracy—Greider's "buried fault line" (capitalistic democracy) quaking.

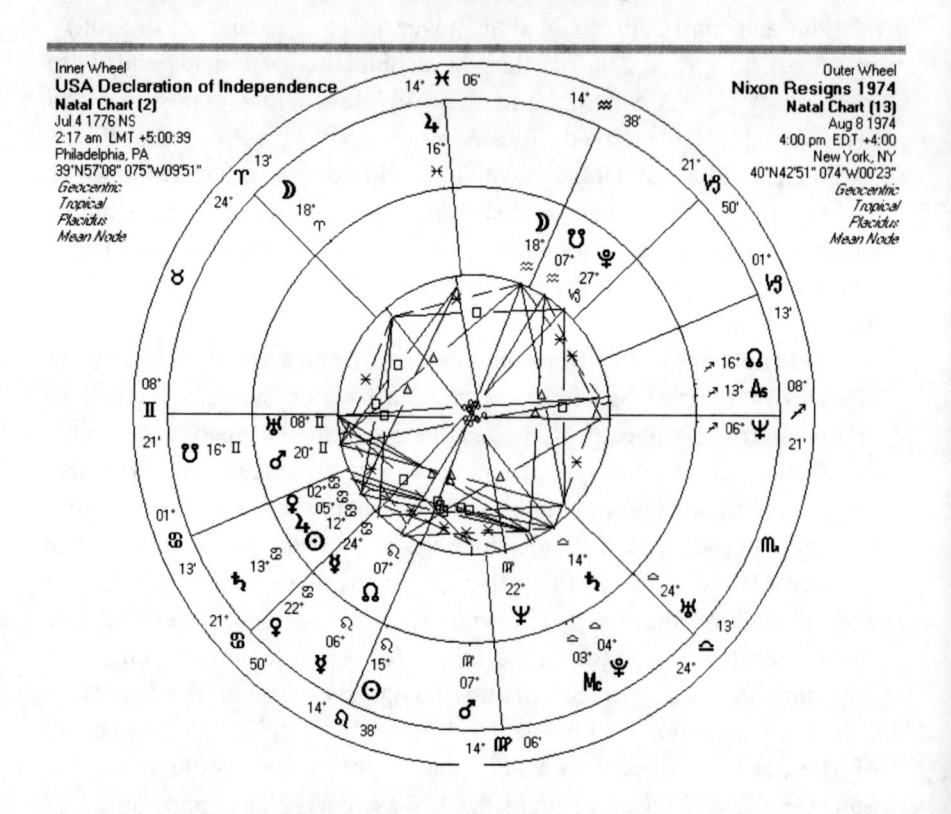

Inner Wheel
USA Declaration of Independence
Natal Chart (2)
Jul 4 1776 NS
2:17 am LMT +5:00:39
Philadelphia, PA
39°N57'08" 075°W09'51"
Geocentric
Tropical
Placidus
Mean Node

Outer Wheel
Nixon Resigns 1974
Natal Chart (13)
Aug 8 1974
4:00 pm EDT +4:00
New York, NY
40°N42'51" 074°W00'23"
Geocentric
Tropical
Placidus
Mean Node

Conservatives Shocked

The forming and then separating of the Uranus-Pluto conjunction lasted through most of the '60s and into the early '70s. That it coincided with a major change of attitude in the American body politic is beyond argument. Those defending the autocracy lurking behind the American mask of democracy were "shock-shock shocked" by the millions of

Time and Money

middle-class and lower-class citizens who rose up to demand rights most had been educated to suppose they already had. When these young protesters were joined by older people, many of them middle class and prosperous, conservatives were panicked, and knew they would have to strengthen and refine their methods of control. Voltaire's progeny were too many to fit in any Bastille.

Forty years later and into the foreseeable future, those words, "The Sixties," remain emotionally charged. Astrologically, this is foretold in the T square formed by Saturn opposite the Uranus-Pluto conjunction and both square Sam's fiery Uranus-Mars pair in Gemini.

The 127-year alignments of Uranus and Pluto historically have seeded new ideas or brought ancient-but-forgotten ideas to the foreground. "Whenever Uranus and Pluto join forces, the status quo is seriously threatened. People jump ahead decades or even centuries and boldly experiment with radically different ways of being and living together." (Meece page 69).

Date Uranus-Pluto Conjunct

1456	13 Leo
1597	20 Aries
1710	28 Leo
1850	29 Aries
1965	17 Virgo

The conjunction of 1456 coincided with the invention of printing and the fall of Constantinople to the Turks.

A scientific revolution began with the conjunction of 1597, and the English decided to colonize North America, beginning with the Lost Colony of Roanoke.

In 1710, Voltaire's works so frightened the protectors of the status quo that they locked him in the Bastille prison. But Uranus-Pluto conjunctions seed revolutionary ideas, and Voltaire's could not be squelched. They spread wide and far "infecting" the minds of America's founders, and the "hippies" of The Sixties.

Robert Gover

Flow of Revolutionary Ideas

In 1850, Voltaire's ideas and the Industrial Revolution led to the ideas of Karl Marx. Socialism was plowed under at first, but its seed ideas continued to germinate.

When Uranus and Pluto formed their next opposition, the Russian Revolution occurred, and since then socialism has undergone many changes and refinements, from "state-run" to "democratic," as in modern Scandinavia. Uncle Sam is not bombing Stockholm or Copenhagen; Volvos and Nokia wireless phones are selling briskly. Americans "hate" socialism but "love" Social Security, and have been largely convinced by corporate public relations that the mission of capitalism and the ideals of democracy are not contradictory.

In 1966, the Uranus-Pluto conjunction hit the USA especially hard because it occurred conjunct the USA's natal Neptune, square natal Mars and Uranus in Gemini, plus the ominous opposition of Saturn moving through Pisces. The keepers of the status quo squelched these radical ideas at first. But, as in the past, they were destined to grow and develop.

Just as the Neptune-Pluto cycle has its phases, so does the Uranus-Pluto cycle have its. Voltaire's radical ideas didn't have their first blossoming till the American Revolution, sixty-some years after Voltaire was first imprisoned. It took about the same length of earth years for Marx's ideas to manifest as the Russian Revolution and then democratic socialism in Scandinavia. Radical ideas seeded in The Sixties are due to manifest during the 2000-teens, when Uranus and Pluto form their next major aspect.

Kings, Commoners, and Gold

Of course varieties of other radical ideas are also seeded during Uranus-Pluto conjunctions. Coinciding with the one in 1850 was the California Gold Rush and subsequent conflict over the Gold Standard, the valuation of paper money based on gold and/or silver.

Time and Money

If the kings of the Old World had been enriched by captured gold in the Americas, why should not the American common man of the mid-1800s strike it rich? Gold as plunder was inextricably woven into the religious culture brought to the Americas from Europe. Earlier monetarists sometimes described their money-based philosophy as the "golden rule" or "golden mean." If a society ventures too far from its golden mean, like Icarus daring to fly too close to the Sun, the feared result is economic chaos.

The "gold standard" was what stabilized economies, it was believed for many centuries. But believing did not necessarily make it so.

Gold and Prices

"Prices, in fact, both rose and fell drastically throughout the nineteenth century—despite the gold standard and sometimes because of it." (Greider page 248). Greider quotes another notable economic theorist, Joseph Schumpeter:

"Capitalist rationality does not do away with sub- or super-rational impulses," wrote Schumpeter, in a review that could be an astrological reading of the Uranus-Pluto conjunction. "It merely makes them get out of hand by removing the restraint of sacred or semi-sacred tradition."

Historian Fernard Braudel described the ancient and enduring competition between gold and silver, sweeping across continents down through centuries: "...one of the two metals would be relatively more plentiful than the other; then, with varying degrees of slowness, the situation would reverse, and so on. This resulted in upsets and disasters on the exchanges, and led above all to those slow but powerful fluctuations which were a feature of monetary *ancien regime*... Ancient theoreticians would have liked a fixed relationship giving gold twelve times the value of silver for equal weights. This was certainly not the general rule from the fifteenth to the eighteenth century (in Europe). The ratio at that time varied frequently around and beyond this so-called 'natural' relationship... At the risk of straining the meaning of the word, we might say that this was an age of gold inflation, which lasted for several centuries."

Robert Gover

During the Nixon Administration, in the wake of the Uranus-Pluto conjunction, the US removed its money from the gold standard, an audacious departure from tradition in the spirit of The Sixties.

Uranus and Acts of God

"Acts of God" are often noticed during Uranus-Pluto conjunctions. Around the time of the 1710 conjunction, brutal hurricanes kept America's early colonists upset and chaotic. In one two-day period of 1706, at least 14 ships were lost off the East Coast; the French and then the Spanish made attempts to capture South Carolina during a yellow fever epidemic in Charleston; 1711 marked the beginning of what would become known as the Tuscarora Indian War; the Pennsylvania Assembly officially banned slavery. All these events were unprecedented and audacious in their time.

As an indication of this conjunction's long-range effects, the one in 1597 was followed closely by the first English colonial settlements at Roanoke, and then Jamestown, indicating a new consciousness developing. Why else would people risk a dangerous voyage of a month or two to cross the Atlantic and go ashore in a new land, where they had to alter the social contract with each other, find ways and means unknown back in their Mother Country to cope in a strange environment of dense forests, vast rivers and estuaries, and people so different as to be considered less than human—"savages," independent, unrulable, seemingly disorganized yet exhibiting an economic well-being and abundance unknown to the new immigrants.

Grisham's Law

The 1597 conjunction also coincides with the Spanish plundering of Central and South American Indian gold and silver. The money supply in Europe, Greider notes, page 249, "was grossly multiplied by the import of precious metals plundered from the Incan mines. A long inflation resulted." Three centuries of gold inflation was then displaced by silver inflation as the value of silver cheapened. "The era produced the paradoxical maxim known as Grisham's law (named for Queen Elizabeth I's counselor): 'Bad money drives out good.' In other words, buyers will always prefer to use a watered-down currency to purchase real goods rather than a more precious one, for obvious reasons."

The effects of the Uranus-Pluto conjunction of the mid-1960s are more immediately and dramatically obvious because of Saturn's opposition to it, and the square both made to Uncle Sam's Ascendant. That the Sixties would also become famous for a new outburst of mind-altering substances and alternative lifestyles and religions is indicated astrologically in the chart for 1965 by the trine from transiting Neptune to a point about midway between Uncle Sam's Sun and Mercury, symbollizing Soul and Mind. Thirty-some years previous, the nation had ended a period called Prohibition, coinciding with the previous return of Saturn to Capricorn. It had been more or less collectively decided that trying to outlaw alcoholic beverages was neither possible nor socially beneficial.

Another Keynesian Stimulus

With the Sixties came an upsurge in the use of such herbs as marijuana, peyote and psychedelic mushrooms, and such pharmaceutical manufactures as LSD and Methamphetamine or "speed," added to the outlawed and fairly widespread use of heroin. This brought forth those opposed to any use of drugs other than tobacco and alcohol and became, in time, another Keynesian stimulus: large sums of tax money invested in "the war on drugs," beefing up police forces all across the land creating the Drug Enforcement Agency, now known worldwide as simply The DEA.

Had it been the American character to merely shrug off the rash of drug use which occurred in the audaciously chaotic years of the Sixties, chances are it would never have become such a huge problem. Other nations ignored it entirely or shrugged it off, and have no drug problem to speak of. But the American temperament, it seems, never met a social problem it didn't believe it could defeat by war, as indicated by Uranus and Mars in Uncle Sam's First House.

Robert Gover

In America, because so many substances were outlawed and such huge investments of money thrown at enforcing laws against all except tobacco and alcohol, something like a cat-and-mouse game developed. This game turned grim as wages began a long trend downward in the middle 1970s, and more and more otherwise-harmless citizens went to prison for drug-related offenses, even though reams of statistics indicated beyond doubt that the two most dangerous and harmful drugs are alcohol and tobacco. Thus we had a couple of decades of Hollywood-produced images of whiskey-drinking, chain-smoking law-enforcement "heroes" hard on the tails of "drug offenders," usually portrayed as people who did not buy their clothes in department stores.

Drug War Casualties

Eventually it would become commonly understood, although not officially acknowledged, that the Central Intelligence Agency contributed to what became a "drug epidemic." Whether this was by secret-but-official decree, bureaucratic corruption, or the nation's innate proclivity to make war on any threats, real or imagined, has yet to be determined. But the "drug war" which began in the Sixties resembled the one launched earlier in the 20th Century against alcohol, known as Prohibition. Both attempts to wipe out mind-altering substances proved futile, although the most recent has residuals: with "privatization," imprisoning millions of poor people has created a profit-making prison industry.

Another residual of the "drug war" was that, when a White youth from a buffer class background was arrested for a drug offense, he or she could be segregated from "them," poor Whites, Latinos and African Americans. The experience of almost winding up doing hard time in prison—almost, because Whites above a certain economic level were not so sentenced—brought a new impetus to class and racial consciousness. The breakdown of segregation which had threatened to unite people during the Sixties was thus nullified, and, happily for the ruling class, rancorous disunity restored.

Plutocrats Fight Back

This "drug war" was but one way in which the Hamiltonian plutocracy fought back against the new tide of democratic passions loosed during the Sixties; there were to be other offenses mounted as The Sixties became the '70s, '80s and '90s.

The anti-war movement of The Sixties was to have a profound effect on what President Eisenhower had labeled "the military-industrial complex," a good old boy network of corporate executives and Pentagon brass who fatten from military Keynesian stimulus, transferring billions of your tax dollars into their own version of free enterprise. The end of the Vietnam War threatened to end, or at least slow, this lush flow of corporate welfare. But the "evil empire," as the Soviet Union was labeled by President Ronald Reagan in the '80s, was still extant, and thus the military-industrial network had the enemy it needed to maintain the habit of plundering the taxpayers for the "national defense."

Communist Menace Bonanza

Earlier in The Sixties, Cuba became a prime candidate for this role of "communist threat" when a small band of musical-comedy-type revolutionaries led by one Fidel Castro—who, as a baseball player, had been an outstanding pitcher—overthrew the American-supported Batista government of that small island 90 miles from Key West. Indeed, the Cuban Revolution, innocuous though it seemed at the time, was a real threat to American business interests, which had dominated the Cuban economy, controlling utilities, mines, cattle ranches, oil refineries, the sugar industry and the public railway system. When the Castro government confiscated over a million acres of Cuban land from three American companies, including United Fruit, the military-industrial complex gained a new and valued enemy, one that would increase the flow of tax dollars to their bank accounts for decades to come.

On April 17, 1961, a CIA-trained force of 1400 Cuban exiles landed at the Bay of Pigs on the south shore of Cuba. They expected to lead a popular uprising against Castro. Instead, the CIA forces were crushed. But one battle does not make a war. Eventually, a variety of anti-Castro projects would greatly enrich Cuban exiles in South Florida. As long as there was a person or group at home or abroad which could be labeled "communist menace," the beneficiaries of this kind of welfare were in high cotton.

Communist Capitalists

"Around 1960," Zinn notes, page 433, "the fifteen-year effort since the end of World War II to break up the Communist-radical upsurge of the New Deal and wartime years seemed successful. The (American) Communist party was in disarray—its leaders in jail, its membership shrunken, its influence in the trade union movement very small. The trade union movement itself had become more controlled, more conservative. The military budget was taking half of the national budget, but the public was accepting this." (And why not? The American propaganda machine had not only successfully portrayed communists as about 45 degrees to the right of Hitler, but the Soviet Communist Party had created a society of rich and poor very much like America's, the difference being that the Soviet rich were a new class of bureaucrats and the American rich were the same old corporate industrialists.)

During the 1960s, the share of wealth held by the richest 1 percent in America was 27.4 in 1962, 31.6 in 1963, 29.2 in 1965, and 24.9 in 1969. This share would balloon dramatically during the next two decades.

Ravi Batra: "A side effect of the growing wealth disparity is the rise in speculative investments. As a person becomes wealthy, his aversion to risk declines. As wealth inequality grows, the overall riskiness of investments made by the rich also grows. It essentially reflects the human urge to make a quick profit. It means margin and installment buying of assets and goods only for resale and not for productive purposes. It means, for instance, increasing involvement of investors in futures markets. When others see the rich profiting quickly from speculative purchases, they tend to follow suit."

Time and Money

Widening Disparity

Through the 1970s and 1980s, despite popping oil prices at times, feverish inflation, a temporary collapse of the commercial real estate market, the rampant failure of savings and loans institutions and the government-forced bailout by taxpayers of these failed S&L's, there was no great depression—just a series of recessions and stock market thrills, while the disparity between rich and poor Americans continued to widen.

The Sixties faded into history with the end of the Vietnam War and the resignation of President Nixon to avoid impeachment. The biwheel chart for Nixon's resignation (page 270) shows some interesting astrological indicators of this troublesome turning point in US history—the grand cross formed by Neptune (3 o'clock) opposite Uncle Sam's Ascendant and natal Uranus, plus the squares made to these two points by Mars (6 o'clock) at 6 Virgo opposite Jupiter (noon) at 16 Pisces but retrograde, tightening this grand cross afflicting Sam's Ascendant, altering the old persona of the USA forever.

Note, too, that Saturn is conjunct Sam's Sun-square-Saturn, and on this day of Nixon's resignation, the Moon in Aries opposite Sam's Saturn forms a T square.

As if all these afflicting aspects weren't enough, transiting Pluto and Uranus straddle Sam's natal Saturn, square Sam's Sun, conjoined by transiting Saturn. There is one school of astrology that focuses exclusively on such midway points as the one between Pluto and Uranus astride Sam's Saturn on this day. And there is evidence that such midpoints are potent in human affairs.

A picture of the resigned President Nixon continues to play on television. It shows Nixon boarding the presidential helicopter and giving that jaunty, phony-confident, stiffly awkward wave to the television cameras. The proverbial picture worth a thousand words: I did all I could for our finest people, Nixon seems to be saying, and it wasn't my fault that the rabble drummed me out of office.

Wall Street Dances, Main Street Weeps

A rare conjunction occurred in the late 1980s and early 1990s: Saturn, Uranus and Neptune were together in Capricorn. Saturn moves into Capricorn every 30 years, approximately. Uranus takes 84 years to circle the Zodiac and Neptune 165 years. Uranus and Neptune form conjunctions once every approximately 171 years. The last time Uranus and Neptune had been conjunct in Capricorn was 1824 when John Quincy Adams was elected President. But at that time Saturn was in Scorpio. Saturn and Uranus had conjoined in Capricorn in 900, 1430 and 1548, and Uranus and Neptune had conjoined there in 1821, but going back to year 1, I found no other instance of all three—Saturn, Uranus and Neptune—together at the same time in Capricorn.

What would this rare conjunction mean for the US economy? Unable to refer to past history for clues, we were left with the classical interpretations of the planets in the Signs and the aspects formed.

Saturn "rules" Capricorn, which is to say that it's "at home" in this Sign. Uranus—eclectic, innovative, surprising, often shocking —is disciplined by Saturn's influence when it's in Capricorn, yet can be expected to deliver surprises nevertheless. Neptune, "the dreamer," named for the god of the seas, brings artistic activity, glamour, religious philosophies. The downside of Neptune, though, is drug addiction, alcoholism, vagueness, escapism, and delusions. Uranus forming hard angles, can bring shocking ruination—for instance, the Crash of '29.

Dreamer and Shocker

Neptune in Capricorn tends to make us nostalgic about the past, or what we imagine the past to have been. Conversely, Uranus in Capricorn makes us want to break out of old routines and discover new methods and technologies. And Saturn's 30-year sojourn through its home Sign is a time of restructuring, which sometimes means periods of difficulty even when it forms no square to another outer planet in Aries.

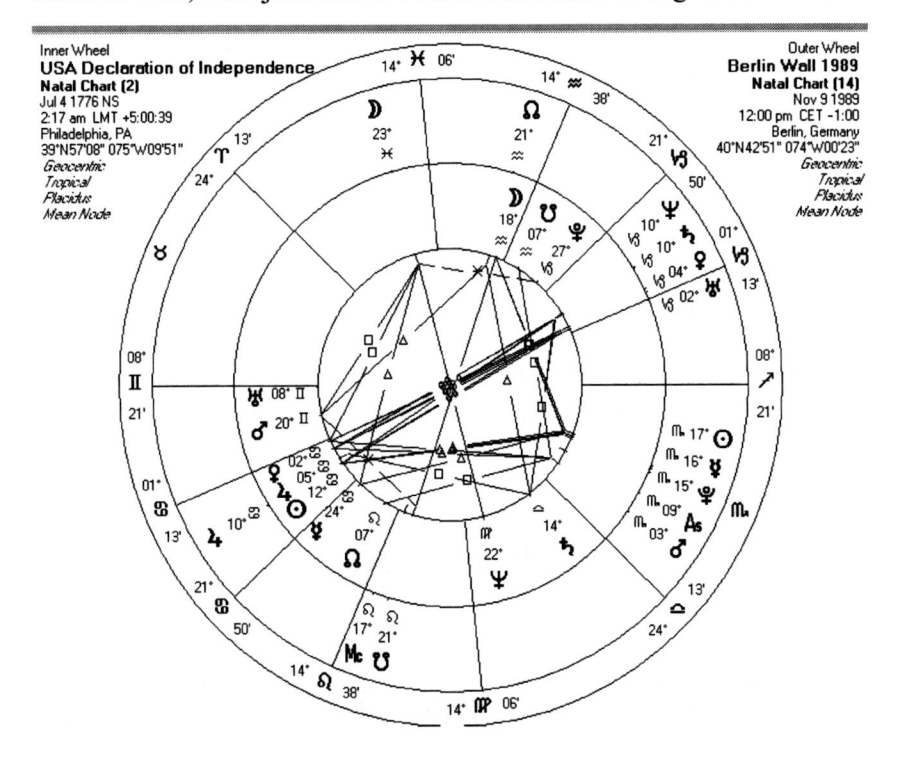

In the first years of the 20th Century, while Uranus was in philosophical Sagittarius before moving into restructuring Capricorn, it played a major role in the panics of 1903 and 1907, and then in the early events leading up to the Russian Revolution. Since this was also when Wall Street financiers were urging Congress to "do something" about the vulnerability of the financial system, Uranus played a role in the creation of the Federal Reserve System, the USA's privatization of the central bank. In 1987, a conjunction of Uranus and Saturn in Sagittarius afflicted the US Mars-Neptune square to bring on the panic of October 1987.

When Uranus moved from Sagittarius into Capricorn, the first major economic event was the tearing down of the Berlin Wall November 9, 1989. This effectively ended the Cold War and led to the reunification of Germany, the "economic engine" of what would soon become the European Union. President Ronald Reagan had famously called for the Russian Premier to "tear down this wall," and soon thereafter the German people did just that.

On November 9, 1989, Saturn and Neptune were conjunct at 10 Capricorn, opposite the US cluster of planets in Cancer, and Uranus was at 2 Capricorn, precisely opposite the US Venus. Jupiter was at 10 Cancer: a celebratory time for Americans and Western Europeans. Pluto at 15 Scorpio was shining a beneficent trine to the US stellium in Cancer and a helpful sextile to Saturn, Neptune and Uranus in Capricorn. All in all, a most auspicious time for the USA.

There was no danger of a great depression when Saturn reached mid-Capricorn in '89 accompanied by Neptune and Uranus, because the only other outer planet, Pluto, was making such helpful angles to both the US Sun and transiting Saturn.

"Desert Storm," February 24, 1991, was the name of the war mounted by President Bush the elder after Iraq invaded Kuwait. By that time, Saturn had moved to 1 degree Aquarius while Uranus and Neptune continued to occupy mid-Capricorn, sextile Pluto. Indicating war at this time was Uranus at 12 Capricorn opposite the US Sun (square US Saturn), and transiting Mars at 11 Gemini, between the US Uranus and Mars (square the US Neptune). Since Bush the elder did not send the US military on to Baghdad to topple Saddam Hussein, this war lasted only a few months. Later, some would see it as a dress rehearsal for President Bush the younger after 911.

The Bull Stumbles

Returning to the '90s, by February 1, 1993, when the bulls stampeded into Wall Street to push stocks up to record highs, Saturn had moved on to 19 Aquarius, trine the US Mars. Suggesting that this new

Time and Money

run-up of stocks was not to be purely wondrous was Uranus and Neptune conjunct at 19 Capricorn opposite transiting Mars in Cancer, with all three forming a square to the US Saturn in Libra. The bull stumbled and some called this the recession of the early 1990s, but it was a comparatively minor glitch and did not really dampen the growing optimism.

The NAFTA trade agreement that would become so controversial in the coming years was signed on January 1, 1994. Both the US natal Pluto and transiting Pluto were prominent at this time. Natal Pluto at 27 Capricorn (opposite the US Mercury) was conjoined by Uranus and Neptune, while transiting Pluto at 27 Scorpio formed a T square with transiting Saturn at 27 Aquarius and the Moon at 27 Leo: as yet hidden trouble for the people.

NAFTA was to become a bonanza for US corporations and a horror for the American working class, but in 1994, few had a full sense of its potential. Speaking to this is a cluster of six planets in Capricorn—Uranus, Neptune, Sun, Mercury, Mars and Venus—all opposite the US cluster in Cancer, and by Sign square the US Saturn in Libra. NAFTA plus developments in computer technology boosted stocks ever higher.

We might imagine Pluto's arrival into prominence in our national life as a parade up Constitution Avenue led by the sprites of Chaos, some so subtle they aren't yet visible, others more obvious but not yet clearly understood. The Lord of the Nether World remains somewhere back in the crowded parade—it's not clear which limo he's in till it clears the crowd. Then he steps out and shows himself to the dignitaries clustered around the Capitol building, who listen to his address, wearing frowns of bafflement and concern, applauding politely now and then. Lord Pluto hasn't been here in 248 years so no one is sure what to expect of him, although his entourage of Chaos Sprites engenders growing unease. His diminutive size (the smallest planet in the Solar System) coupled with his sexy, dapper, grinning Grim-Reaper sort of persona creates emotional dissonance. He's at once the sexiest at the party and the deadliest. The word plutocrat suggests Pluto, god of Hades, the great mystery from whence we come into this world and into which we disappear at death.

Split Trends

A subtle split in the US economy between investors and workers really began in the mid-1970s when tariffs were lowered to facilitate international trade. From that point, wages trended down while stocks trended up, and these trends continued, with minor glitches, through the 1980s and to the present, 2010.

Till the mid-seventies, the American economy had created wealth for the population at large, as tariffs protected the wages of workers, thus providing able consumers for producers. NAFTA was sold to the American public as "free trade," the loaded but vague word "free" being key.

By January 1, 1999, when the European Union issued the euro as the new currency that would replace the need to swap francs for marks and other national European currencies, a sea change in international trade loomed ahead, but few were fully aware of this at the time. Astrologically, Pluto was at 9 Sagittarius opposite the US Ascendant and Uranus at 8 Gemini.

Remember that during the 1960s, Uranus and Pluto had come conjunct in Virgo (square by Sign to both Gemini and Sagittarius) to become the signature of the civil rights and antiwar movements, and other upheavals of those volatile years. The opposition of 1999 indicated another clash of values and breakdown of understanding. This clash would not manifest immediately, as Pluto's effects usually build up with unnoticed subtlety before manifesting dramatically, and when Uranus is involved, the drama can be at once sudden and unprecedented.

Iraq's Switch

Although it was not mentioned by the corporatized media, Iraq's Oil Ministry switched from selling oil for dollars to selling for euros on November 6, 2000. One reason this major change was ignored by the US media was the contested Florida vote count of the 2000 presidential election, which was settled by the Supreme Court in George W. Bush's favor. To arrive at that decision the US Supreme Court reversed its previous habit of deferring to the states to settle such disputes.

Time and Money

At this time, Jupiter was conjunct the US Ascendant and Uranus while Pluto was opposite from 11 Sagittarius. Jupiter's expansiveness was impacting the warrior energy of the US Uranus while Pluto was promising transformative changes looming ahead.

We now know from documents which were not public in 2000 that some in the new Bush Administration—notably those in the Pentagon called the neocons—were planning an invasion of Iraq even as George W. was being sworn in. The neocons had their own agenda, which would not have been salable to the American public at that time: to protect Israel, restructure the politics of the Middle East and protect the dollar as the currency of choice for international trade. If the euro replaced the dollar, it would mean a major change in the world status of the USA, and might put an added economic burden on Americans, if the euro rose in relation to the dollar. It soon did, providing the Iraqis with a 20 percent premium on oil sold for euros instead of dollars.

Speculative Bubble

While this problem was festering "off camera," so to speak, the stock market had built a speculative bubble that broke in the spring of 2000. Using the crash of early April as our marker, we find Pluto at 12 Sagittarius, now within orb of an opposition to the US Mars and square to the US Neptune, the signature of previous stock crashes. Completing a grand cross to the Mars-Neptune square were Mercury and Venus in Pisces, opposite the US Neptune and square the US Mars. To add oomph, the big asteroid Chiron was conjunct Pluto in Sagittarius.

In terms of points, this was a record plunge for US stocks, and ushered in the post-bubble economy of the early 21st Century. I have already mentioned why I read Pluto's movement through Sagittarius and into Capricorn as heralding a long secular bear market leading to a period between 2008 and 2019 when the USA is likely to endure a period more difficult than any in previous history. There are likely to be pops of stock prices during the first decade of the 21st Century but the overall trend will be down, I predict, because the American economy will be undergoing another major transformation, the likes of which we haven't seen since the last time Pluto sojourned through this area during the years leading up to and through the American Revolution of 1776.

Chaotic Health Care System

It soon became clear that George W. Bush, who many Americans believed had been appointed rather than elected, was to be the best president big corporations ever had. To cite just one issue, polls showed that between 80 and 95 percent of Americans would prefer a single-payer health care system; the Bush Administration instead beefed up the hodgepodge of insurance companies which made health care in the USA about twice as expensive per capita as elsewhere in the industrialized world, and infinitely more complex and confusing. It also soon became evident that big insurance companies had discovered a new source of added profits: clerical errors. Providers of health care were obliged to sort through the different systems of various insurance carriers for errors and request corrections in order to get paid. To deal with this, some affluent doctors formed groups to create their own health maintenance organi-zations. Overall, however, no one was happy with this system except the big insurance corporations, which racked up record profits.

Thus the bifurcation between workers and big financial interests that had begun in the mid-1970s grew dramatically. It was, as someone said, "The Mexification of the US economy." Many companies moved overseas for cheap labor and continued to manufacture goods for sale to American workers/consumers, while many others welcomed new cheap laborers from south of the border, further downsizing the wages of native-born Americans.

Faith in Free Enterprise

I hasten to add that the Bushites did not say they created this new economy for mendacious reasons. They believe in free enterprise "supply side" capitalism as the best for all. They are monetarists: increase production and the benefits will spread to all other sectors of the economy—that is their belief, indeed their fervent faith. And, compared to the economic catastrophe which had brought down the old Soviet Union, who was to say that state bureaucrats could run a command-and-control form of capitalism called communism better than elite entrepreneurs could run a social-security protected system called "unfettered free enterprise"? With Saturn, Uranus and Neptune out of harm's way, only subtle Pluto haunted from Sagittarius.

When Saturn moved into Gemini and thus opposite Pluto in Sagittarius, the US economy entered a new and unprecedented phase. Just as George W. Bush's new economic programs were beginning to take hold, the horror of 911 was upon us. Saturn and Pluto move opposite each other, with the Earth between, about three times a century. The previous opposition had coincided with The Sixties; the one before that with The Great Depression. History showed that Saturn-Pluto oppositions marked major turning points, and when they occurred in sensitive points on the USA's natal pattern, such a turn could bring us into a whole new sense of reality.

For most Americans, 911 seemed the product of deranged minds, crazed Arabs who'd lashed out at innocent people who'd done them no harm. Most Americans had no idea what nasty covert operations their tax dollars funded in Arab countries. Those in positions of economic power and influence, however, did not miss the fact that these suicide attackers had targeted the world's most prominent symbol of free-market capitalism, the New York Trade Center's Twin Towers, and the headquarters of free-market military muscle, the Pentagon.

Like the assassination of President John F. Kennedy in 1962, 911 would leave a wake of unanswered questions and speculations, suspicions and rumors, theories and alternative theories. The Saturn-Pluto opposition of 911 squared the one of the 1960s.

No one knows why these hard angles—conjunctions, squares and oppositions—formed by the outermost planets coincide with major turning points in history. Since the advent of modern science, no one has come up with even a theory rational enough to interest scientists. Yet it would be fun to access the super computers at a UC Berkeley, say, to combine Western, Vedic, Chinese and Mayan astrology and find out what ancient secrets this might reveal.

You Get the Vote, We Get Your Oil

The invasion of Iraq began on March 20, 2003 with what Bush operatives dubbed "shock and awe." At this time a grand cross had formed: Pluto at 20 Sagittarius opposite Saturn and both afflicting the US Mars, square the US Neptune. Transiting Neptune, conjunct the US Moon, was forming a grand trine with the US Uranus and Saturn.

It's interesting to note that when Cortez invaded Mexico in 1512, Pluto, Mars and Neptune were then where they would be again for Bush's invasion of Iraq. Cortez was saving the Indians for Christ. Bush was saving the Iraqis for democracy. Those were the justifications. In reality, Cortez captured gold and Bush captured "black gold," oil.

In 2003 Saturn was opposite Pluto (the old assaulted by the new); in the time of Columbus and Cortez, the Saturn-Pluto opposition became exact in 1499 and 1500. In both periods, invaders were imposing the new on established societies. And in both periods, the invaded societies suffered.

The Bushites first sold the invasion of Iraq to the American public by linking the attack of 911 to Saddam Hussein and presenting dubious evidence that Iraq had weapons of mass destruction, including nuclear. When no such link and no such weapons materialized, the Bushites switched their focus to preparing the way for democracy by bombing much of Iraq to rubble. In the time of Columbus and Cortez, the primary weapon was inadvertently biological, as the invaders brought diseases the indigenous peoples had no immunity to.

Armies and Environments

As the American military moved up from Kuwait into Baghdad in 2003, it met very little resistance; the Iraqi military had seemingly evaporated. The toughest resistance came from a sand storm. In the first decade of the 1500s, the toughest resistance encountered by Spanish invaders were hurricanes, high mountains, large estuaries and dense jungles.

Before the Iraq invasion, a worldwide antiwar protest, the largest and most universal ever, had been dutifully downplayed by the American media. Nations such as France and Germany, Japan, Russia and China—expected by the Bushites to "see the light" and back the invasion—refused to join Bush's so-called "coalition of the willing." Resistance to Bush's war was especially strong among the people of the European Union.

In the time of Columbus and Cortez, exploration to find new sources of wealth was popular. The conquistadors were soon shipping loads of gold back to their mother country. In the time of Bush, it was unclear whether or not his invasion would enrich America with "black gold." In the 1500s, gold was the basis of money. By the dawn of the 21st Century, the dollar had replaced gold as the basic form of money, yet the dollar was denominated in barrels of "black gold."

Rise of the Euro

Two very important financial changes had occurred before the US invaded Iraq. On January 1, 1999, the euro replaced national currencies of the new European Union. And on November 6, 2000, as the attention of most Americans and much of the world was focused on the outcome of the US presidential election, Iraq switched from dollars to euros to sell their oil.

Some financial observers were astounded by Iraq's switch and predicted it would have a negative effect on the Iraqi economy. But the euro rose against the dollar so that by the end of 2002, Iraq had made a premium on oil sales. This premium had other oil producing nations contemplating switching from dollars to euros.

Robert Gover

Although the American public was "protected" by the corporatized media from information about this issue, it was widely understood by leading financiers around the world that, push come to shove, there was a bloodless way to defeat the USA's indomitable military: dump dollars and use euros as the new currency of choice for international trade. But if this switch were made suddenly, it would be devastating to the US economy and would have a ripple effect on the world economy. If the switch from dollars to euros was accomplished gradually, the US military would be defeated by economic undermining without doing much, if any, damage to the world economy.

What did the astrological indicators portend?

For the launching of the euro, Pluto was opposite the US Uranus, and Saturn at 26 Aries was opposite the US Saturn but separating. Mars was conjunct the US Saturn. Transiting Uranus was conjunct the US Moon. Jupiter was opposite the US Neptune. Transiting Neptune and Venus were conjunct the US Pluto-opposite-Mercury.

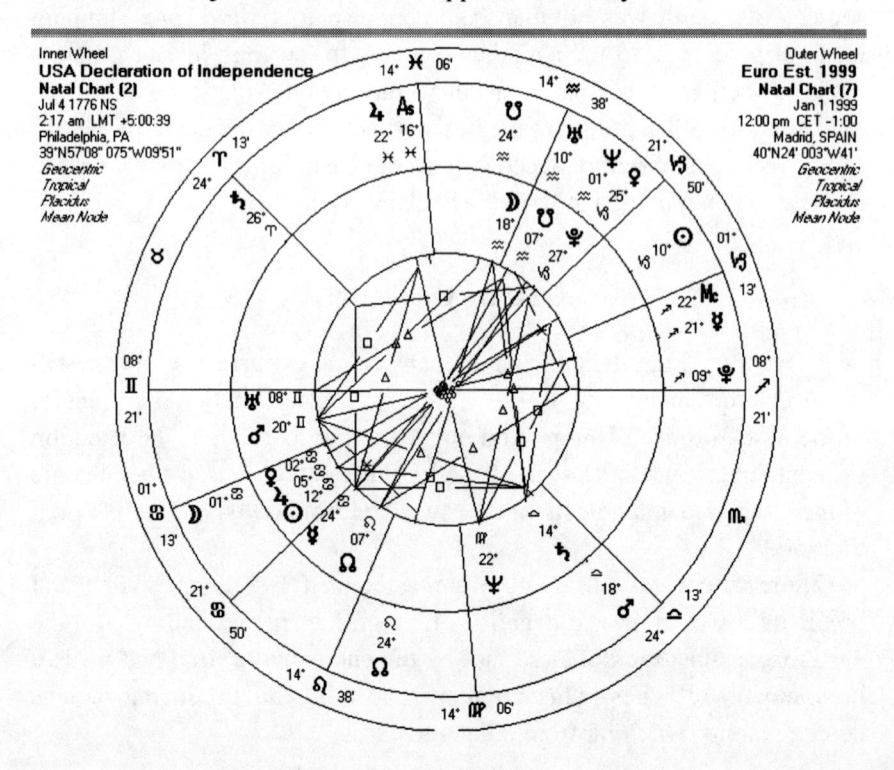

Time and Money

That the US Sun-Saturn square and Mars-Neptune square were both hit by negative aspects at the launch of the euro indicated that this would bring difficulties to the USA. But the most interesting aspect in this biwheel, I believe, is the Neptune-Venus conjunction afflicting the US Mercury-Pluto opposition. Notice Saturn at 26 Aries square the Neptune-Venus pair, creating a T square with the US Mercury-Pluto opposition.

Neptune tends to confuse Saturn's structures and systems. So the Saturn-Neptune square also suggested the EU would have its hands full instituting the euro, and that the euro might blur or bring confusion to the international financial system. There was, in effect, a foreshadowing of possible trouble for oil, ruled by Neptune, the commodity that was now the basis for currency exchanges.

That trouble manifested when Iraq switched from selling oil for dollars to selling oil for euros just after the November 2000 elections in the USA. At this time, a grand cross had formed with the US Mars-Neptune square by Pluto, Saturn, Sun and Mercury. The Moon was conjunct the US Saturn, square the US Sun, opposed at this time by Mars and Chiron in Capricorn.

Although the American media did not inform the public about this switch (Neptune conjunct the US Moon, ruler of the public), some financiers were made very uneasy by it, others were excited by the possibilities. If other oil producers followed Iraq's example, it would eventually do irreparable harm to the US economy, and to the USA's standing in the community of nations.

Saturn-Pluto oppositions usually impact a mix of old and new, established status quo and revolutionary agitation. As the USA brought a new political and economic regime to upset the status quo of Iraq, the increased use of the euro threatened the status quo of the dollar as the world's "reserve currency."

Protecting the Dollar

Even though the American media did not broadcast Iraq's switch from dollars to euros in November 2000, it had to be high on the list of unstated reasons for Bush's invasion of Iraq. While the American public

Robert Gover

had been led to believe that the USA was invading to capture Saddam Hussein's weapons of mass destruction, it was obvious that Bush was intent on capturing Iraq's oil. Less obvious was protecting Israel and the dollar, and the Middle East's most cherished commodity: water. Unlike other Middle Eastern countries, Iraq's two major rivers blessed it with an abundance of water.

Bush was elected to a second term in November 2004. The corporate owned media put out the notion that this was because the American people wanted a restoration of "moral values." The unspoken assumption was that the USA was unconcerned about the slaughter of an estimated 100,000 Iraqi civilians, but highly incensed by a bare tit flashed by Janet Jackson at the 2003 Super Bowl halftime show. Bloody wars were glamorized by the US media; sexual fun was attacked at "moral decay."

A new coalition between fundamentalist Christians and right-wing financial interests had become a "marriage of convenience." During the 1990s the rich right-wingers had thrown Bill Clinton and Monica Lewinski to sexual morality obsessed fundamentalists. When the invasion of Iraq did not turn out as planned, the corporatized media featured Janet's Jackson's bare breast, hours of crime stories and debate over the rights of gays, blocking bad news from Iraq: a new way to censor and maintain control of public opinion.

Dean Koontz caught the mood of the times in his novel *By the Light of the Moon* (Bantam, 2003):

"These were extraordinary times, peopled by ranting maniacs in love with violence and with a violent god, infected with apologists for wickedness, who blamed victims for their suffering and excused murderers in the name of justice. These were times still hammered by the utopian schemes that had nearly destroyed civilization in the previous century, ideological wrecking balls that swung through the early years of this new millennium with diminishing force but with sufficient residual power to demolish the hopes of multitudes."

Poll-Vote Discrepancy

The 2004 presidential election was infected by this poisonous mood. Around 2 million ballots cast by African Americans were "discarded" and not counted. That was not new—resistance to Black civil rights had a long history in the USA. What was new in 2004 was a discrepancy between exit polls and paperless computerized voting machines, especially in Ohio, where the outcome would decide whether Bush stayed in the White House or John Kerry unseated him. Exit polls in Ohio showed Kerry winning 52.1% over Bush's 47.9%. The vote count had Bush the winner by 51%. See http://www.bradblog.com/archives/00001024.htm.

Exit polls are used in many countries to verify vote counts. Exit polls have a proven accuracy of within half a percentage point, as compared to the pre-election polls, which are often wildly wrong. Exit polls ask voters who they just voted for; pre-election polls ask who they plan to vote for. Many voters don't make up their minds till Election Day, sometimes not till they are in the voting booth.

Yet the response of the US media to the discrepancy was to "edit" exit polls and then to declare them unreliable. Some Republicans recommended they be outlawed in future elections. Online sites were abuzz with statistics and academic analyses, and the hot concern of those who realized this could doom the last semblance of democratic governance in the USA. If incumbents of both political parties had the advantage of programmable computerized voting machines which produced no paper record for auditing, it could mark the final coup in the takeover of government by right-wingers, including the manufacturers of these machines, all of whom are conservative Republicans. If exit polls were outlawed, there would be no way to check the vote counts produced by paperless machines. Of course the trouble-free solution to this problem would be for Congress to simplify and standardize voting methods, but American politicians rarely find simple honesty expedient.

Leading up to the election of November 2004, on October 13 there was an eclipse at 21 Libra conjoined by Mars at 11 Libra, putting Sun, Moon, Mars and Mercury conjunct the US Saturn, square the US Sun.

The US natal pattern most heavily impacted this day, however, was the Mercury-Pluto opposition, hit by Saturn conjunct the US Mercury, square the eclipse. This spoke of the plutocratic media owners (Pluto) and the journalists (Mercury) they controlled.

He who sells what isn't his'n,
Must pay the price or go to prison

On election day, November 2, 2004 the US Mercury-Pluto opposition continued to be hit by Saturn square Moon and Mercury in late Libra, and the Libra cluster also square the US Sun in Cancer, plus Neptune continuing to conjunct the US Moon, confusing the public. It's the lingering conjunction of Neptune and the US Moon that speaks to the discrepancy between exit polls and vote counts.

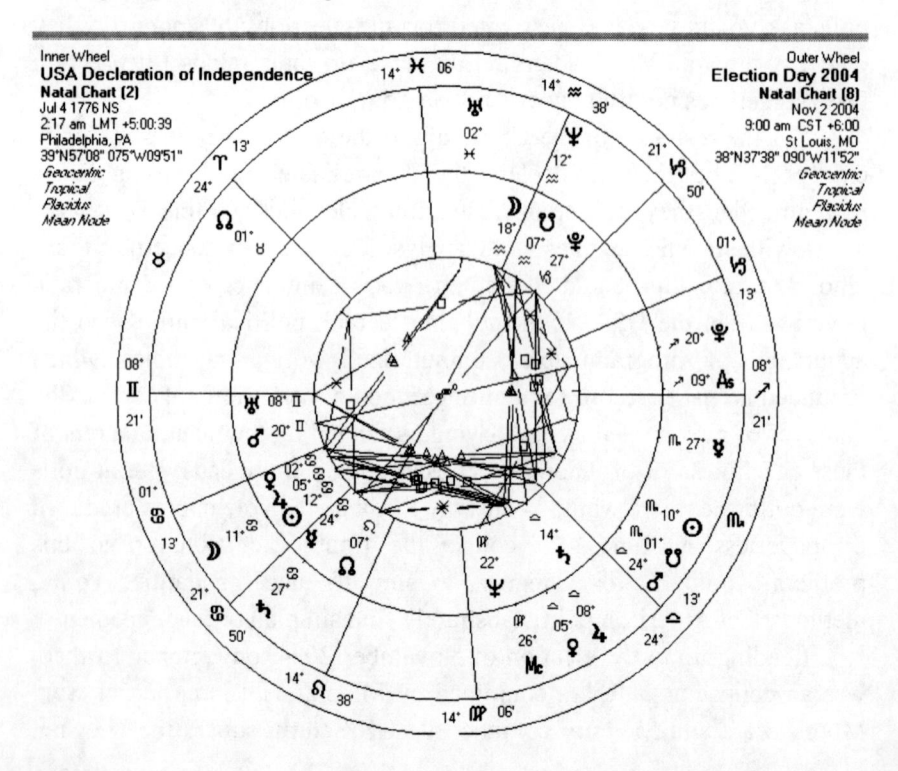

Time and Money

The big money guys (Pluto) were the focus around this time. Dick Chaney, before becoming Bush's Vice President, was CEO of Halliburton, a mammoth multinational making billions of profits annually. Money is power. Halliburton's mission in life is to make more money and wield more power. So the people who run Halliburton find many wonderful ways to sweeten the lives of politicians. This naturally makes the politicians feel beholden. They don't have to ask what the good folks at Halliburton would like in return. They know its corporate mission. What makes the most profits? War! So the neocons at the Pentagon persuaded their President that war is needed in the Middle East. The word "allocate" is used to make it seem "official," something the public could do nothing about. "Authorities allocated" billions to Halliburton and other mega-corporations for the war effort. This was a slick PR way to plunder the American public and deliver interest-free capital to the most generous campaign contributors to Bush and co. None dared call it what it really was for fear of being ostracized as "unpatriotic."

Also given the stamp of official approval was the Federal Communications Commission's sale of the public-owned airwaves to private corporations, creating the big media conglomerates which now own TV, radio, newspapers, magazines, book publishing—every information medium except the Internet. There was a loud outcry of objection to this move, but like the privatized health care system, the democratic will of the people could not overcome that form of Supreme Court created free speech called campaign contributions by the wealthy.

The media reported the cost of the war in Iraq—early estimates ran to about $20 billion, which has since ballooned to over $200 billion—but did not mention whose possession all this money wound up in. Clearly little was devoted to upgrading the equipment of the foot soldiers ordered into dangerous Iraqi cities and towns. They were invaders being attacked daily by so-called "insurgents," some of whom were described as Muslim extremists who saw Iraq as a jihad opportunity to kill Americans. It's safe to assume most of the recipients of those billions for the war lived thousands of miles away from the war.

It's never a good idea for politicians and bureaucrats to sell what belongs to the public without explicit permission by the public. This is the kind of thing that got King George in trouble one cycle of Pluto ago when he decided to tax American colonists, making them pay for his war against France. Rulers usually get away with such moves—except when Pluto moves through Sagittarius and Capricorn, and 33-year-cyclical oppositions from Mars to Pluto trigger impassioned objections. Even then change usually takes a decade or more to happen, so it doesn't seem accelerated to those living through it. But compared to other decades in Pluto's 248-year cycle, change definitely unfolds faster and more furiously during Pluto's sojourn through the wintry signs.

Occupied Iraq Votes

By January 30, 2005, the media had public attention focused on elections in Iraq. Again the major concern was that terrorists would disrupt the elections. Large numbers of Iraqis turned out to cast ballots and again the outcome was billed as a big success for American democracy.

Déjà vu all over again:

"United States officials were surprised and heartened today at the size of turnout in South Vietnam's presidential election despite a Vietcong terrorist campaign to disrupt the voting. According to reports from Saigon, 83 percent of the 5.85 million registered voters cast their ballots yesterday. Many of them risked reprisals threatened by the Vietcong. A successful election has long been seen as the keystone in President Johnson's policy of encouraging the growth of constitutional processes in South Vietnam." - Peter Grose, in a page 2 New York Times article titled 'U.S. Encouraged by Vietnam Vote,' September 4, 1967.

We'll Take Care of Your Oil

In 1967, Pluto was conjunct Uranus at 20 Virgo with both conjunct the US Neptune, square the US Mars.

In 2005, Pluto was square where it had been in 1967 at 21 Sagittarius, square the US Neptune and opposite the US Mars.

Time and Money

The last time Pluto moved through Sagittarius square Uranus in Pisces was during the French and Indian War and the years leading up to the American Revolution, with both afflicting the US Mars-Neptune square—a pattern that will repeat in 2009.

George W., like King George before him, served mercantile interests. He was mainly interested in programs that would guarantee bigger profits for his basic constituents. What the Bush Administration was saying to Iraqis, in effect, is this:

You nice folks go out to the polls and vote and we'll take care of your oil.

Islamic Terrorists and Mother Nature

In early 2005 the dollar continued to fall against the euro and other currencies. Some US commentators said this was a good thing, enabling the US to more easily reduce the budget deficit, national debt and trade imbalance, all at new record highs. Others feared the dollar might sink to a point where it would wreck the US economy, and might even reduce America to third world status, depending on how devalued it became.

The question of the dollar's future has its roots in a more prosperous past. By the end of the virtuous circle economy following World War II, there had arisen an amazing improvisation on the capitalist system: big investors and their political friends had, during World War II, rediscovered the magnificent profits to be made from war. But "war profiteering" was not a nice way to say it, so the dressed-for-church thieves of the military-industrial complex turned to public relations and renamed the War Department the Department of Defense, and "war profiteering" became "defense spending."

By 2000, politicians had staff-written speeches to deliver, extolling "the defense industry as the engine of economic growth." It was sometimes embarrassing to watch on TV as a dapper Congressman stumbled like a first-grader through a recitation of unfamiliar staff-written script. The military-industrial complex President Eisenhower had warned against had grown and prospered till, by 2005, it constituted a kind of massive vampire called "Patriotism," sucking blood and treasure from the nation. It was comparable to the German military-industrial complex created in the 1930s by the Nazi Party led by Adolph Hitler half a cycle of Pluto ago.

Time and Money

In the US this "military Keynesian stimulus" was the result of something that *seemed* valid: that it was World War II which pulled the US out of the great depression of the 1930s. While it's true the military-industrial economy pumped more dollars into the system, this was really another Neptunian delusion: things produced for the military either get destroyed in wars, become obsolete, or rust and disintegrate. The military-industrial complex, despite pumping huge amounts of money into the economy, does not produce goods and services which improve the overall economy by creating real wealth. Jet fighters are fun to play with and can be rented out to make exciting movies extolling the military, but eventually they're either destroyed or scrapped.

"Our Finest People"

By the time this military-industrial complex had ripened, just about every American home had a TV set, through which "our finest people" could persuade the public—with some help from patriotic symbols and sly background music—that it was flag-waving apple-pie mother-loving American.

It was the military power of the Soviet Union which supposedly justified the perpetuation of American military build-up after World War II. In reality, the Soviet military had never been a match for the US military, and after the fall of the old Soviet Union in 1989 (Saturn, Uranus and Neptune conjunct in Capricorn, opposite the US Sun), no other nation could dream of matching Uncle Sam's firepower.

And so it came about that one cycle of Pluto-in-Sagittarius after American colonists used terror tactics on British troops sent by King George, Muslim "insurgents" did likewise to troops sent to Iraq and Afghanistan by George Bush.

Money and Democracy

In a sense, Bush the younger is the historic culmination of the Hamiltonian line of belief: "Anything worth doing is worth doing for money." The Hamiltonians were understandably fearful of "mob rule," as John Adams called unfettered democracy. I say "understandably" because it's quite clear that large populations can be manipulated. And the means of manipulation have never been more powerful than they now are. You can be badly misinformed by watching the evening news.

At one point in the public relations effort to sell the invasion of Iraq, 70 percent of Americans believed that Iraq was behind the attack of 911, that Saddam Hussein had weapons of mass destruction and plans to use them on Americans. The Nazis in the 1930s had demonstrated that big lies are more effective than small lies—back in the days of radio, before television. Now pictures can be transmitted in a wink from Iraq to Indianapolis.

But when pictures of what's happening contradict what the government and media say is happening, political dissonance occurs. Eventually, some people tend to believe what they see rather than what they are told. The Vietnam War came undone due to this form of dissonance. By 2005, public support for "Bush's war" was flagging a bit, but the public relations experts were hard at work, developing new and better ways to manipulate public opinion.

Magical Euphemisms

What the heirs of Hamiltonian thought and Nazi propaganda have perfected is the magic of euphemisms. Call it something nice and the nation will support it. Bush's "Clean Air" legislation has the effect of creating dirty air; "Prescription drugs for seniors" sabotages Medicare and is a giveaway to the pharmaceutical industry; "tax relief for families" enrich the richest 2 percent at the expense of the society at large. More recently, "saving Social Security"—if Bush's plan is enacted—will destroy social security.

These are smart guys, the ones who come up with these PR phrases. But history indicates "events conspire" against their kind and eventually the Uranian unprecedented happens and down the toilet of history they go. For Bush and company, events were conspiring on both economic and ecological fronts.

Time and Money

Watching the dollar steadily drop in relation to the euro and other foreign currencies, some canny investors in 2004 began buying gold and gold mining stocks, and from China to Paris bankers discussed dumping dollars.

From *The Daily Reckoning*, "Greenback Grease Oil" by Eric Fry, January 27, 2005 edition:

"Last night, Fan Gang, director of the National Economic Research Institute at the China Reform Foundation, shocked a standing-room crowd at the World Economic Forum in Davos, Switzerland, when he volunteered, "The US dollar is no longer—in our opinion is no longer—[seen] as a stable currency, and is devaluating all the time, and that's putting troubles all the time."

Fan Gang was by no means the only practitioner of "the dismal science" (economics) who saw trouble ahead.

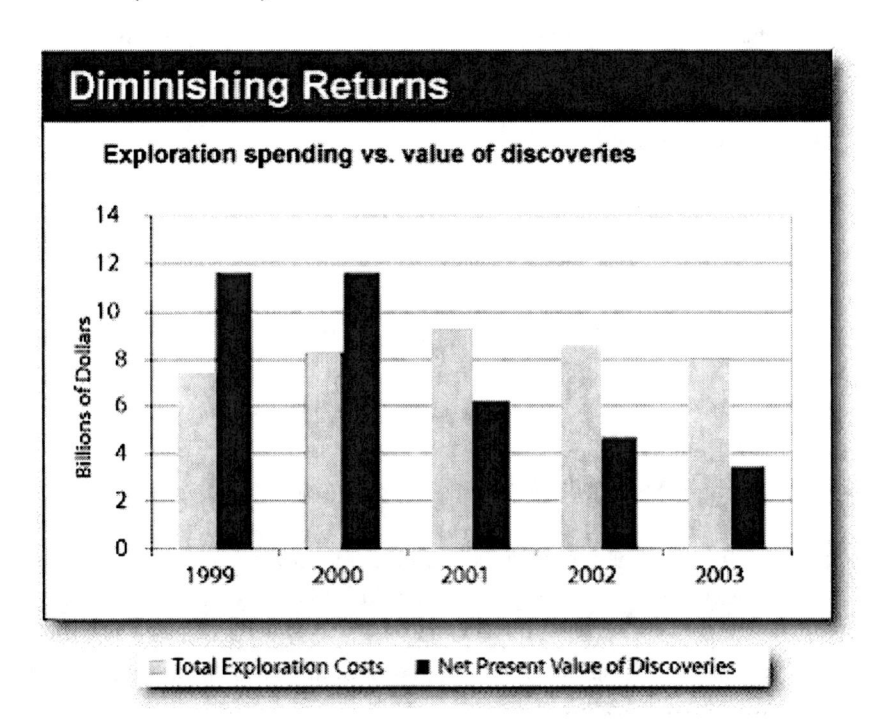

Diminishing Returns

Exploration spending vs. value of discoveries

(Billions of Dollars, 1999–2003: Total Exploration Costs ■ Net Present Value of Discoveries)

"The key to the oil price, we believe, lies not so much in the ratio of reserves to production," observed James Grant, editor of Grant's Interest

Rate Observer, *"but in the position of the dollar in the global economy...The dollar exchange rate is—ultimately—going down."*

Too many dollars chasing too little oil may drive a Neptunian-deluded bull market in oil company stocks, but ultimately no form of currency can buy what is no longer there.

What the above chart indicates is that we've probably discovered most, if not all the oil reserves there are on planet Earth; there's no point throwing good exploration money after bad, but old habits die hard.

Common sense decrees that we get busy yesterday discovering and developing alternative forms of energy. But the Bush Administration was stuck in a medieval feudal mindset. In W's actions—as compared to his words—a strong streak of fundamentalist Christian belief was evident. He was being called "the faith-based president." Just as the English settlers of Jamestown believed Indians would become civilized if they'd put on English clothes, so George Bush, it seems, believed Iraqis would come to love American control of their oil if he could get them to the voting polls. And, with the help of PR power, he did. Iraqi citizens get the vote; Mobile Exxon gets the oil.

Translation Difficulties

But American PR lingo did not translate as intended into other languages. Most of humanity outside the USA watched the action and perceived Bush's feet going one way, his words another. You could still find folks in the American Deep South and Midwest, whose information came from rightwing radio talk shows, who still believed the talk, but even some of them were starting to notice the walk. One of their favorite talk show hosts turned out to be addicted to doctor feel-good drugs. Another was forced to admit he'd been paid by Bushites to propagandize for Bush's "no child left behind" drive, an unfunded law wrapped in the delusion that punishing impoverished school districts would solve the USA's growing illiteracy problem.

Time and Money

Undoing Social Security

Also pointing to future social upheavals was the Bush Administration's scheme to undo Social Security. President Franklin Delano Roosevelt had signed the original Social Security Act into law on August 14, 1935, at or around the depths of the Great Depression. The long-range effect of this act helped narrow the pre-depression record-large discrepancy between rich and poor which had arisen by 1929.

The Social Security Act (H.R. 7260, Public Law No. 271, 74th Congress) became law with the President's signature at approximately 3:30 p.m. on a Wednesday, August 14, 1935.

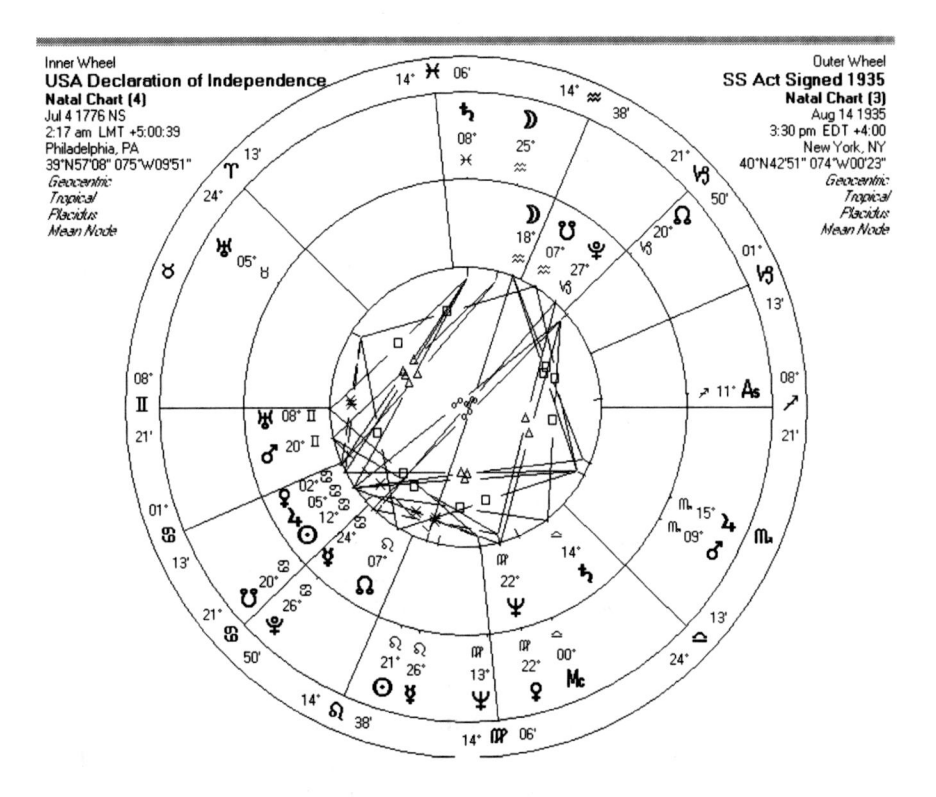

Saturn at 8 Pisces formed an applying opposition to Neptune at 13 Virgo with both square the US Ascendant and Uranus in Gemini, indicating that implementing this new program would be fraught with confusions (Neptune) and difficulties (Saturn) and unprecedented surprises (Uranus). It had strong opposition from conservatives then, and that opposition would continue for the next 70 years.

Saturn in Pisces was also forming a very helpful 120 degree trine to the US conjunction of Venus, Jupiter and Sun in Cancer, indicating that this act would be good for the overall economy, and it certainly has been. Mars and Jupiter, conjunct in Scorpio, completed a grand trine with Saturn to the US cluster of good-luck planets in the US 2nd house of wealth and well-being. Conservatives would have a hard time undoing what they perceived as "a socialist horror."

What's been so surprising about the conservatives' attempts over the years to abolish or, short of that, erode Social Security is that it's been as beneficial to the rich as to the poor. It has enabled poor survivors to pay rents and buy food and a few consumer goods and services which profit wealthy conservatives, the ultimate beneficiaries of all profit-making transactions. Against the weight of this evidence, however, some rich conservatives persisted in pressuring government to downgrade the working class and poor, in the belief that this will provide a larger and more humbled work force, producing bigger profits. Belief trumps evidence and the old beliefs of feudalism die hard.

Heads I win, Tails You Lose

But there were some sharp minds chewing on this latest attempt to "privatize" Social Security, among them Paul Krugman, New York Times columnist, Princeton professor, and author of *The Great Unraveling: Losing Our Way in the New Century*. In an article for the *New York Review of Books*, Krugman pointed out that what the Social Security crisis mongers were doing was like the kid's trick coin toss: "Heads I win, tails you lose." When the Social Security Trust Fund runs a surplus, the crisis mongers don't count it because the money is in US Treasury Bonds, which are part of the government's operating expenses. But when Social Security runs a deficit, it is ballyhooed as an independent entity, separate from the rest of the federal government.

"There are only two ways Social Security could be unable to pay full benefits in 2018," wrote Krugman. "One would be if Congress voted specifically to repudiate the Social Security trust fund, that is, not pay interest or principle on the trust fund's bonds...(but) the trust fund is as real an obligation of the US government as bonds held by Japanese pension funds. The other way would be if the United States found itself in a general fiscal crisis, unable to honor any of its debt. Given the size of the current deficit and the prospect that the deficit will get much bigger over time, that could happen. But it won't happen because of Social Security, which is a much smaller factor in projected deficits than either tax cuts or rising Medicare spending." Not to mention "defense spending."

But President George Bush clearly had no intention of saving Social Security; "his first tax cut would have broken the 'lockbox' all by itself, and his insistence on pushing through another major tax cut after launching the Iraq war made it clear that this wasn't a fluke. But that's not a Social Security problem. Viewed on its own terms, Social Security has been run responsibly and is a sustainable system."

American conservatives may not succeed in their scheme to privatize (and thus sabotage) Social Security in 2005, creating a bonanza give-away to brokerage companies, but you can bet they'll keep trying. They have demonstrated patience and persistence, and they've mastered the art of slight-of-hand public relations.

Keep in mind that from the far right (now an unlikely cabal of religious and fiscal reactionaries), Bush is perceived as the best thing since white bread. The Saturn-Pluto opposition, in its swash, inevitably brings out such diametrically opposed opinions: Rutting wild rams butting horns. Right-wing conservatives love the "glory that was Rome" and romanticize the feudalism of Medieval times when societies were split between autocratic aristocracies and cringing, subservient workers, and the Inquisition dealt harshly with "infidels," anyone who disagreed with the prevailing belief system.

Robert Gover

"Greenspan's Whopper"

But not all conservatives are so brain dead they cannot appreciate the consequences of the Bush Administration's policies and actions, including the policies of the Fed under Bush-supporter Alan Greenspan.

"The US economy faced a major recession in 2001 and had a minor one. The necessary slump was held off by a dramatic resort to central planning. The 'invisible hand' is fine for lumber and poultry prices. But at the short end of the market in debt, Alan Greenspan's paw presses down like a butcher's thumb on the meat scale." ("Greenspan's Whopper" by Bill Bonner, *The Daily Reckoning*, February 16, 2005).

In 2001, Bonner continues, "The Fed quickly cut rates to head off the recession. Indeed, never before had rates been cut so much, so fast. George W. Bush, meanwhile, boosted spending. The resultant shock of renewed, ersatz demand not only postponed the recession; it misled consumers, investors and businessmen to make even more egregious errors. Investors bought stock with low earnings yields. Consumers went further into debt. Government liabilities rose. The trade deficit grew larger. Even on the other side of the globe, foreign businessmen geared up to meet the phony new demand; China enjoyed a capital spending boom as excessive as any the world has ever seen."

Bonner maintains that what Greenspan did was disrupt a natural cyclical correction and "transmorgrify" to create an enormous economic bubble in stocks and real estate.

"A bubble in stock prices may do little real economic damage. Eventually the bubble pops, and the phony money people thought they had, disappears like a puff of marijuana smoke...

"But in Greenspan's bubble economy something remarkably awful happened. Householders were lured to 'take out' the equity in their homes. They believed that the bubble in real estate prices created 'wealth' that they could spend. Many did not hesitate. Mortgage debt ballooned in the early years of the 21st century—from about $6 trillion in 1999 to nearly $9 trillion at the end of 2004. Three trillion dollars may not seem like much to you, dear reader. But it increased the average household's debt by $30,000. Americans still lived in more or less the same houses. But they owed far more on them."

John Law's long shadow, it seems, extends into the 21st Century, confusing money with real wealth. Yet, on the other hand, there were a few who turned their home equity into capital they'd not otherwise have had, and founded businesses which did create real wealth. However, too many workers/consumers paid down credit cards and went out shopping again. I should know: my house bought the car I drive.

"Our own Fed chairman, guardian of the nation's money...custodian of its economy...night watchman of its wealth...How could he do such a thing? And yet he has done it. He turned a financial bubble into an economic bubble. Not only were the prices of financial assets ballooned to excess...so were the prices of houses...and so were the debts of the average household.

"Where does it lead? The force of a correction is equal to the deception that preceded it. Mr. Greenspan's whopper must be followed by a whopper of a slump."

2008 Election

On November 4, 2008 the first exact hit of a Saturn-Uranus opposition afflicts the US Mars-Neptune square, with the Moon conjunct the US Mars acting as trigger for whatever chickens are coming home to roost. The previous Saturn-Uranus opposition heated up the Vietnam War and the antiwar movement. The one before that coincided with World War I, the Russian Revolution, and the early days of the Nazi Party in Germany, among other long-lasting events.

Notice on the outer wheel that on November 4, 2008, Saturn at 10 Virgo is precisely opposite Uranus at 10 Pisces. Forming a grand cross with this Saturn-Uranus opposition is the US Mars opposed by transiting Venus at 20 Sagittarius. Passions will be sky high for this election while the financial markets are in danger of causing panic. On a scale of 1 to 10, I'd guesstimate the chances of a financial crash are around 6. They increase to around 9.5 by February 5, the date of the chart below, when the Saturn-Uranus opposition tightens to within 1 degree square US Mars, and 2 degrees opposite and conjunct US Neptune.

Robert Gover

The Saturn-Uranus opposition on February 5 is also square the Moon at 22 Gemini, afflicting the US Mars-Neptune square, forming a T square with Saturn and Uranus. Also addressing the banking system is Mars and Mercury in late Capricorn and early Aquarius, conjunct the US Pluto, opposite the US Mercury. Transiting Pluto at 2 Capricorn is precisely opposite the US Venus, tying it into an opposition to Sam's good-luck 2nd house of wealth and well-being. Venus at 2 Aries is square both Pluto at 2 Capricorn and the US Venus at 2 Cancer. Neptune at 23 Aquarius is precisely trine the Moon and US Mars, adding inspiration and/or delusion. Even positive angles from Neptune may turn out, in retrospect, to have created delusions, believed at the time to be inspirations.

History tells us that so many hard angles to these sensitive financial points in the US birth chart augur major reshaping events.

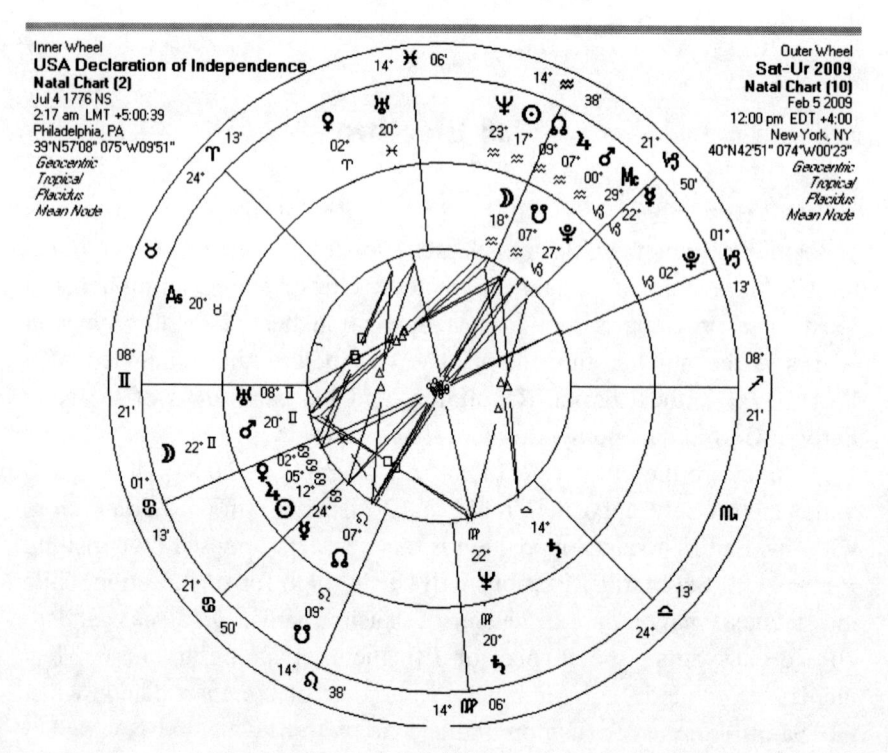

Grisham's Law

Desmond Lachman, a resident fellow at the American Enterprise Institute, in an article posted February 4, 2005, explores what could go wrong, and I would add, according to Grisham's Law, will go wrong, triggering the hard economic period promised by the upcoming Uranus-Pluto square.

"As a result of consistent external deficits since 1982, the United States has moved from a position of being the world's largest creditor nation, with net external assets equivalent to almost 15 percent of GDP in 1982, to being the world's largest debtor nation, with net external liabilities equivalent to 30 percent of GDP by 2004. More disturbing still is the fact that the US net external debt is on a path to exceed over 100 percent of GDP within the next twenty years should the US fail to rein in its presently large external deficit."

Lachman points out that no prior empire was a net debtor. For example at the height of the British Empire, between 1870 and 1914, England ran current account surpluses averaging 5 percent of GDP a year.

"The question that now needs to be addressed," Lachman continues, "is whether the foreign central banks' massive dollar reserve holdings might not place the US in an untenably vulnerable economic position. Might for instance China not be tempted some day to unload its vast dollar holdings to express its displeasure over US policy concerning the Straits of Taiwan? Or might not the OPEC countries be tempted to use their large dollar holdings to register their disagreement over US policy in the Middle East? These considerations would make one think that the days are long since gone (when) US external finances can afford to be treated with the same benign neglect that they have been treated over the past four years."

It's too late for the Bushites to address this problem, even if they showed an awareness of it, which they had not shown by early 2005. For already central banks around the world have begun getting rid of dollars and switching to euros for international trade.

Robert Gover

"Change or Be Changed"

Remember that Uranus and Pluto form their first of many square aspects in 2008—by July they will be within orb of the first hit of their upcoming series of squares, climaxing in 2015 and lasting till 2019. This first will have separated by early 2009 due to Pluto's erratic orbit, but be in the process of reforming later that year. By this time the full impact of international central banks "dumping" dollars and switching to euros is likely to be impacting. In November 2009, Saturn and Pluto will form a waning square, culminating how the USA handled challenges following 911 when Saturn and Pluto were 180 degrees opposite.

I don't think it matters whether it's a Republican or Democrat who moves into the Oval Office in 2009—or if Bush is declared unfit for office or ends his tenure prematurely for other reasons. What needs to be changed is not who sits in the Oval Office, but the economic-political system that has corrupted both Republicans and Democrats. Installing new actors in old roles won't author a new cultural script. True democracy and common sense cannot flourish as long as the government is held hostage by the spawn of Columbus with disdain for the plight of the poor.

Our first revolution, remember, arose and unfolded with Pluto's transit through these same wintry signs of Sagittarius and Capricorn. During Pluto's second sojourn through this area, a second revolution is indicated by the long square to be made between transformative Pluto and the planet of revolutionary passion, Uranus, happening almost simultaneously with the waning Saturn-Pluto square.

The other side of the economic-astrological dialogue is what we believe and thus how we respond to such harsh planetary angles. With both economic and ecological catastrophes indicated by mounting evidence—in dialogue with a ruling elite addicted to free-market capitalism—this will be an opportune time for progressives to present their solutions to economic problems.

Empires and Revolutions

"The unofficial history of America...is not a story of rugged individualism and heroic personal sacrifice in the pursuit of a dream. It is a story of democracy derailed, of a revolutionary spirit suppressed, and of a once-proud people reduced to servitude." —William Kalle Lasn, *The History of Corporations in the United States* (Morrow/Eaglebrook)

"A bit-player in the official history becomes critically important to the way the unofficial history unfolds," Lasn continues. "This player lies at the heart of America's defining theme: the difference between a country that pretends to be free and a country that truly is free. That player is the corporation. The United States of America was born of a revolt not just against British monarchs and the British parliament but against British corporations."

There are three historic turning points in the USA's relationship with corporations: 1) the Boston Tea Party December 16, 1773; 2) a court case called *Santa Clara County v. Southern Pacific*, on May 10, 1886, and 3) another case called *Buckley v. Valeo*, decided by the Supreme Court January 20, 1976.

Boston Tea Party

One cycle of Pluto ago, during the years leading up to the American Revolution, British corporations had a free hand in plundering American colonists. Corporations in pre-Revolutionary America were fewer in number but they were as powerful then as now. King George's relationship with corporations then is similar to an American President's relationship with them today. The anger of American colonists toward the British King and parliament was due mainly to their giving corporations the freedom to exploit the colonists.

The British East India Company imposed duties on its incoming shipments of tea, telling colonists they could buy their tea or do without. The company had a monopoly. American colonists began to react by turning away East India ships at ports up and own the East Coast. This climaxed in the famous Boston Tea Party December 16, 1773, when rebels dressed as Mohawk Indians boarded three merchant ships and dumped the entire cargo of 342 chests of tea into Boston Harbor. This lit the spark that led to the overthrow of British rule by demonstrating that, united, the colonists could stand up to British corporations.

"The Declaration of Independence, in 1776, freed Americans not only from Britain but also from the tyranny of British corporations, and for a hundred years after the document's signing, Americans remained deeply suspicious of corporate power. They were careful about the way they granted corporate charters, and about the powers granted therein," wrote Lasn.

For a century the new nation kept corporations on a tight leash. "They weren't allowed to participate in the political process. They couldn't buy stock in other corporations. And if one of them acted improperly, the consequences were severe. In 1832, President Andrew Jackson vetoed a motion to extend the charter of the corrupt and tyrannical Second Bank of the United States, and was widely applauded for doing so. That same year the state of Pennsylvania revoked the charters of ten banks for operating contrary to the public interest. Even the enormous industry trusts, formed to protect member corporations from external competitors and provide barriers to entry, eventually proved no match for the state. By the mid-1800s, antitrust legislation was widely in place." (Lasn.)

A World-Altering Mistake

In the 1870s, Southern Pacific Railroad refused to pay taxes to Santa Clara County. The sticking point was that the county had included fencing along the railroad right-of-way in their tax assessment, but the fencing belonged to the county. Although the fencing was a tiny fraction of the total assessment, the company refused to pay any of the tax. The case came before a Supreme Court headed by Chief Justice Morrison R. Waite, President Grant's seventh choice to replace Chief Justice Solomon P. Chase. Waite had never been a judge on any court before and was so happy with this appointment that he turned down the Republican Party nomination for President in 1876.

Southern Pacific Railroad's lawyer cited six reasons why his client should not have to pay, including the Fourteenth Amendment, which was enacted after the Civil War, providing former slaves equal rights under the law. The lawyer for Santa Clara County pointed out that to declare corporations persons was illogical. "The whole history of the Fourteenth Amendment demonstrates beyond dispute that its whole scope and object was to establish equality between men—an attainable result—and not to establish equality between natural and artificial beings—an impossible result."

Just before the Court's decision was read on May 10, 1886, Chief Justice Waite said to the contending lawyers, "The court does not wish to hear argument on the question whether the provision in the Fourteenth Amendment to the Constitution, which forbids a state to deny to any person within its jurisdiction the equal protection of the laws, applies...We are of the opinion that it does."

In the Court's written decision, there is no mention of overturning existing laws regulating corporations. In effect, the decision assumes that corporations are persons, and that a government cannot deal with such artificial persons differently than it deals with natural human persons.

Waite's decision freed corporations from tight restrictions imposed by the founders of the USA, and led to the mega-corporate cartels which dominate the world today. That corporations are actually documents, pieces of paper, did not deter the Chief Justice from converting an ideological fantasy into a world-altering reality. The joy of campaign contributions being what they are to politicians, no US President or Congress since has seriously questioned Waite's revolutionary decision.

Pluto at 2 Gemini was moving conjunct the USA's Ascendant and natal Uranus when Judge Waite proclaimed corporations persons. Indeed, this decision was to change how the USA saw the world and was seen by it. Mars at 9 Virgo squared the USA's Ascendant and transiting Pluto. This decision would lead to wars in which big banks and corporations profited from both sides. Saturn was conjunct the money planets Venus and Jupiter, putting a damper on the wealth of the nation, which would henceforth be siphoned off by corporate persons. Transiting Jupiter was conjunct the USA's Neptune, expanding the illusions of those who saw this decision as a benefit for the nation. Transiting Uranus trine its natal position electrified the opportunist aware of what this meant for future corporate expansion worldwide.

Rebirth of Corporate Tyranny

It is ironic, even bizarre, that global corporate dominance has taken root in the USA, a nation forged in a revolution to free Americans from the economic oppression of King George's rule and corporate dominance. One orbit of Pluto later we have President George Bush believing he is as divinely directed as was King George. Belief trumps evidence.

Back then, the British had the mightiest army and navy in the world. American rebels used terrorist tactics against it, much like today's Muslim radicals use terrorist tactics against the US military, whose mission is to protect "American interests," corporations.

For the Boston Tea Party, Pluto was at 3 Capricorn. It arrived there next in March 2009.

Until 1886, corporations in the USA were tightly controlled by government. Since 1886, the rise of corporate domination has been subtle, largely unnoticed, but dramatic—the qualities that describe how Pluto brings conceptions of the new, such as this morphing of ex-slaves and corporations into "persons." Now corporations have all the rights of individuals without all the responsibilities of human individuals. And now much of humanity strives for the profits of a Global Corporate Empire headquartered in Washington and protected by the American military.

It seems every empire has had the mightiest military of its time: Rome, Spain, Britain, Nazi Germany, etc. Note that the duration of each has been shorter than its predecessor. Another fact about empires of the past is that they were gloriously enriching only to a few, oppressive to the many. The Spanish people did not share in the tons of gold brought from the New World 500 years ago. The German people are still dealing with the after-effects of Nazism.

"Corporatized Government"

History repeats but does not duplicate, so on January 20, 1976, the US Supreme Court effectively broke the remaining barrier between the USA as a true democracy, and the USA as what Benito Mussolini proudly called "corporatized government," reprising another old saying: "The road to hell is paved with good intentions."

Following the Watergate scandal that ousted President Nixon, Congress tried to ferret out political corruption without damaging its members. It restricted contributions to political campaigns by setting limits on the amount an individual could contribute. And it required reporting of contributions above a certain level. A Federal Election Commission was enacted to enforce this.

Naturally this prompted a Supreme Court hearing to address the question of whether this restriction violated the First Amendment's freedom of speech and association clause, especially as it applied to those "individuals" called corporations.

"In this complicated case, the Court arrived at two important conclusions. First, it held that restrictions on individual contributions to political campaigns and candidates did not violate the First Amendment since the limitations of the (Federal Elections Commission Act) enhance the 'integrity of our system of representative democracy' by guarding against unscrupulous practices.

"Second, the Court found that governmental restriction of independent expenditures in campaigns, the limitation on expenditures by candidates from their own personal or family resources, and the limitation on total campaign expenditures did violate the First Amendment. Since these practices do not necessarily enhance the potential for corruption that individual contributions to candidates do, the Court found that restricting them did not serve a government interest great enough to warrant a curtailment on free speech and association." (Buckley v. Valeo 424 U.S. 1 (1976) Docket Number: 75-436 Abstract.)

Robert Gover

The Most Free Speech Money Can Buy

This meant, in effect, that campaign contributions were a form of free speech, so both corporations and people could freely express themselves with money as well as spoken and written speech. Since this ruling in 1976, corporations, having the most "free speech" money can buy, have gradually taken control of the US government and thus also American society.

Pluto was opposite and Jupiter conjunct the US Saturn, forming a T square with the cluster of planets in the USA's second house of money. Saturn was opposite the US Pluto. Mars at 14 Gemini was between the US Uranus and Mars, square the US Neptune. The indication is this decision would have unintended and long-lasting consequences detrimental to the nation. One could hardly ask for a worse time to deal with the question of money and politics, as indicated by Saturn's opposition to the US Pluto and Pluto's conjunction of the US Saturn.

It was just a matter of time, I suppose, before the Supreme Court made corporate persons officially superior to natural persons. On January 21, 2010, the Court (*Citizens United v. Federal Election Commission*) decreed that corporations have the right to engage in public debates—meaning corporations are henceforth permitted to throw unlimited amounts of money into persuading voters. Previously, through unlimited amounts of bribe money, they had the extra-legal right to control the elected representatives of the people. Now they have the legal right to control who the people elect—through advertising and public relations techniques which have proven more powerful over the past century than giant earth-moving machines.

Judge Waite's corporate persons now embrace the planet like one giant octopus, extending their tentacles into every facet of our lives from conception to funeral. Acting as a single entity, they constitute a government more powerful than any other on the planet, and a dictatorship more ubiquitous than any in previous history.

For this major turning event, a T square formed by Saturn, Uranus and Pluto afflicted the USA's money planets Venus and Jupiter.

Time and Money

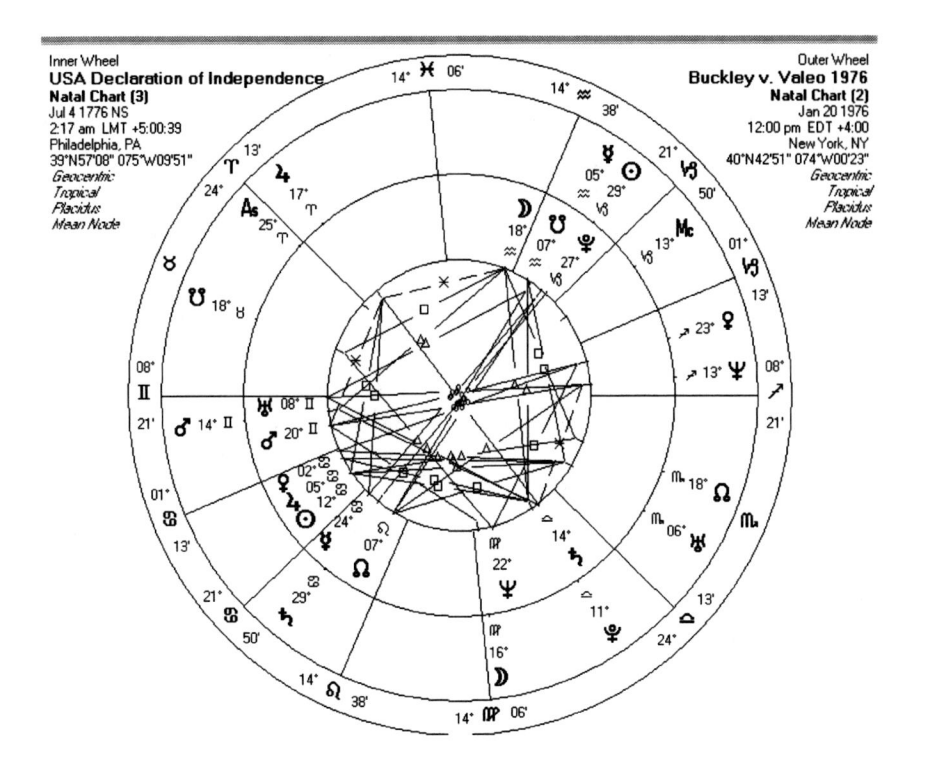

The Corporate "Food Chain"

"At the beginning of the new millennium, of the 100 largest economies on the planet 51 were companies and 49 were countries...The sales of the 500 largest transnational corporations are equal to 47 percent of the gross product of the planet, but they provide employment for only 1.57 percent of the world labor force. Small-scale farmers represent 25 percent of the world population, and they directly feed half the world's people and an even higher percentage indirectly." ("Who's Eating and Who's Being Eaten" by Silvia Robeiro, *La Jornada*, Mexico City, March 1, 2003. Robeiro cites her main information source as The ETC Group, www.etcgrp.org.)

By year 2000, 75 percent of the world's grain trade was controlled by 5 corporations.

By 2002, 90 percent of the world's agricultural chemicals were controlled by 10 corporations.

By 2003, all major media (news, entertainment, etc.) in the US were controlled by six corporations, and this trend was spreading worldwide.

Eventually, agribusiness corporations are expected to be swallowed up by the supermarket chains, the largest of which currently is Wal-Mart.

Corporate control of our lives may soon be accelerated by "terminator technology"—genetically-altered seeds that cannot reproduce and will need to be purchased by farmers every new planting season. Farmers will also need to purchase chemical fertilizers from the same corporate conglomerate. Small farmers who cannot afford to buy a new supply of genetically-modified seed will go out of business, and giant agribusiness operations, subsidiaries of the terminator-tech and supermarket corporations, will supply practically all humanity's food. There have been limp attempts to stop the takeover of humanity's food but such attempts are no match for the battalions of corporate lawyers, lobbyists and beneficiaries in high government positions.

Sea Whales and CEO Whales

Thus, Judge Waite's ideological decree has led to an economic system which generates magnificent profits for the wealthiest 1 percent but brings starvation or worse to billions of humans at the other end of the economic spectrum. Currently in the USA the phrase "top of the food chain" is used to describe those who head huge corporate entities.

Just as whales suck up tons of plankton, corporate empire bosses feed lavishly on humanity's need for food, clothing and shelter. Of course real whales are part of Mother Nature's environmental balance; corporate whales are wrecking that balance at a rapid rate.

There are those who believe a few global corporate conglomerates will soon own everything from drinking water to cemetery plots. Corporate public relations experts are busy persuading us that this is "the American way." When our politicians talk of "freedom and democracy" they mean the freedom of the global corporate empire to dominate.

Time and Money

What is ironic is that today's corporate "libertarians," as they are being called, say they base their devout belief in free-market capitalism on Adam Smith's seminal work, *The Wealth of Nations*. But an examination of Smith's positions shows that he would have strongly opposed the beliefs of the corporate libertarians. Let's run down some of the most obnoxious contradictions:

1) Smith said that labor creates capital; the public relations spin that big corporations "create jobs," implying charity, would have had Smith furious.

2) Smith was against allowing corporations to grow into today's gigantic conglomerates; he opposed any form of economic concentration because it distorts the truly free market's ability to strike fair prices.

3) Smith was opposed to trade secrets of any kind so would have opposed today's intellectual property rights, as claimed by big corporate entities, which have been able to get such laws passed by various governments. The idea that any person or corporation should "own" a lifesaving plant or drug would have sent Smith into paroxysms of rage.

4) Above all, Smith would have been outraged that corporate libertarians attribute to him the idea that unrestrained greed produces desirable economic outcomes. That's John Law's thesis, not Adam Smith's. When Smith wrote of the value of self-interest, he had in mind small farmers, artisans and small companies, not monopolistic corporations backed by an indomitable military.

5) The idea that corporations should be subsidized or capitalized by government transfers of tax money would have sent Smith ballistic. If, on top of that, he had to listen to recipients of corporate welfare crow about being free-market entrepreneurs, there is no telling what horrible crimes he might have been driven to commit.

A World According to Wal-Mart

More contradictions between Adam Smith's truly free market and today's so-called free market dominated by monopolistic corporations can be found in David C. Korton's books, especially *When Corporations Rule the World*.

Adam Smith's free market powered by the self-interest of the many creates a cooperative economy, not a corporate empire. Corporate libertarian devotees of Adam Smith, like fundamentalist Christian devotees of Jesus Christ, put their faith in their own skewed perceptions—and the John-Law-like money creativity of the World Bank and IMF.

Let's suppose, for the sake of argument, that the corporate empire survives beyond year 2015 and Wal-Mart becomes the big whale which has swallowed up all the smaller fish. Its profits in various world currencies are stashed in the world's various central banks, and the multinational central bank, the World Bank, which it owns and controls, along with every other commercial enterprise and government under the Sun. Farmers large or small must buy Wal-Mart's seeds and fertilizers, and sell through its various outlets. Everyone must buy its drinking water. Workers must be employed by it or its subsidiaries or starve; consumers have no choice but to buy from it or its subsidiaries. Faithful to its corporate mission, Wal-Mart's executives must strive to cut costs and maximize profits. How long do you think it will take for this economic freak of nature to devour itself?

Astrology enables us to peer into the future and see when times of major change and/or challenges are due. We can only guess what will change or how challenges will be met, because that depends on how people respond. People respond according to their beliefs. My guess is that by 2009, enough Americans will be aware that they are being abused by the big corporations; agitation for change will begin in late 2008 and accelerate through 2009 to climax around 2015.

Tree of Possibilities

As to surmising what will change, it seems to me the ripest apples on that tree of possibilities are money and the corporations. Corporations were originally the creation of government. During the past century, their changed legal status has enabled them to become the masters of government. The trouble with that is that the mission of corporations is diametrically opposed to the mission of democratically elected government. Corporations seek to acquire as much wealth as possible; democracies seek to spread wealth as equitably as possible.

When Nixon took the dollar off the gold standard in 1971, he inadvertently put it onto the "black gold" standard, oil. Although the world's currencies now "float free" (change ratios to each other practically minute by minute), every industrialized nation must buy oil to fuel its energy-related activities, from heat and light to transportation. So now the cost of a barrel of oil in dollars (or euros) is the "black gold standard." But the amount of oil in the Earth is finite and is being used up at an ever-accelerating rate. As demand for oil rises in China, India and other industrializing countries, the price per barrel will be driven into the stratosphere. The corporatized American rich will still have their World Bank money printing press going, but the poor and middle class won't be there to serve the rich—they won't be able to get to those jobs the corporations so generously created for them. Which will cycle us back to something like the disintegration of the Western Roman Empire around 400-500 when the money of the rich could not buy the goods and services that were no longer being produced by a working class that could no longer survive by doing such work. This situation, remember, followed the Neptune-Pluto conjunction of 411.

Corporatocracy

Meanwhile, gold continues to be mined—at a much slower rate than oil is pumped, of course—and is not being used up because it's immutable; it cannot be transformed into gas to power cars or electric generators. It can't be transformed into anything else, nor can anything else be transformed into gold.

As oil reserves diminish and the dollar or euro price of "black gold" rises in response to dramatically increased demand, we can expect more debtor nations to become more subservient to the alliance of big corporations, banks and governments which constitute the corporatocracy, the new global empire. "Words like *democracy*, *socialism*, and *capitalism* were becoming almost obsolete," writes John Perkins

(*Confessions of an Economic Hit Man*, page 185). "Corporatocracy had become a fact, and it increasingly exerted itself as the single major influence on world economies and politics."

It's no longer possible for any single government to control transnational corporations. "Many of them were incorporated in a multitude of countries; they could pick and choose from an assortment of rules and regulations under which to conduct their activities, and the multitude of globalizing trade agreements and organizations made this even easier."

And what of nations which refuse to knuckle under to the global corporatocracy? That brings us back to 911 and George Bush's decision to invade Iraq.

"Contrary to common public opinion," writes Perkins (page 183), "Iraq is not simply about oil. It is also about water and geopolitics. Both the Tigris and Euphrates rivers flow through Iraq; thus, of all the countries in that part of the world, Iraq controls the most important sources of increasingly critical water...

"In addition to oil and water, Iraq is situated in a very strategic location. It borders Iran, Kuwait, Saudi Arabia, Jordan, Syria and Turkey, and it has a coastline on the Persian Gulf. It is within easy missile-striking distance of both Israel and the former Soviet Union. Military strategists equate modern Iraq to the Hudson River valley during the French and Indian War and the American Revolution. (Pluto then where it is now.) In the eighteenth century, the French, British and Americans knew that whoever controlled the Hudson River valley controlled the continent. Today, it is common knowledge that whoever controls Iraq holds the key to controlling the Middle East."

Humpty Dumpty

The rising tide of resentment by populations around the world is one threat to the corporatocracy. Another threat is that eventually the American people will catch on to what the corporatocracy is doing to bring them under the big global empire umbrella. But the most immediate threat to the corporatocracy is disenchantment with the dollar as the currency of choice for international trade.

Perkins notes: "As long as the world accepts the dollar as its standard currency, this excessive debt (both globally and domestically in the USA) does not pose a serious obstacle to the corporatocracy. However, if another currency should come along to replace the dollar, and if some of the United States' creditors...should decide to call in their debts, the situation would change drastically...

"The euro offers an unusual opportunity for OPEC, if it chooses to retaliate for the Iraq invasion, or for any other reason it decides to flex its muscles against the United States. A decision by OPEC to substitute the euro for the dollar as its standard currency would shake the empire to its very foundations. If that were to happen, and if one or two major creditors (China, India) were to demand that we repay our debts in euros, the impact would be enormous." (For more information about this, check my article "The Dollar and the Euro" www.stariq.com.)

Since Perkins penned those words, the American-dominated global empire has been more and more isolated by diplomatic moves; the European Union has decided to sell high-tech arms to China and to negotiate with Iran regarding its development of nuclear power; China has insisted that Taiwan is its province and it will eventually reclaim it as such, no matter what the US government says or does; in Latin America both President Chavez and President Lula of Brazil are uncoupling their economies from the corporatocracy slowly but surely, and urging other nations in that region to do the same.

"Humpty Dumpty sat on a wall, Humpty Dumpty had a great fall; all the king's horses and all the king's men could not put Humpty together again."

Every great empire has fallen, sooner or later.

Upcoming Uranus-Pluto Square

The virulence of the upcoming Uranus-Pluto square years will depend on which side the US military takes, especially inside the USA once a majority of Americans has learned the details of the global corporatocracy. A tremendous public relations effort will be needed to get American soldiers to point their weapons at their fellow citizens. This

Robert Gover

can be done—cops and soldiers all over the planet obey orders and mow down their fellow citizens almost every day now. But will it succeed in what once was the cradle of democracy, land of the free and home of the brave?

At first, maybe, but not in the long run. Every previous Uranus-Pluto square in American history since 1600, which has simultaneously formed a grand cross with important points in the US natal chart, has brought another turning point in the ongoing class war.

During these past four centuries, democracy (governance in accord with the will of the people) has grown and expanded overall, while plutocratic autocracy has diminished overall, despite periodic surges. The steppingstones of this democratic growth have been the cyclical Uranus-Pluto squares which have simultaneously hit sensitive points in the USA's natal chart. The rise of democracy has been two steps forward, one back, but the overall trend has been forward.

In recent decades, true democracy has been shrouded in a Neptunian fog I call corporatized governance: government of, for, and by the big corporations masked as democracy because people go out and vote—for candidates approved by the corporatized rulers. Thus true democracy has taken another step backwards. But eventually, the people of America and the world will perceive the trick and react. The biggest threat to the corporatized empire is its own success at getting more for less, and less and less and less. Economic imbalance, coupled with dwindling oil supplies, mass migrations of distressed people, and the buildup of horrendous weather events promises to bring out both the best and worst of our human nature.

So the answer to the question, "What's the economy for?" is "the welfare of all, not just the super wealthy few." That goal is aligned with the democratic ideal. Believers in the empire are not likely to go quietly. They are certainly prepared to deal harshly with whatever threatens their wealth and power. Just as certainly Uranus brings unprecedented surprises it's impossible to plan for.

Mind Control

The most fearful weapons of the corporatized empire are subliminal, as the following quotes from an article by Judy Wall makes clear. ("Resonance," Newsletter of the MENSA Bioelectromagnetics Special Interest Group, *NEXUS Magazine*, Oct-Nov 1999):

"The United States Air Force uses aerial mind-control broadcasts against civilian populations as well as enemy troops. Some of these actions against civilians are done with the intent of influencing public opinion and the outcome of elections."

This PsyOps weapon has its insidious effects by "utilizing Silent Sound [TM], in which radio-frequency broadcasts carry subliminal patterns that entrain the listener's brainwaves into a pre-selected emotional state...this technology was used during Operation Desert Storm in 1991, as part of the US Psychological Operations directed against Iraqi troops...To the Desert Storm offensive we can now add several other incidents...Commando Solo was used in Haiti for what was called Operation Uphold Democracy... Instead of butchering a population physically, we can now manipulate them mentally, virtually enslaving their thoughts with a crisscross pattern of flights by an EC-130... We were not at war with the citizens of Haiti, yet the US Government directed military weapons against this friendly, or at least neutral, civilian population. The US Government sanctioned the 'rigging' of the Haitian election by mental control of the people, programming them to cast their votes for the Americans' favored candidate. And they had the nerve to call it 'Operation Uphold Democracy'. Some sense of humor! Stalin would have loved it. Hitler would have loved it. Why is the US Government doing this? Who is behind this flagrant violation of civil liberties?...The rationale is always the same: 'to make the world safe for democracy'. Yet what is democracy if not freedom? Freedom to think your own thoughts; freedom to express your own opinions; freedom to vote for the candidate of your own choice."

It's safe to assume that every empire has developed new ways to control populations, and that every device developed by one side has been duplicated by its opponent. What brought down the British Empire

Robert Gover

was not violent revolutions but British law used by Britain's subjects against their rulers. What brought down the mightiest militaries of Germany and Japan in World War II was a mightier military developed in America.

What's new and different today is that "we the people" are now the opponents of what Perkins calls the corporatocracy, that cabal of corporate-government-military power. Whatever weapons the corporatocracy uses will eventually be used against them. Radio-frequency broadcasts carrying subliminal patterns that entrain the listener's brainwaves into pre-selected emotional states can—and if needed will—be duplicated and used against the rulers of "the new world order."

My dream is that we humans will be zapped with the realization, around 2012, that it's extremely stupid to fight over money and material things, for there's more than enough to go around; if we stop fighting over the scraps, we can all enjoy the whole banquet. No doubt many will find that dream idealistic. I will hold to it, though, because without an ideal to aim for, we drift in a maelstrom of dire possibilities.

Second Edition Addendum

In an earlier chapter titled "Money," I mentioned a Greek myth that illustrates the simple truth that exploitation for immediate financial gain (short-sighted greed) sacrifices the future and leads to self-destruction. My point was that the privatization of our money system with the creation of the Federal Reserve sowed the seeds of self-destruction. The Fed constitutes exploitation for immediate gain by enabling bankers and politicians to collude with the corptocracy in plundering the public and the environment, sacrificing the future.

But few comprehend how the privatized money system works to do this. The vast majority is educated to believe that government creates money—why else would they call it the FEDERAL Reserve? This creates the delusion that the government is to blame if we have a monetary problem. But our government now operates on the "golden rule"—"He who has the gold, rules." And it's the bankers of the Fed who have the gold.

Probably the best source for a comprehension of this system is a book titled *Web of Deb: The Shocking Truth About Our Money System and How We Can Break Free* by Ellen Hodgson Brown, J.D. Here's a sample lifted from Hodgson's web site:

Our money system is not what we have been led to believe. The creation of money has been "privatized," or taken over by private money lenders. Thomas Jefferson called them "bold and bankrupt adventurers just pretending to have money." Except for coins, **all** *of our money is now created as loans advanced by private banking institutions — including the* **privately** *owned Federal Reserve. Banks create the principal but not the interest to service their loans. To find the interest, new loans must continually be taken out, expanding the money supply, inflating prices — and robbing you of the value of your money.*

Robert Gover

Not only is virtually the entire money supply created privately by banks, but a mere handful of very big banks is responsible for a massive investment scheme known as "derivatives," which now tallies in at hundreds of trillions of dollars. The banking system has been contrived so that these big banks always get bailed out by the taxpayers from their risky ventures, but the scheme has reached its mathematical limits. There isn't enough money in the entire global economy to bail out the banks from a massive derivatives default today.

Ballooning Debt

Since the first edition of Brown's book in 2007, some of the predictable consequences of this privatized money system have manifested. The most notable consequence is that the so-called national debt (often also called "public debt" or "sovereign debt") has ballooned astronomically. By 2010, it was estimated that each individual taxpayer in the USA owed $43,000, with the compounded interest growing this debt faster than it can be repaid.

Since our monetary system is debt-based, we cannot pay it all off without removing money from circulation. So it's a catch 22: If we pay off the debt we'll be without enough money to function as a modern society, yet by continuing this debt we enslave ourselves to the bankers of the Fed. The only way to repay it is to de-privatize the Fed and have government sell money to banks rather than the other way around.

The creation of the Fed caused money to morph from our servant to our master. Worse yet, there is no public outcry to change this monetary system which now dominates most of the world. As I write this, the people of France are mounting a nationwide strike to protest their government's cutbacks of social services and pensions to pay down France's national debt. This followed a strike in Greece for the same reason, and is expected to spread soon to Britain and the USA. Government cutbacks are what bankers call "austerity" and tell us is necessary.

What austerity is leading to is a far worse situation by 2015, for it withholds money where it is most needed for economic recovery. This is part of the conflict between the forces of plutocracy and democracy. It will probably lead to what the media calls "unrest," massive protests. The wealthy elites of the world are well prepared with the technology, psychological operations, and obedient troops to suppress protests. But their most powerful weapon is the ignorance of the masses about how the money system really works.

Early in the 20th Century, Henry Ford said, "It is well enough that people of the nation do not understand our banking and monetary system, for if they did, I believe there would be a revolution before tomorrow morning." Since he uttered those words, a lot of knowledgeable people have come to believe there will never be a revolution against the monetary system and the few people who control it. Why? Because the masses don't know or care where their money comes from as long as they have enough to pay their bills and feel superior to those with less. This primate instinct for money-based status pervades our society from the wealthiest to the homeless.

Prediction

My prediction that the present monetary system will be changed is based not on a mass uprising against it, but on the simple fact that it is not sustainable.

The Chinese economy, with its government owned central bank, is leaving Western nations, with their privatized central banks, in the dust. It may take Western elites a decade or more to realize why China's government-run, national debt-free system works to create prosperity. Eventually practical need will overwhelm delusional ideology and bring change.

Posing the Winter Solstice of 2012 as the hinge of change, it's interesting to note that it is the Fed's Sun-Pluto opposition which will be hit hardest by the transiting Uranus-Pluto square, indicating major transformation. That square will trigger the Peoples Bank of China's Mars-Jupiter conjunction, indicting rejuvenation, although not without troublesome surprises. It is the world's monetary system—based on the US Fed—that is most basic to a change in the world economy, and the astrology involved suggests the national debt-creating system is likely to give way to China's national debt-free system. For money-savvy conservatives of today's Western nations, this is an unthinkable thought. And, because the public is largely ignorant of both money systems, it may turn out that change will happen subtlely "behind the scenes" rather than as a dramatic news event.

Cultural Script

The ideological belief in the USA's privatized system is part of what I've been calling the cultural script—all those unarticulated assumptions that together constitute our culture. For instance, the old joke about why thieves rob banks—"because that's where the money is." This joke ignores the fact that less than 3% of what we call money is dollar bills and coins. And then there is the notion that "government is the problem, not the solution." Conservatives ballyhoo "the private sector" as the solution, ignoring the fact that government provides the rules and regulations needed by the private sector to function, and people (taxpayers) provide the labor and buy the goods and services produced by the private sector. Much of the private sector contracts with government, paid with taxpayer money. When rightwing ideology obliterates the fact that the economy is really interdependent, we are down the rabbit hole into a monetary version of *Alice in Wonderland*.

If, tomorrow, all the banks across the country were robbed of all the cash they have on hand, the system would suffer only a brief hiccup. Even if a worldwide electrical failure wiped out all computerized records of credits and debts, the resulting chaos would be temporary, for it would not touch the real wealth money represents: the hard assets, tools, and know-how of the people.

Which brings us to the dire predictions for the Winter Solstice 2012, the Mayan astrologers end of one world and, by inference, beginning of a new world, and the famous Age of Aquarius. During the roughly 2,150 years of the Piscean Age, humanity developed money as means of exchange and measure of value, and those among us who sought power over others, managed to confiscate this primary tool of power: Money.

Time and Money

Medium of exchange money is a boon to civilization, but "love of money" as the old proverb has it, "is the root of all evil."

It was love of money that motivated the Fed's founding fathers when they convened on Jekyll Island back in 1910 to design the system that has brought us to this endgame, this catch 22. Their design was the culmination of centuries of humans scrambling to accumulate as much money as possible in order to—not merely prosper but dominate. During this history, money evolved and grew from precious metals owned only by a small aristocracy to something as necessary to everyone as air and water.

His Own Petard

The super-rich controllers of money are, I submit, soon to be hoisted by their own petard. That saying, used metaphorically by Shakespeare in Hamlet, has an interesting origin. A petard was a bucket of gunpowder used to blow down fortifications. Being hoisted by one's own petard happened when the wielder of this weapon had it blow up in his hands, hoisting him skyward. Although the "money petard" doesn't blow up with the suddenness of gunpowder, it does malfunction and explode in slow motion—although not so slow when viewed from the perspective of humanity's millennial long history with money.

One indication of the money petard blowup began in May 2010 when a California judge made the startling observation that the law does not permit one to transfer or sell what one does not own. (See Case No. 10-21656-E-11, May 20, 2010.) He was referring to deeds to properties in foreclosure. Those deeds, documents proving ownership of the home mortgaged to "homeowners" now in foreclosure because they could not make the monthly payments—those deeds had been resold in the form of mortgage backed securities. Such securities had been "bundled" and mixed together in the process of converting them into securities to be sold all over the world. Now that the homeowners were defaulting on their loans, the banks wanted to foreclose, take back those properties, resell them, bundle them into new mortgage backed securities and perpetuate this nifty business. Until that California judge pointed out that one cannot sell what one does not have. This startling finding hoisted the foreclosure business by its own petard.

What happened to the financial sector (or, as some call it, the financial *industry*) is the subject of a book by Matt Taibbi: *Griftopia: Bubble Machines, Vampire Squids, and the Long Con that is Breaking America* (Spiegel & Grau, New York, 2010). At the end of a chapter revealing the incredible complexities of the subprime mortgage mania—the unraveling of which triggered the crash of 2008 and whatever economic hardships await us in the future—Taibbi summarized with this:

"With the $13-plus trillion we are estimated to ultimately spend on the bailouts, we could not only have bought and paid off every single subprime mortgage in the country (that would only have cost $1.4 trillion), we could have paid off every remaining mortgage of any kind in this country—and still have had enough money left over to buy a new house for every American who does not already have one."

But that would have been "socialism" for the masses, which those who lived in the Marxist bubble at the top of the economic food chain were dead set against. So instead what we got was the Wall Street pump-and-dump schemers able to persuade Congress to throw them a $13-plus trillion dollar lifeline, and impose "austerity" on the American public to pay for it. Or *try* to pay for it. Actually, there is no way "austerity" will enable this humungous national debt to be paid off, for it expands by compound interest too fast. The only way is to change the monetary system that sucked us into this morass. Meanwhile, the victims of this high-finance crime are being punished.

Aristotle was right when he warned two and a half millennia ago that (to paraphrase) money's highest and best use is as a means of exchange. Society's supply-demand balance is lost when the Fed "prints" (electronically) an over-abundance of credit money for big corporations and wealthy investors, and the government sticks taxpayers with the bill for a national debt created by borrowing from the banks of the Fed—then adds insult to injury by sticking taxpayers with the debt incurred when wealthy private investors lose trillions of credit dollars provided by the Fed.

It's this system of the rich living from the unwitting generosity of workers/ consumers/ taxpayers that is unsustainable. It's the world created by this vampire economy that is ripe to end after 2012. It renders the old socialist v. capitalist argument obsolete, for both socialists and capitalists exist in this privatized central-bank-run, debt-based system, with notable exceptions like China. "Communist" China is now seen as the world's most successful capitalist country. It rejected the privatized central bank system and has the kind of system advocated by Ben Franklin and Abe Lincoln.

The old system of voting for Republicans, Democrats or Independents as our representatives has been demonstrated to be obsolete. The political game is rigged. Those who are willing to sell their votes to the highest bidders thrive in our nation's capitol. Honest representatives of the national interest are shunned. Does this mean we have no choice but to either mount a massive rebellion or submit to smarmy crooks? Or does it mean that under the Uranus-Pluto square, events will conspire to cause the corrupt to self-destruct?

From an astrological viewpoint, what we have now is a Piscean Age system that will not work in the Age of Aquarius. From an economic perspective, it's a system that has hoisted itself by its own petard. The old cliché that money is the lifeblood of a society is true. What's needed is a monetary system that provides robust circulation. Which means ridding the body politic of whatever blocks, inhibits or poisons circulation.

Secrets Revealed

By December 2010 a couple of Uranus-square-Pluto twists to the USA's monetary story had surfaced. WikiLeaks, an information website founded by Australian Julian Assange, was publishing volumes of documents the government had classified secret. And Senator Bernie Sanders, Independent from Vermont, had forced the Fed to reveal that it had virtually given away $12.3 trillion to banks and corporations at home and abroad, and stuck American taxpayers with the bill for this giveaway. Julian Assange was being held in a London jail on charges of sexual misconduct brought by two Swedish ladies, but people around the world

Robert Gover

surmised that this was engineered by the US government in an attempt to destroy Assange and shut down WikiLeaks.

As for the $12.3 trillion Fed giveaway to its best friends, bankers and corporate CEOs, Senator Sanders said, "Almost two years ago I asked Chairman Bernanke to tell the American people which financial institutions and corporations received trillions of dollars as part of the Wall Street bailout. He refused. Today, as a result of an audit-the-Fed provision I put into the financial reform bill, we finally learn the truth—and it is astounding."

Equally astounding was how the corporate-owned mass media managed to distort news about Assange and WikiLeaks, and ignore the Fed's $12.3 giveaway like it never happened. This news blackout caused David DeGraw of AmpedStatus to quip,"What if the greatest scam ever perpetrated was blatantly exposed, and the US media didn't cover it? Does that mean the scam could keep going? That's what we are about to find out."

What both WikiLeaks and Senator Sanders' revelations were all about was how unimaginable sums of money were being stolen from the American people and squandered by the wealthy—even while banks were constricting credit for 80 to 90 percent of the American people, practically guaranteeing the crash of 2008 would lead into a great depression during the 2000-teens.

And so it had come about that money, that amazing human inventtion which enabled exchanges of goods and services, had created unprecedented prosperity by the 20th Century, and had been destroyed in the early years of the 21st Century. By 2010, on the cusp of the coming great depression, the rich few were drowning in money while the majority was suffering and dying for lack of it.

Money is indeed mysterious stuff. Widely distributed and used as a medium of exchange, it dramatically raises the prosperity of all. But captured and hoarded by a so-called "privileged few," it destroys as thoroughly as a nuclear holocaust.

Did we need this latest outbreak of massive monetary crime to again prove the old adage, "Love of money is the root of all evil"? Or is the situation we find ourselves in on the cusp of the Uranus-Pluto square the inevitable prelude to a transformation so wide and deep and powerful that it will lift all humanity to a new level social sanity?

The history of past Uranus-Pluto squares tell us that human motive combines with planetary influences to shape the future. The last great depression manifested Hitler in Germany and Roosevelt in the USA, showing a range of motives. The stakes are even higher now as we head into the 2000-teens: Slavery to the controllers of money, or freedom created by a redefinition of what money is and how it must be used.

Gone are the days when gold coins or cowry shells were money. Most money today exists in the form of electronic digits. Also gone is the old squabble between socialists and capitalists, for today both exist in this privatized central-bank run, debt-based system. Today the political battle is between the forces of democracy struggling against the oligarchic owners of money, and traditionally it has been those who control the money who rule. What will arise from the ashes after the present system self-destructs? Can we design a money system of, for and by the people?

Public Utility Money

Of all the various proposals for how to fix the existing money system—you can find an abundance of them on the Internet—the one I find at once the most promising and the most politically difficult comes from someone who worked for the Federal Government. Richard C. Cook retried in 2007 after a remarkable career of 32 years, including analyst at NASA and the Treasury Department. In 2009, he published *We Hold These Truths: The Hope of Monetary Reform* (Tendril Press, Aurora, Colorado).

I was delighted to discover a kindred spirit, for he agrees with me that our presently privatized money system is the root cause of all our economic woes. His basic theme is this: "The political democracy defined by the Declaration of Independence has not been achieved because economic democracy has not been achieved. The attainment of real economic democracy is the next task for the American people."

Cook sees the debt-based monetary system run by private banks as the cause of all our economic misery. And he asserts that this system is just as harmful to the wealthy "who hold their fellow humans in bondage, as it is to the debtors they oppress..." (page 200). What we should do is abolish the Federal Reserve and re-establish constitutional control of credit as a public utility.

This can be done simply by changing back to the kind of system we had during colonial times, when there were no banks, and for most of the USA's early history when democratically responsive government controlled the creation of money.

To those like Senator Ron Paul of Texas who propose a return to the gold standard, based on a distrust of "fiat" money, Cook points out: "The debt-based credit created by the Federal Reserve, often called fiat money, is not money at all. It is simply temporary credit with a lien against it for repayment with interest. But real fiat money, like the Civil War Greenbacks, was true democratic money that was spent into circulation by government and was not inflationary. Rather it allowed commerce to expand and people to prosper. This type of money is actually the key to economic democracy."

No longer are millions of workers required to produce what we need to prosper. High tech machines have made many workers obsolete as far as profitable production is concerned. Yet viable consumers are still needed for a balanced economy. Thus Cook's guaranteed basic income—in effect every family a shareholder in America, Inc.—solves the problem of unemployment.

But not, alas, the problem of status. We humans are status-driven primates, despite our achievements in the arts and sciences, and money is—or has been—how we decide who's on top. Yet even this belief is vulnerable to the transformative revolutionary events we will be moving through in the coming decade.

Winter Solstice Lunar Eclipse

On December 21, 2010, the Winter Solstice, there was a Lunar Eclipse that aligned with the Galactic Center of the Milky Way, what the Mayan called the mother of the universe's vagina and mythologized as the origin of our earth and thus us. Conjunct the Sun on the cusp of Capricorn at the time of this Eclipse was Mercury, Pluto, the Moon's

Time and Money

North Node and Mars. In turn, all this astrological busyness was conjunct the Fed's Sun, opposite its natal Pluto.

This planetary pattern is so rare that it is bound to bring major changes in all areas of our lives. Some astrologers calculated the much-feared Winter Solstice of 2012 had been mistaken due to confusion of the Gregorian and Julian calendars, and the big turning-point date was really two years previous, December 21, 2010.

This powerful, once-ever alignment hitting the Fed's natal Sun-Pluto opposition coincided with two legislative moves against the Fed. The first was the results of an audit launched seven months previous by the amendment tucked into the Wall Street reform Bill by Senator Bernie Sanders, Independent from Vermont, revealing the Fed's $12.3 trillion giveaway to its banker buddies. The second was Bill HR5660 entered into the House of Representatives by Congressman Dennis Kucinich, Democrat from Ohio.

Kucinich's Bill details how the existing system works to create war and poverty, and is the root cause of government corruption, and thus why returning control of money to a government "of, for, and by the people"—as the Constitution provides—is necessary to our survival. Linked to the proposal elucidated by Richard Cook that every citizen has an inalienable right to a share of the nation's wealth, it becomes clear that the Fed and other privatized central banks are on their way to extinction.

The idea that the people have an inalienable right to a share of a nation's collective wealth is presently considered absurd. The people's job is the pay for the lavish life styles of the rich and powerful few. Anyone who objects to this assumption is slammed by the mass media as stirring up "class warfare." But change is the only constant and the never-before-seen planetary alignment of the 2010 Winter Solstice Lunar Eclipse aligned with the Galactic Center is changing that assumption. A new mood is evident, and with it comes a new perspective on money. Actually, it's not new, it's really so ancient it seems new. It overturns money as our medieval master and returns it to our facilitator of life, liberty and the pursuit of happiness.

Bibliography

Astrology and Stock Market Forecasting, by Louise McWhirter, ASI Publishers, 1935.

When Corporations Rule the World, by David C. Korten, Barrett-Koehler Publishers, Inc., San Francisco, 2001.

www.calleman.com for articles by Johann Calleman.

www.iknowwhatyoudidlastelection.com/bush-supreme-court.htm for Mark H. Levine's complete dialogue about Gore v Bush.

Confessions of an Economic Hit Man, by John Perkins, Berrett-Koehler Publishers, Inc., San Francisco, 2004.

Great Depression of 1990, by Ravi Batra, Simon and Schuster, '87.

"The Discovery of the Outer Planets" by Jeff Jawer, www.stariq.com.

"Shay's Rebellion" by Alden T. Vaughan, *Historical Viewpoints*, Harper and Row, 1987.

Horoscope for the New Millennium, by E. Alan Meece, Llewellyn Publications, 1997.

The Twilight of American Culture, by Morris Berman, Norton, 2000.

The Great American Deception, by Ravi Batra, John Wiley and Sons, NY, 1966.

"The May 2000 Astrological Lineup and the Global Economy" by Raymond A. Merriman, The Mountain Astrologer Magazine, Dec. 1999-Jan. 2000.

The Great Crash: 1929, by John Kenneth Galbraith, Houghton Mifflin, 1972 edition.

The *Economist Magazine*, January 8, 2005 issue.

www.amanita.at for more information about the Amanita Newsletter by Manfred Zimmel and Roman Noske.

"The Implications of Saturn in Opposition to Pluto to World Economies and financial Markets" by Raymond Merriman, The Mountain Astrologer Magazine, Nov-Dec 2001 issue.

A Peoples History of the United States, by Howard Zinn, HarperPerenial, 1990.

Bibliography

American Slavery, American Freedom, by Edmund S. Morgan, Norton, 1975.

"Myths that Hide the American Indian," by Oliver La Frage, *Historical Viewpoints,* Harper and Row, 1987.

Encarta, 1998 or later editions, online.

The Future of Capitalism: How Today's Economic Forces Shape Tomorrow's World, by Lester Thurow, Morrow & Co., March 1996.

International Society of Astrological Research, http://www.isarastrology.com.

"**America: Illusion and Reality,**" by J. H. Plumb, *Historical Viewpoints,* Harper and Row, 1987.

Manias, Panics, and Crashes, by Charles R. Kindleberger, Wiley and Sons, 1999.

Silent Depression, by Wallace C. Peterson, Simon and Schuster, 1994.

"**Roanoke: The Lost Colony,**" by Karen Ordahl Kupperman, *Historical Viewpoints,* Harper and Row, 1987.

Planets in Aspect, by Robert Pelletier, Para Research, Inc., 1974.

Everyday Life in Colonial America, by Dale Taylor, Writers Digest Books, 1997.

"**Witchcraft in Colonial New England,**" by John Demos, *Historical Viewpoints.*

Extraordinary Popular Delusions and the Madness of Crowds, by Charles MacKay, Three Rivers Press, New York, 1980.

Secrets of the Temple: How the Federal Reserve Runs the Country, by William Greider, Simon and Schuster, 1987.

"The Privateer Market Newsletter," Google, 2001.

The Crisis of Global Capitalism, by George Soros, Public Affairs, NY, 1999.

The Coming Anarchy, by Robert D. Kaplan, Random House, 2000.

Noam Chomsky in *Class Warfare,* Interviews with David Barsamian, Common Courage Press, 1996.

The American Political Tradition, by Richard Hofstadter, Vintage, 1989.

The End of Work, by Jeremy Rifkin, Tarcher/Putnam, 1996.

The Grapes of Wrath, by John Steinbeck, Benton, 1940.

Bibliography

By the Light of the Moon, by Dean Koontz, Bantam, 2003.

"Bush's Plan to Privatize Society Security," by Paul Krugman, *New York Review of Books*, March 1, 2005.

The History of Corporations in the United States, William Kalle Lasn, Morrow/Eaglebrook, 1999.

"How a 'Clerical Error' Made Corporations 'People'" by Jim Hightower, The Hightower Lowdown Newsletter, April 2003, PO Box 20596, New York, NY 10011.

"Who's Eating and Who's Being Eaten" by Silvia Robeiro, *La Jornada*, Mexico City, March 1, 2003.

The Daily Reckoning, online investors newsletter, several articles and comments by various authors.

The Economist Magazine, various issues.

The Financial Times of London, various issues.

Forgotten Founders, by Bruce E. Johanson, Harvard Commons Press, 1982.

The Wild Beast of Finance, by Alfred Steinherr, Wiley, 1998.

Planetary Economic Forecasting, by Bill Meridian, Foreword by Robert Hand, Cycles Research Publications, 2002.

America: Who Really Pays the Taxes?, by Donald L. Barlett, Simon and Schuster, 1994.

Griftopia: Bubble Machines, Vampire Squids, and the Long Con that is Breaking America, by Matt Taibbi, Spiegel & Grau, NY 2010.

We Hold These Truths: The Hope of Monetary Reform, by Richard C. Cook, Tendril Press, Aurora, Colorado, 2008.

Astrological Charts

Declaration of Independence	22
Federal Reserve	34

Biwheel Charts (USA on inner wheel):

September 11, 2001	22
Fed and USA	38
Winter Solstice 2012	46
Great Depression 1780s	56
Great Depression 1840s	58
Great Depression 1870s	59
Great Depression 1930s	60
No Grand Cross 1901	62
No Grand Cross 1960	63
No Grand Cross 1989	63
Uranus-Pluto Square 2014	70
Stock Market Panic 1903	76
Stock Market Panic 1987	81
2007 CDS	87
Bacon's Rebellion	91
French and Indian War 1754	99
French and Indian War Ends	101
British Stamp Act 1765	102
Boston Massacre 1770	105
Tom Paine 1776	109
Valley Forge 1778	112
British Surrender 1783	113
French Revolution 1789	116
Bastille Day/Eclipse 2015	117
Neptune-Pluto 411	120
Neptune-Pluto 905	121
Neptune-Pluto 1398	122
Neptune-Pluto 1891	123
First Crusade 1099	137
Cortez in Mexico 1518	145

Astrological Charts

Lost Colony Roanoke Island 1590	148
Jamestown 1607	153
Salem Witches 1695	154
First African Slaves 1619	157
John Law's Bubble 1720	161
Bill of Rights 1791	175
US Constitution 1787	179
Federal Reserve 1913	181
Winter Solstice 2012	191
Women's Vote 1920	205
Russian Revolution 1917	220
Crash of '29	229
Great Depression 1930	230
Great Depression Bottom	231
Hitler Chancellor 1933	239
World War II 1941	244
Battle of Midway 1942	245
Hiroshima 1945	246
The Sixties Begin 1960	255
Uranus-Pluto Conjunction 1965	256
Nixon Resigns 1974	258
Berlin Wall Falls 1989	269
Euro Established 1999	278
Election Day 2004	282
Social Security Act Signed 1933	291
Saturn-Uranus 2009	296
Buckley v Valeo 1976	305

INDEX

911 (Sept. 11, 2001), 18, 19, 20, 21, 23, 24, 25, 27, 68, 84, 90, 270, 275, 276, 288, 298, 310
Adams, John, 107, 288
Adams, John Quincy, 268
Afghanistan, 19, 134, 247, 287
African slaves, 158
American colonists, 98, 100, 102, 103, 107, 149, 284, 287, 299, 300
American history, 20, 21, 65, 66, 104, 153, 197, 209, 219, 247, 252, 312
American Revolution, 18, 62, 90, 107, 110, 114, 115, 143, 162, 165, 171, 174, 193, 203, 206, 246, 251, 260, 274, 285, 299, 310
Arab jihadis, 21
Ascendant, 10, 16, 110, 116, 123, 154, 184, 191, 210, 213, 243, 245, 251, 255, 257, 263, 267, 272, 273, 291
astro-economic indicators, 2, 185, 210, 231
astrological perspective, 25, 173, 209, 234
astrology
   definition, 3, 5, 7, 10, 11, 72, 79, 91, 127, 178, 222, 225, 227, 267, 275
atomic bomb, 245
Augustulus, Romulus, 132
Aztec, 144, 145

Bacon's Rebellion, 90, 91, 92, 93, 96, 97, 98, 103, 114, 170, 203, 251, 253
Balfour Declaration, 140
Bartolome de Las Casas, 142
Bastille Day, 115
Batra, Ravi, 51, 64, 67, 222, 225, 266
Battle of Midway, 245
Battleship *Maine*, 24
Belief trumps evidence, 3, 54, 79, 167, 189, 239, 292, 302
Berlin Wall, 11, 65, 270
Berman, Morris, 66
Bill of Rights, 10, 73, 114, 126, 173, 175, 176, 219
biwheel, 9, 21, 52, 53, 54, 55, 61, 62, 81, 84, 120, 154, 161, 182, 208, 267, 279
Black Friday 1873, 75
Black Friday, 1869, 74
Black Monday 1987, 80
Bonner, Bill, 294
Bonus Army, 236
Boston Massacre, 104
Boston Tea Party, 104
Braudel, Fernard, 261
Bribery, 135
British corporations, 300
bubble, 12, 15, 65, 68, 73, 79, 82, 83, 148, 158, 160, 273, 294, 295
Buckley v. Valeo, 299

Index

Bush Administration, 14, 18, 19, 67, 273, 274, 285, 290, 291, 294
Bush v. Gore, 12, 13
capitalism, 119, 130, 131, 193, 194, 195, 196, 197, 201, 203, 207, 208, 209, 211, 212, 213, 215, 216, 220, 242, 260, 274, 275, 298, 307, 309
Capitalism, 130, 133, 134, 193, 195, 196, 220, 242
capitalist, 3, 5, 196, 207, 213, 220, 225, 286
capitalistic democracy, 193, 194, 258
Capitalistic democracy, 130
Castro, Fidel, 265
catastrophe, 5, 228, 232, 241, 275
Central Intelligence Agency, 264
Chaney, Dick, 283
chaos, 18, 84, 129, 136, 196, 257, 261
Chaos Sprites, 271
Chomsky, Noam, 197
CIA, 19, 211, 265
civil rights, 92, 98, 184, 206, 254, 272, 281
Civil Rights Bill, 25
Civil Rights Movement, 250, 254, 258
Civil War, 15, 24, 25, 74, 148, 149, 171, 204, 243, 246
class war, 93, 201
Clinton Administration, 66
Cold War, 64, 65, 83, 183, 219, 247, 254, 270

Columbus, 6, 17, 122, 124, 127, 140, 141, 142, 143, 155, 196, 200, 201, 204, 214, 224, 254, 276, 277, 298
communism, 62, 92, 131, 196, 219, 220, 252, 256, 275
Communist Party USA, 238
computerized voting machines, 281
Confessions of an Economic Hit Man, 27, 310
Congress, 15, 24, 26, 62, 105, 112, 135, 176, 178, 179, 180, 181, 182, 184, 186, 195, 201, 204, 207, 208, 209, 210, 217, 236, 238, 269, 281, 291, 293, 303
Conscription, 217
Constitution, 10, 73, 84, 173, 174, 175, 176, 178, 180, 209, 271
Continental Army, 112, 165, 167, 169
Contract with America, 135
corporate welfare, 62, 135, 265, 307
corporate whales, 306
corporatized, 19, 30, 102, 118, 119, 184, 272, 278, 280, 303, 309, 312
Cortez, 144, 155, 276, 277
Crash of 1920, 77
Crash of '29, 232, 268
Croatoan, 147
Crusade, 137, 139, 140
Crusaders, 23, 121, 139
Crusades, 23, 138
Cuban Revolution, 265

Index

cultural script, 130, 167, 169, 172, 174, 192, 214, 250, 298
Dachau, 239
Daily Reckoning, 289, 294
Dark Ages, 121, 122, 126, 131, 132, 133, 135, 136, 138, 154, 195, 200, 250
Declaration of Independence, 108, 114, 126, 169, 171, 218, 300
defense spending, 286
Déjà vu, 284
democracy, 10, 30, 56, 92, 107, 110, 114, 126, 130, 169, 173, 174, 192, 193, 194, 195, 196, 197, 198, 199, 201, 203, 206, 209, 211, 213, 218, 219, 220, 258, 260, 276, 284, 288, 298, 299, 303, 306, 309, 312
depression, 51
Derivatives, 186
Desert Storm, 270
dollar, 162, 165, 182, 183, 184, 185, 186, 188, 189, 190, 257, 273, 277, 279, 280, 286, 289, 290, 297, 309, 310, 311
Doors, The, 248
dotcom, 82
Dotcom Boom, 160
Dow, 80, 82, 83, 185, 232, 234
Drug Enforcement Agency, 263
drug war, 264, 265
ecological catastrophes, 298
economic crises, 6
economic democracy, 98, 127, 194, 219
economy, 6
English servants, 92, 97
Enron, 84, 187

Espionage Act, 217
euphemisms, 288
euro, 188, 189, 272, 273, 277, 278, 279, 286, 289, 309, 311
euros, 188, 272, 273, 277, 278, 279, 297, 298, 309, 311
Exit polls, 281
Fan Gang, 289
Fed, 180, 181, 184, 185, 186, 187, 209, 210, 211, 212, 213, 214, 294, 295
Federal Communications Commission, 283
Federal Reserve, 62, 79, 85, 163, 180, 209, 213, 214, 217, 224, 228, 243, 269
feudal, 130, 133, 134, 192, 290
Florida Land Boom, 160
foot soldiers, 283
Founders, 10, 115, 166, 169, 171, 172, 174, 178, 179, 180, 181, 201
French and Indian War, 18, 90, 98, 99, 103, 125, 144, 149, 173, 203, 285, 310
French Revolution, 115
Friedman, Milton, 243
Fry, Eric, 289
fundamentalist Christians, 280
Galbraith, 79, 159, 160, 222, 224
GDP, 297
global corporate empire, 306
global empire, 21, 27, 28, 29, 106, 119, 187, 309, 310, 311
gold, 4, 6, 141, 150, 155, 156, 160, 177, 178, 182, 183, 184, 185, 186, 187, 189, 190, 257,

333

Index

260, 261, 262, 276, 277, 289, 303, 309
gold standard, 4, 184, 187, 190, 257, 261, 262, 309
Governor Berkeley, 94, 95, 96
grand cross, 2, 9, 16, 52, 53, 54, 55, 57, 58, 59, 61, 62, 64, 68, 69, 74, 78, 82, 83, 89, 90, 91, 99, 113, 114, 117, 134, 143, 152, 153, 180, 182, 193, 209, 210, 224, 229, 230, 231, 232, 255, 257, 267, 273, 276, 279, 295, 312
grand trine, 22, 83, 104, 105, 110, 116, 117, 179, 182, 221, 276, 292
great depression, 2, 6, 9, 24, 51, 52, 53, 55, 57, 58, 59, 60, 61, 62, 64, 68, 69, 73, 74, 75, 77, 80, 90, 91, 92, 113, 114, 152, 153, 166, 171, 174, 181, 182, 183, 195, 203, 206, 209, 210, 216, 218, 219, 224, 228, 229, 230, 231, 232, 233, 241, 242, 243, 246, 255, 267, 270, 287
Great Depression Defined, 51
Great Depression of the 1780s, 55
Great Depression of the 1870s, 59
Great Depression of the 1930s, 59
great depressions, 2, 9, 51, 52, 53, 54, 58, 61, 64, 65, 68, 74, 75, 77, 79, 180, 193, 200, 226, 227, 228, 257
Greenspan, Alan, 294

Greider, 165, 211, 212, 213, 214, 215, 216, 234, 247, 258, 261, 262
Greider, William, 165, 209
Grisham's Law, 297
Guantanomo, 14
Halliburton, 187, 283
Hamilton, Alexander, 173
Harvard, 29, 152, 172
health care, 196, 274
heathen savages, 153, 164, 172
Herzl, Theodor, 139
Hiroshima and Nagasaki, 246
Hitler, 199, 238, 239, 266, 286
Hofstadter, Richard, 150, 216
Hudson River, 152
Humpty Dumpty, 133
Hussein, Saddam, 19, 23, 270, 276, 280, 288
Immigrants, 134
incantation, 79, 80, 84
Indian, 18, 90, 93, 94, 95, 96, 97, 98, 99, 100, 103, 125, 132, 142, 143, 144, 145, 146, 147, 149, 150, 151, 152, 156, 172, 173, 203, 204, 211, 224, 262, 285, 310
Industrial Revolution, 105, 125, 260
inflation, 4, 155, 186, 247, 261, 262, 267
inner planets, 2, 11, 20
Inquisition, 125, 137, 138, 145, 149, 200, 293
insurgents, 23, 172, 283, 287
International Monetary Fund, 183
Iraq, 19, 23, 24, 26, 106, 115, 187, 203, 217, 247, 257, 270,

Index

272, 273, 276, 277, 279, 280, 283, 284, 287, 288, 293, 310, 311
Iroquois Confederacy, 127
Israel, 124, 140, 273, 280, 310
J. P. Morgan, 216
Jackson, Andrew, 15, 73, 300
Jamestown, 93, 95, 96, 149, 150, 151, 152, 154, 156, 157, 158, 209, 262, 290
Jawer, Jeff, 56, 60
Jefferson, Thomas, 56, 108, 114, 171
Jim Crow, 24, 25, 204
John Law, 158, 159, 160, 161, 162, 163, 164, 178, 184, 187, 190, 212, 243, 244, 295, 307
Johnson, Lyndon, 254
Kaplan, Robert D., 197
Kennedy, John F., 254
Kennedy, Robert, 254
Kerry, John, 281
Keynes, John Maynard, 67, 242
Keynesian, 62, 67, 219, 243, 247, 252, 254, 263, 265, 287
King George, 149, 299, 302
King, Martin Luther, 254
Knox, General Henry, 172
Korton, David C., 307
Krugman, Paul, 292
Lachman, Desmond, 297
Lasn, William Kalle, 299
Lewinski, Monica, 280
Lost Colony, 149, 150, 259
lunation, 228
Malcolm X, 254
market crash, 71, 205, 228, 233, 235
Martyrs, Peter, 141

Marx, Karl, 98, 180, 218, 242, 260
Masons, 10
Maya, 5, 89, 127, 225
Mayan, 4, 5, 89, 190, 275
McWhirter, 74, 75, 77, 225, 226, 227, 228, 231, 232
McWhirter, Louise, 2, 72
media, 19, 23, 24, 27, 30, 65, 110, 173, 194, 199, 200, 201, 213, 215, 218, 252, 254, 272, 277, 278, 279, 280, 281, 282, 283, 284, 288, 306
medicine men, 78
Medieval, 14, 127, 130, 131, 177, 189, 211, 212, 293
Meece, E. Alan, 64, 119, 202
Mekong, 253
Merriman, Raymond A., 71
Mexification, 274
Middle Ages, 132
Middle East, 29, 128, 140, 215, 273, 280, 283, 297, 310
mightiest military, 111, 118, 239, 302
military-industrial complex, 14, 23, 26, 183, 238, 252, 254, 265, 286, 287
Minutemen, 106
Mississippi, 100, 160, 163, 164, 187, 212, 253
Monetarists and Keynesians, 67
money, 3, 4, 5, 6, 10, 28, 29, 30, 57, 72, 111, 118, 136, 159, 161, 162, 163, 164, 165, 166, 169, 173, 177, 178, 179, 180, 181, 182, 183, 184, 185, 186, 187, 188, 189, 190, 195, 198, 201, 209, 210, 212, 213, 214,

Index

225, 234, 235, 243, 244, 254, 257, 261, 262, 263, 264, 277, 283, 287, 288, 290, 292, 294, 295, 304, 307, 308, 309, 314
monotheism, 129
Moore, Michael, 19
moral values, 280
Morgan, Edmund, 93
Morgan, J. P., 208
Morrison, Jim, 249
Mother Earth, 142, 147, 224
Muckrakers, 207
Mussolini, 303
NAFTA, 187, 271, 272
NASDAQ, 82, 83, 234
Native American, 97, 171, 172
Nazi, 219, 238, 239, 245, 286, 288, 295, 302
Nazi Party, 238, 286, 295
Neptune-Pluto Cycles, 16
New Deal, 241, 242, 266
Nixon (President Richard), 183, 184, 186, 189, 190, 249, 250, 254, 257, 262, 267, 303, 309
nuclear, 118, 276, 311
Oil Embargo, 52
Osama bin Laden, 19, 29
Paine, Thomas, 107
Palestine, 139, 140
panic, 71, 72, 73, 74, 77, 79, 80, 85, 86, 160, 161, 208, 224, 232, 233, 270, 295
Panic of 1837, 73, 74
Panic of 1857, 74
Panic of 1893, 52, 75
pantheistic beliefs, 129
Pantheists and monotheists, 130
paper money, 4, 114, 159, 160, 163, 164, 165, 166, 167, 178, 182, 183, 186, 187, 190, 212, 260
Patriot Act, 14
patriotic symbols, 287
Pearl Harbor, 244
Pentagon Papers, 249
Perkins, 27, 29, 30, 188, 189, 310, 311
Perkins, John, 27, 309
Peterson, Wallace C., 146
planetary cycles, 3, 7, 136, 225
Planetary cycles, 1, 6, 82
planetary patterns, 6, 7, 55, 82, 200
Plymouth Rock, 152
pollution, 135
Ponce de Leon, 143
President Carter, 185
President Franklin Delano Roosevelt, 291
President Herbert Hoover, 223, 235
President John F. Kennedy, 275
President Lula, 311
President Roosevelt, 181, 241
President Teddy Roosevelt, 85, 213
Presidential Election, 12
Privateer Newsletter, 185
product of the planet, 305
Prohibition, 263
propaganda, 198, 199, 201
public relations, 19, 130, 195, 198, 217, 257, 260, 286, 288, 293, 306, 307, 311
Puritans, 152
race riots, 251, 254
Reagan Administration, 67
Reaganomics, 14

Index

recession, 51
Revolutionary War, 57, 68, 69, 90, 98, 111, 114, 118, 167, 168, 171, 173, 243
Rich Man's Panic, 1903, 76
Rifkin, Jeremy, 223
right-wing, 280
Rising, 9, 10, 246
Roanoke Island, 147, 148, 157
Robeiro. Silvia, 305
Roman Catholic, 23, 131, 138, 212, 214
Roman Empire, 90, 115, 119, 121, 126, 129, 131, 132, 133, 137, 138, 309
Salem Witch Trials, 154
Santa Clara County v. Southern Pacific, 299
Saturn-Neptune Cycles, 12
Saturn-Pluto Cycles, 14
Saturn-Pluto opposition, 2, 14, 20, 22, 23, 24, 25, 26, 65, 73, 84, 122, 275, 276, 293
Saturn-Uranus Cycles, 11
Scare of 1997, 81
Schumpeter, Joseph, 261
Second Bank of the US, 15
September 11, 2001, 2, 14, 18, 20, 65, 84, 122, 124
Sir Walter Ral, 147
sixties, 27, 90
slavery, 4, 108, 131, 156, 158, 171, 174, 262
slaves, 4, 6, 24, 92, 93, 95, 96, 97, 98, 103, 106, 108, 118, 141, 146, 147, 157, 158, 160, 166, 174, 204, 302
Smith, Adam, 67, 114, 118, 130, 174, 307, 308

Smith, John, 150
Social Security, 195, 196, 201, 242, 260, 288, 291, 292, 293
socialist, 3, 220, 238, 292
Solar System, 1, 17, 22, 56, 61, 129, 136, 138, 200, 222, 225, 227, 257, 271
solstice, 190
Sons of Liberty, 103
Soros, George, 196
South Sea Company, 158, 160
Soviet Union, 11, 83, 183, 218, 219, 221, 265, 275, 287, 310
St. Augustine, 133
Stamp Act, 102
Starving Time, 151
Steinbeck, John, 235
suffragium, 204
supply-side, 14, 67, 223
Supreme Court, 12, 13, 14, 15, 169, 217, 272, 283, 299, 303
synodic cycles, 11
T square, 9, 23, 73, 74, 75, 77, 78, 79, 81, 137, 139, 157, 175, 176, 182, 229, 255, 257, 259, 267, 271, 279, 296, 304
Taylor, Dale, 152
Teddy Roosevelt (President), 209
Terkel, Studs, 237
terminator technology, 306
The Doors, 249
The Sixties, 2, 15, 16, 20, 25, 26, 61, 80, 202, 247, 248, 249, 250, 251, 254, 257, 259, 260, 262, 265, 267, 275
Third Reich, 24
Tombaugh, Clyde, 60
Treaty of Paris, 100, 114, 115

Index

Tulip Mania, 159
Turkish Empire, 65
unemployment, 29, 51, 66, 103, 195, 216, 219, 222, 224, 235, 241, 242, 247
Uranus-Neptune Cycles, 15
Uranus-Pluto Cycles, 15
Vietnam, 20, 23, 24, 25, 26, 62, 92, 130, 183, 184, 217, 247, 249, 250, 251, 252, 254, 257, 265, 267, 284, 288, 295
Virginia Colony, 94
Virginia Company, 150
Volcker, Paul, 185, 211
Wagner Act, 241
Wagner-Connery Bill, 238
Wall Street, 21, 61, 73, 74, 79, 84, 211, 212, 269, 270
Wal-Mart, 306, 307, 308
waning squares, 12
War Department, 286
war on terror, 26
wars, 2, 9, 14, 15, 20, 65, 104, 127, 149, 151, 155, 218, 226, 227, 243, 246, 257, 280, 287
Washington, George, 99, 114, 172
water, 30, 85, 141, 146, 150, 151, 153, 160, 196, 234, 280, 306, 308, 310

Watergate, 184
Watt, James, 83, 105, 114
waxing square, 12, 14, 15, 90
We The People ..., 166
Witchcraft, 155
women's vote, 203
workers/consumers, 68, 274, 295
World Bank, 30, 163, 183, 187, 308, 309
World Trade, 2, 14, 18, 21, 25, 65, 84, 124, 138, 139
World Trade Center, 2, 18, 21, 65, 84, 124, 138, 139
World Trade Organization, 14
World War II, 22, 25, 115, 149, 171, 183, 217, 219, 231, 241, 243, 246, 247, 257, 266, 286, 287
Worldcom, 84
Yorktown, 112, 114
Zinn, 97, 103, 104, 106, 108, 146, 150, 151, 155, 156, 167, 168, 169, 176, 207, 217, 235, 237, 241, 242, 252, 253, 266
Zinn, Howard, 93, 96, 141, 146, 173, 207, 208, 216, 240
Zionist Movement, 124

About the Author

Robert Gover grew up in an endowed orphanage, Girard College in Philadelphia, received a BA from the University of Pittsburgh, became a best-selling novelist at age 30, lived most of his life in California and now lives in a Delaware beach community. He has published seven novels and other works of fiction and non-fiction. A new edition of the American cult classic, ***One Hundred Dollar Misunderstanding***, has been published by Hopewell Publications.

As I pursued my curiosity about economic and planetary correlations, dozens of intelligent, accomplished people have told me, often with a condescending smirk, "The planets have nothing to do with the economy." When I've asked why they are so sure of this, they have usually recited either a basic tenet of modern science or a Bible verse.

If you believe that only modern science or your particular religion has captured the whole Truth, this book is not for you. This book is for the incorrigibly curious, all who realize our perception of Truth is an ongoing human adventure.

- Robert Gover 2005

**Read Gover commentary and articles at
http://robert-gover.blogspot.com/**

CPSIA information can be obtained at www.ICGtesting.com
Printed in the USA
LVOW12s1819111213

364884LV00002B/467/P